Japanese Educational Productivity

Center for Japanese Studies
The University of Michigan

Michigan Papers in Japanese Studies
Number 22

JAPANESE EDUCATIONAL PRODUCTIVITY

edited by

Robert Leestma and Herbert J. Walberg

Ann Arbor

Center for Japanese Studies
The University of Michigan

1992

© 1992

Center for Japanese Studies
The University of Michigan
108 Lane Hall
Ann Arbor, MI 48109-1290

The excerpt on pp. 240-41 is from Thomas Rohlen's *Japan's High Schools*. Copyright © 1983 The Regents of the University of California. Used by permission of the publisher.

Library of Congress Cataloging in Publication Data

Japanese educational productivity / edited by Robert Leestma and Herbert J. Walberg.
    p. cm.--(Michigan papers in Japanese studies; no. 22) Includes bibliographical references and index.
   ISBN 0-939512-55-6 (alk. paper)
   1. Education--Japan. 2. Educational productivity--Japan. I. Leestma. Robert. II. Walberg, Herbert J., 1937- . III. Series.
LA1312.J326   1992
370'.952--dc20   91-32032
                                                              CIP

The paper used in this publication meets the requirements of the ANSI Standard Z39.48-1984 (Permanence of Paper).

Printed in the United States of America

TABLE OF CONTENTS

FOREWORD

Japanese Education Today, the first volume resulting from the U.S. Study of Education in Japan, made important contributions to our understanding of Japanese education in cultural context. It helped us rethink our own national education situation by providing a fresh sense of possibilities and alternative approaches to various education objectives, tasks, and dimensions.

For example, the Japanese experience shows that it is possible to establish national education goals based on the public interest and to develop a curriculum for common learning that embodies high average expectations, standards, and achievement. Among other things, the Japanese experience also illustrates the importance of: parental involvement in education, having children start school ready to learn, specific attention to cultural literacy and character development, and instilling in students accountability for their own learning. The education outcomes include world class performance in science and mathematics and, indeed, the setting of international standards of excellence for these subjects.

The rapid rise of Japan in the brief span of less than fifty years to major international status dramatizes the power implicit in a learning society that has a clear sense of purpose and a strong national resolve. Whatever the problems and weaknesses on the Japanese scene, complacency is not a national characteristic that plagues school or society.

All of these thoughts are relevant to the problems facing the United States today as we as a nation gear up to meet the challenges of human development and economic competition that characterize the dawn of the twenty-first century. Education has crucial contributions to make to both. It is an imperative of the information age that we do a better job of developing the full potential of the mind and spirit of American youth. America 2000, President Bush's bold, long range plan for the renaissance of American education--new schools for a new world and a new century--provides the strategy and framework for, in the president's words, "making this land all that it should be."

Anything we can learn from the experience of others is grist for our mill of improving American education. In my view, *Japanese Educational Productivity*, this second and final volume of the U.S. Study of Education in Japan, makes as much of a contribution in its own terms as the initial report did to our understanding of an education system that is quite different from our own. The research focus of the present book is of special significance, not just in the further depth of information and insight it provides on what works in education there and why, but also in helping chart the course for research needed to fill the gaps in existing knowledge and probe further the frontiers of effectiveness in education.

I am particularly taken with the potential for cooperative studies that is sketched in the concluding section of Dr. Leestma's final chapter. The U.S. and Japan continue to have much to learn from each other in education. There are implications throughout this book for research on American education as well as on Japanese education.

The Department of Education is grateful to the Center for Japanese Studies at the University of Michigan for making this important work available to the scholarly community in the U.S. and abroad.

Lamar Alexander
Secretary
U.S. Department of Education

PREFACE

As many readers are aware, in 1983 President Reagan and Prime Minister Nakasone of Japan initiated a cooperative research project designed to enable both countries to better understand one another's education system. By mutual agreement, the studies were conducted under the general sponsorship of the United States-Japan Conference on Cultural and Educational Interchange (CULCON), a continuing forum of government and private-sector leaders that is charged with fostering cooperation in education, culture, and public affairs.

The Japanese Ministry of Education, Science and Culture was responsible for Japan's study of American education, and the U.S. Department of Education was responsible for carrying out the study of Japanese education. Each side had full autonomy to set its own research agenda and to conduct its study as it saw fit. Each study team received important assistance from a distinguished group of advisors and consultants of its own choice.

The basic reports of both national research teams were published concurrently in January, 1987. The U.S. report was entitled *Japanese Education Today*, and the Japanese report, *Educational Reforms in the United States*. Both studies have received widespread public attention in both countries and each is now available in both English and Japanese.

The principal purpose that the Department of Education established for the U.S. study was to develop a comprehensive yet accessible understanding of Japanese education in cultural context--to find out how and why the system works, and how the Japanese accomplish what they do in education. The report was intended for a broad audience of American educators, policy officials, parents, and other citizens concerned with education and its improvement. The aim was to present enough authoritative information in sufficient perspective to enable Japanese education to speak for itself--so that interested Americans could draw their own conclusions about the relevance of the Japanese experience to their situations.

The utility of the report was enhanced by an insightful epilogue by then Secretary of Education William J. Bennett, wherein he shared his own analysis of the possible implications for American education. The points he made were not prescriptive. Rather, they were intended to stimulate the reader to reexamine the goals, doctrines, practices, and performance of American education in the light of Japanese experience.

It is clear from the critical acclaim of the scholarly community as well as the widespread positive reaction from the public, the education profession, and the mass media that *Japanese Education Today* hit the mark we had set for it. This report is now widely considered the most informative and readable summary of Japanese education in cultural context that is currently available in English.

One reason for the accuracy and comprehensiveness of the initial report is indicated by the contents of this volume, which contains briefer, and in some cases updated, versions of six of the eighteen research papers prepared by outside scholars under commission from the National Institute of Education (chapters 3-7 and 9), and four from members of the Department of Education team that produced *Japanese Education Today*. As the U.S. study developed, it became clear that, in addition to our original plan for a general audience report (which was all that was required under the bilateral agreement with Japan), we were accumulating some important scholarly work that should be made available in its own right. Professor Herbert Walberg of the study's Advisory Committee deserves credit for the idea of producing this second volume by drawing on some of the best of the background research material associated with the study. Dr. Robert Leestma, director of the U.S. study, was responsible for bringing the material together in its present form, including the development of additional chapters by team members.

Three criteria determined which papers would be included here (usually in revised form). The editors selected those papers whose content:

1) was related to the productivity theme of this volume,

2) was primarily focused on Japanese education or on an actual comparison between aspects of Japanese and American education, and

3) would be of interest to more than a few scholars and policymakers.

The concept of productivity that provides some thematic unity to this collection of research papers is well explained in Professor Walberg's cogent introduction. The volume concludes with Dr. Leestma's perceptive review of weaknesses in our present knowledge of Japanese education and some thoughtful ideas concerning further research needs and opportunities. It is a fitting final chapter to the U. S. Study of Education in Japan.

With the publication of this volume, the Department of Education considers its involvement in the special cooperative study with Japan to be officially completed. The experience was a fruitful and altogether worthwhile undertaking with which we were pleased to be associated at every level: intergovernmental, scholarly community, education profession generally, and the concerned lay public. In the process of learning more about Japanese education, we also achieved some fresh insights into the potential and problems of education and education reform in the United States.

My appreciation to all who contributed in both countries, whether represented in this final volume or not, remains strong and sincere. I thank them all. Special recognition is due Betty George, a coauthor of the first volume, who rendered yeoman editorial service on several chapters of this one. Commendation is also in order for subsequent important contributions by Cynthia Dorfman and Helen Wiprud of the Department of Education, Barmak Nassirian of the American Association of State Colleges and Universities, and the good offices of AASCU. The final credit line goes to Dr. Leestma and the Center for Japanese Studies at the University of Michigan, particularly Managing Editor Bruce Willoughby and his staff, for bringing this book into print.

Chester E. Finn, Jr.
Professor of Education and Public Policy
  Vanderbilt University, and former
Assistant Secretary for Educational Research and
  Improvement and Counselor to the Secretary
U. S. Department of Education

INTRODUCTION

Herbert J. Walberg

During the past century, education expanded quantitatively, providing more years of education to ever greater numbers of students. Throughout the world, the fractions of national populations successively completing primary, secondary, and tertiary programs have increased enormously. Today, education is expanding in the form of preprimary programs on the one hand, and, on the other, in the form of postsecondary education, on-the-job training, recurrent education, leisure and retirement courses, and other programs for adults. Also, we realize today the decisive educational influence of the larger world outside the conventional classroom, especially as exercised through the family, the media, and the community.

Those concerned with education cannot remain content with mere quantitative expansion. In an age of rapidly expanding knowledge and world economic competition, they must be concerned not only with diplomas and degrees but also with how much students have actually learned and the degree to which their knowledge, skills, and attitudes have prepared them for occupations, civic participation, and constructive leisure pursuits. They must be concerned as well with the quality of the educational experience and the conservation of human time in learning, since our days on earth are severely limited.

For these reasons, educators must examine curricula and ask what knowledge is of greatest worth. They must avoid teaching what students already know and what they are yet incapable of learning. They must also ask what teaching methods and instructional media and systems accomplish the most in the shortest periods of time at least cost. Finally, they must ask about the most efficient ways of governing, financing, and organizing education.

To respond to these challenges, educators cannot rely on a single discipline. Anthropology, economics, history, political science, psychology, and sociology--all have useful insights and facts that can be brought to bear. In addition, innovations in practice often outrun what academia is able to systematize; educators need to be informed of efficient breakthroughs wherever they originate.

In this interdisciplinary, practical spirit we need to enlarge, compile, and systematize knowledge about educational productivity. We need to know more about the theory of educational systems in the United States and in other countries, more about the research underlying their design, and their effectiveness as implemented.

Japan represents a case of special importance. This country has risen from the devastation of World War II to the first or nearly the first rank among nations by several objective indicators. With close to the highest income per capita, highest life expectancy, lowest infant mortality, very low crime rates, excellent goods and services, and top rankings on various other indicators of the quality of life, Japan exemplifies exceptional progress in modern times.

We cannot assume that education alone made for such prosperity and welfare, but it is reasonable to think that the country's extraordinary accomplishments in education, broadly defined, must have been among the important forces for progress in other spheres. For example, consider elementary and secondary education in international perspective: the United States has taken pride in a mass system that aims at graduating all students from high school and actually graduates about three-fourths. Europe traditionally had elite standards, but since World War II has succeeded in enlarging opportunities through the use of comprehensive secondary schools.

Japan, however, seems to have achieved the best of both--an elite system for the great mass of students. Almost 90 percent of Japanese students graduate from secondary school, and, in many important subjects, notably science and mathematics, they achieve the highest or nearly the highest average achievement scores among affluent countries. These exceptional accomplishments alone make it worthwhile for us to examine the distinctive features of Japanese education, especially as they compare with practices and policies in the United States and other countries.

Overview

Nobuo Shimahara begins the main body of this book with his chapter, "An Overview of Japanese Education," which analyzes the structure, policies, and current issues of education in Japan. He further sets the stage by noting several highlights of the modern history of Japanese education since the Meiji Restoration of 1868, which ended the feudal era. He describes the spirit of hard work, credentialism, and meritocracy that influenced the formation of school policies and curricula. He then describes the centralized control, monitoring of industrial needs, moral development, and diversity and choice that have further shaped educational policies.

With Lois Peak's "Formal Pre-Elementary Education in Japan," we turn to the considerable learning experience Japanese children acquire in the form of preschool (or day care) and enrichment lessons in activities such as piano and swimming. Many Americans have long known that Japanese get large amounts of education of a high standard starting in elementary and secondary schools, but it is equally impressive to find that children gain a head start by careful, humane lessons in socialization during the early years.

Tokuo Kataoka, in "Classroom Management and Student Guidance in Japanese Elementary and Lower Secondary Schools," describes two techniques that are thought to be among the keys to high academic achievement among Japanese students. He explains the operation of Japanese classrooms and how small groups of children assume considerable responsibility for the social order of learning. He gives several examples that illustrate how management and guidance constructively influence moral development and academic interest in the special context of group life in Japanese schools. He also specifies the allocation of curriculum hours and a calendar of special events and activities during the school year. Student planning of assemblies seems geared toward both moral development and high standards.

Harold Stevenson and Karen Bartsch, in "An Analysis of Japanese and American Textbooks in Mathematics," report on detailed and careful analysis of the content of lessons in textbooks ranging from first through twelfth grades. Mathematics, of course, is the language of science and much commerce, and mastery gives students an edge and special insights in many fields. The comparative rigor and fast pacing of Japanese texts may have been expected. What is especially interesting, however, is their brevity, which puts a burden on students and teachers to make links and develop concepts on their own.

Willard Jacobson and Shigekazu Takemura (with Rodney Doran, Shigeo Kojima, Eve Humrich, and Masao Miyake, and contributions by Arthur Schneider), in "Science Education in Japan," describe elementary and secondary science curricula and two comparative studies recently completed. Although students in Japan and the United States differ in their achievement scores, the correlates of and possible influences on achievement appear to be similar. Books in the home, interest in science, active experimentation, textbook use, homework, interesting teaching, and the general quality of school life are associated with higher achievement in both countries.

Leigh Burstein and John Hawkins, in "An Analysis of Cognitive, Noncognitive, and Behavioral Characteristics of Students in Japan," analyze distinctive cognitive and noncognitive traits. They compile a considerable amount of research on the comparative performance of Japanese students, notably those conducted by the International Association for the Evaluation of Educational Achievement. They review many studies and commentaries on the causes of exceptional performance of Japanese students. They conclude with their own interpretive account of family, educational, and social factors that lead to high Japanese achievement, especially in science and mathematics.

Catherine Lewis, in "Creativity in Japanese Education," reviews psychological literature on the definition, assessment, and promotion of creativity. In the light of this research, she discusses Japanese education. She concludes that creativity may be construed differently in Japan and the U.S., but that several creativity-enhancing and inhibiting factors can be identified from studies of Japanese childrearing and education.

Robert August, in "*Yobiko*: Prep Schools for College Entrance in Japan," reviews a subject of great interest in Japan and the United States. Since, as he says, "there is strong and pervasive emphasis on one's academic background in Japan," entrance examinations play a decisive role in matriculation to prestige universities that confer corresponding advantages in postgraduate life. "Cram" schools aim to prepare students to pass entrance examinations. Yet, as August points out, the successful cram schools build up a substantial knowledge base in students' minds, and some schools concern themselves with a deeper and longer view of learning and culture.

Koji Taira and Solomon Levine, in "Education and Labor Skills in Postwar Japan," attribute individuals' level of education to an indirect but decisive role in recruitment, training opportunities, compensation, and promotion. Yet, of even greater importance in Japanese labor skills, they find, is direct, on-the-job training. They describe examples of training procedures in various firms and cite data showing that Japanese workers are the most experienced at their present jobs among workers in countries surveyed. Not only can greater experience lead to greater expertise, but also companies can afford to invest more in the human skills of their workers if they are to be employed for comparatively long periods.

Robert Leestma, in the concluding chapter, "Further Research: Needs, Opportunities, and Perspectives," draws on the experience of conducting the U.S. Study of Education in Japan to provide a candid assessment of what we *don't* yet know about Japanese education. While the study resulted in considerable knowledge and a fresh perspective useful for the United States (and possibly other countries as well, we can hope), we need to acknowledge uncertainty about some topics, and there is much more that we would like to know. Leestma points the way in identifying some major needs and opportunities for further research. He also provides some insightful perspectives on the interrelationship of school, society, and educational change in Japan.

CHAPTER 1

OVERVIEW OF JAPANESE EDUCATION: POLICY, STRUCTURE, AND CURRENT ISSUES

Nobuo K. Shimahara
Rutgers University

Introduction

Formal education has been central to the formation of modern Japan. Modern Japan dates from 1868, when the Meiji Restoration repudiated the feudal system of the Tokugawa era, which had prevailed since 1603. Schooling proved a formidable tool throughout the nation's early modernization, and the leaders of the Meiji period used it skillfully as they forged the new nation. No less formidable since then, schooling has shaped Japan's industrial development since World War II. Indeed, the evolution of Japanese education closely parallels the growth of the Japanese economic and sociopolitical structure. In brief, Japanese education both anticipates and responds to the country's critical needs.

Japan is probably without peer in the community of nations in relying extensively on formal education to modernize and industrialize, to develop character, and to cultivate the moral and cultural sensitivity of its citizens. From its fledgling days in the nineteenth century to its enviable position in the twentieth, Japanese education has remained a pivotal institution. The nation's commitment to schooling has never been diluted, and the Japanese faith in education and in its benefits to the commonweal flows from that unswerving tradition.

In 1872, just four years after the Restoration, Japan promulgated the Fundamental Code of Education, its first comprehensive plan for a national education system. Implementing that system, though fraught with repeated trial and error, eventually established centralized education. In 1886, ordinances defined primary, middle, and normal schools and the imperial university, and by the early 1900s the Meiji government had established the educational system that became the bedrock of Japanese education until 1945.

Establishing a national system in such a relatively short period was possible for two reasons. The first was a tradition of learning. Schooling had been extensively developed during the Tokugawa period in the form of private academies, officially organized schools, and Terakoya, a widespread institution of learning for commoners. This tradition provided a cultural ambience conducive to a school system under state control. The second, more significant, reason was the Meiji leaders' adaptability and sensitivity to the nation's urgent needs for modernization. They actively sought Western education models and guidance, notably in the United States, Germany, France, and Britain, and emulated them.

A second comprehensive reform occurred immediately after Japan's surrender to the Allied Forces in 1945. No less radical than the Meiji reform, it fundamentally altered the structure and superstructure of prewar education. Incorporating recommendations of the United States Education Mission in early 1946, Japan undertook a drastic reform of its education system that had a lasting impact upon postwar education. The Fundamental Law of Education and the School Education Law, enacted in 1947, provided the framework of postwar education, defining the democratic ends and means of a new nation. As a result, the nation's school system became not only democratic, but also egalitarian and efficient at all levels. Although these reforms were somewhat modified shortly after Japan's independence in 1952, the fundamental structure of schooling has remained relatively unchanged as it has supplied the necessary human resources for industrial and social development.

Since the early 1970s, Japan has been in the midst of what some consider its third reform. The reformers intend to reshape education to better satisfy newly emerging needs, including the greater diversity, flexibility, and internationalization demanded by a complex postwar industrial society. This concern culminated in the National Council on Educational Reform, an advisory body appointed by the Prime Minister in August, 1984, and charged with developing recommendations for reform.

Over the last century, Japan has created a meritocracy. A citizen's social mobility is determined largely by education and competition, and the consequent credentials are essential to employment, promotion, and social status. Historically, as the Meiji Restoration repudiated the ascribed status system of the Tokugawa period, it introduced a meritocratic system that deemed individual achievement crucial to status. Understandably, to fill strategic, bureaucratic positions with educated and competent citizens, the new

Meiji government stressed achievement in employment and promotion. Meritocracy became indispensable to building a modern nation. Today, however, Japan's meritocracy means intense educational competition for credentials among youths from all social classes.

Several salient factors combine to develop credentialism in a society (Aso 1981, 2-26). First among these is a longstanding respect for education and the view that diligence in school is the key to success. A second factor is the belief that educational credentials are indispensable to gain employment and to determine individual mobility in the hierarchy of a work organization characterized by lifetime employment and a rigid seniority system. Third, Japan's social structure, just like the hierarchical structure of its universities and the status hierarchies of its work organizations, fosters possession of educational credentials. This contributes to the modern stress on "school credentials," credentials from particular schools valued by industrial firms, rather than general educational credentials. That hierarchy of higher education generates intense competition among secondary students seeking admission to universities. Finally, 31 percent of the high school graduates now have access to higher education, making a university certificate a common symbol attainable by anyone with sufficient motivation and commitment. It is this meritocracy that drives youths to study diligently and to compete for better credentials.

Educational Orientation and Policies

Japan has established high standards of student performance. Japanese students have consistently achieved very high scores in international tests, including those administered by the International Association for the Evaluation of Educational Achievement (IEA). In the IEA tests conducted in 1983, for example, Japanese seventh and eleventh graders outperformed students from participating nations in almost all categories of mathematics.

What are Japan's educational policies and the orientation responsible for this high performance in school? Most significant are the national standards for curriculum and related aspects. The Ministry of Education, Science and Culture (shortened hereafter to the Ministry of Education) exerts firm control over these standards and their effective implementation. For example, it carefully monitors the curricula at all levels throughout the nation, and it requires that textbooks comply with the ministry's course of study. To assure that they do, the ministry has charged two advisory bodies, the Council on Textbook Authorization and Research and the Curriculum Council, to examine all textbooks and curricula. Furthermore, the ministry expects every Japanese teacher to follow the course of study irrespective of local differences and preferences, thus making the content and sequence of teaching uniform. This assures that students at all socioeconomic levels and in all geographical areas are exposed to the same basic skills and knowledge.

Because curriculum is the critical vehicle of knowledge transmission and personality development, the ministry periodically evaluates the relevance of the curricula to the changing needs of industry and society. So far, every decade has shown significant economic and social transformation, and each evaluation has changed the curricula appropriately. This monitoring function of the ministry is essential to systematically improving curricula. The following four major curriculum reforms reflect the social, economic, and political conditions since World War II.

The first curriculum revision took place under the strong influence of American education during the Occupation. It replaced the nationalistic curriculum with a new one. The new curriculum was characterized as experience-based and student-centered, because it encouraged applying problem-solving methods to student experience and community activities. The ministry issued a first course of study in 1947 and an improved version in 1951. Intended to help teachers and local schools build their curricula, this was a guide, not a framework of officially binding criteria. During those years the ministry left teachers considerable freedom to determine curricula relevant to their local schools and students. The experience-oriented curriculum was widely criticized, however, the chief contention being that student performance had deteriorated.

Accordingly, the ministry thoroughly reviewed that curriculum in the early 1950s and, in 1958, devised a fundamental revision for the primary and secondary levels that took effect during 1961-63. During the 1950s, through legislation, the ministry regained firm control over local schools. Subsequently, it issued a course of study that became legally binding throughout the nation and established more rigorous and scrupulous standards to ensure that commercial textbooks matched the ministry's philosophy. The primary thrust of the revised curriculum was to improve moral education, academic achievement, science and technical education, and vocational education (Kinoshita 1983, Yamaguchi 1980, and Yanagi

1984). As a result, a discipline-centered curriculum displaced the experience-oriented curriculum and simultaneously quashed local adaptations. At this same time, stimulated by the outbreak of the Korean War, the Japanese economy was growing rapidly, and industry was demanding more competent and diversified human resources to meet its needs. Japan's independence in 1952 also generated a new political climate that favorably influenced both education and industry. By responding to all these emerging economic and political conditions, the ministry established strong standards suited to the times that would nonetheless affect later curriculum development.

The 1960s witnessed industrial and economic expansion unparalleled in Japanese history. Personal incomes tripled, as did international trade. Industry was desperate for ever greater numbers of better-trained people, and it demanded that education be upgraded. Reflecting the tenor of those times, enrollments in high schools and four-year colleges increased from 57.7 and 9.2 percent respectively of all youths in 1960 to 82.1 and 20 percent in 1970, a phenomenal change within a single decade. Responding to the demands of industry, the Curriculum Council began to research and deliberate upon the content of a third curriculum reform in 1965. The council submitted its recommendations in 1967, and in 1968 the ministry announced its third comprehensive revision--one intended to improve scientific and technical education and to enhance students' adaptability to a changing society. The reformed curriculum called especially for upgrading education in mathematics and science (Kinoshita 1983 and Yamaguchi 1980).

A wag once observed that anything worth doing is worth doing to excess, and that comment has a limited applicability to Japanese education in the 1970s. High school enrollments rose above 90 percent in the early 1970s, causing a number of problems. To cite just two of them, a disconcerting lack of continuity became apparent between the curricula of elementary and secondary schools. In addition, critics pointed out that high school curriculum requirements had been pulled out of thin air; they failed to coincide with the abilities and skills of high school students. Awareness of these problems, and others, led to the curriculum revision of 1977-78, which took effect in 1980 at the elementary level and in 1981-82 at the secondary level. This was a response to the perceived rigidity and excessive requirements of the previous reform. In a nutshell, the overhauled curriculum emphasized the importance of more flexibility and diversity in curricula, to "humanize" student life at school.

From the foregoing discussion several distinct policies that influence education in Japan today can be gleaned. The first is centralized control which standardizes educational practice and promotes uniformity in curricula and similar aspects of schooling. Centralized control also contributes to efficient education and egalitarianism in compulsory education. Educational policy shifted drastically from decentralization to centralization and from diversity to uniformity. Japan's centralized system is composed of three tiers having different degrees of power in actually implementing policies and standards: the Ministry of Education, the prefectural board of education, and the municipal board of education. These levels of educational control are hierarchically ordered, and, although prefectural and municipal boards of education have appreciable independence in a formal sense, they are functionally under the supervision of the ministry. The dramatic transformation in the pattern of control occurred after a series of measures ignited a succession of controversies between conservatives and reformists, the Ministry of Education and the Japan Teachers Union, and the ruling and opposition parties. Among these measures were: a law enacted in 1954 to protect the political neutrality of education, a law enacted in 1956 to replace elected school boards with appointed boards, an administrative measure in 1956 that increased the ministry's power over textbook authorization and the course of study, and another administrative measure in 1957 that enforced the performance-rating system for teachers.

Second, monitoring industrial development and needs has been central in formulating the educational policies promoted by the ministry. The ministry has an apparatus through which it monitors and responds to changing social problems and industrial trends. The apparatus includes the Central Council of Education, an important advisory body that makes broad policy recommendations to the Ministry of Education. Consisting of diverse appointees, including some representing industry, the council is a primary link between education and society at large. The predecessor of today's Central Council was the Education Reform Committee, which drafted the immediate postwar reform. Another important body of the ministry is the Curriculum Council, whose function is to make recommendations to the education minister concerning curricular matters. The functions of both councils are critical in developing broad educational and curriculum policies.

Third, moral education has been a crucial area addressed in every curriculum revision. In 1958 moral education was formally incorporated as an independent area of instruction, parallel with other subjects and special educational activities, including extracurricular activities. This was an expression of the policymakers' persistent concern for the need to develop a moral basis for the position of the individual in society. The ministry conceived moral education not only as an instructional area, but also as a basic factor in the general process of socialization, which involves all aspects of schooling. Therefore, articulating the purpose of moral education and its relation to other elements of the curriculum continued to be debated in every decade.

Fourth, a new policy direction began to emerge in the early 1970s, one that stressed the need for diversity and student choice in education. This policy orientation developed as a reaction to the rigid uniformity and standardization of curriculum and schooling, especially in the secondary schools. Though standardization contributed to the upgraded schooling throughout the nation and made the training of the human resources needed by the expanding economy more efficient, Japan's economic affluence and increased social differentiation created critical problems that challenged the previous policy of uniformity. When 94 percent of all adolescents were enrolled in high schools, policymakers had to consider differentiating high school education to meet the needs of students with a wide range of abilities and aptitudes. Moreover, as Japan was attaining ever higher levels of industrial sophistication, marked by the onset of the information industry, policy planners began to suspect that the rigidly standard education would be incapable of adapting to rapid industrial change (Aso and Amano 1983, 89-93).

The Central Council of Education unambiguously recognized these problems in 1971 in its long, detailed report. The report presented comprehensive recommendations for what it called the third education reform, an initial outline of education reform leading to the reform movement in the 1980s (Ministry of Education 1980, 337-44). A report on Japanese education in 1971, by an education mission of the Organization for Economic Cooperation and Development, stressed the same theme: it called for diversification of the Japanese educational system and freedom of choice. The OECD examiners who wrote the report urged Japanese policymakers to pay critical attention to what they perceived to be excessively standardized education developed in the interests of egalitarian and rigid central control (OECD 1971).

Higher education, too, was expanding rapidly in the 1960s and 1970s, but was leaving its stratified and rigid structure largely unaltered. Rates of youths attending colleges and universities increased dramatically. Ninety percent of these increased demands for higher education were met by private institutions alone, which expanded rapidly in the 1960s. The national (public) institutions did little to meet those demands and expanded hardly at all. Lacking government support, private institutions had to rely solely upon tuition for their revenues, and these comparatively modest sums were inadequate to pay for facilities and programs equal to those at the national universities. Considering such substandard education a serious problem, the National Diet passed an important measure in 1970 to subsidize the operating costs of private institutions. Nonetheless, proliferation did not sufficiently meet demands for diversification, and, anticipating the diverse demands of the 1970s, the Central Council of Education urged that higher education be diversified and fully accessible to the public. As Aso and Amano state:

> Higher education, with its stratified and rigid structure, can be said to have been well suited to the demands of rapid modernization. By concentrating the investment of limited resources in a few institutions, it became possible to nurture the talent needed for the modernizing process in a highly effective way. However...it became increasingly difficult to maintain such a rigid system of higher education. This is considered the principal cause of the problems that Japanese education faced, such as academic careerism and excessive emphasis on examinations, the so-called "examination hell" (Aso and Amano 1983, 45).

All in all, the call for diversification of Japanese education was continuously debated in the 1970s, for diversity challenged the traditional stress on central control and uniformity. Even today, diversification is a central concern of the National Council on Educational Reform.

The Educational System Structure

More than 97 percent of high school students and 90 percent of college and university students complete their education. Japan gives its citizens high quality, disciplined schooling for a prolonged period. Today twenty-eight million children and youths, a quarter of the national population, participate in the nation's educational enterprise. Ninety-two percent of four- and five-year-olds attend kindergarten and day care centers. Literally 100 percent of the age groups at the elementary and lower secondary levels attend school, and 94 percent of the high school age group are enrolled in upper secondary schools. Fully one-third of the upper secondary graduates advance to college and university or some form of postsecondary institutions.

Two pivotal national laws, the Fundamental Law of Education and the School Education Law, provide the legal basis of education and define broad aims, functions, and structure of formal education in Japan. Postwar reform democratized Japanese education by converting a multitracked structure to a single-track structure, which promotes equal educational opportunity and meritocratic competition--an efficient and egalitarian system that has contributed to the nation's industrialization.

The academic year begins on April 1 and ends on March 31, corresponding to Japan's fiscal year. During the academic year elementary and secondary students attend school for 240 days, including half days on Saturdays, of which approximately thirty days are devoted to noninstructional activities. Compulsory education is provided for nine years, from ages six to fifteen; six and three years each at the elementary and lower secondary school. Japan has three kinds of schools, different in the source of their funding: national, financed by the national government; public, financed by local municipalities and prefectures; and private, financed by private organizations.

Preprimary education is noncompulsory and is offered at two types of institution: kindergartens, operating under the supervision of the Ministry of Education, and day nurseries, run by the Ministry of Welfare. Kindergarten is intended for children aged three and older, and day nurseries, defined as "child welfare facilities" under the Child Welfare Law, enroll infants from birth to five years old who need institutional care. Today about 30 percent of preprimary children aged three to five are enrolled in day-care facilities.

All children six years old must attend elementary school for six years; when they complete the elementary course they proceed to lower secondary school or middle school for three years. Unlike kindergartens, 73 percent of which are established by private organizations, 99 percent of elementary and 95 percent of lower secondary schools are run by local public authorities.

The nationally determined curriculum for elementary education includes: Japanese, social studies, arithmetic, science, music, drawing, handicrafts, physical education, moral education, special activities, and homemaking for the final two years. For the lower secondary school, the prescribed subjects are Japanese, social studies, mathematics, science, music, art, health and physical education, industrial arts and homemaking, moral education, special activities, and English, an elective that is ordinarily taken by all students. The term "special activities" refers to student activities, including classroom assemblies, student council meetings, and club activities; activities involving student guidance; and such school events as formal ceremonies, cultural performances, physical activities, study trips, health- and safety-related functions, and work-related opportunities.

Since 1974 over 90 percent of the students who finished lower secondary school have attended upper secondary school (or high school). Entry to upper secondary schools is determined on the basis of both competitive entrance examinations and the academic record of each applicant. Upper secondary schools in Japan are generally categorized into academic, vocational, and comprehensive institutions. Although the postwar upper secondary school was modeled on the American high school, it did not become a fully comprehensive school, enrolling students with various academic and vocational interests from the immediate community. Instead, Japan adopted a system whereby applicants were to be selected by written examination from a large district. This system has resulted in competitive admission and the practice of ranking schools based on their competitiveness within a given district, less competitive academic schools and vocational schools being relegated to lower ranks. In addition, competitive private schools are ranked at the top of the high school hierarchy. Thus, Japanese students first experience the intense pressure of the entrance examinations at the lower secondary level.

Students enrolled in the academic programs account for 72 percent of the total. Different kinds of courses are offered in each category to meet student needs: full time, part time, and correspondence. The full-time course lasts three years, and part-time and correspondence courses, four years or longer. Seventy-six percent of the upper secondary schools are run by local public authorities, and about 24 percent by private organizations; only a small number of schools, 0.3 percent, are institutions under the direct control of national universities. No matter what programs students are enrolled in, they must cover a set of common requirements, including Japanese, social studies, mathematics, science, health and physical education, and fine arts. In addition, nearly all students take English as a foreign language. Girls are also required to study home economics.

The education system provides special elementary and secondary schools for the handicapped of each age group. Included in this category are schools for the blind, deaf, mentally retarded, physically handicapped, and health-impaired. Children with comparatively mild disabilities are ordinarily enrolled in special classes in elementary and lower secondary schools.

Higher education includes universities, junior colleges, technical schools, special training schools, and miscellaneous schools. Universities usually offer four-year programs and six-year programs in medicine and dentistry. Two-year programs are normal at junior colleges. Admission to universities and colleges is ordinarily by a competitive entrance examination, although a growing number of institutions, especially low-ranking private colleges and universities, admit applicants solely on the basis of recommendations from high schools and interviews (Amano 1985). In 1983 the number of students admitted on the basis of recommendations accounted for 31 percent of all admitted students.

In 1985-86, Japan had 460 four-year institutions, of which only 95 and 34, respectively, were national and local public universities. Private universities, totaling 331, enrolled 73 percent of Japan's university students, whereas the relatively more prestigious and better financed national universities enrolled only 24 percent. Enrollments of female students vary considerably among these institutions: 21.9 percent at the national universities; 32.8 at the local public; and 56.3 at the private. Japan's 536 junior colleges are similarly dominated by private institutions, which constitute 84 percent of the total, and 90 percent of the students are female. Universities are ranked in a traditionally established hierarchy that places national universities and a handful of private universities above the rest of the institutions; therefore, the top institutions are rigidly ranked by prestige and reputation. There is also considerable inequality in the geographical distribution of the universities, causing

an imbalance of access to them. Tokyo alone has one-third of the total students. A striking contrast between national and private universities in student/teacher ratios may also be noted: eight to one
for national institutions and twenty to one for private institutions in
1982.

In addition to these institutions, there are technical colleges
founded in 1962 to provide a high level of vocational training; they
specialize in several industrial courses and mercantile marine studies. Eighty-seven percent of the sixty-two technical colleges are national institutions. Graduates of lower secondary schools are admitted to technical colleges, and their curricula require 5 to 5.5 years,
depending on fields of study. Finally, the special training schools, or
senshu-gakko, and miscellaneous schools, or *kakushu-gakko*, both offer vocational training for about one year. However, the former offer more technically oriented and concentrated programs than the
latter. In 1985, there were 7,315 of these, most of which are privately organized. Training is offered primarily to graduates of lower
and upper secondary schools.

Moral Education

The Japanese attach enormous importance to moral education, and it is of special interest to Americans. Like formal education itself, the development of moral education has paralleled the
evolution of Japan's modernization.

Strongly influenced by Confucianism, moral education attained its central position as early as 1880, just a dozen years after
the Meiji Restoration. Textbooks on moral education had already
been introduced by 1904. Before World War II, the themes of moral
education evolved in different stages. For example, hard work, diligence, honesty, endurance, and progress characterized the Meiji period. The early twentieth century emphasized Confucian ethics,
such as filial piety and loyalty to the emperor. Nationalism and pa-
triotism dominated in the 1930s and 1940s (Karasawa 1976). Immediately after the war, the authorities abolished moral education,
because its orientation had turned extremely nationalistic, but it
emerged again, redefined and incorporated into social studies, a new
subject that stressed citizenship education. Debate on the orientation of moral education and its proper place in the curriculum increased in the 1950s and culminated in reaffirmation of its importance. Since 1958, moral education has been a compulsory element

of the official curriculum. Elementary and lower secondary schools must allot one hour per week for moral education.

The new moral education developed in the postwar period is quite different from the moral training, or *shushin*, that existed before the war. Nevertheless, it responds to the values the Japanese have articulated from the Meiji Restoration to the present day, such as basic discipline, sound character formation, and sensitivity to social bonding and interdependence.

The Japanese want moral education to pervade all aspects of schooling. Hence the course of study stipulates that it be provided "throughout all the educational activities of the school." It stresses that moral education is involved in all dimensions of teaching and learning, especially "special activities."

There are twenty-eight moral education themes at the elementary level and sixteen at the lower secondary level. Every year each school plans to cover these themes in all grades during a thirty-five-week period (the period is only thirty-four-weeks in the first grade). Notice that this is in addition to the hours of informal moral education included in special activities (thirty-four to thirty-five for grade one through three, and seventy for grades four through nine).

The twenty-eight themes roughly fall into six categories. The first involves the importance of order, regularity, cooperation, thoughtfulness, participation, manners, and respect for public property. The second stresses endurance, hard work, character development, and high aspirations. Such moral attributes of human life as freedom, justice, fairness, rights, duties, trust, and conviction are central concerns in the third category. The fourth examines the individual's place in groups, such as the family, the school, the nation, and the world. The fifth category focuses on harmony with and appreciation of nature and the essential need for rational, scientific attitudes toward human life, and the sixth emphasizes originality.

Each school annually identifies central goals in moral education. Individual teachers, too, develop their own goals for their classes. For example, one elementary school in Okayama City stresses thoughtfulness and endurance as its central moral goals for 1985; at that school all the teachers establish common emphases and are responsible for organizing instructional materials. Unlike other subjects, no textbooks are used in moral education. Teachers often use educational television programs, expressly developed for moral education, and commercially available materials to promote students' discussion on moral issues.

The Japanese are highly critical of their education, despite its remarkable accomplishments that are envied in the United States. Educational reformers and Japanese policymakers insist today that moral education is insufficient to cope with what the National Council on Educational Reform characterizes as "the state of desolation" of Japanese education. The deterioration of schooling, in their view, is manifested in a number of ways, including increasing bullying and school violence. The council considers enrichment of moral education central to ameliorating the present state of education. It suggests that greater attention ought to be given to teaching "basic manners and customs," to developing "self-restraint and willingness to follow social norms in daily life," and to cultivating moral sensitivity to life (National Council on Educational Reform 1986, 16-17).

In the meantime, the Curriculum Council of the Ministry of Education, which is considering the curricular revision forthcoming in 1992, has begun to deliberate on moral education. Preliminary reports suggest that the council intends to strengthen moral education, especially at the elementary level, underscoring the importance of developing "fundamental living habits" (Asahi Shimbun 1986). Thus, as we have repeatedly pointed out, the Japanese faith in fusing moral training into every aspect of formal education is unlikely to diminish.

University Entrance Examinations

Applicants generally win admission to universities and colleges on a competitive basis, though a third of entrants to universities and an even larger proportion of entrants to junior colleges gain admission via recommendations from high school principals (Amano 1986). Most applicants, however, especially those seeking admission to relatively prestigious institutions, are required to compete among themselves.

In 1983, applicants totaled 879,969, of whom 204,104 were *ronin*, high school graduates who, having initially failed to gain entry to the universities of their choice, spent a year or more preparing to try again. In that year, 604,329 applicants, including 154,918 *ronin*, were admitted; 62 percent of the university applicants won admission.

The university entrance examinations are currently one of the most persistent sources of tension in Japanese life. The pressure they exert on adolescents and secondary schools to meet the requirements of the high school and university entrance examinations has become a common source of perpetual, but culturally expected anxiety for students, parents, and teachers. For most applicants entrance examinations carry the greatest weight in deciding admission to universities. They alone determine admission to the national and public universities, while other kinds of relevant information, such as high school scholastic records, teachers' recommendations, and aptitude, are little considered. However, university entrance examinations have positive effects as well. They are one of the central and most persistent forces that drive Japanese students to high performance, and they contribute to disciplined study habits. Indeed, the entrance examinations are a centerpiece of high school education.

There are three significant factors, among others, that contribute to intense competition in the university entrance examinations. The first is the existence of an entrenched hierarchy of universities, which makes admission to prestigious universities highly competitive. The second factor, more culturally significant, relates to Japan's social mobility pattern. The ideal pattern of social mobility involves vertical enhancement within work organizations offering lifetime employment, rather than horizontal mobility across these organizations, in search of further rewards and recognition. Vertical mobility requires that individuals gain access to desired organizations immediately after their graduation from university, so that they may readily commit to an organizational orientation. Once they become employed, their social status becomes correlated with the social prestige of their companies (Nakane 1972, 104-20). The social prestige and rank of the university from which youths graduate tend to determine their opportunities for employment by the corporation or government organizations that they choose. Therefore, winning admission to prestigious universities is crucial for the futures of young people and guarantees that they will obtain employment at a socially prestigious and stable corporation. This accounts for the unusual pressure to excel on the entrance examinations. The third, and last, factor is Japan's social structure, which stresses school credentials.

The intense entrance examinations in Japan are not a recent practice peculiar to the postindustrial setting. They began early in the course of Japanese modernization, shortly after the Meiji education system had been firmly established, in the late nineteenth century. They were introduced as an objective, meritocratic method of selecting applicants for secondary and higher schools. Former *ronin* constituted 43 percent of the enrollees in the higher schools as early as 1906. Competition for entrance to these schools intensified in the 1910s and 1920s (Amano 1982, 165). Applicants converged in the competitive middle schools, which provided better chances for admission to prestigious higher schools, leading to the best university. Although graduates of higher schools were admitted to universities without entrance examinations, their ambition was to win admission to the most prestigious institution, making entry to it very competitive. The prototype of today's fierce entrance examinations developed early in the twentieth century, as a response to the development of a hierarchy of schools ranked by reputation and competitiveness in gaining employment in government.

School Finance

Another unique feature of Japanese education is the relative equality of financing throughout the nation. Variations in operational expenditures per student at the compulsory level are less than 20 percent between the wealthiest and the poorest public school districts (Cummings and Kobayashi 1985, 425). The role of the central government is critical in equalizing school financing, as in other aspects of schooling. The responsibility for financial support of public education is shared by the national government and the prefectural and municipal governments. At each level, funds for financing public schools are generated from taxes and other governmental revenues. National subsidies are earmarked for national institutions at all levels and for municipal and prefectural schools; national subsidies are also provided for private institutions.

The national government subsidizes one-half of the cost of compulsory education at the local level, paying for salaries and allowances of teachers and other personnel, teaching equipment, school building construction, and facilities. Moreover, it provides free textbooks for compulsory education. In 1984, the national treasury's share of the nation's total expenditures for compulsory education was 53.3 percent, including 8.1 percent as capital expenditures for local public school facilities. Put differently, nearly one-half of the total public expenditures for elementary and lower secondary education is funded by the national government, and the remaining half is funded evenly by prefectural and municipal sources.

In summary, Japan's school financing provides extraordinary equality in school facilities, teacher salaries, and per pupil expenditures, regardless of locality. This reflects the general pattern of the Ministry of Education's commitment to egalitarian education.

Industry and Education's Response

Economic and political imperatives dictate the development and shape of formal education in the modernization of nations. Meiji Japan is a classic example of the vital significance of education in economic development. In the postwar era, too, those same imperatives guided the course of educational development, which parallel the nation's experience a century earlier. In both eras, the central government played a key role in stimulating and planning educational development in response to industry's needs, just as it played a central role in promoting economic growth.

The unparalleled success of Japan's industry has been significantly assisted by the expansion of formal education since the late 1950s. Indeed, the nation's educational expansion can be best viewed as a function of economic development and a response to industry's needs for human resources. Since the middle of the 1950s the interests of private industry have been a highly crucial factor in shaping educational policy.

What has been identified as manpower theory, stressing the development of human capital, has been a guiding paradigm underlying educational expansion in Japan, especially since 1960. That paradigm has served well and was useful to educational planners during the rapid economic growth. Several agents stimulated educational expansion, including several powerful industrial organizations serving as spokesmen to promote private industry's interests: the Economic Council, an advisory body to the prime minister; the Ministry of Education; and the Central Council of Education, functioning as a vital link between the Ministry of Education and the public and private sectors. Although those agents fulfilled different functions, representing varied interests, they concertedly contributed to forming the basic policy of educational expansion.

As early as 1952, almost immediately after Japan's independence, Nikkeiren (Japan Federation of Employees) began to urge the central government to move away from the postwar emphasis on common academic studies and citizenship and toward more specialized and vocational training, as in the prewar era. In its repeated recommendations to the government in 1952, 1954, 1956, and 1957, it stressed the need for functional differentiation of secondary and higher education, so as to upgrade training, especially in science and engineering (Yokohama National University Institute for Modern Education 1983, 249-57). Moreover, in its recommendations to the government in 1956, Nikkeiren issued a stern warning reminding the nation to measure further manpower needs against the background of the latest technological innovations in the advanced nations. It articulated a critical awareness of the vital linkage between industry's demands for human resources and education and set forth initial strategies for other industrial organizations, such as Keizai Doukai (the Committee for Economic Development), to follow. In fact, between 1952 and 1969, industrial organizations made a dozen recommendations outlining goals and strategies for enhancing human abilities and promoting science and engineering (Yokohama National University Institute for Modern Education 1983, 249-57). A report on expanding upper secondary education, compiled by the Central Council of Education in 1966 and submitted to the Minister of Education, reinforced the views of industry.

    In the meantime, the government played no less significant a part in emphasizing the importance of the human factor in economic growth. Its national income-doubling plan, an ambitious economic program announced by Prime Minister Ikeda in 1960, virtually transformed the pace of both industrial and educational development. That plan delineated the educational investment and manpower needs to accomplish the goals. A report prepared in 1960 by the Economic Council of the Economic Planning Agency, shortly before the plan was announced, was influential in defining the role of education in implementing the plan. Titled "Report on the Long-Range Educational Plan for the Doubling of Income," it maintained that "economic competition among nations is a technical [technological] competition, and technical competition has become an educational competition" (Shimahara 1979, 133). The income-doubling plan required an additional 170,000 scientists and engineers and 440,000 technicians. The Ministry of Education responded by calling for enhanced training in those fields. In its Education White Paper published in 1962, the ministry concluded: "The economic theory of education had been accepted positively among the planners of educational policy as well" (Aso and Amano 1983, 81).

In the 1960s those plans stimulated increased investment in education. For example, university enrollments in science and engineering increased from 108,788 in 1960 to 325,745 in 1970; enrollments in technical training in upper secondary schools similarly grew from 237,328 in 1960 to 565,508 in 1970. In addition, in response to the demand for middle-level engineers, nineteen technical colleges appeared in 1962; by 1970 their number had increased to sixty. Furthermore, the increased numbers of university students in science and engineering led to a significant change in enrollment patterns: those students represented 18.2 percent of the total university enrollment in 1960 and 23.2 percent in 1975. The national universities showed the same patterns: science and engineering students rose from 24 to 33 percent.

The economic context in which educational expansion took place can be further illuminated by the growth of Japan's gross national product. In the late 1950s, its share of the world gross national product stood at about 3 percent, but it rose dramatically to 6 percent by 1973. The nation achieved an average annual growth rate of 11 percent from 1961 to 1969, accomplishing the income-doubling plan in only five years. By 1969, Japan's gross national product was 3.7 times that of 1960.

Rapid educational expansion came nearly to a halt shortly after the oil crisis of 1973 brought economic recession. The percentage of high school graduates advancing to colleges and universities reached 34.2 percent in 1975 and has been declining since then. The reason for this seems to be associated with the fact that the gap between the career earnings of university and high school graduates has narrowed, providing a disincentive to individual investment in university education (Ushiogi 1986). Likewise, the high school enrollment rate rose to 93.5 percent in 1976 and then headed upward only slightly.

Problems and Reform in the 1980s

One of the long-standing national goals since the Meiji Restoration has been to catch up with the industrialized nations in the West. Japan has successfully achieved that goal with respect to its education and economy. In particular, the phenomenal development of industry in the 1960s and early 1970s led to an expansion of education that has surpassed that of all industrialized nations but the United States.

Japan has developed an efficient national system of elementary and secondary education based on uniformity. The Japanese deemed uniformity essential to promote egalitarianism and to upgrade the adaptive competencies of the entire population to be compatible with the needs of a developing industry and higher standards of living. Japan's educational policy has been remarkably successful in the postwar period in encouraging its citizens to participate in all levels of formal education. Both economic and educational expansion has enhanced social mobility. Upper secondary education has become almost universal although not compulsory, and higher education is no longer only for the elite, but for the masses as well.

Japan, thus, has a highly trained and well-disciplined work force that contributes to its dominant economic role in the international marketplace. Its per capita income is one of the highest in the world. However, as repeatedly pointed out by the National Council on Educational Reform, a task force that is deliberating what reformers consider to be Japan's third comprehensive reform since the Meiji era, Japan is now at a different stage of development, a stage where the development and needs of individual citizens call for greater attention and where society is dominated by information, requiring divergent skills, creativity, and diversified participation in sophisticated industry. Thus, the longstanding emphasis on the efficient training of citizens with uniform competencies is challenged today. In the words of the council:

> Most important in the educational reform to come is
> to do away with the uniformity, rigidity, closedness,
> and lack of internationalism, all of which are deep-
> rooted defects of our educational system, and to es-
> tablish...the principle of putting emphasis on individ-
> uality (National Council on Educational Reform
> 1985, 26).

Indeed, as aptly pointed out by an observer of Japanese education, "Japan seems like an anthill, busy, well-organized, and competitive, but unable to foster individual expression or to support idiosyncratic or uncommon talents" (Rohlen 1986, 36). As stated earlier, Japan's past educational policies are now being challenged by the very accomplishments they sired. The council unambiguously recognizes the nation's obsession with growth and output, accomplished through what it now regards to be defective means, namely the imposition of rigid uniformity on all levels of education.

The council's declaration that "the principle of putting emphasis on individuality" is its foremost consideration is very significant. That premise is, however, a compromise of a more progressive position initially enunciated by those members of the council who advocated radical liberalization of standards and regulations controlled by the Ministry of Education. Nevertheless, even the compromised declaration points to the need for individual choice, decentralization, and an educational structure that facilitates individual choice at all levels. Philosophically, the council's recommendation reflects some elements of the immediate postwar reforms, rejected in the 1950s, and the aforementioned recommendations of the Central Council of Education in 1971. Some of the reform proposals made by the Japan Teachers Union are similar to these recommendations, although the union and the council have quite different ideological perspectives. Thus convergence of views on some vital educational issues is highly relevant to the reform movement (Japan Teachers Union 1983).

The "uniformity," "rigidity," and "closedness" of Japan's educational system have contributed to intensifying competition for entrance to upper secondary schools and especially to universities. On the one hand, over 70 percent of all ninth graders felt anxious about failing the entrance examination to the upper secondary level, according to a recent survey (Fukaya 1983, 164). On the other hand, what Amano calls the "structuration" within and between the Japanese educational and economic systems is exerting a negative impact upon young people's aspirations (Amano 1986, 24). As the recent trend of stratification within the educational and economic structures evolved, it produced polarized consequences. Although intense competition for university entrance increased among ambitious youth, apathy and unwillingness to compete increased among less motivated youth.

Another source of concern is the increasing polarization of upper secondary education into academic and vocational tracks: academic schools for scholastically able students and vocational schools for students who are academically less motivated--a criterion not based on individual aptitude. Moreover, increasing numbers of students in academic schools are unable to meet the rigid standards because their abilities and aptitudes vary considerably. Rigidity and uniformity appear to be further associated with one of the most sensitive current issues in Japanese education: student misbehavior, encompassing widespread bullying, school violence, juvenile delinquency, and an adamant refusal to go to school.

Still another problem is the quality of higher education. As a Japanese scholar points out, "the prevailing view among university professors is that neither the general education nor the professional education is complete" (Amano 1986, 35). These two curricula constitute the undergraduate program in Japan. Graduate training is also criticized. Because professional training is stressed at the undergraduate level in Japan, graduate education is not considered a functionally distinct and more specialized level of professional training than it is, for example, in the United States. This view is responsible for underdeveloped and undemanding graduate programs.

To offset the effects of these programs, the National Council on Educational Reform is pressing for "diversity" and "flexibility" in education; a more coherent relation between lower and upper secondary education; improvement of instruction in basic knowledge and skills and moral education; decentralization of educational administration; and the upgrading of the quality of teachers through improved teacher education and rigorous internship. The council is also recommending provisions for developing distinctive and diverse institutional structures and programs at the undergraduate and graduate levels and increased access to training at the master's and doctor's levels.

Several relevant events that precipitated the establishment of the National Council on Educational Reform constitute an important background of the reform campaign as a political commitment.

To begin, the Liberal Democratic Party's Task Force on Culture and Education was already deliberating reform issues as early as 1981 and produced a report focusing on policy recommendations to restructure Japan's school system. Historically, working closely with ministry officials, this task force has been a dominant influence on the Ministry of Education and educational legislation. In the same year the Minister of Education charged the Central Council of Education with recommending a revised curriculum that would reflect important changes in society.

In 1982 when the Nakasone Cabinet was first formed, the nation's mood for school reform was growing rapidly. A perceptive and astute politician, Nakasone wasted no time in appointing an advisory panel on education and culture. The panel, chaired by Marasu Ibuka, founder of the Sony Corporation, was to advise him on reform and to formulate a set of conceptually broad categories of reform issues. The panel prepared a document delineating the scope of work to be considered by a task force on reform (Conference on Culture and Education, 1985). As anticipated, the panel became immensely important; not only did it become the key organization Nakasone relied on to develop his views on education, it also helped generate further impetus for the movement.

Three members of the panel were subsequently appointed to the reform council, one as acting chairman, and another as head of the division deliberating upon Japan's education for the twenty-first century. There was an obvious ideological influence by the panel on the council. In late 1983, the so-called Kyoto Seminar on Educational Reform (Kyoto Zakai) convened under the sponsorship of a private organization, the powerful Matsushita Electric Company (known as Panasonic in the United States). Its seven-point recommendation instantaneously gained national visibility and contributed to the acceleration of the movement. Its 1984 report, resulting from the seminar, reflects the views of the prime minister's panel (Kuroha 1985, 23-27).

Meanwhile, Nakasone was successfully marshalling support from other political parties. In 1984, at Nakasone's request, the Vice Minister of Education also prepared a memorandum outlining a broad range of urgent areas to be considered. Nakasone received his pledge to promote the movement.

By the spring of 1984 Nakasone had become thoroughly acquainted with the critical issues of Japanese education and was ready to move ahead. Preparation of the national bill to establish the council was already underway, and the bill passed in the Diet in the summer of 1984.

As established by law, the council consists of a panel of forty-five members, assisted by thirty full-time staff members. Its four divisions focus upon education for the twenty-first century; activating the educational functions of society; reforming elementary and secondary education; and reforming higher education.

The council was established as a national task force under direct control of the prime minister and completely independent of the Ministry of Education. This status allows two interesting political insights. First, Nakasone was interested in exercising direct personal influence on the reform council. Second, independence from the bureaucratic Ministry of Education let the council develop audacious reform proposals unconstrained by the ministry's views, which

Nakasone regarded as too conservative. Thus, the reform movement became clearly identified with Nakasone's political interest.

A Final Remark

Having begun deliberations in September, 1984, the council presented its first report in June, 1985, its second in April, 1986, and the third in April, 1987. Because the news media extensively covered the council's deliberations, the reports captured the nation's attention and stimulated extensive public reaction. Thus far, the reports have generated more questions for further inquiry and public debate than specific proposals. Careful review of the reports reveals that they have at least three things in common. First, the council envisions comprehensive reforms of formal and informal education at all levels and in all categories, including the home and community. Second, the council addresses an extraordinarily broad range of issues, and, perhaps because of that, its deliberations tend to remain at a general, abstract level. Third, there are relatively limited specific proposals to be considered for implementation; the recommendations made by the council thus far focus upon the problems referred to earlier.

Japan is coming full circle. Decentralization and individuality, which interest today's reformers, were two of the pivotal points presented in the report of the United States Education Mission to Japan during the Occupation period.

Subsequent to the mission's report, the Japanese Reform Committee drastically altered Japan's educational administration in order to implement lay and local control of schooling. Meanwhile, to encourage independent thinking and to develop personality, as stressed by the mission, American progressive education was introduced to Japan. By the early 1950s, however, decentralization, local diversity, and progressive education came under intense attack. As mentioned earlier, educational policy shifted from decentralization to centralization, from diversity to uniformity, and local freedom to central control.

It is interesting to note that school reform movements in the 1980s in Japan and the United States are developing in opposite directions. One the one hand, the American movement seeks greater compatibility across the United States in curricula, student performance, fiscal standards, teacher certification, and in other areas. On the other hand, Japanese reformers are interested in eliminating rigid uniformity and standardization--a mark of centralized control by the Ministry of Education. They are attempting to pave a way toward diversifying education and decentralizing educational administration. Keeping in mind that Japanese education has been centralized since the nineteenth century, to what extent is Japan committed to altering the current system of schooling and administrations?

References

Amano, I. 1982. *Education and Selection* [Kyoiku to senbatus]. Tokyo: Daiichi Hoki.

-----. 1985. "Higher Education and Student Enrollment Selection in Japan." Paper presented at the International Seminar on Education and Reform, Tokyo.

-----. 1986. "Educational Crisis in Japan." In W.K. Cummings, E.R. Beauchamp, S. Ichikawa, V.N. Kobayashi, and M. Ushiogi, eds., *Educational Policies in Crisis*, pp. 23-43. New York: Praeger.

Asahi Shimbun. 1986, June 7. A daily Japanese newspaper.

Aso, M. 1981. "The Structural Pathology of Japanese Credential Society" [Nippon gata gakureki shakai no kozo to byori]. In H. Takeuchi and M. Aso, eds., *The Transformation of Japanese Credential Society* [Nippon gakureki shakai wa kawaru], pp. 2-26. Tokyo: Yuhikaku.

-----, and I. Amano. 1983. *Education and Japan's Modernization*. Tokyo: Japan Times.

Central Council of Education [Chuo kyoiku shingikai]. 1971. *Basic Policies for Comprehensive Expansion and Improvement of School Education* [Kongo ni okeru gakko kyoiku no sogoteki na kakuju seibi no tameno kihonteki shisaku ni tsuite]. Tokyo: Monbusho.

Conference on Culture and Education. 1985. "Report to the Prime Minister." *Education Week*, February 20, p. 34.

Cummings, W.K., and V.N. Kobayashi. 1985. "Education in Japan." *Current History* 84, 422-33.

Fukaya, M. 1983. *The Alienation of Children* [Koritsuka suru kodomotachi]. Tokyo: Nippon Hoso Kyokai.

Japan Teachers Union. 1983. *Educational Reform in Present Japan: Report of the Second JTU Council on Educational Reform.* Tokyo: Japan Teachers Union.

Karasawa, T. 1976. *Japan's Modernization and Education* [Nippon no kindaika to kyoiku]. Tokyo: Daiichi Hoki.

Kinoshita, S. 1983. "The Postwar Curriculum" [Sengo no kyoiku katei]. In M. Okazu, ed., *The Encyclopedia of Curriculum* [Kyoiku katei jiten], pp. 25-36. Tokyo: Shogakkukan.

Kuroha, R. 1985. *The National Council on Educational Reform* [Rinkyoshin]. Tokyo: Nippon Keizai Shimbunsha.

Ministry of Education. 1980. *Japan's Modern Educational System.* Tokyo: Monbusho.

Nakane, C. 1972. *Japanese Society.* Berkeley: University of California.

National Council on Educational Reform [Rinkyoshin]. 1985. *First Report on Educational Reform.* Tokyo: Government of Japan.

-----. 1986. *Summary of Second Report on Educational Reform.* Tokyo: Government of Japan.

Organization for Economic Cooperation and Development. 1971. *Reviews of National Policies for Education: Japan.* Paris: Organization for Economic Cooperation and Development.

Rohlen, T.P. 1986. "Japanese education." *American Scholar* 55, 29-43.

Shimahara, N.K. 1979. *Adaptation and Education in Japan.* New York: Praeger.

Ushiogi, M. 1986. "Transition from School to Work: The Japanese Case." In W.K. Cummings, E.R. Beauchamp, S. Ichikawa, V.N. Kobayashi, and M. Ushiogi, eds., *Educational Policies in Crisis*, pp. 197-209. New York: Praeger.

Yamaguchi, S. 1980. "The Modernization of Curricular Content and its Critique" [Kyoka Naiyo no Gendaika to Sono Hihan]. In Y. Shibata, ed., *The Making of Curriculum* [Kyoiku Katei Hensei no Soi to Kufu], pp. 190-206. Tokyo: Gakushu Kenkyusha.

Yanagi, H. 1984. "Modern Problems of the Curriculum" [Kyoiku Katei no Gendai Teki Kadai]. In S. Sato and H. Inaba, eds., *School and Curriculum* [Gakko to Kyoiku Katei], pp. 46-52. Tokyo: Daiichi Hoki.

Yokohama National University Institute for Modern Education [Yokohama Kokuritsu Daigaku Gendai Kyoiku Kenkyusho]. 1983. *Central Council of Education and Educational Reform* [Chukyoshin to Kyoiku Kaikaku]. Tokyo: Sanichi Shobo.

CHAPTER 2

FORMAL PRE-ELEMENTARY EDUCATION IN JAPAN

Lois Peak
U.S. Department of Education

Acknowledgments

Data collection for this chapter was generously supported by a Japan Foundation Fellowship and a Sinclair Kennedy Travelling Fellowship from Harvard University. Data analysis and writing were made possible through the assistance of the Office of Educational Research and Improvement, U.S. Department of Education. I am indebted to Dr. Shigefumi Nagano for his guidance and advice during the data collection process, to Keith Stubbs and Tom Litkowski for their technical support during data analysis, and to Robert Leestma for his comments on an earlier draft of the chapter. The views and ideas expressed in this chapter are those of the author and do not necessarily reflect the position or policy of the U.S. Department of Education.

Introduction

Japanese children receive considerable formal learning before entering elementary school. This experience is of two primary types: preschool (or day care) and enrichment lessons. Nearly all children attend one if not two years of preschool or day care. Many children also attend enrichment lessons of various types. These lessons are unrelated to the preschool or day care programs and typically consist of weekly private or small group lessons. Swimming and piano lessons are currently popular.

Despite the widespread realization that early education is important in Japan, Western students of Japanese education still lack a good quantitative understanding of the formal early educational experiences Japanese children bring with them to first grade. With a few exceptions (Boocock 1987), reports to date in the English language have been based largely upon fragmentary reporting of

Japanese official statistics, Westerners' personal observations, and anecdotes derived from Japanese news media and the experiences of Japanese individuals. Furthermore, there is virtually no information regarding how Japanese children's early educational experiences are affected by family background, or by urban or rural residence patterns.

This paper provides some preliminary quantitative information regarding Japanese children's formal preprimary educational experience. It also provides descriptive information concerning enrichment lessons. The first section presents information about preschools and day-care centers and official enrollment statistics. The second section reports the results of a questionnaire survey of Japanese children's enrollment in preprimary enrichment lessons. In addition to describing the basic characteristics of Japanese preschool children's enrollment in enrichment lessons, some tentative relationships between enrollment patterns and family background and urban or rural residence are noted. The third section describes a typical lesson in two types of enrichment lesson centers. The chapter concludes with recommendations for future research.

Preschool and Day-Care Centers

Enrollment

The overwhelming majority of Japanese children attend two years of preschool or day care before entering first grade. Preschools (yochien) are sometimes translated as kindergartens, although they bear little resemblance to American institutions of that name. Most preschools offer classes for three-, four-, and five-year-olds and are almost always structurally and administratively separate from elementary schools (Peak 1987, 72). Neither public nor private preschools are free of charge, although both receive government subsidies. In 1983, the average parent paid approximately 100,000 yen ($670 at $1.00 = 150 yen) annually in tuition and fees to send their child to a public preschool and 200,000 yen ($1,340) for a private one. Roughly 60 percent of Japanese preschools are private (Leestma, August, George, and Peak 1987, 77).

Day-care centers (hoikuen) are officially translated as nursery schools. By definition they are established to serve the children of working mothers. Although children may be enrolled in infancy, in fact, most children are three, four, or five years of age at entrance. Approximately 60 percent of day-care centers are public (Leestma et al. 1987, 77). Both public and private day-care centers are subsidized by the government. Tuition and fees are determined on a sliding scale based on parental income (National Council of Day Nurseries 1986, 5). Although the amount a family pays for tuition depends upon its financial circumstances, enrolling a child in day care is usually cheaper than enrolling the child in preschool.

Preschools are under the jurisdiction of the Ministry of Education, Science and Culture, and day care centers are administered by the Ministry of Health and Welfare. Despite the fact that they are controlled by different government agencies, they provide a basically similar learning experience for the child. From the child's point of view, the primary difference is that day-care centers are in session from 7:00 a.m. until 6:00 p.m., while preschools operate only between 8:30 and 2:00. Both require attendance six days a week.

Many mothers of children enrolled in preschool state that they initially wished to enroll their children in a day-care center because it is less expensive and the children are cared for all day (Peak 1987, 87-88). However, due to a shortage of facilities, day-care centers strictly enforce an eligibility criterion that the mother must be employed or otherwise incapable of caring for the child. Because day-care centers serve almost exclusively the families of working mothers, students tend to be drawn from a somewhat lower socioeconomic strata than children who are enrolled in preschools.

Licensed preschools and day-care centers must meet the ministries' standards concerning staffing and physical facilities. In addition to licensed centers, there are an undetermined but growing number of unlicensed facilities (Boocock 1987, 5-6). Table 1 shows the number of children enrolled in officially licensed preschools and day-care centers in 1984.

Table 1 indicates that virtually all Japanese children attend at least one year of formal preprimary education at a licensed institution, and the vast majority of children attend for two years. Specialists on Japanese early education agree that preschool or day care for four- and five-year-old Japanese children has acquired the status of "semi-compulsory education" (Boocock 1987, 5). Although these extra years of schooling are neither legally required nor free of charge, the very high percentage of children enrolled attests to

TABLE 1

Number of Children Enrolled in Licensed Preschool and Day-Care Facilities as a Percentage of Population Age 0-5 by Type of Institution (1984)

Age	Population cohort	Preschool attendees		Day-care attendees		Preschool & day-care attendees	
		# of children	% of cohort	# of children	% of cohort	# of children	% of cohort
0	1,498,000	--	--	18,353	1.2%	18,353	1.2%
1	1,511,000	--	--	92,377	6.1%	92,377	6.1%
2	1,513,000	--	--	180,429	11.9%	180,429	11.9%
3	1,529,000	202,871	13.3%	337,758	22.1%	540,629	35.1%
4	1,579,000	855,701	54.2%	494,127	31.3%	1,349,828	85.5%
5	1,632,000	1,074,370	65.8%	511,558	31.3%	1,585,928	97.1%

SOURCE: For Preschools: Monbusho 1984, 416-17. For Day-Care Centers: Unpublished data supplied by Ministry of Welfare, drawn from annual reports of the Ministry of Welfare.

the high value Japanese parents place on early learning experiences.

Curriculum

Both preschools and day-care centers follow the same official curriculum (Kodama 1983, 9). The daily classroom routines and typical learning activities are similar. The main goals of the official preschool and day-care curriculum are explicitly nonacademic. Rather than emphasizing basic reading and number skills, the curriculum is geared to group life, basic self-sufficiency, and personal management skills (Peak 1987, 101).

The six areas of the official preschool curriculum (health, society, nature, language, music, rhythm, and arts and crafts) generally reflect the traditional subject matter divisions of the elementary school curriculum. However, closer examination of the curriculum and observation of the way in which it is typically implemented in Japanese preschools reveal that these six areas are primarily media through which the more important goals of training in group behavior and basic habits of daily life are achieved (Peak 1987, 102).

The Ministry of Education's official curriculum does not encourage the teaching of letter recognition and number skills in preschools and day-care centers. The ministry's detailed specification of appropriate preschool curriculum content makes no mention of teaching letter recognition, phonics, or basic reading skills. It notes, "concerning letters, it is desirable that the level of instruction remain within that which is naturally acquired through daily life experiences, in accordance with the child's age and developmental level" (Monbusho 1975, 12; see Peak 1987, 108 for translation). Concerning numbers it notes, "Quantity should be treated in accordance with children's age and developmental level, using concrete objects, within the context of everyday life and play. Moreover it is not desirable to purposelessly have children learn numerals or to count large numbers of things" (Peak 1987, 108).

The official curriculum encourages preschools and day-care centers to recognize and maintain the distinction between preschool and elementary education. The nature of preschool education is to provide "integrated instruction based on the experiences of children's daily life" (Peak 1987, 101). In common practice this is interpreted to mean that preschool instructional activities should be structured around extended projects such as planting sweet potatoes or preparing for the school sports day, rather than around pencil and paper activities providing practice in reading and counting skills.

The professional consensus among preschool, day-care, and elementary school teachers and principals is that the rule of thumb for the upper limit of preschool and day-care training is to teach children no more than to recognize and write their own names and to count as far as ten. Although a few preschools and day-care centers ignore ministry guidelines and do teach basic letter recognition and number skills, the majority do not teach these things (Peak 1987, 110). Few Japanese preschools and day-care centers are as content oriented as American kindergartens.

Japanese preschools and day-care centers do, however, provide important experience in school-relevant skills other than reading and counting. Learning to live, work, and play as a group, manage personal belongings, take responsibility for assigned tasks, and enjoy coming to school are all outgrowths of the preprimary experience. These skills unquestionably facilitate the Japanese child's transition to elementary school life.

Enrichment Lessons

Enrichment lessons are another popular source of formal educational experience for preschool-aged children in Japan. A wide variety of lessons such as swimming, piano, English conversation, calligraphy, arithmetic, and examination preparation come under this heading. In Japanese, a distinction is usually made between *okeikogoto* or nonacademically-oriented lessons such as swimming and piano, and *juku*, such as arithmetic and examination preparation, that are explicitly designed to assist students' academic progress. This distinction is less meaningful for the types of lessons provided for the preschool age group. For the purpose of this study, both *okeikogoto* and *juku* are included within the term "enrichment lessons."

Enrichment lessons are not sponsored by preschools or elementary schools and do not take place on school property. They are chosen and financed entirely by the family and take place in a variety of settings. For example, piano lessons may occur at a piano teacher's house or at a music lesson center operated as a private business. In general, teaching in lesson centers is more common than teaching in private homes. Typically, children attend lessons once a week for about an hour.

Virtually no systematic information is available in either English or Japanese regarding enrichment lessons for pre-elementary-aged children. Therefore, an exploratory questionnaire survey was conducted to gather basic information regarding Japanese children's participation in these lessons. The primary goal was to collect preliminary estimates of enrollments, the age at which children begin lessons, and the most popular types of lessons. A secondary goal was to gain some understanding of the effect of family background and urban or rural residence on children's attendance patterns.

Due to the modest scale and exploratory nature of this initial survey, results should not be interpreted as representing reliable national averages. It is hoped, however, that these preliminary results will be useful to other researchers planning more comprehensive studies of the field.

Description of the Study

In order to study Japanese children's pre-elementary enrichment lesson experiences, it was decided to obtain a complete record of the subjects' lesson attendance from birth through entrance to the first grade. Therefore, as soon as practical after the beginning of the school year, mothers of first grade students completed a questionnaire that elicited a history of their child's enrollment in enrichment lessons.

The decision to sample newly matriculated first graders was made for two reasons. It provided a more complete history of pre-elementary learning experiences than would have been possible through sampling students in the last months of preschool. Also, it proved more efficient to obtain a sample of approximately one thousand students by contacting eleven elementary schools than the thirty or more preschools that would have been required to obtain a sample of a similar size.

The questionnaire was developed following twelve months of field experience in Japanese pre-elementary education and in conjunction with interviews of mothers whose children were enrolled in enrichment lessons. It was written in Japanese by a bilingual research team and repeatedly revised and refined on the basis of trial administration to mothers. A pilot test involving one hundred first grade students in two schools was performed, and results were analyzed before the final draft of the questionnaire was developed. The data reported here comprised only one section of the entire questionnaire that queried mothers concerning a broad variety of their children's early educational experiences.

The final questionnaire was administered to mothers of 1,150 newly matriculated first grade students in eleven schools in three different prefectures in Japan, early in the third month of the 1984 school year. All children were in the first grade and between six years and three months and seven years and three months of age at the time of the survey.

As is the custom in Japan, the researcher's contacts with surveyed schools were established through the introduction of various acquaintances. Once permission to perform the survey was secured, the principals were requested to have classroom teachers distribute the questionnaire to all first grade students. Parents completed and returned the questionnaire anonymously through the child to the classroom teacher, who returned it to the researcher. A total of 1,082 codable questionnaires were returned. Response rate varied by school, ranging between 82 percent and 100 percent.

Although a secondary goal of the study was to acquire information on the effect of family background on Japanese children's participation in enrichment lessons, it was not possible to study this directly by collecting information on parental income, occupation, and educational level for individual children. To request such individual information is a sensitive social issue in Japan, particularly within the school setting. Therefore, it was impossible to obtain data which would have allowed a student-by-student analysis of the relationship between family background and attendance at enrichment lessons.

However, to obtain a rough approximation of the effect of family background, schools were carefully selected to represent a range of types of socioeconomic neighborhoods and typical parental occupations. To provide some comparison with metropolitan Tokyo, small towns and farming communities were also included. Once selected, the socioeconomic characteristics of each school were further defined by asking the principal to describe the school, the neighborhood, and the typical family background of the student body as a whole. The descriptions of schools which follow are based upon the principals' reports. Names of schools have been changed to provide anonymity and facilitate description.

Elite Girls' Elementary

>Prestigious elite private girls' school in an historic section of Tokyo. Entrance is determined by examination and interview. One in ten applicants to the elementary school is accepted. Students are typically drawn from long-established affluent upper and upper-middle class families. (Only one-half of one percent of all Japanese elementary students are enrolled in private schools.)

Showcase Laboratory School

>Famous public laboratory school attached to a national university in Tokyo. Entrance is by examination and lottery and only one in twenty applicants is selected. A high proportion of graduates eventually enter elite universities. With a few exceptions, children are from upper-middle class families. (Approximately 0.4 percent of Japanese elementary schoolchildren attend national public schools.)

Executive New Town Elementary

>Neighborhood public school in a newly built prosperous professional suburb of Tokyo. The neighborhood is almost exclusively company housing for management-level employees of large multinational companies and the national government, occupations which represent an elite track within Japanese society. One in five graduates of New Town Elementary enter elite private junior high schools. Families are well educated, prosperous, upwardly mobile, and educationally conscious members of the middle and upper middle class.

Downtown Elementary

>A small public school in a densely crowded downtown area of Tokyo. The neighborhood is a mixture of comfortable condominiums on prime commercial property and small, inexpensively priced wooden

apartments. The area is in the process of transition from a residential to a commercial neighborhood. Families represent a combination of white collar and blue collar workers. The principal estimates that 10 percent of students' mothers work at night as hostesses or waitresses in the nearby entertainment district.

Retail District Elementary

A public school in a middle-class residential area of Tokyo honeycombed with small shopping arcades. Many students are the children of small shopkeepers, who typically live in small, single-family homes or a suite of rooms at the rear of the family shop. Many families have lived in the neighborhood for generations. The principal estimates that, including women who assist in the family shop, over half of students' mothers work at part-time jobs while the children are in school.

Suburban Elementary

A neighborhood public school in a postwar suburb of Tokyo. Children are drawn from middle-class families living in condominiums, apartments, and small single-family homes. The principal reports that fathers typically commute to salaried jobs in the city or work in the electronics-related industries in the neighborhood.

Dockside Elementary

A medium-sized public elementary school in a dilapidated industrial area of Tokyo, less than a mile from a huge shipyard and railway station. The neighborhood is a mixture of superhighways, storage yards, modest homes, and inexpensive wooden apartments. Parents typically perform wage labor in factories or work as temporary employees. Few are office workers. The junior high school into which these students matriculate experiences school violence problems.

Provincial City Elementary

> A public elementary school in a modern provincial city of four hundred thousand in Nagano Prefecture. Located in a newer section of the city, the school enrolls children from a mixture of types of families: university faculty, shopkeepers, officeworkers, and wage laborers.

Small Town Elementary

> One of two public elementary schools in a mountain town of five thousand people located in Fukushima Prefecture. Most families have lived in the town for generations and are involved in shopkeeping or tourist-related business. The town is comparatively traditional in both architecture and lifestyle and lacks the range of early educational opportunities available in larger urban areas.

Farmland Elementary

> A public school in rural Nagano Prefecture rising abruptly from the middle of rice fields between two small towns. The principal estimates that 90 percent of the students' families are rice or vegetable farmers. As is typical of contemporary Japanese farmers, most farms are managed by the mother and grandparents, while the father provides cash income through wage labor in local factories or light industry.

Mountaintop Elementary

> A tiny isolated school in Nagano Prefecture, high in the Japanese Alps in a small hamlet of four hundred people. There are only eighteen students in the first grade. Ninety-five percent of the students' families live in widely dispersed households, farming steeply terraced fields which much of the year are under deep snow. Most fathers supplement the family

income through seasonal road construction or
lumbering work. The principal estimates that fewer
than half of the students' fathers completed high
school. The area is economically depressed and
steadily losing its population to cities and towns.

Because the various types of communities surveyed were
represented by only one school each, considerable caution should be
exercised in interpreting the results. It is unclear how representative the surveyed schools are of others of their type. The survey's
results should not be considered definitive characterizations of the
average experience of children from various types of backgrounds.
Nor should the aggregated results be viewed as national averages.
However, the data may provide some preliminary evidence regarding the general range of variation in contemporary Japanese
preschool children's enrichment lesson experience. It is hoped that
this preliminary study can lay the groundwork for further research
of a more comprehensive and rigorous nature.

Enrollment in Enrichment Lessons

As shown in Table 2, in almost all of the schools surveyed,
half or more of the students were currently enrolled in some type of
enrichment lessons. Approximately four out of five children from
more affluent backgrounds were enrolled. Even in a working-class
school such as Dockside, and a rural school such as Farmland, at
least 40 percent of the children attended some type of lessons. Only
in extremely geographically isolated Mountaintop Elementary were
no children attending enrichment lessons (According to the principal,
no such classes or teachers existed in the community).

The high enrollment rates across a broad range of family
backgrounds and types of communities suggest that contemporary
Japanese parents perceive enrichment lessons to be a valuable
experience for preschool-aged children. Parents' willingness to pay
for these lessons in addition to regular preschool or day-care tuition
attests to the degree to which enrichment lessons are viewed as an
important part of children's informal early education.

Table 2 also shows that the newly matriculated first grade
child took one or two different types of lessons. Children from more
affluent backgrounds and those living in Tokyo tended to take more
different types of lessons.

TABLE 2

New First Graders' Participation in Enrichment Lessons, by School

	Number of students surveyed	Percentage currently attending lessons	Number of different lessons per child	Average age lessons began (yrs. mos.)	Percentage attending exam prep class
Tokyo Area Schools					
Elite Girls'	86	93%	2.10	4.10	44%
Showcase Laboratory	157	84%	1.62	4.7	57%
Executive New Town	150	85%	1.55	4.11	2%
Downtown	82	80%	1.28	5.1	6%
Retail District	69	70%	1.12	5.2	2%
Suburban	142	55%	.90	5.3	1%
Dockside	120	47%	.62	5.8	1%
Schools Outside Tokyo					
Provincial City	65	58%	.87	5.6	2%
Small Town	98	47%	.53	5.6	0
Farmland	97	40%	.46	5.10	0
Mountaintop	16	0	0	--	0
All Schools Combined	1,082	66%	1.12	5.1	13%

Detailed examination of the frequency distributions upon which Table 2 is based shows that in Elite Girls', Showcase Laboratory, and Executive New Town Elementaries, the modal child took two different types of lessons. In Downtown, Retail District, and Suburban Elementaries, the modal child took one. Of the 1,082 children sampled in this study, only one child attended six different lessons per week, and one attended five. Only slightly over 1 percent of all children attended as many as four different lessons per week. Despite articles in the Japanese popular press recounting stories of preschool children whose over-zealous mothers take them to a different enrichment class every day of the week, children who take as many as four different lessons per week appear to be extremely rare. The vast majority of Japanese mothers in this sample seemed to maintain the number of outside lessons for their children within reasonable bounds.

Table 2 also shows that most of the first graders who were taking lessons had enrolled while they were students in preschool or day care. Either they enrolled as five-year-olds or shortly before turning five. Only 8 percent of the children currently taking lessons had enrolled during the three months which had elapsed between the time the children entered first grade and the administration of the questionnaire. Therefore, the results can be assumed to be roughly representative of Japanese children's pre-elementary educational experience.

A significant minority of Japanese children enroll in enrichment lessons at a very early age. Thirty percent of the children surveyed had enrolled at age three or younger, and 6 percent had enrolled at age one or two. Although due to the sampling limitations of this study these percentages should not be considered national averages, they do indicate that a small, but significant, number of children under the age of three are enrolled.

In each of the Tokyo city schools surveyed, between 30 and 40 percent of the students who were taking lessons by the third month of first grade had begun those lessons *before* enrolling in preschool. In schools outside the Tokyo area, this percentage was less than 10 percent. There is a clear tendency for children from more affluent backgrounds and those in metropolitan Tokyo to begin enrichment lessons at a younger age. This may be the result of both more available money to spend on enrichment lessons and these families placing a higher priority on early education.

Table 2 also shows that attendance at examination preparation classes is common only in Elite Girls' and Showcase Laboratory

Elementary schools. This is because Elite Girls' Elementary is a private school and Showcase Laboratory Elementary is a national public school. These are the only types of elementary schools in Japan which have a selective screening process. Together these two types of schools account for approximately 1 percent of the Japanese elementary population (Leestma et al. 1986, 77). The remaining 99 percent of students attend local public elementary schools that accept all students within the school's designated boundaries. Therefore, the students have no need to attend special classes in preparation for entrance examinations and screening interviews. The small percentage of students in regular public schools who have attended examination preparation classes are likely to be students who tried and failed to enter private or national public elementary schools.

Types of Enrichment Lessons

The questionnaire asked mothers to complete a history of all lessons that their child was currently taking and all those in which he or she had previously been enrolled and later discontinued. Table 3 shows the eleven most popular types of lessons ever attended by students. Swimming and piano were the two most popular lessons in every school studied, except Small Town Elementary and Mountaintop Elementary, whose communities did not have a pool. Calligraphy was either the third or fourth most popular type of lesson in every school studied. Although the other types of lessons listed were not as overwhelmingly popular, at least a few children in every school sampled attended them. The only type of lessons which exhibited extreme differences in enrollment pattern by school were examination preparation lessons, which were almost exclusively limited to students from elite elementary schools.

Popular press reports (for example, Simons 1987) that suggest that the large numbers claimed for Japanese children attending examination preparation classes for entrance to elementary school are probably overstated. The data in Table 2 from the two types of schools which require examinations suggest that only approximately half of the 1 percent of Japanese children who successfully entered these types of schools attended exam preparation classes. Even allowing for some children in regular public schools who attended examination preparation lessons in an attempt to enter elite schools but failed, it can be inferred that the exam preparation phenomenon

TABLE 3

Most Popular Types of Enrichment Lessons for Newly Matriculated Japanese First Graders, Amount of Maternal Lesson Observation and Home Practice

	Number of students ever enrolled	Number of students currently enrolled	Percent enrollees who are girls•	Modal frequency mother observes	Modal frequency of home practice
Swimming	389	303	47	Almost always	Almost never
Piano or organ	382	364	78	Sometimes	Every day
Calligraphy	137	134	56	Rarely	Almost never
Gymnastics	81	42	51	Almost always	Almost never
Art/drawing	77	53	50	Rarely	Almost never
English conversation	73	61	37	Rarely	Almost never
Music room /rhythmics	70	54	60	Almost always	Every other day
Arithmetic	68	65	38	Rarely	Every day
Ballet/modern dance	52	35	100	Sometimes	Almost never
Intelligence development	39	39	41	Sometimes	Almost never
Exam preparation	37	0	64	Almost always	Almost never

Total Number of Students Surveyed: 1,080

• Only coeducational schools are included in this calculation.

for entrance to elementary school probably affects only a tiny percentage of the total preschool-aged population.

Some types of lessons, like ballet, gymnastics, music room, and examination preparation show a comparatively large number of children who were once enrolled and then later discontinued lessons. This is primarily because these lessons are perceived as more appropriate for very young children. For example, many of the children who initially enroll in music room classes transfer in a year or two to regular piano lessons. In the case of examination preparation, children are typically enrolled for only a brief period of time (three to six months) immediately before the examination, and discontinue the lessons as soon as the exam is over. Generally speaking, ballet, gymnastics, and music are popular with younger children, and calligraphy, arithmetic, and intelligence development are usually begun as children near elementary school age.

Gender Differences in Enrichment Lesson Experience

Among newly matriculated first graders, girls are more likely than boys to be enrolled in enrichment classes. Among the ten coeducational schools surveyed, 73 percent of the first grade girls were currently enrolled, compared to 55 percent of the boys. Furthermore, some types of lessons are more popular with girls than with boys. Girls are more likely to take piano and ballet, which are perceived as typically feminine accomplishments. Boys are more likely to take academically-related subjects such as English conversation and arithmetic. Enrollments in swimming, gymnastics, and art are approximately evenly balanced by gender.

There is a moderate tendency for more girls than boys to be enrolled in examination preparation classes. Although this information is based only on data from children in Showcase Laboratory Elementary School (Elite Girls' Elementary lacking boys for comparison), it agrees with the reports of directors of examination preparation lesson programs. Directors report that some parents who strongly desire to provide their daughter with an elite education and a good chance at access to a top-ranking high school and university attempt to spare them the rigors of examination preparation at the junior high and high school level by enrolling them in an elite elementary school which will automatically promote them through senior high school graduation. By receiving assistance to enter the elite track at the transition from preschool to elementary school,

their daughter will be able to move smoothly through the system
without undergoing high school entrance examinations. Many parents consider the rigors of adolescent examination preparation less
appropriate for girls than for boys.

Maternal Participation and Home Practice

Mothers were asked to report how frequently they observed
in the classroom during their children's enrichment lessons and how
much their children practiced the lesson material at home. Table 3
shows considerable variation in these factors, depending on the type
of lesson. Interestingly, frequency of maternal class observation and
frequency of home practice are not highly correlated. For example,
most mothers whose children were enrolled in piano lessons reported that they observed their children's weekly lesson only sometimes, but that their children practiced every day. Yet mothers of
children in gymnastics typically almost always observed their
children's lessons, but children almost never practiced at home.

Importance to the parent of the material to be learned is apparently not a critical factor in determining the amount of home
practice. Examination preparation courses, which can be assumed
to be very important to the parent, were almost never practiced,
while music room lessons were reportedly practiced every other
day. Because the amount of practice for each given type of lesson
was highly similar across different cities and different lesson teachers, both parents and teachers appear to have common cultural expectations regarding the amount of practice appropriate for certain
types of lessons. Some types of lessons, such as music room or piano, are commonly expected to be practiced regularly at home,
while other types, such as calligraphy or exam preparation, are
usually not. The data from this study suggest that aside from children who are enrolled in music lessons or arithmetic, pre-elementary children almost never practice enrichment lesson material at
home.

Interestingly, except for calligraphy, all of the eleven most
popular types of lessons are derived from the Western artistic or
athletic tradition. Few contemporary Japanese preschool or first
grade children study traditional Japanese disciplines. Table 4 lists
all different types of enrichment lessons reported in this study, except school subjects such as arithmetic, Japanese language, and examination preparation. Categorizing the lessons according to

TABLE 4

**Origin of Subject Matter of Enrichment Lessons and Number of Newly
Matriculated First Grade Students Ever Enrolled**

Western-derived lessons	Number of students ever enrolled	Asian-derived lessons	Number of students ever enrolled
Swimming	389	Calligraphy (shuji)	137
Piano and organ	382	Japanese fencing (kendo)	9
Gymnastics	81	Abacus (soroban)	7
Art/drawing	77	Classical dance (nihon buyo)	6
English conversation	73	Karate	5
Music room/rythmics	70	Aikido	3
Ballet/modern dance	52	Folk dance (minyo)	2
Sports (soccer, tennis, skiing)	29	Wrestling (sumo)	1
Violin	24	Recitation (rodoku)	1
		Judo	1
Total	1,177	**Total**	172

Western or Asian origin of the subject matter, the overwhelming
popularity of Western-derived subject matter for the pre-elementary
age group is clear.

With the exception of calligraphy, very few preschool-aged
children are enrolled in enrichment lessons derived from the Asian
tradition. This may be due to the declining popularity of traditional
Asian disciplines, the belief that Asian-derived disciplines are more
appropriate to older children and adults, or both. Although a small
number of individuals who studied piano lessons as a child may
later take up the koto as an adult, by choosing Western-derived
lessons for their children in preference to classical dance or kendo,
contemporary Japanese parents may be inadvertently contributing
to the gradual erosion of interest and participation in traditional
Japanese arts.

Examples of Typical Enrichment Lesson Centers

Music room and examination preparation lessons are less
popular than swimming, piano, and calligraphy for this age group.
However, the classes and centers described here are typical of the
music room and examination preparation lessons observed in approximately ten other centers of these types. In addition to being
representative of type, these lessons are illustrative of typical
teaching style and format of those types of preschool enrichment
lessons in which the mother observes. Names of individuals and institutions have been changed throughout.

A Music Room Class

The Nippon Music Plaza lesson center is located on the
fourth and fifth floors of a small and unpretentious office building
near the train station in a middle-class suburb of Tokyo. Nippon
Music Plaza is owned and operated by Nippon Music, Inc., a large
corporation which is internationally known as a manufacturer of
musical instruments. Nippon Music Plaza is one of a nationwide
network of music lesson centers. This particular center is located
several blocks from a large grocery store and shopping complex.

The lesson center offers music room classes for preschoolers
and private piano and organ lessons for older students. The floor
space is subdivided into large classrooms designed for group lessons,

and small individual cubicles for private music lessons. In the center of the first floor is a large waiting area with a reception desk and benches where mothers and children gather to wait for class to begin. Families whose children are enrolled in this center are mostly middle class and live in the surrounding neighborhood.

Preschool children attend the center accompanied by their mothers, and all classes for preschoolers require the mother's attendance. Almost all preschoolers are enrolled in the music room program, which consists of three different levels corresponding to the child's first, second, and third year of lessons. Classes are held once a week, for fifty minutes per lesson. Monthly tuition for four lessons is 4,500 yen ($30.00 per month) and the one-time application fee upon entering the program is 3,000 yen ($20.00). This makes the lessons affordable for most middle-class families.

Children can begin the music room program at age four, five, or six. The goals of the preschool music room program, as stated by the teachers, parallel the goals described in the advertising brochures. The purpose of the program is to help young children learn to enjoy music through the following five types of activities: listening, singing after the teacher, playing the electric organ, reading music, and learning to accompany and improvise.

Music room classes at Nippon Music Plaza are held in large group classrooms. Each room is equipped with ten electric organs arranged in rows facing the front of the room. At the front of the room is the teacher's organ, a blackboard ruled with the musical staff, and a circle of child-sized chairs. This excerpt from class observation notes in a first-year class illustrates typical music room activities. At the time of the observation, students were four, five, and six years of age and had been taking music room lessons for approximately ten weeks.

> The classroom door opens ten minutes before the hour to allow the previous class to exit and the next class to begin. Ten children and their mothers enter the room and quickly prepare for class. Each child sits at an organ, and the mother sits on a stool beside the child and prepares the child's books for the lesson.
>
> After the children, mothers, and teacher bow to each other in unison, the lesson immediately begins. The teacher instructs the children to look at the ♩♩♩♪ rhythm on the board and to play it

repeatedly "on the blue key" while she plays a simple familiar march. She then changes rhythms and plays another song while the children accompany her in a similar manner.

After ten minutes of this practice, she calls the children to the circle of chairs in the front of the room. She sings "doh mi soh" and asks the children to imitate her in turn. She then sings "ti fa la" and the children again attempt to imitate her individually. When children sing the intervals incorrectly, the teacher repeats the pattern to them and they try again. Then she claps simple rhythmic patterns and asks the group of children to imitate her.

Children then return to their seats at the organs. The teacher puts the notes "fa doh re" on the staff on the blackboard and asks the children to whisper to their mothers the names of the notes displayed. She then rearranges the notes and asks the children several more combinations. She concludes by reminding them "be sure to practice hard with your magnet boards at home."

The class is then instructed to open their books and to play the ♪♪♪♪ rhythmic pattern of a song with castanets while the teacher plays the song on a tape recorder. The teacher plays castanets along with the children. Next, the children come to the front of the room again to sing a children's song in unison and then as a round. Then they repeat it changing the words to "so la so fa mi," etc.

Finally, the children return to their seats to practice reading the three-note series "fa doh fa" in their books, singing and counting the notes off one by one with their fingers in the book. Next, they play the pattern in unison on their color-coded keyboards. When transferring the pattern to the keyboard, the teacher refers to it as "red blue red." Finally, they sing and clap the rhythm.

The lesson concludes with the teacher assigning the page numbers in the book that they are to practice at home. In addition to practicing the singing and clapping exercises, working with the magnetic board, and practicing on their organ at home, the children are assigned two pages of writing notes in their music copy books. The assignment for today is "do mi do mi..." Mothers record the homework assignment in their notebooks. The teacher calls the children to the front of the room, where they receive attendance stickers. Then the children hold hands in a circle and bow together with the teacher to end the lesson.

After class, the teacher explained the purpose of the lessons in terms of developing the children's appreciation of music:

We want the children to enjoy music and become able to play music themselves. A few parents come because they hope that their child will get better grades in music, but most just hope that their child will become able to play the organ. We try to teach them to read music and learn the fundamentals of the instrument, as well as the enjoyment of singing. We try to make it fun for the children.

Lessons are believed to be easier to teach if the children's mothers attend. The same teacher reports:

It's best that the mother come with the child to the lesson, at least until the child is in elementary school. The children are happier when they are with their mothers. The mothers sing together with the children and it makes a louder and warmer sound. They also keep track of the homework, so we ask that the mothers attend with their children.

The content-oriented format and relatively serious attitude of this music room lesson are typical of most other types of enrichment lessons for Japanese preschool children. Expectations for children are comparatively high, and both teachers and mothers seem to be confident that even four- to six-year-old children can make real progress in learning to read music and in playing the organ. Although the component tasks in the learning process have been broken into small, easily learnable pieces, even preschool-aged children are treated as serious students learning a real and important skill.

The teacher states that learning to enjoy music is the primary goal of music room lessons, and says that she tries to make the lessons "fun" for the children. However, within the context of Japanese teaching and learning situations, age-appropriate "fun" for preschool children is rarely of an infantile sort. Rather than encouraging children to laugh and call out excitedly during lessons, or to engage in self-expressive large-motor activities, children are encouraged to focus on the task of learning to play the organ. The implicit message is that there is sufficient enjoyment in the learning and practice of the skill itself, and that there is no need to disguise the subject matter with childlike amusements for it to be appealing to young children.

This comparatively businesslike approach to teaching children has been noted in other Japanese early educational contexts (Peak 1986). Although it is in sharp contrast to the relaxed and boisterous structure of Japanese preschool and day-care centers, it is typical of the more focused and content-oriented teaching style of enrichment lessons. The following description of an examination preparation class further illustrates this serious and content-focused teaching style, carried to the extreme, that is typical of examination preparation classes.

An Examination Preparation Class

The Yamamoto Development Center occupies one floor of a building in a centrally located, upper-middle-class neighborhood of Tokyo. The classrooms are comfortable and nicely appointed with child-sized chairs and tables. The mothers and children are fashionably dressed. Like the teachers, the mothers speak refined, upper-middle-class language. All children are five-year-olds in their last year of preschool.

Children come to the center once a week, for an hour-long lesson. Most enroll six to eight months before entrance examinations are held. The one-time application fee upon entering the program is 80,000 yen ($530.00) and tuition for four hour-long lessons per month is usually around 20,000 yen ($133.00). Such high tuition is typical of examination preparation centers, which are notoriously one of the most expensive types of enrichment lessons in Japan.

Most families choose an examination preparation center that is designed to help children prepare for the examination to a particular elementary school. This both ensures that the child's training is appropriate to the content of the examination and that the parents can benefit maximally from the director's advice on admission strategies.

Lesson activities at Yamamoto focus on providing children experience in several key skills that are important in entrance examinations. Training typically attempts to develop a cheerful, confident self-presentation, care and precision in following directions, familiarity with typical test items, and experience with the testing routine. Some classes also have children construct things using scissors and paste or practice motor skills that are required on some entrance examinations.

Interestingly, instruction in reading and writing, letter and numeral recognition, and simple arithmetic skills are not usually a part of examination preparation lessons. This is because the examinations include only very simple letter recognition and counting skills, focusing primarily on broader classroom skills such as planning, concentration, and ability to follow directions.

The official position of the Ministry of Education is that training in basic reading and arithmetic skills is not an appropriate part of the preschool curriculum. Therefore, even highly selective elementary schools are reluctant to have it appear that they flout the ministry's guidelines and preferentially select children who have received prior instruction in reading and number skills. Consequently, examination questions typically require children to do no more than recognize a few letters and phonetic sounds, count up to ten objects, and make simple combinations. In fact, most children's reading and counting skills are far more advanced than these. Parents and teachers widely acknowledge that most children, particularly those from such educationally conscious backgrounds as those who sit for the elite elementary school entrance examinations, can read quite well and have considerable arithmetic skills when they enter first grade.

In a typical lesson at Yamamoto Development Center, children are seated at their desks and mothers sit in a line of chairs at the back of the room. The teacher begins the lesson by having each child rise to attention, announce his or her name loudly and clearly, and then sit down again. The ability to say one's name and basic greetings such as hello, goodby, and thank you in a clear, polite, and energetic voice is considered an important social skill by Japanese parents and teachers. Children who are shy or imprecise in their replies are at a disadvantage in an interview situation.

The main part of the lesson involves practicing sample test questions from mimeographed work sheets. Children are given experience not only in understanding the format of typical questions, but also in how to listen carefully and follow directions accurately. An excerpt from class observation notes at Yamamoto gives a flavor of how these lessons are presented:

> The teacher passes out mimeographed papers with three letters written at the top of the page, and fifteen pictures beginning with those sounds in random order beneath them. Bringing the children to seated attention and telling them to listen carefully, she gives directions only once. Speaking slowly and clearly she tells them, "Circle the 'su' with green. Circle the 'se' with red. Circle the 'so' with orange. Now you may color." At this signal, children pick up their crayons and circle the letters quickly with the appropriate color. After finishing, they line their crayons up again carefully.
>
> "Now look at the pictures underneath. Draw a green circle around the things that start with 'su'... Draw a red circle around the things that start with 'se,' and an orange circle around the things that start with 'so.' Now you may start." The teacher moves around the room correcting children who make mistakes.
>
> Following this exercise, the teacher passes out another mimeographed page with a series of domino-like figures on it (see Figure 1). Again, calling the children to seated attention she gives instructions only once. "Count the number of dots in each box. Draw one more than that number of circles in the small spaces below. Begin." She again moves about the room giving suggestions to children who make mistakes. "Use your finger when you count. How many dots are there? How many did you draw? You're looking around the room, which is why you're making mistakes." After children have finished they lay down their crayons and quietly await the next exercise.

FIGURE 1

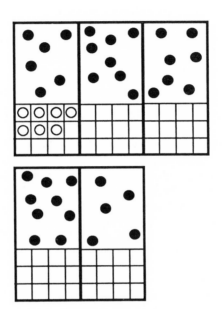

The content of the assigned tasks is relatively easy in that, given the children's much higher degree of familiarity with reading and basic arithmetic, it requires comparatively little sophistication in letter or number skills. However, the instructions that accompany the tasks are deliberately complex. Each child must pay careful attention to understand the teacher's instructions to the group and remain alert throughout the task to avoid making a mistake. Hearing and remembering the directions accurately the first time they are given, keeping one's green, red, and orange crayons straight, and correctly counting random dots and remembering to add one to the total tests children's concentration, planning, and ability to follow directions. Clearly, children facing an examination of this kind benefit considerably from familiarity with the testing format.

Why do some Japanese parents send their children to these examination preparation classes? This excerpt from an interview with the mother of a five-year-old girl who had attended such an examination class reflects typical themes in upper-class parental decision making about examination preparation classes and their relation to entrance to elite elementary schools.

> I sent Mika to an examination preparation class to try to help her get into Forest Green Elementary School. That's a nice private girls' school which both her father and I wanted her to attend. Actually, I'm a graduate of that school, and so is her papa's mother. Many families want their daughters to go to that school, and so there's a very selective test. I thought that to enter first grade, examination preparation training was just too much, but what can you do? It seems everyone else is doing it and all the children that get in have had examination preparation lessons.
>
> Some mothers start their children a year or two early, but I couldn't bring myself to do that. The entrance exam is in November, and so I started her in September. Mainly they train them how to do the problems fast and accurately, so that the children have an automatic response to quickly do exactly what the teacher tells them to. It has nothing to do with intelligence.

Mika has good concentration but she isn't very quick in her movements so she didn't pass the entrance exam. The first round of the examination is a group paper test, and then the second round is an interview. She didn't even make it to the second round.

Her father was really angry when Mika didn't get in. He thinks the system is really terrible. He thinks they ought to enroll the children of graduates like they used to and not make little children take such ridiculous training to get in. These days, to get into elite schools, families really have to put themselves all out. It's not good. The people who want this kind of education are society's elite. These days there are also a lot of *nouveau riche* families who've made a lot of money recently.

Examination preparation classes cost 5,000 yen ($33.00) or more for each lesson, and the lesson centers make you attend from four to eight lessons per month. That kind of expense for six months or a year is not possible for regular salaried families. But it's too bad that these days the *nouveau riche* can get into these schools just by buying the examination preparation lessons for their children. The whole thing has become an economic proposition. Most families who want elite education for their children send them to these preparation classes. There's too much competition in Japan these days, everyone trying to get to the same place.

(Interviewer: Who are the society's elite that you mention?) They're from elite families. Sometimes the parents themselves aren't yet old enough to be elite. But the grandparents and great grandparents were Diet people, presidents of large companies, professors, and people like that. Our family used to be retainers to the Shogunate. These days it's considered best if the children are going to elite schools like the one we wanted Mika to go to.

A teacher in one of the five-year-old classes at Yamamoto Development Center corroborates this mother's view:

(Interviewer: How do children benefit from studying
at Yamamoto Development Center?) These days, in
Japan, society is like a war. I don't like the war, but
it's out there. That's reality. So here we are
preparing weapons, so that children will be prepared
when they enter battle. Here we are nurturing
Japan's elite.

It is a common misunderstanding that examination preparation lessons are widespread among Japanese preschool children, and
that the utilitarian focus of these classes on getting children into
elite elementary schools is a preoccupation typical of most Japanese
parents. Although further research on this subject among a range of
families of different social types is needed, the preliminary evidence
presented in this study indicates that the examination preparation
phenomenon is limited to a small minority of socially and financially
fortunate families.

Indeed, the effectiveness of examination preparation programs may rely in large part on their exclusivity. As long as only a
small number of families can afford the extremely high tuition fees,
these children will receive maximum advantage from their added
familiarity with the testing format and counseling on admissions'
strategies. If examination coaching becomes standard practice for
all prospective applicants to elite elementary schools, the advantages accruing to the students who receive such training would be
neutralized.

Examination preparation classes have often been implicitly
represented as the model paradigm for Japanese preschool enrichment lessons (Simons 1987), because it was assumed that parents'
primary goal in selecting enrichment lessons for their preschool
children was to help the children get ahead in the academic race.
This may be so for a small minority of parents for whom social
mobility or maintenance of a hereditary position among society's
elite are overriding concerns, but it is not accurate for the vast
majority of Japanese families.

The findings of this preliminary study suggest that the goal
of the vast majority of Japanese parents in enrolling their preschool
child in enrichment lessons is expressive rather than utilitarian.
The five most popular types of enrichment lessons for this age
group are swimming, piano, calligraphy, gymnastics, and art. These
would hardly be the choices of parents bent on giving their children

a head start in core academic subjects, or getting their children into the fast lane in the race to a good university.

Instead of being academically oriented, enrichment lessons for preschool children appear to serve as an introduction to the recreational and personally expressive aspects of life. Through an introduction to music, art, calligraphy, and sports during the preschool years, Japanese children have the opportunity to develop an interest that may lead to a lifelong hobby and source of personal enjoyment and recreation. Developing their children's appreciation of the finer things in life appears to be a more important parental priority than improving future academic standing in choosing enrichment lessons for children of this age.

This expressive, rather than utilitarian, goal for enrichment lessons is consonant with the downplaying of academic content which is characteristic of Japanese preschool and day-care programs. In this least regulated and most parent-responsive phase of Japanese education, parental objectives for a child's learning in preschool and day-care programs are primarily social rather than academic (Peak 1987). Preschool is above all a place to learn to enjoy the company of friends and adjust to life in a group.

Because of its noncompulsory nature, pre-elementary education enjoys the greatest latitude for experiment within the entire Japanese system. In particular, preschools and day-care centers operate with considerable freedom to determine the degree to which the style and content of their curriculum will adhere to the guidelines set by the Ministry of Education. Private individuals and commercial educational enterprises are relatively unconstrained by the need to make their classes appear useful in helping children improve their academic standing. Because choice of a given preschool, day-care center, or enrichment lesson program is entirely at the discretion of individual parents, pre-elementary education is more market controlled than any other phase of schooling in Japan. The choices they make and types of programs they support may be closer to their own true beliefs and values concerning education than the more utilitarian and content-oriented nature of compulsory education at the upper levels.

Japanese pre-elementary education has often been assumed to be a downward extension of the university examination race. The evidence indicates otherwise. The pre-elementary period needs to be conceptualized in its own terms. This includes listening to the voices of everyday mothers, preschool teachers, and enrichment lesson program instructors, who structure and choose the types of learning experiences they consider most appropriate for their preschool children. Their voices tell us that their goals for children's pre-elementary development are far broader than merely getting a headstart in elementary school.

Conclusions and Suggestions for Future Research

The data reported in this study provide some preliminary estimates regarding Japanese children's enrollment in formal pre-elementary education. Almost all Japanese children attend one or two years of preschool or day care, and pre-elementary enrichment lessons appear to be widespread across a broad range of social classes. Based on these findings, several interesting and important directions for future research can be identified.

Detailed analysis of Japanese children's academic achievement (Stevenson 1986) shows that Japanese first grade children arrive at school better prepared than their American counterparts in reading and arithmetic. This is the case even though most preschools apparently adhere to the Ministry of Education's guidelines that specific teaching of reading and arithmetic skills is to be avoided in the preschool and day-care curriculum. Precisely where children learn these skills is unclear. As we have seen through our analysis of common types of enrichment lessons, it is unlikely that a significant number of children learn reading and arithmetic from these weekly lessons. If not primarily in preschool, day care, or enrichment lessons, then where are these skills acquired?

The answer to this question is not yet known. Television, maternal instruction, and the generalized effect of a content-rich environment are other possible sources of basic reading and arithmetic skills. Although it is frequently asserted that Japanese mothers spend considerable time instructing their children in reading and writing skills at home, these reports are not based on systematic observation of actual childrearing practices in a wide variety of types of Japanese homes. We still are a long way from understanding the full context of learning experiences typical for Japanese pre-elementary children.

Another important question to be explored is the effect of family background on Japanese children's pre-elementary learning experiences. A standard finding of sociological studies of education in many cultures is that parental socioeconomic status and urban or rural residence has an important effect on families' educational attitudes and children's educational participation and achievement. This issue has received little attention in contemporary studies of Japanese education.

This study gives some preliminary evidence that even a rough measure of families' social background has a strong relationship to both the number of enrichment lessons children are enrolled in, and the age at which those children begin lessons. Additionally, attendance at examination preparation classes was found to be limited to a small number of children from upper and upper-middle-class families whose families desire to enroll them in elite elementary schools.

These preliminary bits of evidence support the not-unexpected hypothesis that family background may have an important determining effect on Japanese children's early learning experience. However, there is no evidence available on what these effects might be, and in what way they may influence children's later academic progress. This lack of perspective seriously limits the understanding of social variation in Japanese childhood experience and later education.

Japanese pre-elementary education is a particularly rich area of study not only as a prelude to the high academic achievement characteristic of the elementary and secondary system, but also as an unusually varied and vigorous phase of the Japanese educational process. Because it remains largely free of the centralizing effect of compulsory school regulations and university examination pressure, it more fully reflects the variety of parental beliefs and educational approaches than do other phases of schooling in Japan. The next decade of research in Japanese elementary education should be exciting because so much is yet to be learned.

References

Boocock, S. 1987. "The Privileged World of Little Children: Preschool Education in Japan." Paper presented at the annual meeting of the Comparative and International Education Society, Washington DC.

Kodama, T. 1983. *Preschool Education in Japan* (NIER Occasional Paper). Tokyo: National Institute for Educational Research.

Leestma, R., R. August, B. George, and L. Peak. 1987. *Japanese Education Today*. Washington, DC: U.S. Government Printing Office.

Monbusho [Japanese Ministry of Education, Science and Culture]. 1975. *Yochien kyoiku yoryo* [Guidelines for Preschool Education]. Tokyo: Monbusho.

-----. 1984. *Gakko kihon chosa hokokusho* [Report on basic survey of schools]. Tokyo: Monbusho.

National Council of Day Nurseries. 1986. *Day Nurseries in Japan 1985*. Tokyo: National Council of Social Welfare.

Peak, L. 1986. "Training Learning Skills and Attitudes in Japanese Early Educational Settings." In W. Fowler, ed., *New Directions for Child Development: No. 32. Early Experience and the Development of Competence*, pp. 111-23. San Francisco: Jossey Bass, Inc.

-----. 1987. *Learning to Go to School in Japan: The Transition from Home to Preschool Life*. Doctoral dissertation, Harvard Graduate School of Education, Cambridge, MA.

Simons, C. 1987. "They Get by with a Lot of Help from Their Kyoiku Mamas." *Smithsonian* 17:12, 44-53.

Stevenson, H. 1986. "Learning to Read Japanese." In H. Stevenson, H. Azuma, and K. Hakuta, eds., *Child Development and Education in Japan*, pp. 217-35. Hillsdale, NJ: Earlbaum.

White, M. 1987. *The Japanese Educational Challenge: A Commitment to Children*. New York: Free Press.

CHAPTER 3

CLASS MANAGEMENT AND STUDENT GUIDANCE IN JAPANESE ELEMENTARY AND LOWER SECONDARY SCHOOLS

Tokuo Kataoka
Hiroshima University

Introduction

This chapter examines the guidance students receive for schooling and life that is conducted through class management and student guidance activities throughout elementary and secondary education. *Japanese Education Today* defines "student guidance" as "the direction provided by the classroom teacher to help students establish fundamental attitudes and behaviors necessary for successful school life" (Leestma et al. 1987, 27). This guidance is an important aspect of education in Japan that has attracted wide attention and is believed to be an important factor in the high academic achievement of the country's students. In addition to describing the ways teachers and schools direct students, this article explains guidance through the presentation of a number of concrete examples from specific elementary and lower secondary schools.

Every teacher and school, and the educational administration at all levels, provide guidance throughout the entire Japanese educational system. Guidance occurs during the course of regular academic instruction, as well as in special activities specifically designed to provide such guidance. Guidance activities, for better or worse, strongly influence the students' academic work, moral consciousness and attitudes, and behavior in daily life. This all-pervasive guidance helps students develop such desired attributes as docility, diligence in order to accomplish a given objective or assignment, cooperation, loyalty, and responsibility in carrying out assigned collective work. However, these attributes can also be disadvantageous. For example, docility might discourage creativity, and cooperativeness might foster uniformity.

Although guidance is considered important at all levels, it is most actively provided in compulsory education, which consists of the six-year elementary school course and the three-year lower secondary schools. Although the theory and practice of this guidance is similar at the elementary and lower secondary levels, it has been most ardently pursued and has gained greatest success in the elementary schools, with the lower secondary schools ranking second in this pursuit. The upper secondary schools lag far behind.

There are three reasons for the differences at the different levels. The first concerns the mental development of elementary school-aged children. As indicated in the old saying "strike while the iron is hot," the younger a child is, the easier and more effective it is to give moral, social, and behavioral guidance. The second reason is that there are different staffing systems. In an elementary school, the homeroom teacher also teaches almost all subjects and thus has very close contact with pupils in the homeroom on a daily basis. In a secondary school, on the other hand, a homeroom teacher usually teaches the homeroom class one subject or none; there is less contact between the teacher and the children. The third reason concerns different views of the teaching profession. While elementary school teachers tend to consider character education and student guidance as important as subject instruction, lower and upper secondary teachers are likely to view student guidance as somewhat less important, probably because of the attention and resulting accomplishments of the elementary years. Nevertheless, even among the upper secondary school teachers much attention has recently been given to guidance beyond the limits of their specialized subjects in order to cope with present difficulties and various deviant behaviors within the student body.

In Japan, it is commonly accepted that guidance should be carried out through class management and in all curricular areas. Both the Course of Study for Elementary Schools and the Course of Study for Lower Secondary Schools, which are promulgated by the Ministry of Education in Japan's nationally directed system and have a powerful influence, provide for a school curriculum consisting of three areas:

1) Regular subjects (the Japanese language, social studies, mathematics, science, music, fine arts, and physical education),

2) Moral education, and

3) Special activities.

The class hours allotted annually to each area in each grade of elementary and lower secondary schools are shown in Table 1.

The class hours allotted for special activities account for less that 10 percent of the total in elementary and lower secondary schools. Nevertheless, although student guidance is conducted in all three curricular areas, it receives particular emphasis in special activities.

This chapter focuses first on guidance provided through methods and techniques of class management and then on guidance provided in regular subjects (discussed briefly) and special activities, the area in which most guidance is provided.

Class Management

Homeroom Teachers

Some elementary and lower secondary teachers in Japan are, as homeroom teachers, interested and skilled in class management and student guidance, and others are not, just as some are skilled in teaching subjects and others are not. An effort is made here to sketch a picture of an average or above average homeroom teacher. There is also an example of outstanding class management.

When a teacher is assigned to a class, the teacher first tries to memorize every name and face of the students as soon as possible. The pupils also try to understand each other. For example, they introduce themselves to others through speeches and short essays about their hobbies, personalities, families, future dreams, and so on.

The teacher asks the children such questions as, "What would you like this class to be like?" By asking this question, the teacher intends to collect the pupils' opinions about group life in the class and about common moral objectives. The teacher may also suggest some exemplary hopes and needs to the class. Sometimes both approaches are combined. The result is that the class chooses a slogan that may be hung on the front wall of the classroom. Among slogans often seen in Japanese classrooms are "friendliness," "cheerfulness," "consideration," and "effort."

TABLE 1

LEVEL	GRADE	CURRICULUM AREA			TOTAL CLASS HOURS
		Subjects	Moral Education	Special Activities	
Elementary	1	782	34	34	850
	2	840	35	35	910
	3	910	35	35	980
	4,5,6	910	35	70	1,015
Lower Sec.	1,2,3	945	35	70	1,050

Note: One class hour is forty-five minutes in elementary schools and fifty minutes in lower secondary schools.

FIGURE 1

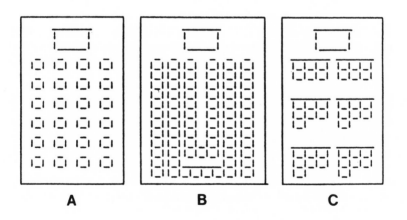

A   B   C

Seating Arrangements

Meanwhile, seating arrangements are decided for each class. Usually, there are three types of arrangements, as illustrated in Figure 1.

The most popular type is A. The A type is most suitable for a teacher to communicate with all pupils when teaching. The B type, which is often seen in the classroom assembly, is suitable for class discussion. The C type, in which a class is usually divided into subgroups of about six members, is convenient for discussion and collaborative activities by each subgroup. This C type is much more effective in promoting collaboration and group consciousness than A or B.

Formation and Responsibilities of Han

Each subgroup in the C type classroom is a basic unit both in instruction and in class life. This unit is commonly called *han* or *gurupu* in Japanese, and is usually made up of four to six pupils. The arrangement of seats is variable in the C type classroom; sometimes seats are rearranged into the A type or B type. In any case, each member maintains a strong consciousness as a part of *han* or *gurupu*.

These subgroups share various responsibilities within the class, including planning and carrying out such projects as producing class books and class newspapers, organizing recreational activities, and providing assistance to teachers. Additionally, these *han* are also used for one term of the year to discuss such academic assignments as reading and comprehension and calculation.

Han are organized in several ways:

1) By lot, physical height, or order of roll call, for example,

2) By existing personal relationships among the children,

3) By having the leader choose the members of the group, or

4) By shared interests of students.

Two Junior High School Examples

Almost every class divides itself into several subgroups and assigns a portion of the classroom work to each. Thus, a unity of all members in the class is further strengthened through the unification of each subgroup. In short, each member, sharing and making a contribution to portions of classroom work and other activities assigned to the subgroup, can accept responsibility for and allegiance to both the subgroup and the larger class. At the same time, the student can develop such attributes as diligence and team spirit through the shared work which must be done by each subgroup.

Two examples of *han* are shown below. Table 2 presents data for a second-year class of a lower secondary school (grade eight). This class is grouped into seven *han* of about six members each. There are boys and girls in each *han*. Members of each *han* share the responsibilities for both subject-related and class life-related duties so that students can help their teachers with teaching as well as the smooth running of the classroom (Nomoto 1984).

Table 3 presents data for another second-year class of a lower secondary school. In this example, an additional category of responsibilities, recreational and cultural activities, is given to each *han* (Magari 1978).

The example of the Magari class, with every *han* additionally having its own tasks in the recreational and cultural area, is rare.

An Example of Outstanding Management

The following, which appeared in an article entitled, "Ideas for the Classroom-Sweet Potatoes, Print, and Slides," in a journal on fostering good group relations, gives one example of outstanding class management. It shows how students achieve unity as a class through the cooperative work of *han*, with a homeroom teacher as the leader, and how harmony is achieved between creativity and collaboration or individuality and solidarity (Yamanaka 1985).

> On the first day of April 1984, when I met the students of my second grade class in the junior high school, I spoke to them like this, "Let's think about what we will do on the last day of school next

TABLE 2

The Nomoto Class (Sekiya Junior High School)

Subgroup	Responsibilities	
	Subject-related	Class life-related
1	Science	Classroom discipline
2	Fine arts/Homemaking/Industrial arts	Recreation
3	Music/Physical education	Health and Hygiene
4	English	Class books
5	Social studies	Public relations
6	Japanese	General affairs
7	Mathematics	Beautification

TABLE 3

The Magari Class
(Yasuoka Junior High School in Shimonoseki)

Subgroups	Responsibilities		
	Subject-related	Class life-related	Recreational and cultural-related
Tulip	Moral education	Classroom discipline	Writing a detective story
Study 7	Social studies	Gardening	Cultivating watermelons and making a detailed report
Eight	Japanese	Health & hygiene	Writing a scenario of a play, "A Life in a Jr. High School"
Seishun (Young Life)	Mathematics	Recreation	Making a class newspaper
The Kanazuchi (Stones in Water)	English	Maintenance	Making a future life table of the class
4 Gorillas & 003	Science	Planning	Making a wall newspaper

March." For a while, they didn't understand what I meant. They were almost all strangers to each other and my question had no meaning for them at first. The silence continued.

So, I suggested an idea about cultural activities for this class for that academic year.

There was no response from them. I told them to think about this idea until the next day. The next morning they said they agreed to it, but with almost no emotion.

The first term--grow sweet potatoes. (There is a small piece of waste field behind the school building, which belongs to our class. We'll make it there.)

The second term--make a calendar of wood-cut printing.

The third term--take 120 slides of our life for this year. (We'll arrange transcription by adding music and words to them and bid farewell after seeing it.)

There were forty-two students in my class. The class was divided into six subgroups with boys and girls mixed. The members for each subgroup were decided by lot. Each subgroup had to share work such as planning, beautification, notice board, school lunch, the growing of the sweet potatoes, etc. These duties were rotated every two weeks. Each group elected its own leader by vote, who was also changed every two weeks. Every member in the subgroup was also given duties such as delivering messages from teachers, distributing handouts, taking the chair in the assembly, keeping records, etc. These roles were again changed every two weeks. Through these subgroup activities, everyone in the class was expected to have the chance to be responsible for group activities, to be independent of others, to encourage and help each other, and to endeavor to carry out his/her responsibility.

We started to grow the sweet potatoes in the first term by plowing the eight-square-meter field. At first, this was done by the subgroup in charge of the sweet potatoes, assisted by me. But this job was more suited to the boys and soon some boys from other subgroups helped us. On May 28, we planted the seedlings of sweet potatoes. They were prepared all free by the courtesy of a farmer, living in a remote place, through introduction of a student's parents. Nine sweet potato cuttings were distributed to each subgroup and planted by the six subgroups.

We wrote thank you letters to the farmer. However, the students having never written such a letter took a great deal of time to start. Only after I showed them how, could they manage it. We got a reply from the farmer and some lightning bugs. The students were very delighted with the bugs. We dug the sweet potatoes at the end of November. On December 6, we cooked and ate the potatoes. It was the girls' turn this time. We offered the dish to other teachers. The students wrote letters to the farmer. This time they could write them satisfactorily.

Concurrently with the sweet potato growing, in the second term, we made calendars out of woodcut prints. I introduced the printing of the calendar for the following reasons. First, we can keep the work longer as a memento. Second, boys and girls can work on it cooperatively. Third, when they make the very first printing, the children are beaming with joy. I like this activity for these reasons, memory, cooperation, and excitement.

The common theme of the class that year was "festivals." Each of the six subgroups was further divided into half and made twelve temporary smaller groups. Each of them was in charge of one of the twelve months of the year and competed with each other over creativity, inventiveness, and the appropriateness of their design and selection of the festival of the month in their charge.

The students collected the information and materials for the calendar in September and discussed the subject selection and design in October. In November, those designs were exhibited in the cultural festival of the school and the carving and printing were completed in December.

On December 15, after taking a good three hours to finish printing all the woodcuts, the students all cried out with joy. The representatives of our class, a boy and a girl, went to the principal's office and presented one set of the work. Previously, we had rehearsed in the class with laughs and cheers the correct manner and how to present the gift to the principal. The class got a few words of thanks and pleasure from the principal.

This teacher's effective use of class management in providing student guidance is evident. The most impressive part of the report is the scene of the first day of the class. The teacher was forceful at first, but the students gradually became enthusiastic. They fulfilled their responsibilities by carrying out their own duties. They cooperated with each other. The collaboration of each *han* enhanced their consciousness of belonging. The rotation of roles so that everyone was responsible for various duties can also be seen as contributing to deeper mutual understanding. Also impressive is the fact that these educational effects were achieved through creative activities such as sweet potato production, cooking, or woodcut printing, and the pupils learned about manners, the etiquette of writing a thank you letter, and greeting a principal. Discipline and moral education were taught in a pleasant atmosphere of original activities. This is why this teacher's practice rises above the usual level.

Regular Subjects

Guidance is given also during instruction in the regular school subjects. In terms of time, such guidance is more important than other forms. This instruction in regular subjects is not only a good opportunity to teach communication skills in each subject, but also an opportunity to conduct effective moral education.

The excerpt from a student manual below, similar to that distributed by many schools in Japan, is typical of the type of guidance given during regular subject instruction provided in any class of any Japanese school.

About Learning

"Why do you climb mountains?" asked the mountaineer.

G.L. Mallory said, "Because there are mountains there [sic]."

This is a well-known story. Interesting in this story is that he never thought of climbing as instrumental for strengthening his mind and body. He challenged the mountains because they never stopped charming him.

"Why do you study?"

"Because I want to know."

This should be the right answer for studying. Study should not be done for a practical reason such as getting high marks or becoming a great man, which only makes study irksome to you.

Your every day should begin with study and end with study. You must go on climbing for each summit. You approach it step by step through unprecedented paths with a desire for conquest.

In mountain climbing, a single accident can lead to death of all the party. In learning, too, it is important to be cooperative. We should not leave any friend behind. Let's make sure we advance together with encouragement and cooperation.

...The center of learning is certainly the classes at school. Concentrate on them. Please do not forget the basic manners and etiquette for learning.

1) Sit down on your seat the moment a chime rings to start class.
2) Respond "yes" at once when your name is called.
3) Assume a correct posture during class.
4) When making a remark, speak clearly until the end of your speech, facing each other.
5) Ask any questions when you wonder. When answered, say, "I understand. Thank you."
6) Listen to others until they finish (Genyo Junior High School 1983a).

In this excerpt, guidance is obvious, with reference to both morality and daily attitude. Students read in this excerpt that learning is like a team advancing together, and that it is not to be pursued just for the practical purpose of personal or social success. They learn it should be achieved through solidarity and cooperation. They also read about how to transform what is written in an itemized form into practical manners and etiquette during class.

The reason for including this excerpt is not to evaluate the extent to which these policies, philosophies, and expectations of the school described in the manual actually influence the students. Rather, it is to illustrate the essential educational thought of Japanese school teachers.

Class slogans, often hung in front of a classroom in an elementary or lower secondary school in Japan, are generally related to manners and etiquette. Most of them are especially concerned with communication skills and morality.

A sample of class slogans from various schools shows that they can be classified into three categories (Kataoka 1981).

1) How to listen

> Gaze at a speaker.
> Listen to a speech until the end.
> Refrain from conversation when others make a speech.
> Listen to others, comparing what is said with one's own opinion.
> Listen with correct posture.

2) How to speak

> Speak with an appropriate voice for each occasion.
> Speak facing listeners.
> Speak moderately.
> Speak articulately and in a relaxed manner.
> (For upper grades) Speak to the point and take a clear position.

3) General attention

> Keep seated during class.
> Don't forget necessary things at school.
> Don't make fun of others' remarks.

Learn from others' good points.
Be considerate of others and look at yourself critically.

The attention items enumerated above indicate what should be most emphasized when a homeroom teacher teaches regular subjects. They show that it is important to have an orderly class, to establish a network of personal relations in a group, and to cooperate for a common goal and objective.

Elaborate skills must be used when a teacher gives guidance to students in the class. For example, one teacher may make all members of the class concentrate on their slogans in the morning and evening. The teacher may also make them reflect on whether or not they keep these rules. Another teacher may do more than this. One method is to post a score chart on the wall in the classroom to show how many times a subgroup or an individual student breaks the class rules during a certain period. In this way, orderliness and discipline in a class are generally maintained.

Japanese education has been criticized for putting too much emphasis on orderliness and discipline, thus stifling individual freedom and creativity. Most school children who have returned to Japan from the United States have frequently faced the cultural problem of making the adjustment from freedom to order in a classroom.

The traditional scene in a Japanese classroom is one in which the teacher speaks and students listen. Recently, the situation has been changing. Children have been more active in their presentations, and discussions have been encouraged. Despite such communication changes, order in a classroom is still strictly maintained. Not only do teachers watch rigidly over their students, but the school administrators (principals and boards of education) also do the same over the teachers. Order and discipline are double-edged. While they may generate desirable behavior and attitudes such as obedience to a group and authority and consideration and esteem for others, at the same time they engender limited individual freedom and personality growth.

Special Activities

Objectives and Components

The objectives of special activities of the Course of Study for Elementary Schools and the Course of Study for Lower Secondary Schools are:

> ...through desirable group activities, to promote harmonious development of mind and body, to develop individuality, to enhance consciousness of being a member of a group and to cultivate a self-reliant, independent, and practical attitude to enrich the school life in cooperation with others (Ministry of Education 1977a, 1977b).

Three educational objectives are to be achieved through special activities. The first objective, as expressed by "harmonious development of mind and body" and a "self-reliant, independent and practical attitude," fosters efforts to solve problems independently. The second, as expressed by "desirable group activities," "self-consciousness of being a member of a group," and "cooperation with others," nurtures a sense of responsibility and allegiance to the groups to which one belongs. The third, as expressed by "to develop individuality," develops self-esteem and individual personality. The last element, however, is stressed the least.

Using these objectives, both the Course of Study for Elementary Schools and the Course of Study for Lower Secondary Schools prescribe three components of special activities: students' activities, school events, and classroom guidance. The activities included in the first and second components and some of those included in the third are as follows:

Student Activities

Classroom Assembly
Student Council
Clubs

School Events

> Ceremonies
> Academic events
> Physical education
> Excursions
> Events related to health and safety education
> Events related to work and production

Classroom Guidance

> Adapting to classroom and school life
> Health and Safety
> Fulfilling academic work
> Choosing future courses

Perhaps the activities most conducive to developing attributes of diligence, effort, and allegiance to groups are the activities of classroom assembly and classroom guidance. The activities of classroom assembly are designed to encourage students to solve problems within the classroom and to let them share responsibility. Classroom guidance is designed to help students adjust to school life, with special emphasis on interpersonal relations, and to acquire academic skills and abilities, with special emphasis on motivation and attitudes.

Student council activities and school events conducted by the whole school regardless of grade and class, can help develop effort and allegiance. Through these activities, students have the opportunity to plan and cooperate in dealing with common problems within the school.

"To develop individuality" is an objective of club activities. Clubs are organized by all pupils in grades four to six in elementary schools and by all students in lower secondary schools who are interested in the same subject. The objective is to have activities of common interest and concern to the members regardless of the classroom and grade to which they belong.

Although the development of individuality is not confined to club activities (the whole area of special activities and every aspect of group activities is, to some extent, committed to the development of the individual personalities of students), club activities are the only ones where the objective of individual development is explicitly stated. In other areas, individuality may be only obliquely implied.

The Japanese are prone to standardize themselves and to neglect individual personality and creativity. For this reason, the importance of developing the individual personality should be emphasized and articulated more in the current courses of study.

Implementation of Special Activities

In what ways are the special activities prescribed in the courses of study implemented nationally? Useful data come from a May 1985 Ministry of Education study that includes information collected from 39,000 Japanese public schools at all levels (Narita 1985). Table 4 presents relevant data from the study.

As the data from the above-mentioned implementation report show, "special activities" in Japan are not abstractions. In fact, they hold a special place in Japanese education. Although it cannot be asserted that special activities are universal (as shown in item 1, nearly 20 to 30 percent of all schools have no general plans for special activities), there is reason to speculate that they are regarded as effective in schools where they take place. For instance, items 2 and 3 indicate that special activities (classroom assembly and classroom guidance together) are conducted for more than one class hour a week. Also, items 5 and 6 show that the annual school hours allotted for school events are never less than ninety, and almost all schools conduct educational school trips.

Student Activities

There are three components of student activities: classroom assembly, student council, and clubs. This section focuses on the first two.

Classroom Assembly

An example as fine as the sweet potato project described above contrasts with the most common guidance lessons that tend to be moralistic or disciplinary. Typical of this type of guidance are classroom assembly activities that include short-term homeroom activities, generally called "morning meeting" and "afternoon meeting" and held for ten or fifteen minutes every day, and

TABLE 4

| Item | School Level | | |
	Elementary	Low. Second.	Upp. Second.
1. Percentage of schools which have general plans for special activities	76.2	73.4	82.3
2. The greatest annual class hours for classroom assembly	35 and more	15-19	—
3. The greatest annual class hours for classroom guidance	15-19	20-24	35
4. Percentage of schools implementing club activities	99.2	—	98.2
5. Average annual class hours for school events	90.7	103.8	119.4
6. Percentage of schools which conduct educational trips	84.7	96.5	89.3
7. Top objective and its percentage of classroom guidance	Basic behavior and customs	Consciousness as a member of group as well as an individual	A full group life
	74.7	68.0	32.3
8. Top component and its percentage which must be considered as the most preponderant in guidance.	Class guidance	Class guidance	Class assembly
	32.8	—	—

NOTES: Items 1 to 3 are from 1985 data. Items 4 to 8 are from 1984 data.

long-term homeroom activities that are weekly, one-hour homeroom meetings.

Short-term classroom assembly activities include:

A. Morning meeting at an elementary school:

    1. Class song.
    2. The day's schedule and motto of the class.
    3. Health check.
    4. Notices from any pupil in charge.
    5. Speech by a pupil.
    6. Comment from the homeroom teacher.

("Speech by a pupil" is included to give any child in the class an opportunity to speak in front of others. Pupils usually speak about what they think, or they read their diaries or short essays on any subject.)

B. Morning meeting at a lower secondary school:

    1. Morning greeting and roll call.
    2. Discussion about the day's class activities and study.
    3. Notices from *han* and students in charge or personal messages.
    4. Submitting *han* notebooks and other assignments.
    5. Arranging the classroom.
    6. Special programs of the day.
    7. Comment from the homeroom teacher.

("Special programs of the day" may include recreational games, discussion about class problems, or activities of subgroups.)

C. Afternoon meeting at a lower secondary school:

    1. Reflection of each subgroup upon the day.
    2. Reflection of the class upon the day.
    3. Notices from students in charge.
    4. Special programs of the day.
    5. A word from the homeroom teacher.

The following examples of what is actually done in the classroom is from the Murakami class in Shimenhigashi Junior High School in Fukuoka Prefecture (Murakami 1985):

Monday: Speech about a wonderful experience on Sunday
Tuesday: A communication game
Wednesday: A short quiz on Chinese characters
Thursday: An instructive story from the homeroom teacher
Friday: An instructive story from students
Saturday: Songs

These are activities in which all pupils can participate and develop their individuality. However, even in these activities, too much emphasis is apt to be put on awareness of, or reflection upon, moral and disciplinary mottoes of a day (such as whether or not members of the class should refrain from private conversations during class, should act in cooperation with other members of a subgroup, or be on time for each class). In addition, pupils often become overly critical about others' faults or breaches of the rules. A Japanese mother who recently came back from Sydney, Australia, gave the following report:

They had a period of show-and-tell time in that elementary school in Sydney, during which time the children speak about their wonderful experiences of the day or day before and show their treasures. Children who listen to those stories also give a big applause to the speaker, saying, "Wow, it's wonderful!" and sharing the same pleasure without any envy. They are really open-minded. On the other hand, we have an "evening meeting" in the elementary school in Japan and look back on what has happened during the day. It is O.K., but they try to find the slightest faults with others and attack each other even among friends. I hate this because it seems to me to be somewhat very insular and narrow!

There is more, of course, to this story than the difference between narrowness and open-mindedness. There is the difference between discipline and spontaneity. In the atmosphere of Japanese short-term classroom assemblies, excessive discipline may limit a child's natural spontaneity.

Another important role of a homeroom teacher is managing long-term homeroom activities, namely the one-hour classroom assembly every week. How it is planned and presented is often influenced by the educational policy and philosophy of individual homeroom teachers. The general procedures are as follows:

1) A committee of the classroom assembly first discusses and determines topics to be posed in the next classroom assembly.

2) An assembly is run primarily by a chairman, a keeper of records, and members of the committee.

3) The other pupils of the class express their opinions about the topics.

4) A homeroom teacher avoids giving direct advice, but provides indirect advice and assistance.

5) Topics posed for discussion usually concern problems to be solved in the class or planning for school and class events.

The committee of a classroom assembly usually consists automatically of the subgroup leaders or *hancho*. This means that only certain students of the class can participate in the committee. So, recently, another method of selection has been accepted. The subgroups take turns in forming the committee, and thus all members of the class have the experience of being on the committee. Every time a different subgroup forms the committee, different students assume the roles of chairman and keeper of the records. Thus, as many students as possible participate in the committee and serve as an officer of the committee.

The topics for discussion are generally classified in two categories: those concerned with problems and difficulties in the course of daily class life, and those concerned with planning for ceremonial events. In the case of the latter, students can put forward ideas and map out a tentative plan for a given period. In the case of the former, they may come up with an idea to solve a problem for a given period, but very often they must go on trying to improve one idea after another until they find the right one. Because of many trials and errors, this process takes much longer than a one-hour discussion. The distinction between the two types of subjects and the discussion they require is rarely acknowledged by Japanese school teachers, and they usually have time for only one type of discussion. As a result, there can be little expectation that the child's problem solving abilities will be developed. This may be one of the reasons for the Japanese preference for formality.

Nevertheless, the once-a-week classroom assembly greatly contributes to the exposure of Japanese children to democratic attitudes, problem-solving practice, and especially the ability to participate in discussions on a subgroup basis.

Student Council Activities

Table 5 is an annual schedule of activities of the Student Council of Genyo Junior High School (Genyo Junior High School 1983b, 1983c).

The principles of guidance are conveyed through this schedule of events:

1) Students identify problems and make efforts to solve them on their own.

2) Students cooperate with each other in an organization and achieve the goals efficiently.

3) Students responsibly carry out their own roles.

4) All students create a "we-feeling" of unity.

School Events

The following is a schedule of annual events and assemblies of Furuta Elementary School (Furuta Elementary School 1985):

Month	*Events and Assemblies*
April	Entrance ceremony/school excursion
May	Welcome assembly for the first graders*
June	Athletic meet*
July	Ceremony ending the first term

TABLE 5

Month	Event	Activities
April	Welcome to the new entrants	Assist preparation for the entrance ceremony/Decorate the newcomers' classroom
	Introduction ceremony	Speech by the president/Introduce a school song and play music
	Orientation	Introduce the members of the Council and the committees and various events
	Introduction of after-school club activities	Explain about clubs and how to register
May	"Pep rally" for the students who attend the Spring Prefectural Athletic Meet	Speeches by the representatives of the players and the Student Council/Sing a school song in chorus
July	Class match	Interclass match in each grade
September	Athletic meet	Determine collective games and individual games/Select the necessary members for the meet
October	Cultural festival	Determine a theme or a slogan of the festival/Share the roles by each class
November	Election of the Council members	Establish the election committee/Counting of votes
December	Year-end charity	Raise contribution money
January	Inauguration of the new Council	Introduce the new executive members
February	Beautification of the school	Repair and arrange desks, chairs, bulletin boards, etc.
March	Farewell assembly for the graduates	Present flowers/See the graduates off to the school gate

September	Ceremony starting the second term/athletic meet
October	Draw-a-picture day/ presentation-of-essays day
November	Cultural performance day*
December	Ceremony ending the second term
January	Ceremony starting the third term
February	Club activity day/farewell assembly for the sixth graders*
March	Graduation/ceremony ending the academic year
Every month	Classes in each grade have separate assemblies

The school events and assemblies marked with an asterisk are specifically organized to achieve effective student guidance. Through these activities, the school intends "to deepen interaction among classes and grades, to tighten pupil solidarity, to make school life more pleasant and richer for pupils, and to promote their consciousness of affiliation with the school, interdependency, and socialization, which therefore can be said to be part of moral education" (Furuta Elementary School 1985).

Some of these special activities are described in further detail as follows:

Welcome Assembly for the Newcomers in May

The Student Council plans and puts it into practice. All upper grade pupils gather in lines at the auditorium and welcome the first graders with songs. The council sponsors events and games and explains major school events of the year.

Athletic Meet in June

An original plan is prepared by the Student Council executive committee, and the class representative committee examines it and determines a final plan. According to this plan, the whole school participates in the meet to enjoy sports, become friends, and keep rules. The objectives of the meet are to develop athletic abilities and to nurture an awareness of affiliation and solidarity with the class or school.

Cultural Performance Day in November

The executive committee of the Student Council draws up an original plan, and the class representative committee examines and determines a final plan. According to this plan, the whole school participates in the creative activities to deepen personal contacts and develop an awareness of affiliation and solidarity with the school and class.

Farewell Assembly for the Sixth Graders

The Student Council executive committee, excluding the sixth graders, plans and carries out the assembly. Each grade decides what to perform in the assembly. The fifth graders present handmade ribbons to the sixth graders. The sixth graders in return sing in a chorus or play in a concert.

The following is a list of some major school events held in Genyo Junior High School (Genyo Junior High School 1983b, 1983c). It indicates the student guidance roles such events are expected to play.

School Trip for the Third graders and a One-Day Bus Tour for the First and Second Graders in May

The objectives are:

> To let students not only widen their knowledge and experience and to commune with nature, but also to deepen friendship and create good memories of school life, and

> To let them get accustomed to a collective action as well as to let them learn public manners and morality.

Cultural Festival in October

The objectives are:

> To develop the subjective attitudes of students,

> To bring out their morale,

> To make the most of their cooperation, and

> To make the most of their perseverance.

School Marathon in December

The objectives are:

> To foster tolerance,

> To let students challenge their own physical limits, and to let them be careful in case of an accident.

Through these school events, the intention is to develop effort, tolerance, creativity, and cooperation, although in the area of creativity there may be big differences among schools.

Classroom Guidance

The programs for the first two components of special activities, student activities and school events, are developed on a school-by-school basis. This is also true of the third component, classroom guidance. Table 6 is an annual plan for classroom guidance at one elementary school (Furuta Elementary School 1985).

These subjects are intended "to establish the fundamental behavioral patterns necessary for school and classroom life and to develop the individual internal consciousness or the morality of each child, and they are also intended not only to solve problems in actual life, but also to promote effectiveness of moral education..." The topics designed to foster cooperation, diligence, and responsibility are mostly listed under "adjustment," that is, "a clean school," "making friends," "class duties," "cooperation with others," and so on.

Classroom guidance classes are of two types: one full class hour and one-half class hour.

TABLE 6

| Month | Field | | | |
	Adjustment	Safety & Health	School lunch & Books	Others
April	Becoming a pupil in the x grade	Health check		Greetings
May	A clean school	Dangerous games	Preparation for lunch	The signal of the chime
June	Making friends	Prevention of bad teeth	Making the most of books	Making the most of public property
July	Reflection on the first term	Cautions for swimming	Classification of books and their arrangement	Summer vacation coming up soon
September	Start of the second term	Physical exercises and injuries	How to eat	A joyful athletic meet
October	Class duties	Eye check	How to read books	How to speak politely
November	Cooperation with others	Rules when walking road & street	Eating with gratitude	Beautification of school
December		Sickness & safety in winter	Putting things back in order after use	How to spend days during winter vacation
January	Start of the third term	Prevention of the flu	Rests after lunch	
February	School recesses	Emergency preparation & drills		Nicknames
March	Promotion to the next grade		Arrangement of readers' notebooks	Farewell to the 6th graders

The plan for one class hour of guidance on the subject "a clean school" for a fifth grade class in the same elementary school follows (Furuta Elementary School 1985).

1) (Subject) School cleaning.

2) (Reasons for its choice) A month has passed in the fifth grade. The sites of cleaning assigned to the class have increased by two--a classroom of the first graders and the east stairway besides our own classroom. In other words, they are required to be of service to the welfare of the whole school. Some sort of skills in cleaning are also required. On this occasion, I let the class reflect on the cleaning this month and identify some problems, and consider better methods for efficient and cooperative cleaning. I also let them develop the attitude and consciousness as upper graders that they must take an initiative to promote the beautification of our school and to make a comfortable environment for the lower graders.

3) (Objectives) The objectives of the cleaning are to let pupils become aware of the importance of cooperation and responsibility, and to let them develop the motivation to put the theory into practice.

4) (Preparation)

> a) Problems of each cleaning site.
> b) A list of reflections on cleaning.
> c) Diary by pupils.
> d) Voice of a teacher in charge of the first graders (tape recorded).

5) (Procedure)

> a) Introduction: Reflect on the daily cleaning and comprehend problems.
> i) Point out trouble areas.
> ii) Suggest the bad points.
> iii) Suggest the good points.

b) Development: Discuss and think about causes and measures in each cleaning subgroup.
   i) Distribution of duties.
   ii) Procedures for cleaning.
   iii) Individual responsibility.
   iv) Reflection meetings after cleaning.
   v) Each subgroup presents its ideas about improving the methods, etc., and about collecting opinions from the entire class.
c) Effect: Heighten motivation for cleaning from now on.

In Japan, unlike other countries, school cleaning has great educational significance (Okihara 1978). Through this process, pupils can comprehend the moral significance of cleaning, that is, its spiritual value, the responsibility involved, and the cooperation needed. This cleaning activity is an example of how theory is linked with practical tasks. It is most important in classroom guidance to link theory with practice.

Table 7 is an annual plan for classroom guidance in a third grade class in a lower secondary school (Genyo Junior High School 1983b, 1983c).

These activities, especially the activities shown in field 1, make it clear that development of a cooperative attitude in a group activity is an essential educational goal and objective. In field 2, effort and diligence in academic work are again and again emphasized. In spite of such elaborate plans, as noted earlier, classroom guidance in the lower secondary schools is generally given less attention than in elementary schools.

Conclusion: Summary, Effects, and Problems

The courses of study stipulate the educational aims of the three components of special activities: student activities, school events, and classroom guidance. Those educational aims are summarized as the acquisition of the attributes of effort and diligence, the attitudes of allegiance to and cooperation in groups, and the development of individual personality.

TABLE 7

Month	Field			
	1. Consciousness as an individual as as well as a group member	2. Complete academic life	3. Future course selection	4. Health & safety-related life, etc.
April	Organization of the class	Objectives of and readiness for learning		
May	Cautions for a a school trip		Academic career and occupation	Group action during a school trip/Traffic safety
June	Educational counseling	How to study each subject and make a long-term plan for examinations	Future course selection	
July	Reflection on the first term/A daily plan for summer vacation/ Preparation for an athletic meet			Secure life, especially cautions for swimming
September				
October	Preparations for a cultural festival	Reviewing one's learning plan		
November	Educational counseling		Future course survey	Sex education for youth
December	Reflection on the second term/A daily plan for winter vacation			
January	Reorganization of the class		Cautions for the examinations	
February	Memories		Individual counseling	
March				Beautification of the environment

Skillful Japanese teachers almost always attempt to organize their classes into several subgroups and to foster creativity, cooperativeness, and sharing in each subgroup. They also try to develop a child's independence and willingness to collaborate through classroom assemblies, and they try to enhance individual efforts and increase understanding of collective rules and discipline through instruction in regular subjects as well.

Adjustment to a collective life is emphasized in both an annual schedule of school events and a plan for classroom guidance. Allegiance to groups and a sense of unity are nurtured through school events and classroom assembly activities. Independence, a sense of responsibility, and the ability to solve problems are also expected to be developed in student-initiated council activities.

In short, the most salient feature of guidance as actually practiced is the encouragement of problem-solving attitudes and abilities, cooperation and collaboration, and respect for discipline.

How effective are these educational methods in achieving the intended results among Japanese students? Some data concerning effectiveness have become available through recent surveys.

In a survey conducted in Tokyo, senior high students indicated they considered the most significant aspects of a cultural festival to be:

a) Presenting and showing academic
   achievement   10.0%
b) Having fun away from studying   17.7%
c) Independent and student-initiated
   planning and administration   24.3%
d) Implementing collaborative work   37.0%
e) Friendship between teachers and
   students as well as among students   7.7%
   (Takai 1985)

The highest percentages of the students considered collaboration and independent activity as the most important aspects of a cultural festival.

The following data show the results of a questionnaire about class management and student guidance that was given to a fifth grade class in an elementary school (Kanzaki 1982). Most pupils liked school events and, in particular, assembly activities:

a) A classroom assembly is necessary	Yes 100%
	No 0%
b) I like the activities in the assembly	Yes 50%
	No 0%
	Don't know 50%
c) I like the discussions	Yes 47%
	No 6%
	Don't know 47%
d) I like the shared work	Yes 82%
	No 0%
	Don't know 18%
e) I like school events and assembly activities	Yes 94%
	No 0%
	Don't know 6%

A sample of responses of individual members of the class include:

a) The classroom assembly is necessary for improving the sense of unity of the class.

b) It is good to discuss matters with each other.

c) The classroom assembly is fun and inspirational.

d) The assembly is an opportunity to find out the different good qualities of friends through the various activities.

e) We can work together to achieve goals by speaking, listening, thinking, and acting.

f) The teacher should not interrupt during the classroom assembly.

g) It is up to us to make the assembly work successfully.

These statements by the pupils make it clear that the goals of special activities, particularly those of the classroom assembly, are, in the main, successfully achieved.

In the debate of the National Council on Educational Reform (a temporary advisory committee to the prime minister, which began a thorough review of Japanese education in September, 1984), one of the controversial issues has been the inadequate development of individual personality and creativity. Since individuality is related to individual freedom, independence, and responsibility, emphasizing individuality will promote both the integrity of the individual and the vitality of the group. The issue of whether or not to individualize education affects special activities most of all.

Some reasons for the problem can be pointed out. First, the courses of study do not specifically state that special activities must be conducted with the same emphasis on building individual personality and creativity as on building effort and diligence and allegiance to and cooperation in a group. Second, Japanese education has traditionally set greater value on obedience than on independence. Yet, at home, most Japanese parents would like to raise more self-reliant children, while Americans want more obedient ones. The reality is the reverse, however (Masuda 1969). Third, the Japanese tend to have a standardized idea about groups: that the individuality of each member must be subordinate to the needs of the group, and each member should try to adjust to its uniformity. However, according to a comparative cultural theory, Japanese are more individualistic than Chinese and Russians, but less so than Europeans and Americans (Umesao 1967).

Traditional Japanese student guidance has often been criticized (Kataoka 1975). "Individual-based collective guidance" has been gaining new attention. The mainstream of current Japanese theories about special activities and class management is concerned with how to combine individual personality and creativity with collaboration and collectiveness (Uruta 1981).

The guidance conducted by almost all Japanese schools and teachers is more or less conducive to fostering diligence, allegiance, and collaboration. However, the way that guidance is conducted is so group-oriented that an individual must be totally immersed in the group. As a result, the problems of the development of individuality and the individualization of groups have been left to be solved later.

References

Furuta Elementary School, Hiroshima. 1985. *Kenkyu kiyo 1985* [Research bulletin 1985]. Hiroshima: Furuta Elementary School.

Genyo Junior High School, Shimonoseki. 1983a. *Gakushu no tebiki* [Lesson handbook]. Shimonoseki, Japan: Genyo Junior High School.

-----. 1983b. *Kenkyu kiyo 1983* [Research bulletin 1983]. Shimonoseki, Japan: Genyo Junior High School.

-----. 1983c. *Nenkan keikaku to shiryo* [Annual plan and data]. Shimonoseki, Japan: Genyo Junior High School.

Kanzaki, M. 1982. *Hancho no iru gakkyu kara hancho no inai gakkyu e* [From a class with a leader to a class without leaders]. Nagoya, Japan: Reimei Shobo.

Kataoka, T., ed. 1975. *Shudan shugi kyoiku no hihan* [Critique of Japanese collectivism in education]. Nagoya, Japan: Reimei Shobo.

-----. 1976. *Ko o ikasu shudan zukuri* [Group formation for respecting individuality of members]. Nagoya, Japan: Reimei Shobo.

-----. 1981. *Zen'in sanka no gakkyu keiei handobukku* [Handbook of class management for participation of all members]. Nagoya, Japan: Reimei Shobo.

Leestma, R., R. August, B. George, and L. Peak. 1987. *Japanese Education Today*. Washington, D.C.: U.S. Government Printing Office.

Magari, H. 1978. *Yutori to sozo no shoshudan katsudo* [Creative small group activities]. Nagoya, Japan: Reimei Shobo.

Masuda, M. 1969. *Amerika no kazoku: Nippon no kazoku* [Family in America: Family in Japan]. Tokyo: NHK Press.

Ministry of Education. 1977a. *Chugakko gakushu shido yoryo* [Course of study for lower secondary schools in Japan]. Tokyo: Monbusho.

-----. 1977b. *Shogakko gakushu shido yoryo* [Course of study for elementary schools in Japan]. Tokyo: Monbusho.

-----. 1985. *Koritsu shochu-koto gakko ni okeru tokubetsu katsudo no jissi jokyo ni kensuru chosa ni tsuite* [Regarding research on special activities in public primary and secondary schools] (Official notification for the elementary schools, No. 162). Tokyo: Monbusho.

Murakami, S. 1985. "Kyosahitsu no aidea: Kodomo ga tsukuru gakkyu bunka" [Ideas for the classroom: Class culture that students create]. *Nakama Zukuri to Jugyo* 5.

Narita, K. 1985. "Tokubetsu katsudo no jissi jokyo to sono kaizenten" [Some comments about special activities and areas for improvement]. In Ministry of Education, ed., *Shoto kyoiku shiryo* [Data about primary education]. Tokyo: Monbusho.

Nomoto, S. 1984. *Watashi no gakkyu keiei* [My class management] (A research report to the Niigata Board of Education). Niigata, Japan: The Board of Education.

Okihara, Y. 1978. *Gakko soji* [Research on school cleaning in the world: From the perspective of comparative education]. Tokyo: Gakuji Shuppan.

Takai, N. 1985. "Seito o henyo sasu gakko soji" [School activities for changing students' attitudes]. In Study Group on Special Activities, ed., *Tokubetsu katsudo no kenkyu* 23.

Umesao, T. 1967. *Bunmei no seitaishi-kan* [Ecological-historical view of civilizations]. Tokyo: Chuo Koronsha.

Uruta, K. 1981. *Tokubetsu katusdo-ron* [The theory of special activities]. Tokyo: Daiichi Hoki.

Yamanaka, K. 1985. "Kyoshitsu no aidea: Imo to hanga to suraido to" [Ideas in class management: Sweet potatoes, prints, and slides]. *Nakama Zukuri to Jugyo*, 5.

CHAPTER 4

AN ANALYSIS OF JAPANESE AND AMERICAN
TEXTBOOKS IN MATHEMATICS

Harold W. Stevenson and Karen Bartsch
University of Michigan

Mathematics is an important academic discipline, and plays a critical role in nearly all forms of scientific inquiry. In a scientific era it is important that a nation's citizens possess a solid understanding of the fundamentals of mathematics. Such knowledge is not only important to those who pursue careers in which mathematics is a basic tool, but also to those who seek to understand the operations of modern science and commerce. It is a matter of serious concern, therefore, when the fundamentals of mathematics are not being acquired effectively by a nation's children. A lack of knowledge of the concepts and operations of mathematics seriously impedes their ability to adapt to a world in which mathematics plays an increasingly important role. Such is the case with America's children and youth. They have consistently demonstrated an understanding of mathematics that is inferior to that of students in other industrialized nations.

This chapter examines the evidence supporting one possible basis of the poor performance of American students: the content of the textbooks that are used in their classes at school. Mathematics textbooks used in Japan and in the United States from the first through the twelfth grades are analyzed in detail. Before describing this analysis, the international studies of mathematics achievement that led to the current national concern will be discussed.

International Studies

First International Study

The inadequate performance of American students in mathematics first received attention with the dramatic results of the international comparison of mathematics achievement conducted in

1964 (Husen 1967). This study involved thirteen-year-olds and pre-university students from twelve countries, including Japan and the United States.

Detailed tests of mathematical concepts and operations were given to four groups of adolescents. Of the American and Japanese students, the following groups were tested: a) thirteen-year-olds from 381 schools in the United States and from 210 schools in Japan; b) all students other than thirteen-year-olds in the classes in which thirteen-year-olds were enrolled; c) students in their preuniversity year who were taking mathematics in 149 schools in the United States and 91 schools in Japan; and d) students in their pre-university year who were not taking courses in mathematics in 155 schools in the United States and 349 schools in Japan.

On none of the sixteen tests did the American students obtain scores comparable to those of their Japanese counterparts. Total scores of the Americans were consistently below the average for the twelve countries; those of the Japanese were consistently above the average. For example, among thirteen-year-olds, the average z score for the Americans was -.25 and for the Japanese, .76; among the preuniversity students taking mathematics courses, the corresponding z scores were -.90 and .38; and of the preuniversity group not taking mathematics courses, the z scores were -.90 and .34. A z score represents the degree of departure in standard deviation units of an individual score in a distribution with a mean of 0. The standard deviation for each of the four sets of comparisons was computed from a distribution of scores of participating students from all countries. The z score can also be interpreted in terms of percentiles. A z score of 1 would be at the 84th percentile; a score of 0, at the 50th percentile, and a score of -1 at the 16th percentile.

Average scores for the American and Japanese groups differed, as did scores for the top students in each country. For example, of the top 4 percent of the preuniversity students in mathematics classes, Japanese students solved an average of forty-four problems and the American students, thirty-three. Perhaps the most devastating comparisons were those involving the percentage of American students whose scores fell at various percentiles in the distribution of scores derived from all countries. It would be expected that 75 percent of the students would be at or above the 25th percentile, 50 percent at or above the 50th percentile, and so forth. Of preuniversity students taking mathematics courses, 82 percent of the Japanese, but only 36 percent of the Americans, obtained scores that were at or above the 25th percentile for all students taking the test. At the lower percentiles, therefore, the American students were below the Japanese students but did not perform especially badly in comparison to students from other countries. However, 63 percent of the Japanese students, but only 18 percent of the American students, obtained scores above the 50th percentile; 43 percent of the Japanese students, but only 9 percent of the American students, obtained scores above the 75th percentile. Thus, the relative inferiority of the scores received by the American students was more notable as the overall percentiles increased.

Rural students in both countries fell behind city students, but whether the students were from rural areas, towns, or cities, the Japanese children excelled. Similarly, children from families of the lowest occupational group in each country received lower scores than children from families in the highest occupational group; again, however, the differences always favored the Japanese students. In fact, students from families in the highest occupational groups in the United States received scores similar to those of Japanese children from the lowest occupational groups. The respective scores, in terms of percentage of items passed, were 26.8 and 27.7.

Efforts were made to categorize the problems in different ways, but the results were consistent. Scores for the American students were as depressed for items involving routine application of what had been learned as for items requiring applications of knowledge in solving novel problems. Differences between the American and Japanese students were just as great for verbal problems as for problems involving only computation. Mathematical skills of American adolescents simply were not competitive with those of their Japanese peers.

Second International Study

The situation has not improved over the past two decades. Preliminary analyses of a second international study of eighth graders and high school seniors reveal a large gap between the scores of American and Japanese students (McKnight, Crosswhite, Dossey, Kifer, Swafford, Travers, and Cooney 1987). Eighth grade students from twenty countries and twelfth grade students from fifteen countries participated. The students were tested during the 1981-82 school year. Nearly 12,000 American students from 250 public and private high schools participated in this study. Among eighth graders, Japanese students received the highest average scores on all five of the tests given: arithmetic, algebra, geometry, statistics, and measurement. The status of American students ranged from eighteenth (in measurement) to eighth (in statistics). Among high school seniors, the Japanese students were surpassed only by students from Hong Kong on each of the following tests: sets and relations, number systems, geometry, algebra, probability and statistics, and elementary functions and calculus. Again, the American students performed more poorly on all of the tests than the Japanese students did. The American students ranked fourteenth in algebra and twelfth in all other areas except sets and relations, where they were tenth. In general, the scores of the Japanese students were from 10 to 20 percentage points above those of the American students.

As in the earlier study, the top American students were not competitive with top students from other countries. For example, of the students in precalculus courses, American students tended to be at or below the 25th percentile for all countries. Among those who were enrolled in calculus classes, a group that contains approximately 2 percent to 3 percent of all American high school students, performance was at or near the average level for students from all the participating countries.

Some of the items on the 1981 test were the same as those that had been used in 1964. On the thirty-six items common to the tests given to eighth graders, the American students showed a modest decline in performance. American students in 1981 passed 3 percent fewer of the items than the American students did in 1964. The decline was somewhat greater for problems involving comprehension and application (-4 percent) than for computational problems (-2 percent). At the twelfth grade level, there was a slight improvement between the two testing periods: American students solved 6 percent more of the problems in 1981 than the American students solved in 1964.

Elementary School Children

The poor academic performance of American children in mathematics does not begin in junior high school. Even during kindergarten, American children perform significantly worse than Japanese children, and differences between the children's scores from the two countries increase between the first and fifth grades (Stevenson, Lee, and Stigler 1986). The study, conducted in Japan,

Taiwan, and the United States, included 288 kindergarten, 240 first grade, and 240 fifth grade children in each country. The results were startling. For example, among the one hundred students from all three countries who received the lowest scores, there were 56 American students at first grade; at fifth grade, 67. Among the top one hundred first graders in mathematics, only 15 were American. Only one American child was among the fifth graders receiving the top one hundred scores. American children performed as poorly on problems involving the routine use of mathematical operations as in problems requiring the application of concepts and operations in problem solving.

Elementary School Textbooks

One of the many questions that arises in attempting to interpret the large difference between American and Japanese students' performance in mathematics is whether the content of the mathematics textbooks used in the two countries is comparable. If it is not, the better performance of Japanese children could be attributed to more comprehensive coverage of mathematical concepts and operations or to their earlier introduction in Japanese textbooks.

The analysis of textbooks used in elementary schools in Japan and in the United States was completed in the spring of 1985. The procedure was based on an earlier analysis of elementary school textbooks (Stigler, Lee, Lucker, and Stevenson 1982). Both sets of analyses were undertaken to provide information about the mathematics curricula that was needed in order to construct valid cross-cultural tests of mathematics achievement. These tests were to be used in research projects in Japan, the United States, Taiwan, and China. One series of mathematics textbooks from each of the countries was selected for the analyses.

The Japanese textbook series was *Atarashii sansu* (New mathematics), published by Shoseki Kabushiki Kaisha. The American series was the 1985 edition of *Holt Mathematics*. Both are among the most popular textbooks used in each country. The Taiwan textbook series, *Shuxue* (Mathematics, third edition), published by the National Translation Institute in 1984, and the second edition of *Shuxue*, published by the Beijing Publishing Company in 1983, were also included in the analyses. The comparisons between Japan and the United States will be discussed first.

The first question was the definition of mathematical concepts and operations. There was little utility in adopting so global a definition that elementary school mathematics could be described by a relatively small number of concepts and operations, or in making them so specific that thousands of concepts and operations would have to be included in a description of the textbooks. Definitions of intermediate levels of inclusiveness were, therefore, adopted. For example, if a lesson in the text discussed how to write the numerals from 1 to 10, each numeral was not considered as a separate concept. Nor was the lesson considered as part of a more global concept, writing numerals. Writing numerals from 1 to 10 was, therefore, entered in the list of concepts, as were such concepts and operations as writing numerals from 11 to 20, writing and counting to 50, writing large numbers, and writing numerals for words, each of which constituted a discrete section in the text. Our level of classification was determined, therefore, by the intent of each lesson as well as by its content.

Each textbook was examined page by page by native speakers of each language in order to obtain the lists of the concepts and operations. These three examiners worked closely with each other in making these lists in order to obtain maximal agreement about the level of complexity of the concepts and operations that should be included. An effort was made to be as specific as possible in describing the concepts and operations and by providing examples of the types of problems that illustrated these concepts and operations. Concepts and operations were listed for the curriculum according to the grade and semester in which they first appeared.

A master list was then created. Before this could be done, it was necessary to organize each of the individual lists. As a preliminary step, the concepts and operations were grouped into twenty-nine general topics, such as addition, subtraction, fractions, and decimals. Within each topic, the concepts and operations were listed according to the year and semester in which they appeared within each of the curricula. If a concept or operation was not found for one of the series of textbooks, a second search was made through the textbooks to see if the operation or concept was missing or merely had been overlooked.

General Impressions

Many differences between the textbooks and the curricula of Japan and the United States are readily apparent to anyone who spends a few hours looking at these books. One of the most obvious differences between the textbooks of Japan and the United States is in the appearance of the books and the general way the material is presented. Two textbooks, one for each semester, are published in Japan for each year of elementary school. Each book contains approximately one hundred pages. The American textbooks, in contrast, are thick volumes of several hundred pages, and are designed for use throughout one full year of elementary school. The American textbooks are colorful, complete with photographs at the beginning of each chapter and illustrations and figures on nearly every page. The illustrations and supplementary comments are used, it appears, in an effort to engage the interest of the student. Japanese textbooks, in contrast, are shorter, paperback books with closely printed problems and text and few illustrations. There is little diversion, either by the text or the illustrations, from the central issues of each lesson.

The terse style of the Japanese textbooks is in marked contrast with the step-by-step approach frequently found in the American textbooks. For example, addition problems with two three-digit numbers involving carrying never appeared in the Japanese textbooks, although later problems clearly assumed this knowledge. Japanese textbook writers place more reliance on the teacher to assist children with discussion and elaboration of the content of the lesson than in the United States. The writers of Japanese textbooks also seek to engage the child's active participation in the development of understanding to a greater degree than American writers seem to believe is necessary or possible. For example, the solutions of problems are often presented so that Japanese children must actively work to bridge gaps between steps in an argument, whereas American children often have each step laid out for them.

Although some concepts may be introduced earlier in American textbooks, they seem not to be as sophisticated as those appearing in the Japanese textbooks. For example, probability concepts are introduced in the second semester of the fourth grade in American textbooks, and not until the sixth grade in Japanese textbooks. However, in contrast to the American textbooks, inferential skills are immediately discussed when probability concepts are introduced in the Japanese textbooks.

The importance of repetition and review appears to be a guiding principle underlying the presentation of material in the American textbooks. The textbooks tend to present problems at each grade level that are related to many different topics, such as geometry, addition, and measurement, and to repeat the discussion with some elaboration at later grades. The Japanese textbooks, in contrast, seem to be developed on the assumption that knowledge should be cumulative from semester to semester; if the concept or operation is taught well the first time, it is unnecessary to repeat the discussion at a later time.

The contrast between the curricula is great. The American curriculum is often described as a spiral in which topics reappear in successive years at more and more advanced levels. This "spiral" curriculum has been criticized as being repetitive and inefficient in comparison to the "concentric" curriculum that appears in Japanese textbooks. In the concentric curriculum there is an ever-increasing expansion of knowledge that is dependent upon, but not repetitive of what has been taught earlier. Indeed, without careful examination of an American textbook, it is often difficult to guess the grade at which it is to be used. This is not the case with the Japanese textbooks.

Finally, a number of topics receive greater emphasis in the Japanese than in the American textbooks. Overall, there appears to be more emphasis in the Japanese books on large place values--even into the thousand trillions. Japanese textbooks place greater emphasis on proportions, ratios, and on "mixed" calculation. Problems such as (4 x 6) - 3 are common in Japanese textbooks, but are nearly nonexistent in American textbooks.

Earlier and more frequent examples of the conversion of numbers, shapes, and other concepts are found in the Japanese more often than in the American textbooks. For example, conversion from decimals to fractions is not presented in American textbooks until the second half of fifth grade, but occurs earlier in Japan. Illustrations of how shapes can be converted into other shapes or constructed out of various materials, such as ribbon or matches, are much more common in Japanese than in American textbooks.

In Japanese textbooks, there appear to be more problems that require reading and inferring information from graphs, charts, and tables. In geometry topics, the Japanese textbooks seem to have more problems concerning three-dimensional figures and the concept of symmetry. Japanese children are also taught to place more emphasis on accuracy than American children are, but American children are given more practice in estimating. For example, while Japanese children may be taught to carry out the division of a fraction such as 1/3 to many decimal places, American children may be taught to estimate how many balls are contained in a colored photograph of a box of balls.

Differences between Elementary School Curricula

A total of 497 different concepts and operations appeared in American and Japanese textbooks (see Table 1). All are not taught in each country nor are they taught at the same time. Some appear in the Japanese but not in the American textbooks, and some appear in the American but not in the Japanese textbooks. Nevertheless, 411 of the 497 concepts appear in the Japanese textbooks, and 408 in the American textbooks. Thus, nearly identical percentages of the total concepts are represented in the textbooks of each country: 82.7 percent and 82.1 percent, respectively. As a consequence, relatively small percentages of the concepts and operations appear solely in the textbooks of one country: 17.9 percent in the Japanese textbooks and 17.3 percent in the American textbooks. Generally, then, children in neither country are placed at a disadvantage of having fewer concepts and operations introduced in their textbooks.

Concepts tend to be introduced earlier in the Japanese than in the American textbooks. This is true in 30.4 percent of the cases. Concepts are presented earlier in the American textbooks in only 18.5 percent of the cases. Differences in the time of introduction of the concepts are often quite large. The concepts appear two semesters or more earlier in the Japanese than in the American textbooks in 38 percent of the cases (Table 2). The concepts that appear this much earlier in the Japanese textbooks are: addition, subtraction, decimals, dimensions of solids, decimals and fractions, time, money, relation of circle and sphere, triangle, the relation of the square to other forms, and calculation of area. Only 25 percent of the concepts appear a year or more earlier in the American than in the Japanese textbooks. These include ratio and proportion, problem solving, fractions, and weight. Only 15.9 percent of the concepts were introduced at the same time in the two countries.

Differences in the percentage of concepts and operations appearing first in either the Japanese or American textbooks are small for several topics. These include the concept of number; multiplication; division; mixed addition, subtraction, multiplication, and division; tables and charts; and volume and capacity. The remaining topics, mixed addition and subtraction, mixed multiplication and division, and the use of coordinates, are represented by only a few concepts and operations.

The number of concepts found in each of the major topics appears in Table 3. The distributions are comparable for most of the topics, with some noteworthy discrepancies. In several cases, for example, one of the textbook series includes as many as four or more concepts or operations in illustrating a particular topic than are included in the other series. Japanese textbooks depart from American textbooks to this degree in their presentation of mixed addition, subtraction, multiplication, and division; three-dimensional solids; reading data, tables, and charts; and volume and capacity. Discrepancies of the same magnitude favor the American textbooks in the following four categories: concept of number, addition, length, and time.

Comparisons with Other Curricula

Comparisons are not limited to those made between Japanese and American textbooks, but also include comparisons of textbooks from China and Taiwan. Comparisons with the two textbook series in Chinese are no more favorable to the United States than are the comparisons involving Japan. The results are summarized in Table 4, where the data are broken down according to arithmetic and geometry.

Fewer arithmetic concepts and operations are omitted from the two Chinese curricula than from the American curriculum, and the concepts are more likely to be introduced earlier in the Chinese curricula. The Taiwanese curriculum also tends to introduce more arithmetical concepts than the Japanese curriculum and to introduce them somewhat earlier. Arithmetical concepts tend to be introduced earliest in the Chinese curricula.

The American textbooks are also more likely to omit geometrical concepts than the Taiwanese curriculum and to present the concepts somewhat later. Although the Chinese curriculum tends to introduce concepts in arithmetic earlier than the Japanese

TABLE 1

**Comparison of When Concepts and Skills are Introduced
in Japanese and U.S. Elementary School Textbooks
in Mathematics**

When Concepts Introduced	Number	Percent
Total concepts in textbooks	497	100.0
Japan earlier than U.S.	151	30.4
U.S. earlier than Japan	92	18.5
Same time	79	15.9
Japan, but not U.S.	89	17.9
U.S., but not Japan	86	17.3

TABLE 2

**Comparison of When Concepts Are Introduced in Japanese
and U.S. Elementary School Textbooks, by Semester**

	Semester							
	1		**2**		**3**		**>3**	
	Number	Percent	Number	Percent	Number	Percent	Number	Percent
Country								
Japan earlier	60	25	36	15	24	10	31	13
U.S. earlier	32	13	36	15	12	5	12	5

TABLE 3

Distribution of Number of Concepts and Skills in Japanese and U.S. Elementary School Mathematics Textbooks, by Topic

Concept or Skill	Japan	U.S.
Addition	26	35
Subtraction	21	18
Multiplication	20	22
Division	25	27
Mixed addition and subtraction	3	2
Mixed multiplication and division	1	0
Mixed addition, subtraction, multiplication, and division	8	4
Concept of number	35	39
Factoring	5	7
Ratio and proportion	11	7
Fractions	35	33
Decimals	27	25
Three-dimensional solids	15	6
Coordinates	1	4
Length	10	15
Integers, decimals, and fractions	11	8
Data, tables, charts	20	14
Time	14	24
Money	6	7
Problem solving	15	18
General concepts	23	21
Circle and sphere	8	6
Triangle	8	10
Square, rectangle, parallelogram, rhombus, polygon	13	11
Symmetry	4	5
Area	13	10
Volume/capacity	19	15
Weight	11	12
Other	3	3

curriculum, much less emphasis is given to geometrical concepts in the Chinese than in the Japanese curriculum. In short, the Japanese curriculum is not the most inclusive or advanced of the three Asian curricula, but the American curriculum tends to be less inclusive and to develop at a slower pace.

Conclusions

The curriculum represented in the elementary school textbooks is somewhat more advanced in Japan than in the United States. Concepts and skills are likely to appear earlier in Japanese textbooks, thereby giving Japanese children a greater opportunity during the elementary school years to practice these operations and use these concepts than is possible for the American children. Relatively few concepts and skills are introduced during the same semester in the two countries, and neither country introduces a number of concepts and skills that is notably greater than the other. The emphases given to various topics in the two countries differ, but more notable than the differences are the similarities in the mathematical concepts and operations that appear in the elementary school textbooks. The major difference lies, therefore, not in the content of the curricula, but in the manner and timing in which the curricula are presented in the textbooks.

Secondary School Textbooks

The study of the mathematics textbooks written for students from the seventh through the twelfth grades in Japan and the United States consisted of several phases. The first phase involved selecting the books that were to be analyzed.

Analysis of the secondary school mathematics textbooks was undertaken as part of the United States Study of Education in Japan. The three most popular textbooks currently being used in each country at each grade were analyzed, because they were representative and there was concern that there would be greater diversity among the secondary school textbooks than among those used in elementary school. This decision was easily implemented in Japan, but selecting the most popular textbooks in American junior high and high schools proved to be an extremely complicated problem. For example, staff members of the National Association of

State Boards of Education indicated that they had no statistics related to this question. The lack of a standard curriculum and the independence of school districts in the United States have permitted the proliferation of textbook series by many publishing companies. There are scores of textbooks for each topic, such as algebra, geometry, and calculus, covered from the seventh through the twelfth grades. Moreover, within each grade there are textbooks covering a large number of topics, ranging from consumer mathematics to calculus. No current, comprehensive, national statistics concerning the frequency with which the various textbooks are used in the United States are available.

Selecting the American Textbooks

Illinois Study

A list of frequently used textbooks was compiled by Dr. Kenneth J. Travers of the University of Illinois in 1981-82, but this list included only the textbooks used in the eighth and twelfth grades. Travers obtained his data from a national sample of mathematics classes in these two grades. The rank orders of the five most popular eighth-grade textbooks were *Mathematics Around Us* (Scott-Foresman); *Modern School Mathematics* (Houghton Mifflin); *School Mathematics* (Holt, Rinehart and Winston); *School Mathematics* (Heath); and *Mathematics for Mastery* (Silver-Burdett). The most popular textbooks for the twelfth grade were: *Advanced Mathematics* (Harcourt Brace Jovanovich); *Modern Trigonometry* (Houghton Mifflin); and *Modern Introductory Analysis* (Houghton Mifflin).

National Statistics

Although there is little information about the textbooks that are used, data from the Center for Education Statistics (U.S. Department of Education) indicate the classes taken by a national sample of students who graduated from public and private schools. Information about the courses in which the students were enrolled in 1982 was collected from the time they were in their sophomore year. The courses and the percentage of students enrolled in the courses appear in Table 5. The percentage of students enrolled in

TABLE 4

Comparisons of Content of Japanese Elementary School Textbooks With Content of Textbooks from China, Taiwan, and the United States

Concepts	Japan	China	Taiwan	U.S.
	Percent of total number of concepts			
Arithmetic				
Not included	21.9	21.9	17.6	24.8
Earliest	15.0	33.3	13.7	16.0
Latest	17.0	17.0	19.6	25.5
Only in	3.9	2.0	2.6	7.5
Geometry				
Not included	27.9	49.5	15.3	31.5
Earliest	25.2	8.1	36.9	18.9
Latest	19.8	18.9	14.4	28.8
Only in	4.5	0	9.9	6.3

TABLE 5

Percentage of Students Enrolled in U.S. Secondary School Mathematics Courses

Course	Percent enrolled
General mathematics	2.5
Pre-algebra	14.7
Algebra I	63.2
Algebra II	31.2
Advanced algebra	8.0
Geometry	48.2
Trigonometry	7.4
Calculus	5.6
Other advanced courses	13.4
Unified mathematics (algebra, geometry, calculus)	1.4
Statistics	1.2

prealgebra may be an underestimate; many students may have
taken this course in the eighth grade.

Publishers

The obvious source of information about the use of textbooks
within the United States is the publishers of mathematics textbooks. Obtaining such information is not easy, however. Because of
the financial implications of such statistics for their companies,
publishers generally are not interested in providing data about the
frequency with which various books are used. However, in an effort
to obtain as much information as possible, the national offices of the
seven major publishers of junior high and high school textbooks in
mathematics were contacted.

During a telephone call, the purpose of the study was outlined to a representative of the company. The representative was
asked which were the company's best selling books for the average
level mathematics classes and which book was being used most frequently in classrooms. The representative was also asked if the
company would be willing to compare the sales of its books to those
of other companies. There were varying degrees of willingness to
answer these questions. Some representatives claimed to have no
information about sales and would not answer the questions; others
were cooperative and provided information about their sales and
those of other companies.

After obtaining as much information as possible from
the publishers, a list of what appeared to be the five most popular
textbooks at each grade level was put together. The validity of these
lists was checked with the representatives who had been the most
responsive to the requests for information. On the basis of their
feedback, three of the five textbooks at each grade level were picked
for analysis. As a final check on the validity of these judgments, the
opinions of several leading mathematics educators were obtained.

Textbooks Selected

Textbooks in the United States typically are divided into
three series: those for elementary schools, junior high schools, and
high schools. There are series, however, for grades one through
eight and grades nine through twelve. Schools tend to adopt a series
for one of these segments. Moreover, students tend to enroll in a
sequence of classes that includes algebra I, geometry, algebra II,

and some type of twelfth-grade mathematics. The series that were most popular for grades seven and eight and for grades nine through twelve were, therefore, chosen. These textbooks are listed in Table 6, along with information about their length.

Table 6

U.S. Secondary School Textbooks Selected for Analysis

Heath Mathematics (D.C. Heath, 1985)
    Seventh grade: 13 chapters; 404 pages
    Eighth grade: 13 chapters; 404 pages

Mathematics Today (Harcourt Brace Jovanovich, 1985)
    Seventh grade: 15 chapters; 440 pages
    Eighth grade: 15 chapters; 438 pages

Mathematics Structure and Methods (Houghton Mifflin, 1985)
    Seventh grade: 12 chapters; 437 pages
    Eighth grade: 12 chapters; 465 pages

Grade 9

HBJ Algebra I (Harcourt Brace Jovanovich, 1983)
    14 chapters; 534 pages

Algebra Structure and Methods (Houghton Mifflin, 1983)
    12 chapters; 484 pages

Merrill Algebra I (Merrill, 1983)
    16 chapters; 512 pages

Grade 10

HBJ Geometry (Harcourt Brace Jovanovich, 1984)
    16 chapters; 626 pages

Geometry (Houghton Mifflin, 1985)
    12 chapters; 543 pages

Merrill Geometry (Merrill, 1984)
    14 chapters; 470 pages

Grade 11

HBJ Algebra II with Trigonometry (Harcourt Brace Jovanovich,
    1983)
    16 chapters; 626 pages

Algebra and Trigonometry Structure and Method: Book II (Houghton
    Mifflin, 1984)
    16 chapters; 637 pages

Merrill Algebra II with Trigonometry (Merrill, 1983)
    17 chapters; 571 pages

Grade 12

HBJ Advanced Mathematics (Harcourt Brace Jovanovich, 1984)
    14 chapters; 856 pages

Modern Introductory Analysis (Houghton Mifflin, 1984)
    15 chapters; 700 pages

Advanced Mathematics Concepts (Merrill, 1981)
    15 chapters; 564 pages

Selecting the Japanese Mathematics Textbooks

    Obtaining information about the most commonly used
Japanese textbooks was relatively simple. Although textbooks are
published by a number of companies, all texts must adhere to the
national curriculum in mathematics established by the Ministry of
Education. Information is compiled by the Japanese Publishers'
Union (*Nihon Shuppan Kyokai*) about the yearly sales of textbooks
in Japan. The union was able to provide information about which
textbooks are used most frequently from grades seven through
twelve. The three most popular textbooks at each grade level were
selected for analysis. These textbooks were published by: Tokyo
Shoseki Kabushiki Kaisha, Keirinkan, and Gakkotosho Kabushiki
Kaisha for grades seven, eight, and nine; and Suken Shuppan

Kabushiki Kaisha, which replaced the Gakkotosho series for grades ten through twelve. The textbooks used in the analyses for Japan appear in Table 7.

Table 7

Japanese Secondary School Textbooks Selected for Analysis

Grade 7

Atarashii sugaku [New mathematics] (Tokyo Shoseki, 1985)
    7 chapters; 183 pages

Kaitei sugaku [Mathematics, revised edition] (Keirinkan, 1984)
    7 chapters; 175 pages

Chugakko sugaku [Middle school mathematics] (Gakkotosho, 1985)
    7 chapters; 172 pages

Grade 8

Atarashii sugaku [New mathematics] (Tokyo Shoseki, 1985)
    8 chapters; 192 pages

Kaitei sugaku [Mathematics, revised edition] (Keirinkan, 1984)
    8 chapters; 199 pages

Chugakko sugaku [Middle school mathematics] (Gakkotosho, 1985)
    8 chapters; 188 pages

Grade 10

Sugaku I [Mathematics I] (Tokyo Shoseki, 1985)
    5 chapters; 230 pages

Sugaku I [Mathematics I] (Keirinkan, 1984)
    7 chapters; 216 pages

Sugaku I [Mathematics I] (Suken Shuppan, 1985)
    7 chapters; 223 pages

Grade 11

Daisu. Kika [Algebra. Geometry] (Tokyo Shoseki, 1985)
    4 chapters; 158 pages

Kisokaiseki [Fundamental calculus] (Tokyo Shoseki, 1985)
    4 chapters; 162 pages

Daisu. Kika [Algebra. Geometry] (Keirinkan, 1985)
    4 chapters; 144 pages

Kisokaiseki [Fundamental calculus] (Keirinkan, 1984)
    5 chapters; 144 pages

Daisu. Kika [Algebra. Geometry] (Suken Shuppan, 1985)
    5 chapters; 166 pages

Kisokaiseki [Fundamental calculus] (Suken Shuppan, 1985)
    5 chapters; 167 pages

Grade 12

Kakuritsu. Tokei [Probability. Statistics] (Tokyo Shoseki, 1985)
    4 chapters; 148 pages

Kakuritsu. Tokei [Probability. Statistics] (Keirinkan, 1984)
    5 chapters; 120 pages

Kakuritsu. Tokei [Probability. Statistics] (Suken Shuppan, 1985)
    4 chapters; 166 pages

Bibun. Sekibun [Integral and differential calculus] (Tokyo Shoseki,
    1985)
    3 chapters; 174 chapters

Bibun. Sekibun [Integral and differential calculus] (Keirinkan,
    1985)
    6 chapters; 160 pages

Bibun. Sekibun [Integral and differential calculus] (Suken Shuppan,
    1985)
    6 chapters; 191 pages

Procedure for Analysis

Groups of native speakers of Japanese and English undertook the analyses of the textbooks. The four coders of the Japanese books were graduate students familiar with the mathematics contained in the textbooks they were assigned. Five American graduate students coded the American textbooks. Again, all were familiar with the material contained in the textbooks they analyzed.

One person analyzed the three textbooks selected for each grade or semester. It was much easier to analyze the second and third textbooks than to become familiar with the materials appearing at another grade or semester. The advanced books were assigned to the individuals who had been enrolled in the greatest number of courses in mathematics.

Coders were assisted in defining the concepts and operations by individuals who had done so with the elementary school textbooks. They were told that when they were in doubt about a concept, it should be coded.

The coders listed each concept on a separate card, along with an example of the concept from the textbook. The grade, semester, and page number at which the concept appeared also were recorded. This master set of cards for each grade constituted the basic data for the study.

In some ways it was easier to develop a master list of concepts for the secondary school textbooks than it had been for the elementary school textbooks. In elementary textbooks, it was sometimes difficult to assess what topic of information the writers were attempting to impart; in the secondary textbooks, the purposes of a section or a chapter typically are stated explicitly.

After the master list had been compiled, all of the cards were reviewed by one person. The purpose of this review was to compile a single list of concepts by eliminating redundant entries, and by deciding whether the concepts were represented at an appropriate level of generality and at a similar level across the textbooks from the two countries.

In order to obtain a manageable list, the concepts were organized into general topics. Narrow, specific concepts were subsumed under more general ones. When limits in a function were represented in terms of limits approaching from the right hand and from the left hand, for example, the two concepts were combined as limits of a function; the matrix expression of a linear transformation was subsumed under "linear transformation"; the reciprocal of a complex binomial (a + b*i*) was subsumed under "reciprocals." Variations or applications of the same concept to different content areas were included under the more basic concepts.

A new master set of cards was then constructed. Each card contained the concept, a brief explanation of the concept, and one or more examples of the concept. In addition, the grade(s) and semester(s) at which the concept appeared were represented in a matrix defined by grade and publisher. If it was not clear to the reviewer whether the same concept defined by two different coders represented the same mathematical idea, the pages of the textbooks on which the concept appeared were consulted. It was not difficult to decide whether or not the two or more concepts matched, once the concept was located in the textbook within the context of the lesson. This type of check was performed for approximately one-third of the cards.

At times it appeared unreasonable that certain concepts would appear in the textbooks of one country but not in the textbooks of the other country. In these cases, the original books were reviewed to ascertain whether the concept was present but had been missed by the original coder. It was necessary to recheck approximately one-fourth of the cards to be confident that the concept had not been missed. Concepts were located in approximately half of these cases, but in the other half of the cases the concept was, in fact, missing.

A second type of checking was necessary for some of the basic concepts. It was possible that these concepts had been taught before the seventh grade, and thus would not be found in the junior high and high school textbooks. One of the coders of the elementary school textbooks reviewed all of these cases and identified those concepts that had appeared in the elementary school textbooks.

The final list contained a total of 485 concepts, a number very close to the total of 497 concepts and operations derived from analyses of the elementary school textbooks.

General Impressions

The American textbooks are much longer than those published in Japan. The average number of pages in the American textbooks is 540. No American textbook examined had fewer than 400 pages, and the longest book had 856 pages. Japanese textbooks are much shorter. None of those examined had more than 230 pages, and the average length was 178 pages. Japanese textbooks tend to be tersely written, while the American textbooks contain information that is not necessary for developing the concepts under consideration.

American textbooks are more concrete in their mode of presentation of information than the Japanese textbooks. American writers attempt to engage the readers' interest by describing practical problems, discussing the use of information in everyday situations, and presenting biographical information about eminent mathematicians and scientists. Problems are often personalized and placed in a particular situation. Japanese textbooks tend to be more abstract; there is little effort to place the problems in concrete, everyday settings. Japanese textbooks present the essence of the lesson, with the expectation that the information will be elaborated upon and supplemented with other materials when it is presented in class by the teacher. American textbooks appear to be written so that understanding the content of the lesson is less dependent upon what happens in mathematics classes.

Problems presented in the Japanese textbooks tend to be more complex than those in the American textbooks. Although each exercise begins with simple problems, problems rapidly become difficult. Below are three word problems, from the seventh, tenth, and eleventh grades, respectively:

Between 7 and 10 o'clock, bus A leaves every 10 minutes, bus B leaves every 15 minutes, and bus C leaves every 12 minutes. At 7:05 the three buses left at the same time. What will the time be when they next leave together?

Points A and B are located on the side of a hill. The elevation of Point A is 160 meters above that of Point D. The angle formed by a line drawn from A to B and a line, AC, parallel to the ground is 21 degrees. What is the altitude of Point B?

There are 100 g of salt water in each of two vessels. The density of these are x percent in A, and y percent in B. Now, 30 g of the salt water are taken out from each vessel and transferred to the other vessel. The density of these then becomes x' percent in A,

and y' percent in B. Show that the mapping (x,y)-
(x',y') is a linear transformation.

Problems presented in the American textbooks tend to be
less complex. It appears that the questions in American textbooks
are written at a level of difficulty such that most students should be
able to solve them. This is not the case in Japan; problems are included that will be solved by very few.

American textbooks give drills, exercises, and examples; answers to many of the problems can be found in the back of the book.
Much smaller numbers of problems follow each Japanese lesson,
and in only a few of the books is it possible for students to check the
accuracy of their answers. As a consequence, Japanese students
cannot adopt a routine, mechanical approach to the solution of
problems, but often must evaluate the correctness of their solution
themselves.

As was the case with the elementary school textbooks,
many of the early steps in the development of concepts are omitted
in the Japanese secondary school textbooks. American textbooks
tend to present the information step-by-step, and all details are
specified. For example, an American textbook might contain the
statement that one of the sides of a triangle is shorter than the
other two sides. An explicit statement of such a fundamental fact
would not generally appear in Japanese textbooks; the students
would be expected to make this common sense deduction by themselves or it would be pointed out incidentally by the teacher.

One of the strongest impressions one gains in examining the
two sets of textbooks, therefore, is that American textbook writers attempt to relate mathematics to the everyday world and to engage the student's interest. Explanations are much longer
and problems are simpler and more repetitive than those found in
the Japanese textbooks. Japanese textbook writers, on the other
hand, appear to strive to present the information in
brief discussions that emphasize the abstract nature of mathematical concepts and engage the child's active participation in the
derivation and development of the mathematical concepts.

Results of the Analyses

Analyses of the mathematical concepts in the textbooks
from grades seven through twelve followed the same general

pattern used in the analyses of the elementary school textbooks. However, since three books rather than a single book for each semester or grade were analyzed in each country, consideration can be given to the degree to which the concepts are represented in each of the textbooks for a given grade. If each concept appeared in each of the textbooks, there should be 1,455 entries in the total list of concepts: three times the total number of 485 concepts. The total number of entries was 1,240, indicating that some concepts appeared only in a single text.

When Concepts Were Introduced

Each concept was categorized according to the time at which it was first introduced in the textbooks of the two countries. The results of this analysis appear in Table 8.

Only 11 percent of the concepts were introduced in the same semester in the Japanese and American textbooks. Concepts appeared earlier in one country than in the other 57 percent of the time. Among these, concepts appeared earlier in Japanese than in American textbooks 34 percent of the time and appeared earlier in the American textbooks 23 percent of the time.

There was not a strong tendency for more concepts to be introduced in the textbooks of either country. Eighty-five percent appeared in the Japanese textbooks, and 83 percent appeared in the American textbooks. It is clear that differences in performance in mathematics cannot be attributed to the introduction of a greater number of concepts in Japanese textbooks.

Time of Introduction of Concepts

How much earlier are concepts introduced in Japan than in the United States and vice versa? Of the 276 concepts introduced earlier in one country than in the other, 41 percent appeared one year or more earlier in the Japanese textbooks than in the American textbooks and 27 percent appeared one year or more earlier in the American textbooks (see Table 9). Thus, the advantage in favor of the Japanese students is often a year or more in length. As was hypothesized with regard to elementary school children, earlier introduction of concepts may allow greater opportunities for practice, thereby translating this advantage in time into higher levels of performance.

The data were analyzed in a different fashion. In Table 10, the number of concepts that appeared in all three Japanese textbooks at a given grade or in all three American textbooks at a given grade are presented. Many more concepts appeared in all three of the Japanese than in all three of the American texts. The large difference in the frequency with which the concepts appeared in all three textbooks of a given grade appears to be directly attributable to the national curriculum in Japan that defines the curriculum and stipulates when concepts will be introduced. All textbook writers in Japan are strongly influenced by the content and order of the material described in the national curriculum. In the United States, the order and time for introducing concepts are more a matter of the teacher's or writer's individual choice.

Topics Already Covered in Elementary School

Some of the concepts introduced in the secondary school textbooks in one country did not appear in the secondary school textbooks of the other country. To assess whether these concepts had already appeared in the elementary school textbooks of each country, a search was made of the elementary school textbooks. An overlap of thirty-four concepts was discovered; that is, thirty-four concepts discussed in secondary school textbooks of one country had been discussed earlier in the elementary school textbooks. Of these thirty-four concepts, thirty-two were included in the Japanese elementary school textbooks, and nineteen in the American elementary school textbooks.

Two concepts appeared in the American, but not in the Japanese elementary school textbooks, but fifteen concepts found in Japanese elementary school textbooks had not appeared in the American elementary school textbooks. (Seventeen concepts had appeared in both sets of elementary school textbooks.) Thus, concepts that appeared in American secondary school textbooks were more likely to have appeared in Japanese elementary school textbooks than was the opposite case.

Concepts within three topics--measurement, decimals, and probability--were introduced in the Japanese, but not in the American elementary school textbooks. Concepts that were included in the elementary school textbooks of both countries fell within the following topics: addition and subtraction; percentages, proportions, and ratios; fractions; and factoring.

TABLE 8

Comparison of When Concepts Are Introduced in Japanese and U.S. Secondary School Mathematics Textbooks

	Concepts	
When Concepts Introduced	Number	Percent
Total concepts in textbooks	485	100
Japan earlier than U.S.	163	34
U.S. earlier than Japan	113	23
Same time	53	11
Japan, but not U.S.	73	15
U.S., but not Japan	83	17

TABLE 9

Comparison of When Concepts Are Introduced in Japanese and U.S. Secondary School Curricula, by Semester

	Semester							
	1		2		3		>4	
	Number	Percent	Number	Percent	Number	Percent	Number	Percent
Country								
Japan	50	18	58	21	13	5	42	15
U.S.	40	15	40	15	6	2	27	10

TABLE 10

Comparison of When Concepts Are Introduced in Japanese and U.S. Mathematics Textbooks at Each Grade of Secondary School

When Concepts Introduced	Japan	U.S.
Total concepts	279	162
Japan earlier than U.S.	106	58
U.S. earlier than Japan	89	32
Same time	40	18
Japan, but not U.S.	44	—
U.S., but not Japan	—	54

Representation of Concepts

Table 11 presents the total number of 485 concepts divided into nineteen major topics. Generally, concepts are represented with equal frequency in the two sets of textbooks. There are areas, however, in which greater emphasis is given to a category in one country than in the other.

The difference between the textbooks of the two countries in the number of concepts appearing in each topic was determined. A difference of three or more concepts was considered to indicate greater emphasis on a topic of mathematics in one country than in the other. According to this criterion, American secondary school textbooks give greater emphasis to fractions, percentages, and ratios; addition and subtraction; measurement; decimals; general geometry; and geometric triangles and angles than do the Japanese textbooks. Japanese textbooks, on the other hand, give greater emphasis to graphing functions, three-dimensional figures, equations and sets, probability and statistics, and calculus. When a differential emphasis was given to the topics in the two countries, emphasis appeared to be placed on more advanced topics in Japan than in the United States.

Repetition of Concepts

Although it was impossible to evaluate the level of sophistication with which each concept was introduced, it was possible to assess how frequently the textbooks returned to particular concepts after they had been introduced in an earlier year. The frequencies are summarized in Table 12.

The American spiral curriculum was evident in this analysis. A great majority of the concepts (72 percent) were repeated at least once in the American textbooks after their initial introduction. Nearly a quarter (24 percent) were repeated twice, and 9.9 percent were repeated three times. These values are in striking contrast to those obtained from the Japanese texts. There was some tendency to return to a topic once; this occurred for 38 percent of the concepts. Very few (6 percent) were repeated more than once.

The philosophy underlying Japanese secondary textbooks, as in the textbooks for elementary school students, appears to be that the student should master the concept in its initial presentation or with one repetition at most. This is not the guiding philosophy of American authors of mathematics textbooks. They apparently

TABLE 11

Frequency with Which Concepts Are Represented in Each Major Category of Japanese and U.S. Secondary School Textbooks

Concepts	Japan	U.S.
	Number	
Multiplication/division	12	14
Fractions	11	19
Irrational numbers	15	14
Graphing functions	44	41
Factoring	27	29
Inequalities	8	8
Percentages/ratios	4	12
Equations	2	1
Circles, 3-dimensional	27	24
Equations, sets	27	24
Addition/subtraction	12	21
Measurement	4	13
Problem solving	16	15
Decimals	4	13
Probability/statistics	46	32
Exponential/polynomials	22	22
General geometry	31	35
Geometric triangles and angles	23	27
Calculus	48	28

TABLE 12

Frequency with Which Concepts are Repeated in Japanese and American Textbooks

Country	Times Repeated				
	1	2	3	4	5
Japan	189	26	3	1	—
U.S.	347	115	48	7	1

assume that repetition facilitates learning. In view of the American students' performance, the alternative hypothesis that repetition may lead to boredom and to a failure to master the concept must also be entertained.

Conclusions

American textbooks may form an obstacle to the learning of mathematics by American students. The books are long, wordy, and repetitive. There is basis for the statement often made by American teachers that there is no possibility of completing the coverage of the textbooks within a year. Overwhelmed by the length of the texts and aware that the concepts will be encountered by students again at a later grade, many teachers may exert little effort to cover the material contained in the elementary and secondary textbooks.

The American textbooks neither make high demands on the students in terms of difficulty of the concepts presented nor encourage independent thinking in solving problems. Expectations appear to be different in Japan. Textbooks appear to be written with the assumption that students can master the content within the school year. The textbooks are short, definitive, and conducive to intensive study. Teachers are expected to supplement the materials contained in the textbooks by elucidating their content and offering students opportunities for practice and drill with supplementary problems and exercises. American textbooks are self-contained and require little elaboration by teachers.

Although American textbook writers try to make the material meaningful, their efforts may distract the students from appreciating the abstract representation within mathematics. Problems within each lesson tend to follow common patterns of solution; answers are readily available to the students. The problems presented in Japanese textbooks are more varied, both in level of difficulty and in mode of solution. Japanese children appear to appreciate the practical applications of mathematics, but these applications are emphasized by the teacher rather than in the textbooks.

Japanese textbooks seem to be more advanced than the American textbooks in the level of the concepts included. The number of concepts is no greater in the Japanese than in the American textbooks, but in both elementary and secondary school, concepts tend to be introduced earlier in the Japanese textbooks. Japanese children are expected to master complex concepts more rapidly during the first twelve years of schooling than are American children.

Improved performance in mathematics by American students will depend upon altering many current practices in American elementary and secondary schools. Although many of the Japanese innovations in teaching mathematics followed the development of the "new mathematics" curriculum in the United States, the ways in which Japanese educators have modified and are utilizing ideas from this curriculum should be particularly informative to American mathematics educators. Moreover, continued analyses of Japanese textbooks in mathematics may be productive in view of the outstanding success of Japanese students in mathematics.

References

Husen, T. 1967. *International Study of Achievement in Mathematics: A Comparison of Twelve Countries*. New York: Wiley.

McKnight, C.C., F.J. Crosswhite, J.A. Dossey, E. Kifer, J.O. Swafford, K.J. Travers, and T.J. Cooney. 1987. *The Underachieving Curriculum: Assessing U.S. School Mathematics from an International Perspective*. Champaign, IL: Stipes Publishing Co.

Stevenson, H.W., S.Y. Lee, and J.W. Stigler. 1986. "Mathematics Achievement of Chinese, Japanese, and American Children." *Science* 231, 693-99.

Stigler, J.W., S.Y. Lee, G.W. Lucker, and H.W. Stevenson. 1982. "Curriculum and Achievement in Mathematics: A Study of Elementary School Children in Japan, Taiwan and the United States." *Journal of Educational Psychology* 74, 315-22.

CHAPTER 5

SCIENCE EDUCATION IN JAPAN

Willard J. Jacobson
Teachers College, Columbia University

Shigekazu Takemura
Hiroshima University

with

Rodney L. Doran
State University of New York at Buffalo

Shigeo Kojima
National Institute for Educational Research, Japan

Eve Humrich
Teachers College, Columbia University

Masao Miyake
National Institute for Educational Research, Japan

With contributions by Arthur E. Schneider, a Research Associate on the Second IEA Science Study-U.S.

     This chapter includes a description of science curricula at the elementary and secondary levels as well as of the influences of American science education innovations. It includes summaries of two comparative science education studies (Jacobson 1985 and Miyake 1985). It also includes discussions of factors that correlate with science achievement, teachers and teacher evaluation, students' opportunity to learn, and the influence of tests and testing.[1]

Science Curricula In Japan

Education in Japan is centralized. Essentially the same curriculum is implemented throughout the nation, and science is an integral part of this curriculum.

Science is one of the major subjects in both the elementary and secondary schools.[2] The overall elementary and secondary science program in Japan is shown in Figure 1. Science is a compulsory subject for all students in the elementary and lower secondary schools (grades one through nine). The pattern is similar to that of many school systems in the United States. In Japan, Science I, which is an integrated science course for four unit hours in the tenth grade, is also compulsory. In grades eleven and twelve the following science subjects are electives: physics, chemistry, biology, and earth science. Table 1 reflects the percentage of students at the eleventh and twelfth grade levels who enroll in chemistry and physics.

It is clear that there are important differences in enrollment in chemistry and physics in the upper secondary school. A larger percentage of Japanese students are enrolled in chemistry and physics than in the United States (see Table 1).

Science in the Elementary School

As stated by the Ministry of Education, Science and Culture (1983a, 56), the overall objectives for science in the Japanese elementary school are: "To develop the ability in and attitude toward making inquiries about nature through observations and experiments as well as to enhance [students'] understanding of natural things and phenomena, thereby nurturing a rich sensitivity to love nature." For the science at each grade level there are more specific objectives. Most of these objectives can be categorized as nature study with attention given to the plants and animals in the child's environment. Starting in the third grade, there is a gradual introduction to simple physical science, such as the study of air, sunlight, magnets, solutions, electric current, water, and astronomical phenomena.

In both Japan and America, elementary school science is generally taught in self-contained classrooms by the general classroom teachers. The classroom teacher teaches most of the subjects that children study in the elementary school. While

FIGURE 1

Science Program
Japan

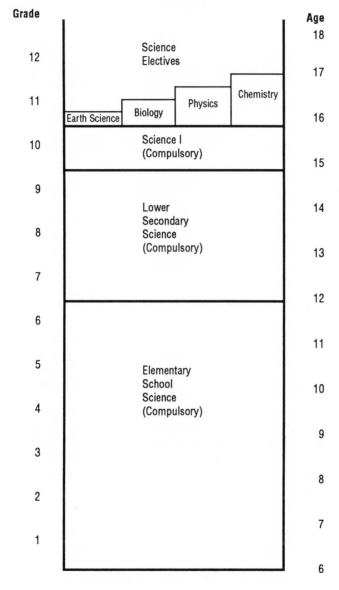

TABLE 1

Average Percent Enrollment in Chemistry and Physics, Eleventh and Twelfth Grades, Japan and the United States

Subject	Percent Japanese Average 11-12th Grades	Percent United States Average 11-12th Grades
Chemistry	42	35
Physics	25	16

(Composite from Jacobson et al. 1986 and Jacobson and Doran 1988) elementary science educators in both countries emphasize the importance of hands-on experiences in which children actually handle science materials and manipulate science equipment, one of the authors of this study has made extensive observations of elementary science classes in both countries. He believes that children in Japan actually have more hands-on science experience. There should be further information on this point from the Second International Science Study (SISS). The longer school year in Japan undoubtedly also contributes to Japanese students having more opportunity to experience science.

Japanese students have assignments that are supposed to be completed during the summer holiday. Some of these assignments are in science. In the fall, the children come back to the same teacher and report to this teacher on the studies carried out during the summer. Some observers of Japanese education have expressed the belief that these summer assignments reduce the amount that is forgotten over the summer break.

Science in the Lower Secondary School

As stated by the Ministry of Education (1983b, 44-60), the overall objectives for lower secondary school science are: "To develop students' ability in and positive attitude towards making inquiries about nature through observations and experiments as well as to enhance the understanding of matters and phenomena in nature. Thus, to have students realize the relationship between nature and human beings." In the lower secondary school, there is emphasis on observation, experimentation, and problem solving as approaches to learning. Students have science experiences dealing with matter and energy and elements, and an attempt is made to develop an appreciation and respect for life and the influence of the natural environment of humans.

In these grades in both countries, most of the science is taught by specialist science teachers. Obviously, these science teachers usually have had considerably more science training than the general classroom teacher who has responsibility for science instruction in the elementary school.

Again, there is a striking difference between the Japanese lower secondary school science and the science in the American junior or middle school: there appears to be a much greater emphasis on positive attitudes toward other living things and the natural environment. While this is certainly an important dimension of American science education programs as well, it is usually not as specifically emphasized.

Comparison of Upper Secondary School Science Programs

As stated by the Ministry of Education (1983c, 49) the overall objectives for science in the upper secondary school are: "To develop students' ability and positive attitude to inquire into nature through observations and experiments, to enhance their understanding of fundamental concepts of matters [sic] and phenomena in nature, and to develop students' scientific view of nature."

The science subjects offered in the upper secondary school include such standard courses as physics, chemistry, biology, and earth science, as well as integrated science courses. The courses appear to cover the well-known, traditional topics associated with these sciences. There seems to be no indication that Japanese science educators have chosen any particular approach to biology or physics, for example. In the U.S., by contrast, there are biology courses that emphasize an ecological approach and physics courses that concentrate on a historical and philosophical approach. It could be argued that in a nation where there is a centralized school system, with courses of study that are used by all, a general and traditional approach has to be taken. In a large nation with a heterogeneous population where many curriculum decisions are made at the local and state levels, it may be less risky to try out new and different approaches.

While Japanese science education is undergoing considerable criticism, it is a part of an educational program that has demonstrated great holding power, with almost 90 percent of Japanese young people graduating from the upper secondary level (Takemura and Overly 1986, 14). Japan has made investments in education, including science education, that have contributed to economic growth. As Aso and Amano (1983, 82) have said:

> ...the theory of investment in education became one of the officially accepted theoretical bases for determining the direction of education policy, and investment in the training of scientists and technicians

as strategic manpower influencing the speed of economic growth came to receive priority.

Important changes have taken place in Japanese science education since 1950. Even greater changes are taking place now. These changes are best understood if they are placed in the context of earlier experiences. Table 2 by Shigekazu Takemura (1983, 153) shows the shifts in emphasis that have taken place, and indicates the directions in which science education is moving in Japan.

Student Achievement in Science

While there are a limited number of sources of information in the English language about Japanese science education, both Japan and the United States have participated in the Second International Science Study (SISS), conducted under the auspices of the International Association for the Evaluation of Educational Achievement (IEA). This study provides a base of information with which some comparisons can be made. In this study, international core achievement tests were administered to students in both countries. In the United States, the tests were administered to students in the fifth and ninth grades, physics students in the twelfth grade, and twelfth grade students who were not currently studying any science. In Japan, these populations, as well as twelfth grade students studying earth science, biology, and chemistry, were tested. The results are summarized in Figure 2. In addition to the achievement tests, students and teachers provided further information in questionnaires.

The SISS data have been used extensively in the analyses and comparisons made in this chapter. Also, the authors have been educated in the Japanese and American systems of science education, and they have taught science in their respective educational systems. Thus, the authors have been able to check many of the statements made in this study against their varied backgrounds of experience.

Fifth Grade Students

In the Second International Science Study (SISS), the same achievement test was given to fifth graders (Jacobson 1985 and

TABLE 2

Historical Development of Science Education

Science Education in 1950-65	Science Education in 1965-80	Science Education in 1980-
1. Democracy, individual freedom	Economic growth, science-technological advancement	Social welfare, love for human beings
2. Democratic citizenship, maximum growth	Manpower-oriented, utilitarian, competition	Society-oriented, individually-oriented cooperation, self-development
3. Experimental curriculum, child-centered curriculum, units curriculum	Discipline-centered curriculum, scientific concepts, process skills	Interdisciplinary curriculum, integrated science based on the nature of science, society and learners
4. Reflective thinking, social problem solving	Intellectual competency	Creation, affection, willpower
5. Problem-focused studies, comprehensive studies, functional thinking, scientific thinking, interests, needs, activities	Interpretive and theoretical science, logical thinking with models, concept formation and systematic framework	Observation of objects and natural phenomena, discovery of regularity and broad fundamental-conceptual schemes, doing science and applying science
6. Guided by pedagogist philosopher and teacher job analysis	Guided by scientists and modern learning psychology as academic derivation	Wide-ranging cooperation of science, history of science, sociology, anthropology, psychology, pedagogy, etc.
7. Learning activities based upon child's felt needs, learning by doing, socially responsible, democratic process	Understanding in inquiring into a discipline, learning a way of knowing, specific behavioral objectives, evaluation of stated inquiry skills	Group project and pacing, curiosity and excitement, not "cool" learning but "hot" learning
8. Individualized to socialized, unified structure, environment, life aspect, project methods	Linear discipline, highly structured laboratory and classroom, discovery methods, teacher dominating	Cross-disciplinary, loosely structured, field, lab, and classroom doing science methods, teacher's managing

SOURCE: Takemura 1983, 153.

FIGURE 2

Comparison of Science Scores of Four Populations of Japanese and American Students

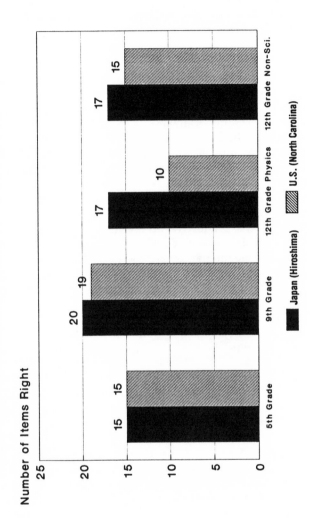

(From Mattheis, Spooner, and Coble 1985)

Miyake 1985). There were twenty-four items in this test, and, if rounded to the nearest whole number, the mean number of items correct in both countries was fifteen. But Japanese and American students differed as to which items they were most likely to get right. There were differences (of 5 percent or more) between Japanese and American students responding correctly to fifteen items. On eight of these items, Japanese pupils did better. On seven of these fifteen items, pupils in the United States had better scores. Of the four items on which there were the greatest differences between the scores of Japanese and American children, the Japanese children had a higher percentage of correct scores on three. One involved interpreting a table; another involved measurement. A third item on which Japanese pupils did much better was a knowledge item asking what is required for seed production. The one item on which U.S. students did much better dealt with the difference in evaporation rate of water and gasoline.

Seven of the grade five achievement test items have been classified as assessing science process skills. On five of these items, Japanese pupils had higher means, while U.S. pupils had higher means on two items. While these data have limitations, they do support the thesis that Japanese children achieve greater command of science process skills.

Ninth Grade Students

In the Second International Science Study, ninth graders in Japan and the United States were tested with an international test consisting of thirty items (Jacobson 1985 and Miyake 1985). The mean number of correct items for Japan was twenty while the mean number correct in the United States was nineteen. Ninth grade students in Japan and the United States differed regarding which items they were most likely to get right. There were differences (of 5 percent or more) between Japanese and American students responding correctly to twenty-two of these thirty items. On fourteen of these twenty-two items, Japanese students scored higher, and U.S. students scored higher on eight. The item on which there was the greatest difference favoring Japanese students (grade nine) was an item involving the interpretation of a table of temperatures. This was the same item on which fifth grade students in Japan did much better than fifth grade students in the United States. Like the fifth graders, American ninth grade students did much better on an item involving the interpretation of an experiment studying differing evaporation rates.

Japanese students did best (95 percent correct) on an item asking how batteries should be inserted into a flashlight and poorest, with 20 percent correct, on a question asking what particles are gained, lost, or shared during chemical changes. American students did best (92 percent correct) on an item asking why milk in a refrigerator does not go sour for a long time, and poorest (29 percent correct) on a question asking them to choose the circuit inside a box to explain the observations that have been made (a "black box" question). Ten items in the grade nine test have been classified as science process items. While students in both countries appear to have done better on these items than on others, the Japanese students did better than their American counterparts on nine out of the ten items. Again, it appears that Japanese schools are effective in teaching science process skills.

Upper Secondary School Students

In both Japan and the United States, twelfth grade students were tested with an international core science test (Jacobson 1985 and Miyake 1985). On the thirty-item international core test the Japanese physics students had a mean of twenty-four items right, and the U.S. physics students had a mean of nineteen items right. Further, Japanese physics students had a mean of seventeen items right on the thirty-item international physics test, while the U.S. physics students had a mean of ten items right. This is a large difference. This information tends to support those critics who suggest that all is not well with physics in U.S. high schools.

Students who were not studying any science in the twelfth grade were given a thirty-item test in which many of the items dealt with the science that would be helpful for the citizen to know. The mean number of items right for the Japanese nonscience students was seventeen, and for the American nonscience students it was fifteen. This was not as striking a difference as with the physics scores, but still the Japanese nonscience students had a better mean score than their American counterparts.

Overall in the SISS, each sample of Japanese students tested had higher mean scores, except in the fifth grade where Japanese and American scores were essentially equal (see Figure 2). The differences at the ninth grade level were not great, but

favored the Japanese students slightly. It is in the upper secondary
school where the greatest difference in Japanese SISS science and
achievement scores occur. Of particular interest and concern are the
higher Japanese achievement scores in physics.

Reasoning Skills

     One aim of effective science education is the development of
reasoning skills. Some of the characteristics of reasoning have been
identified, and ways have been developed to test for reasoning skills.
One instrument is the Group Assessment of Logical Thinking
(GALT), developed by Roadrangka, Yeany, and Padilla (1983).
Another instrument is called the Integrated Process Skills Test II
(TIPS) (Okey, Wise, and Burns 1982). These are American
developed instruments, and they have been used to test seventh,
eighth, and ninth grade students in Hiroshima, Japan and in North
Carolina. The results of these testings are of special interest in
Japanese-American comparisons of science education.
     The Group Assessment of Logical Thinking measures six
logical operations. The first is *conservation* in Piagetian terms, such
as the relationship between a ball of clay and an equal mass of clay
that has been flattened. The second is *proportional reasoning*, in
which students have to determine such proportions as those between large and small glasses of water. Third is *controlling variables*, such as the variables that have to be controlled if the effect of
changing the weight of a pendulum bob is to be studied. Fourth is
probabilistic reasoning, such as determining the probability that
certain sizes and shapes of objects will be pulled out next from a
cloth sack. Fifth is *correlational reasoning*, such as determining
whether there is a relationship between the size of the animals
captured and the color of their tails. Sixth is *combinatorial reasoning*, such as determining the possible dance partners when there are
three boys and three girls. In the GALT instrument, there are two
items for each of these logical operations.
     As reported in Mattheis, Spooner, and Coble (1985) and
Takemura (1985), respectively, the Group Assessment of Logical
Thinking instrument was administered to about 3,500 students in
grades seven, eight, and nine in North Carolina and to 4,397
students in grades seven, eight, and nine in Hiroshima. The results
for each of the logical operations, as well as the total for all of the

operations, are given in Figure 3, from the report by Takemura (1985, 9).

Strikingly, Hiroshima students did better on all of the logical operations except one. Neither the Hiroshima nor the North Carolina students did very well on correlational thinking. The Hiroshima students did much better on proportional thinking, control of variables, probabilistic thinking, and combinatorial thinking. Actually, on some of these logical operations, more than twice as many Hiroshima students answered items correctly than their North Carolina counterparts. These are striking results, and certainly, the North Carolina researchers are right when they suggest that these logical operations and how students can master them need to be studied further.

The Integrated Process Skills Test II (TIPS) consists of thirty-six items that are designed to measure five process skills. The first process skill is *identifying variables*, such as identifying the variables that may be related to the strength of football players. The second process is *identifying and studying hypotheses*, such as identifying the hypothesis that should be tested when studying the speed of objects falling to earth. The third process is *operationally defining* such terms as auto efficiency. The fourth process is *designing experiments*, such as designing an investigation of how air pressure in a basketball affects the height of bounce. The fifth process skill is *graphing and interpreting* data, such as graphing and interpreting data collected in a study of the effect of temperature on the growth of bacteria.

TIPS II was administered to junior high school students in Hiroshima and North Carolina, and the results, which were reported by Takemura (1985, 27), are portrayed in Figure 4. The Japanese students outscored their U.S. counterparts on every process skill. The differences are not as great as with the GALT scores, but there are differences favoring the Hiroshima students for each process skill.

These differences occurred even though some of the items in TIPS might be construed to be culturally biased toward U.S. students. (There is an item dealing with football, and, in one item, volume is stated in gallons.)

In this Hiroshima-North Carolina Study, an attempt was made to determine the Piagetian level at which the student was operating (Mattheis, Spooner, and Coble 1985, 41). It was found that 42 percent of the Hiroshima ninth grade students were

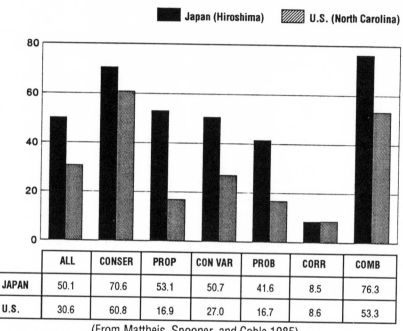

FIGURE 3

Group Assessment of Logical Thinking
(percent correct)

Japan (Hiroshima)   **U.S. (North Carolina)**

	ALL	CONSER	PROP	CON VAR	PROB	CORR	COMB
JAPAN	50.1	70.6	53.1	50.7	41.6	8.5	76.3
U.S.	30.6	60.8	16.9	27.0	16.7	8.6	53.3

(From Mattheis, Spooner, and Coble 1985)

FIGURE 4

The Integrated Process Skills Test (TIPS)
(percent correct)

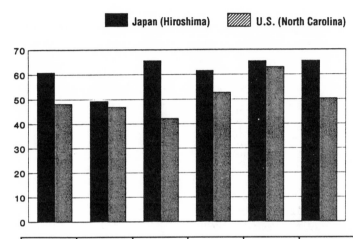

	ALL	ST HYPO	ID VAR	OPER DEF	DESI EXPERI	GRAPH
JAPAN	60.9	49.3	65.7	61.6	65.5	65.6
U.S.	48.2	46.9	42.2	52.7	63.0	50.3

(From Takemura 1985)

at formal operations, while 13 percent of the North Carolina ninth grade students were considered formal.

Gains were made by both groups of students in the junior high school years, but there was a large difference in the scores of seventh grade students in the two countries. This large difference was carried on through grade nine. Mattheis, Spooner, and Coble (1985, 41) concluded: "The implication is that the low scores in grade seven for the North Carolina students is the cumulative result of the education of these students in the elementary school (grades K-6)."

The differences in the TIPS II scores were similar. There was an increase in scores from grades seven to nine in Hiroshima and North Carolina with the greatest increase between grades eight and nine. Again it is suggested by Mattheis, Spooner, and Coble (1985, 41): "The inability of the North Carolina students to handle the integrated process skills may reflect the lack of experience these students have had in their educational experiences in Grades K-6."

Gender Differences in Science Achievement

In a number of investigations of science achievement, it has been found that males tend to do better in science than females. For example, males achieved higher scores than females in the First International Science Study (FISS), and the differences between the sexes increased as the level of education increased. This led Comber and Keeves, the authors of the report of the FISS, to comment, "For those who believe that girls are not given fair treatment, the IEA findings provide dramatic evidence of the scope of the problems" (Comber and Keeves 1973, 299).

In 1983, sex differences in science achievement were found in both Japan (Miyake 1985, figures 4-6 and 4-13) and the United States (Jacobson and Doran 1985, 414-17). The differences in mean science achievement scores of males and females in the United States, 5.7 percent in grade five and 6.4 percent in grade nine, were greater than those in Japan. In Japan, the difference favoring the males was 1 percent in grade five and 5 percent in grade nine (see Table 3).

In both countries, the sex difference increased from fifth grade to ninth grade. In the United States, the difference between males and females in the twelfth grade population studying physics

TABLE 3

Male/Female Differences in Percent Correct on International Core Test

Level	Japan	U.S.
Grade 5	Male 64.8 Female 63.8 Difference 1.0	Male 61.3 Female 55.6 Difference 5.7
Grade 9	Male 69.8 Female 64.8 Difference 5.0	Male 64.7 Female 58.3 Difference 6.4
Grade 12 physics students	Male 81.3 Female 80.0 Difference 1.3	Male 67.8 Female 58.7 Difference 9.1
Grade 12 students not taking science	Male 66.7 Female 56.3 Difference 10.4	Male 46.2 Female 41.4 Difference 4.8

(From Jacobson et al. 1986)

was even greater (9.1 percent). (The gender difference for physics students in Japan was small: 1.3 percent.) Apparently, in the United States the longer males and females continue in school, the greater the differences between them in science achievement. The one exception to this in the U.S. was with grade twelve students not studying science, where the male/female difference was 4.8 percent. The sex differences in Japan also increase with grade except for grade twelve students studying physics, where the difference was 1.3 percent.

Such sex differences have been found in many of the countries reporting on science achievement in the SISS. Many American science educators and others will be surprised and concerned to learn that, in general, there were greater differences in science achievement between males and females in the United States than in Japan.

Variables Correlating with Science Achievement

In the SISS, carried out in Japan and the United States, students were asked to give information about themselves, about science and school, and about their science experiences in school (Miyake 1985, figure 4-24, and Jacobson 1985). Correlation coefficients have been calculated for many of these variables and science achievement on the international core test. Correlations are available for the fifth grade and the ninth grade. As usual, the reader should be cautioned that correlations can indicate possible relationships but do not indicate a causal effect.

The correlations for grade five are given in Table 4 and for grade nine in Table 5.

There is considerable similarity between the correlations for the two countries. In both countries, "Books in the home," "I like science," "Ease of science learning," and, at the ninth grade level, "Homework on all subjects" are variables highly correlated with scores on the international core achievement test. There are also similarities on the low or negative correlation of "Students choose topics," "Students work on topics by themselves or with teacher," and the "Discussions of careers."

There are notable differences with regard to laboratory work, tests, and homework in the ninth grade. The correlations with achievement for U.S. students are higher for "Students do experiments," "Students do lab work in small groups," and "Write

TABLE 4

Science Teaching and Learning Variable Correlations
with Mean Score on Fifth Grade International Core Test
Arranged in Descending Order of U.S. Correlations

Variables	U.S. correlations	Japanese correlations
Books in the home	.244*	. 253*
Student's view of importance of science	.233*	.090*
"I like science"	.200*	.088*
Ease of learning science	.192*	.173*
Use textbooks	.153*	.114*
Have science tests	.133*	.147*
Students do experiments	.093*	.118*
Teacher makes lessons interesting	.093*	.051*
General quality of school life	.024*	.144*
Use library books	-.002	-.089*
Students do lab in small groups	-.012	-.152*
Watch teacher do experiments	-.039*	-.099
Teacher uses ideas	-.095*	-.082
Choose topics for study	-.102*	-.218*

*Indicates significance at the .05 level.

(From Jacobson et al. 1986)

TABLE 5

Science Teaching and Learning Variable Correlations
with Mean Score on Ninth Grade International Core Test
Arranged in Descending Order of U.S. Correlations

Variables	U.S. correlations	Japanese correlations
Ease of learning science	.338*	.273*
Books in the home	.295*	.292*
"I like science"	.285*	.287*
Students do experiments	.255*	.039*
Student view of importance of science	.248*	.119*
Students do lab work in small groups	.240*	.092
Write up lab reports	.226*	.026
Career interest in science	.194*	.133*
Homework on all subjects	.185*	.257*
Teacher gives instruction for lab work	.174*	.081
Adoption of scientific attitude	.134*	.162*
Use of hand calculators	.105*	-.174
General quality of school life	.101*	.118*
Teacher makes lessons interesting	.098*	.119*
Use textbooks	.095*	.030
Have science tests	.074*	.188*
Watch teacher do experiments	.064*	.070*
Field work outside classroom	.049*	.008
Hours science homework	.047*	.162*
Teachers help with difficulties in science	.043*	.082*
Use library books	.030	.006
Teacher explains relevance	.017	.035
Teacher discusses careers	-.053*	-.077
Students work on problems with teacher	-.151*	-.060
Students work on problems with own method	-.153	-.066

* Indicates significance at .05 level.

(From Jacobson et al. 1986)

up lab reports." Japanese correlations are somewhat higher for "Science tests" and "Hours science homework." These results might indicate that there is more attention to laboratory work in the United States, particularly in the ninth grade, and more attention to tests and homework in Japan.

There are interesting differences in the use of hand calculators. At the ninth grade level, there is a significant correlation of .105 with achievement in the United States, while in Japan, there is a significant negative correlation of -.174. A Japanese view of the use of hand calculators is given by Miyake: "Calculators are not used in elementary and junior high schools so this contributes to helping children develop their mental abilities" (Miyake 1985).

In brief, then, there are a number of significant similarities and differences in student achievement in Japan and the United States. At all levels tested in the SISS, Japanese students scored higher on the science achievement tests. Japanese students tended to do better than their American counterparts on items classified as science process items. On logical thinking and integrated process skills tests administered to the junior high school students in Hiroshima and North Carolina, Japanese students did better on all categories except one, where there was no difference. In both countries, males scored higher than females with the differences being greater in the United States than in Japan. In both countries, the differences were greater at the ninth grade level than at grade five. In both countries, students at all grade levels did better on the same items in 1983 than in 1970.

Teachers and Teaching--Students and Learning

The significance of teachers and teaching for students and learning is stressed in the science education literature in both Japan and the United States. Major sources of information for this section are Japanese government documents and data collected by the SISS.

In both countries, the teachers of fifth grade, ninth grade, and secondary school physics have similar patterns of college preparation. Most of the fifth and ninth grade teachers have had five to six years of college preparation. In both countries, the physics teachers have had more college preparation with a mode of seven or more years. With regard to the amount of science background, elementary school teachers in both countries reported that they had studied science but it was for less than 25 percent of their college education. Japanese ninth grade science teachers reported slightly less of a concentration on science subjects than the U.S. teachers. In the United States, 67 percent of the responding physics teachers reported that more than 50 percent of their college education involved science subjects. In both countries, the mode for teaching experience was eleven to twenty years, with ninth grade teachers and physics teachers being somewhat more experienced than their elementary school colleagues.

The teachers also reported on ways that teachers can keep up-to-date and improve their teaching. In both countries, the elementary school teachers seldom belong to a science teacher organization or a science association. In both countries, teachers occasionally read periodicals related to teaching in general, somewhat more so for elementary school teachers than others. In both countries, the teachers who specialize in science are more likely than their elementary school colleagues to read periodicals on science subjects. In the United States, for example, 83 percent of the physics teachers report reading a science periodical each month or more often. More than 70 percent of the elementary school teachers in the United States report less than one day of inservice education during the past year. Japanese teachers appear to devote more time to inservice education with an estimated two to three days a year. In both countries, junior high school science teachers report devoting more time to inservice education than teachers at other levels.

There are both similarities and differences in approaches to teaching in the two countries. Teachers in both countries at each level report that they use question-and-answer methods. Similarly, teachers in both countries at the elementary and junior high school levels report that they occasionally lecture, but that the twelfth grade physics teachers lecture frequently. Teachers in both countries tend to depend on the textbook to determine what to teach. In both countries, audiovisual materials are used more often in the elementary school than in the lower or upper secondary; somewhat greater use of audiovisual materials is reported from the United States than from Japan. In both countries, most of the teachers report that field trips are rarely or never used. When used, field trips are more likely to take place in the elementary school than at other levels.

Perhaps because it is a centralized school system, Japanese teachers are more likely to use standardized tests. American teachers are more likely to use teacher-made, objective (short answer) tests. Japanese teachers, especially grade twelve physics teachers, make more use of teacher-made essay tests. U.S. teachers, especially at the junior high school and grade twelve physics level, are more likely than their Japanese counterparts to use homework assignments or laboratory exercises and projects in assessing the work of their science students.

Teacher Preparation

Teachers in Japan must be certified, and the teacher certificates are granted by prefectural boards of education. There are two kinds of certificates: temporary and regular. Regular teaching certificates are valid in all prefectures and are valid for life. Temporary certificates are honored for three years only and are valid only in the prefecture by which they were issued.

A bachelor's degree or its equivalent is now generally required of all new teachers at the compulsory education level. Teachers in the upper secondary school (U.S. senior high school equivalent) are expected to have a master's degree or thirty credits beyond the bachelor's degree. In their preservice training, prospective teachers are required to take general education subjects and professional and specialized subjects. In general education, twelve credits each are required in the humanities, social sciences, and natural sciences. There is also a requirement of eight to twelve credits in foreign languages and four credits in health and physical training. To become a science teacher in lower or upper secondary school, a total of forty credits in science is required, including credits for physics and physics laboratory, chemistry and chemistry laboratory, biology and biology laboratory, and earth science and earth science laboratory. This can be compared with a state such as New York, where thirty-six credits in science are required, with at least fifteen credits in the science that is to be taught, and collegiate-level study in at least two sciences. In professional studies, the future Japanese teachers are required to take pedagogical theory, educational psychology, teaching materials, methods of teaching a subject, teaching practice, moral education, and electives. These requirements are somewhat more specific than those in a state such as New York, where twelve semester hours in the professional study of education and a college-supervised student-teaching experience are required.

Science Education Centers

As Takemura (1984, 67-69) has indicated, Science Education Centers are among the most important organizations concerned with science education in Japan. The main objectives of the Science Education Centers are to reeducate teachers and to carry out science education research on such topics as teaching materials, teaching techniques, and educational aids. Compared to the more or less academic studies of universities, the Science Education Centers aim at the advancement of science education from a more practical point of view.

For teachers, the Science Education Centers provide inservice programs. They deal with such topics as teaching materials and techniques, the production and operation of educational aids, the safe handling of chemicals, and guiding children's voluntary studies or inventions. They also organize lecture series, which are usually given by university staff members.

Some Science Education Centers provide "A Science Room for Children." Here children are guided to have experiences in science and to have the pleasure of making tools and toys. The centers encourage and commend voluntary studies on the part of children. Occasionally they hold exhibitions of the children's work.

The centers bring essential teacher aids and educational materials to remote schools so that students in these remote schools can have suitable science programs. There are annual meetings where representatives of the centers exchange ideas and discuss the results of studies.

In the United States, there are many organizations, such as museums, zoos, botanical gardens, nature centers, and teacher centers that make important contributions to the science education of children and provide inservice education opportunities for teachers. While these institutions carry out many of the same functions as the Japanese Science Education Centers, there is no nationwide system of centers that provides systematic support for teachers, special opportunities for children and young people, conducts science education research, and disseminates the results of studies.

Student Backgrounds and Expectations

In the SISS, students in Japan and the United States responded to a questionnaire soliciting information about their backgrounds. Some of their responses are now available in the two national reports (Jacobson 1985, 9-16, and Miyake 1985, 9-16). The responses are interesting and cast light on various aspects.

Sex

As might be expected, about half the students in grades five and nine are male and one half are female. But in the United States 63 percent of the students in twelfth grade physics courses are male; in Japan the comparable figure is 68 percent. Of the twelfth grade students who are not studying any science, in the United States 56 percent are female compared to 65 percent female in Japan.

Family size

The students were asked, "How many brothers and sisters do you have?" American families tend to be larger. In both countries, the largest percentage of students had one brother or sister: Japan 22 percent and the U.S. 24 percent. But 17 percent of the U.S. students replied that they had two or more siblings as compared to 5 percent in Japan.

Like Science

Students were asked whether they liked science more, about the same, or less than most other subjects. There were similar reactions to this question in both countries. In Japan, about 35 percent of the students said that they liked science better than other subjects as compared to 31 percent in the United States. But 23 percent in both countries liked science less than other subjects.

Future Science Education

The students were asked about plans for further education, including science education. In both countries, almost all of the students expected to complete secondary school (twelfth grade). Many more Japanese ninth graders than U.S. ninth graders (48 percent to 11 percent) did *not* expect to go on beyond high school. The twelfth grade students studying science in the United States set their sights high with 55 percent of the students expecting to complete more than four years of study after high school; the comparable figure in Japan was 13 percent. However, 57 percent of the Japanese twelfth graders studying science expect to have three to four years of postsecondary school study. Of the twelfth grade students studying science, 85 percent in the United States and 61 percent in Japan expect to include science subjects in their further education.

Homework

In some studies, a positive correlation has been found between the amount of time devoted to homework and achievement. The students were asked, "About how many hours a week do you usually spend on homework?" The Japanese students, with a mean of 3.9 hours, reported somewhat more total homework than the U.S. students, who had a mean of 3.2 hours. In both countries, the twelfth grade students studying science were the students who reported the most homework with a mean of 4.4 hours in Japan and 3.5 hours in the United States.

The students were also asked, "How many hours a week do you usually spend on homework or other schoolwork out of class for science subjects?" Here, the mean of 2.4 hours in the United States was more than the Japanese mean of 2.1 hours. Again, the twelfth grade students studying science reported the most science homework with a mean of 2.6 hours in Japan and 2.5 hours in the United States.

Books in the Home

Another variable that has been found to correlate with individual achievement is the number of books in the home. The students were asked, "How many books are there in your home?" The mode reported by Japanese students was 26 to 100 books. The mode reported by the U.S. students was 101 to 250 books. In both countries, twelfth grade students studying science reported the most books in the home.

Opportunity to Learn Science

In the SISS the teachers of the tested students were asked to indicate the opportunity that the students had to learn the concept indicated by each item. Because the opportunity-to-learn (OTL) data were collected and interpreted in slightly different ways, the mean opportunities to learn in Japan and the United States cannot be directly compared. However, interesting insights can be gained by identifying the ten items on which students did best and the ten items for which students had the best opportunity to learn.

Miyake (1985, 5,7) reported that in Japan, eight of the ten items on which fifth grade students did best were also on the list of the ten items on which the students had the greatest opportunity to learn. This could indicate a fairly strong relationship between achievement and the opportunity to learn. Jacobson (1985, 5,7) reported that in the United States, of the ten items on which fifth grade students did best, five were on the list of ten items on which the students had the greatest opportunity to learn. This would seem to indicate a somewhat weaker relationship between achievement and the opportunity to learn in U.S. schools.

At the ninth grade level, there was no opportunity to learn achievement correlation differences between Japan and the United States. In the core test, there were thirty test items. The ten items with the highest achievement and the ten items with the highest opportunity to learn were identified. In both countries, there were five items on both lists.

In general, in IEA science studies there has been a fairly high correlation between science achievement and opportunity to learn. In Japan and the United States, the mean science achievement scores for grade five and grade nine were quite similar. There apparently is also considerable similarity between the opportunity to learn scores.

It has been pointed out that, "...one of the central and most persistent forces driving Japanese students to high performances is the college entrance examination system. Today's high school education in Japan is largely dictated by the requirements of the entrance examinations" (Shimahara 1985). Since entrance to and graduation from prestigious universities, or failure to gain entrance, can affect the student's entire life, many students and their families will devote a great deal of time, energy, and money to try to gain entrance to preferred high schools which, in turn, may make it possible for them to enter a prestigious university. Many observers of Japanese education point to the entrance examinations and preparation for them as being key factors in Japanese education. The great importance Japanese national education policy accords to science and mathematics in combination with the influence of university entrance examinations obviously affects the opportunity Japanese students have to learn science (and mathematics).

Effect of Examinations on Science Education

The entrance examinations have a wide impact upon education, including science education (Nomura 1980). The nature of university entrance examinations may have a greater influence on what science is actually taught than the course of study, although the two are closely correlated. The university entrance examinations have become more and more difficult.

A Joint First-Stage Achievement Test has been introduced. It is claimed that this tests fundamental knowledge, general ability, and the science that students have studied in upper secondary school. The questions are composed by ten university professors for each subject. This examination is the first stage test for entrance to public universities. The second stage is provided by the individual universities. There is some movement toward a "common test."

To try to improve chances on the examination, cram schools (*juku*) and tutoring services have been developed. (This subject is treated in some detail in Rohlen 1980 and by August in Chapter 8, "*Yobiko*: Prep Schools for College Entrance in Japan.") There is concern about the impact of the *juku* upon the quality of adolescent life and the goal of equity in Japanese life.[3] Japanese science educators have agreed that the intensity of the cram schools and tutoring does affect science education in Japan.[4]

Use of Microcomputers in Science Education

A National Institute for Educational Research paper (NIER, Japan) (1984) reported that as in the United States, microcomputers are being used more and more in Japanese schools with interesting applications in science education. The greatest use is in the upper secondary schools, with fewer uses in the lower secondary and elementary schools. Computer Assisted Instruction (CAI) is most popular in the elementary schools, where the computers are used for such functions as presenting teaching materials during class. In the secondary schools, Computer Managed Instruction (CMI) is most popular. Some examples of computer use in science education are constellations, three-dimensional molecular models, and the calculation of calories in foods. At all levels, computers are also used in club activities.

Innovative uses of microcomputers in chemistry have sometimes been reported, as in an article by Shimozawa (1981). Using a student response mechanism where each student has a terminal, microcomputers were used to evaluate a new high school chemistry curriculum. This was a fast and efficient way of collecting student feedback before it could be "interpreted" by the teachers. Microcomputers also sometimes have been used to study dynamic phenomena, of which there are many in chemistry, such as the molecular vibration of the water molecule. They have also been used for the study of electron densities using probability functions, such as the time-dependent variable. This gives more meaning to probability than the traditional dotted cloud models shown in textbooks.

Influences of United States Science Curricula and Directions of Japanese Science Education

It has been suggested that innovations in science education in Japan were influenced in the 1960s by the introduction of materials from such American projects as the Physical Science Study Committee (PSSC), Harvard Project Physics (HPP), Chemical Bond Approach Project (CBA), Chem Study (CHEMS), and the Secondary Mathematics Study Group (SMSG). The conceptual structure of the disciplines was used in planning the curricula as were the inquiry processes that generate scientific knowledge. Attention was also given to the hierarchical concept of curriculum organization in the sequencing of learning materials. Takemura (1983, 154-55) states:

> Innovation model was research, development, and diffusion. Academic background was behavioral psychology and pure science. Implicit value was competition. Relevance was seen in manpower-orientation and utilitarian consideration. Taxonomic domain was cognitive. Teaching technique was

inductive-heuristic and stressed discovery methods. The teacher had the dominating role. The form of work organization was conventional class groups. Subject matter were linear disciplines. Mode of materials was highly structured. View of knowledge was by subject disciplines. Humanity was viewed as manipulable and people were regarded as things. Evaluation techniques were tied to attainment of prespecified goals. The curriculum in science at all levels was organized around representative conceptual systems, their major supporting concepts, and the processes of science as they related to developing further economic growth.

Certainly, this view is not consistent with the views of many of those involved in the American science curriculum projects in the 1950s and 1960s. Perhaps one of the lessons that has been learned is that new science courses and materials will be viewed and used in many different ways. The views and uses cannot be completely foreseen.

It has been suggested that while it was, in part, fruitful to imitate the American projects, it was a mistake to do so superficially, because it led to the need to teach large quantities of more difficult knowledge. It has been alleged that "...curricula demanding voluminous knowledge and high-level quality increased the number of stragglers and pupils who disliked science..." (Imahori 1980, 140). Contrary to the spirit of the innovators, laboratory work came to be neglected and the process of inquiry was taught by "dry" laboratories, using data shown in texts.

More research and development in science education was undertaken in Japan. This involved teams of researchers and repeated tryouts of experimental curricula to provide feedback that could be used for further improvement.

To correct the apparent inadequacies of the science curriculum of the 1960s and 1970s, a new orientation has been designed with the following broad objectives:

1) To develop the pupil's ability to think for himself and to cultivate creative intelligence and skills.

2) To develop strong willpower and to cultivate a self-reliant spirit.

3) To cultivate love and appreciation for nature and mankind.

4) To cultivate a proper attitude toward labor.

5) To cultivate practical sociability based on consciousness of solidarity and a spirit of service to the society.

6) To exert efforts to train a healthy and strong body.

7) To grow up into a Japanese citizen with love for people everywhere in the world in order to obtain the trust and respect of international society (Takemura 1983, 155-56).

In this new direction, we see the interesting emphasis upon the love and appreciation for nature and mankind, practical sociability, consciousness of solidarity and a spirit of service to society, and the concern for the trust and respect of international society. The effectiveness of Japanese education has been demonstrated. What will the impact of these new directions be upon science education and upon the Japanese citizens of tomorrow who are in Japan's science classrooms today?

Summary and Conclusions

The primary purpose of this analysis was to find ways to improve the experiences that children and young people in both countries have in science. "Japanese people have always adopted, adapted, coopted--or even borrowed the best from the West and East, yet sometimes discarded the borrowings to think and act according to their own unique characteristics" (Takemura 1983, 153). A similar and related approach might be taken by the United States. Because of its great heterogeneity in population and education, it is probably more important for the United States to study and come to know itself. But, based upon this knowledge of ourselves and our education, we should try to learn from others.

Surely, we will improve if we study ourselves and others and "learn, adopt, adapt, extend, and grow."[5]

Similarities far outweigh differences in elementary school science curricula in Japan and the United States. There is an important emphasis in the elementary and lower secondary schools in Japan on developing a sensitivity to and love for nature. Developing a respect for life is also stressed. This dimension of science education is certainly present in U.S. elementary and junior high school science programs. The increased interest in environmental education in the United States has, in part, similar goals. However, these humanistic goals are not made as explicit in U.S. elementary science programs as they are in the Japanese.

There is greater variety in upper secondary school science programs in the United States than in Japan. In biology in the United States, for example, programs have been developed that have had different emphases. One program emphasizes an ecological approach, another an organismic approach, and yet another includes more molecular biology. It may be that experimenting with a variety of approaches is more difficult in a centralized school system that is much influenced by university entrance examinations. The importance of studying and adapting before adopting is underscored by Japanese criticisms of new American programs. The new American programs often emphasize inquiry. But, if they are not used in an inquiry mode, they can be nothing more than compendiums of facts to be read and memorized. This is certainly contrary to the aims of the program developers and does not contribute very much to the improvement of science programs anywhere.

The achievement scores at the fifth grade level in the two countries are similar. However, at the elementary school level we begin to see evidence of the effectiveness of the Japanese schools in developing science process skills.

At the ninth grade level, the Japanese students had scores on the IEA international core achievement tests that were slightly higher than those of the U.S. students. Again, the Japanese students did much better on items classified as science process skill items.

At the twelfth grade level, the Japanese students did slightly better on the international core test, but on the thirty-item international physics test, the Japanese students had a mean of seventeen items right, while the U.S. physics students had a mean of ten items right. This is a very large difference in means.

There was not as wide a gap between twelfth grade students in the two countries who were not studying science. When tested on a thirty-item test containing items on science subjects that it would be desirable for future citizens to know, the twelfth grade Japanese students had a mean of seventeen right and U.S. students fifteen.

The differences in scores on two instruments assessing reasoning skills are striking and should cause concern. These instruments assess logical thinking and integrated process skills. In every category, the Hiroshima lower secondary school students did better than their counterparts in North Carolina. This is dismaying because most of the new elementary and junior high school science programs in the United States have as one of their goals the development of science process skills. Are these new programs being used? Are they being used as they are intended? Are American elementary and junior high school students actually having as many hands-on, minds-on science experiences as are called for in modern science programs? Certainly, these results in critically important areas should be investigated further.

In both countries, males tend to do better on science achievement tests than females. The differences are greater in the United States than in Japan. Disturbingly, the differences at the ninth grade level are greater than at the fifth grade level. In the United States, the differences between sexes on the twelfth grade tests were even greater. Thus, it appears that the sex differences in science achievement scores tend to increase as the grade level increases. Both Japan and the United States face a challenge to improve the science achievement of females.

A major reason that Japanese students tend to score better on various kinds of achievement tests may simply be that more time is devoted to education. The number of days of classroom instruction in a school year is greater, more effective use is made of the scheduled class hours, and more time is devoted to study outside of formal school hours. The special testing and coaching schools, *juku*, also contribute. As a Japanese colleague has said, "In the coaching schools, Japanese students learn what has to be learned to score well on tests."[6]

High school is a problem. There is not a great difference between the achievement scores of Japanese and American students at the fifth and ninth grade levels. But the differences in scores on the basic high school physics tests are striking. There are many who believe that education in physics is of special importance for young people. In fact, some knowledge of physics is helpful, perhaps essential, in learning other sciences. Only a small percentage of U.S. high school students elect to study physics. Those who did choose to study physics did not do very well on an international physics achievement test when compared with Japanese students. Physics is so basic and the achievement of U.S. physics students is so poor that it would seem essential that something be done to improve high school physics in the United States.

In Japan, there is greater emphasis on entrance examinations and preparation for them. Students and their families devote a great deal of time, money, and energy to preparation for the entrance examinations. These entrance examinations and preparation for them are being subjected to searching criticism by groups proposing reforms in Japanese education.

There are interesting and perhaps important similarities and differences in student backgrounds in the two countries. In both countries, more males than females elect science in the twelfth grade. Roughly the same percentage of students in the two countries say they like science better than other subjects. Exactly the same percentage of students in the two countries respond that they like science less than other subjects. Japanese students reported somewhat more hours a week devoted to homework, but in both countries it was the twelfth grade students studying science who did the most homework. U.S. students reported the presence of more books in the home. In both countries, almost all students expect to complete secondary school. Substantially more American twelfth graders expect to complete more than four years of study after high school. More U.S. twelfth grade students expect to include science subjects in their further education.

Teacher education in science is quite similar in Japan and the United States. In general, a bachelor's degree is required of all teachers, and at the upper secondary (senior high) level, a master's degree or equivalent is strongly preferred, if not required. In Japanese teacher education, there may be somewhat more attention given to such professional subjects as pedagogical theory, educational psychology, and methods and materials of teaching.

There seems to be general agreement that continuing education or inservice education is essential for teachers, perhaps especially for science teachers. In fact, continuing inservice education in Japan is mandated. Some of the inservice education of teachers of science takes place in Science Education Centers. While there are many institutions in the United States engaged in continuing education, there are few, if any, that are strictly comparable to the Japanese Science Education Centers. American observers tend to agree with Japanese science educators that these centers make important contributions. In both countries, questions are raised as to what kind of inservice education is the most useful.

Intensive science curriculum development took place in the United States from the late 1950s to the early 1970s. This intense activity led to the development of several new programs at the elementary, junior high school, and senior high school levels. These new programs came to the attention of Japanese science educators. Some were adopted and more adapted. Apparently there have been few overall evaluations of the effectiveness of these new programs in Japan. But at least one report suggests that the implementation of the parts of one program led to effects that were quite contrary to those anticipated by the developers of the program. The textbooks and other materials in the new programs were often intended to stimulate and develop students' inquiring abilities. But the materials contained a great deal of modern scientific knowledge that previously had not been in science programs. One Japanese critic has stated that this just provided more information to be assigned and memorized. An examination of Japanese science curricula suggests that little of these new programs remain in the current curricula.

"Know yourself--then study, learn, adapt, extend, and grow." The word "adapt" is of special importance when innovations from other cultures and educational systems are considered. It is almost a truism, but extremely important, that the characteristics of the society and culture be considered in the development of science education.[7] For example, one of the reasons that Japanese schools have more time for teaching and learning is that they have a five-and-a-half day school week. A quick response from an American critic might be that American students and their teachers should go to school five-and-a-half days a week. But many, including students and teachers, argue that this would be a mistake in the United States. They contend that a much more effective way in the United States is to give greater encouragement and support to the wide range of voluntary activities that take place on Saturdays-- from honors programs in universities to ecological studies at the local nature center. For American students and teachers, these voluntary approaches to further study in science may be more effective. More effective use of available class time would also help.

Certainly, we can learn much from the study of science education in Japan. But for a large country with a heterogeneous population and decentralized education, it may be especially important to "know yourself." Then American educators can "learn, adapt, extend, and grow."

Notes

1. For a more extensive analysis and comparison of science curricula in Japan and the United States, see Jacobson and Takemura 1986.

2. The following brief description of the science program for grades one through twelve is adapted from Takemura 1984, 11-16.

3. Perhaps the best discussion of the examination competition and the struggle for equity in Japanese life is found in Cummings 1980.

4. Communication from Masao Miyake and Shigekazu Takemura.

5. Some of the suggestions included in this chapter are drawn from Miyake memorandum (1985).

6. Personal communication from Masao Miyaki.

7. This point is developed further in Jacobson 1984.

References

Aso M., and I. Amano. 1983. *Education and Japan's Modernization.* Tokyo: The Japan Times, Ltd.

Comber, L.C., and J.P. Keeves. 1973. *Science Education in Nineteen Countries.* New York: Wiley.

Cummings, W.K. 1980. *Education and Equality in Japan.* Princeton, NJ: Princeton University Press.

Imahori, K. 1980. "Problems of Innovation in the Japanese Science Curricula." *Journal of Science Education in Japan* 4:4, 139-48.

Jacobson, W.J. 1984. *Science Education for the 21st Century--The Great Debate.* New York: Second International Science Study.

-----. 1985. *National Report: U.S.A.* New York: Second International Science Study-U.S.

-----, and R.L. Doran. 1985. "Second International Science Study: U.S. Results." *Phi Delta Kappan* 66, 414-17.

-----, and R.L. Doran. 1988. *Science Achievement in the United States and Sixteen Countries: A Report to the Public.* New York: Second International Science Study, Teachers College, Columbia University.

-----, and S. Takemura. 1986. *Analysis and Comparisons of Science Curricula in Japan and the United States.* New York: Second International Science Study-U.S.

Mattheis, F.E., W.E. Spooner, and C.R. Coble. 1985. *A Study of the Logical Thinking Skills, Integrated Process Skills, and Attitudes of Junior High School Students in North Carolina.* Greenville, NC: East Carolina University.

Ministry of Education, Science and Culture. 1983a. *Course of Study for Elementary Schools in Japan.* Tokyo: Monbusho.

-----. 1983b. *Course of Study for Lower Secondary Schools in Japan.* Tokyo: Monbusho.

-----. 1983c. *Course of Study for Upper Secondary Schools in Japan.* Tokyo: Monbusho.

Miyake, M. 1985. *National Report: Japan.* Tokyo: National Institute for Educational Research.

National Institute for Educational Research. 1984. *The Use of the Computer in Education in Japan* (NIER Occasional Paper 03/84). Tokyo: National Institute for Educational Research.

Nomura, Y. 1980. "The Impact of Examination on Science Teaching in Japan." *Journal of Science Education in Japan* 4, 163-66.

Okey, J.R., K. C. Wise, and J.C. Burns. 1982. *Integrated Process Skills Test II*. Athens, GA: University of Georgia.

Roadrangka, V., R.H. Yeany, and M.J. Padilla. 1983. *Group Test of Logical Thinking*. Athens, GA: University of Georgia.

Rohlen, T.P. 1980. "The *Juku* Phenomena: An Exploratory Essay." *Journal of Japanese Studies* 6, 207-42.

Shimahara, N.K. 1985. "Japanese Education and Its Implications for U.S. Education." *Phi Delta Kappan* 66, 419.

Shimozawa, J.T. 1981. "Use of Microcomputers in Chemical Education." *The Journal of Science Education in Japan* 5:4, 177-87.

Takemura, S. 1983. "People, Society, and Science Education Japan." In D.E. Hadary and M. Vincentini, eds., *Proceedings of U.S.-Italy Joint Seminar on Science Education for Elementary School Children*. Washington, DC.: The American University.

-----. 1984. *Study on the Position of Science Education in Japan*. Hiroshima: Faculty of Education, Hiroshima.

-----, et al. 1985. *A Study of Reasoning Skills in Junior High School Students (Grade 7-9)*. Hiroshima: University of Hiroshima.

-----, and N.V. Overly. 1986. *Science Curriculum in Japan*. Hiroshima: University of Hiroshima.

CHAPTER 6

AN ANALYSIS OF COGNITIVE, NONCOGNITIVE, AND BEHAVIORAL CHARACTERISTICS OF STUDENTS IN JAPAN

Leigh Burstein and John Hawkins
Graduate School of Education
University of California, Los Angeles

Acknowledgments

This paper is a considerably shortened version of a larger manuscript commissioned by the U.S. Japan Study team operating under the auspices of the Office of Educational Research and Improvement (OERI), U.S. Department of Education. We would like to thank our project monitor, Dan Antonoplos, for assistance and guidance in the preparation of the original report. Other colleagues and students were generous in providing reactions to our ideas and manuscript drafts and in providing insights from which we have borrowed freely. Obviously, neither they nor OERI is directly responsible for what we have discussed herein. The research reviewed in preparing this report covered a period through 1985, and it was not possible to update the report to incorporate more data.

Introduction

Recently, a Japanese government commission was appointed to assess Japan's educational system and report back to the executive branch how it viewed the educational system against world standards. The twenty-five-member commission reported that the current Japanese educational system was outmoded, uncreative, rigid, and inhibiting. More specifically, the commission reported that:

> Despite its merit, the main thrust of this country's education has been to have students memorize

> information and facts. The development of the ability
> to think and judge on one's own and the development
> of creativity have been hampered. Too many
> stereotyped persons without marked individuality
> have been produced (Haberman 1985).

Although there has been a spate of similar commentaries on
the educational system in the United States, the report described
above was commissioned by the Japanese government to assess its
own system; the results were quite negative. This criticism comes
at a time when those in the United States are seeking answers to
many educational problems and in many cases are looking to the
Japanese as a model for possible answers.

The contrast is interesting--the United States seeking
models and answers from the Japanese and the Japanese are
questioning their own system, often reflecting on the U.S. system as
more humane, creative, and advanced. Analysis of the Japanese
experience comes from many quarters: Japan scholars and
educators in the United States, international teams studying
educational performance, and Japanese commentators themselves.
This document assesses the quality, quantity, scope, content, and
general usefulness of much of the literature, in order to put the
current debate on education in the United States vis-a-vis the
perceived "educational miracle" in Japan into perspective.

This chapter is based on a review and conceptual analysis of
the literature on the characteristics of Japanese students and of the
factors influencing those characteristics. Qualitative and
quantitative information from English and Japanese sources about
cognitive, noncognitive, and behavioral characteristics of students
and factors influencing them were used. This information was
collected about students from both elementary and secondary levels
and for special populations of dropouts, gifted, learning disabled,
and private education students. In addition to the literature
analysis, the quality and credibility of each citation source were
judged.

In some cases, the reports simply were not obtainable within
a reasonable time frame; this proved to be true for certain
governmental reports (typically written in Japanese) and fugitive
drafts from ongoing studies of Japanese students. In other instances, there were hardly any data to begin with; rather, the
judgment or interpretation about some aspect of Japanese students
was based only on the observations and impressions of a

knowledgeable observer of Japanese society and its educational system. While reports of the latter type may be no less accurate than those based on empirical data collections across a number of students and, preferably, locales, the fact remains that often it was hard to document the source of the interpretations generated.

In the end the decision was to conduct an analysis of the contemporary literature on characteristics of Japanese students with explicit emphasis on empirical evidence that would allow comparison with similar attributes of students in the United States. This chapter summarizes the more extensively documented analysis conducted.

Cognitive Characteristics

Virtually every newspaper article, book, and popular account of the achievements of Japanese students point to the pattern of exceptional Japanese performance in comparison to that of students from other countries. For the most part, these judgments (by Cummings 1980, Lerner 1982, Rohlen 1983, Schiller and Walberg 1982, and Walberg 1983, among others) are based on secondary interpretations of the overall test performance results from the First International Mathematics Study (Husen 1967) and the Six Subjects Science Study (Comber and Keeves 1973), conducted by the International Association for the Evaluation of Educational Achievement (IEA). Thus the primary basis for most contemporary judgments about Japanese schooling rests on highly aggregated data in a limited range of subject matters from studies conducted over fifteen years ago.

Several specific questions that get to the heart of the issue of whether the evidence of Japanese academic superiority is solid or illusory can be asked:

1) Are recent accounts of the Japanese performance on the earlier IEA studies an accurate and complete portrayal of the data from those studies?

2) If so, do the Japanese accomplishments in the earlier IEA studies persist, as reflected in more recent IEA data?

3) Is there comparative evidence, separate from the IEA studies, that corroborates or contradicts this body of work?

4) With respect to a given content area (for example, mathematics), is the performance of Japanese students uniformly or differentially exceptional?

5) Is the performance of Japanese students uniformly exceptional (comparatively) across all content areas?

6) Is the performance of Japanese students uniformly exceptional for all age groups?

7) Aside from measures of academic achievement, what evidence is available about the comparative cognitive abilities of Japanese students?

8) How uniform is the performance of students within Japan? Do certain segments (defined by sex, social class, or ethnicity) exhibit higher achievement than others?

The evidence considered in the course of the analysis that was designed to address this set of questions was derived from the seven studies described briefly in Table 1. In the remainder of this chapter, the basic results from each study are summarized and the results are synthesized across studies to respond to the questions regarding cognitive performance of Japanese students.

IEA First International Mathematics Study

The First International Mathematics Study (FIMS) produced data on mathematics performance and other characteristics from students, teachers, and other school officials from twelve countries including Japan and the United States (Husen 1967). Taken as a whole, the evidence from FIMS supporting the exceptional performance of Japanese students is substantial. Regardless of whether one considers average scores for countries or the entire distributions, the younger population or the older cohorts (taking selectivity into account), or various subscore categories, Japanese students show high levels of achievement. Even though the performance within Japan is more variable than in most other countries, the weakest Japanese students compared favorably with those from other countries (see Figure 1). Additionally, in almost

TABLE 1

Sources of Data on the Cognitive Characteristics of Japanese Students

Source	Dates	Age/Grade	Type of measure
IEA: First International Mathematics Study	1964	13 years	Mathematics (lower er process)
		Grade 12	Mathematics (lower process, higher process, word problems, computational, new mathematics, algebra, geometry, analytical geometry, calculus, analysis, sets, logic)
IEA: Six Subjects Survey	1969-1970	10 years 14 years	Science (earth science, biology, chemistry, physics, practical [14 only], behavioral levels, test of understanding of science)
IEA: Second International Mathematics Study	1980-1981 (Japan) 1981-1982 (U.S.)	Grades 7-8 (Japan) Grade 8 (U.S.)	Mathematics (arithmetic fractions, ratio, proportion, and percent), algebra (integers, formulas, and equations), geometry, measurement, statistics
		Grade 12	Mathematics (sets and relations, number systems, algebra, geometry, elementary functions/ calculus, probability and statistics, finite math)
Harnisch/Sato	1981-1982	Grade 11	High School Mathematics Test (ETS) (algebra, geometry, modern math, data interpretation, probability)

(continued)

TABLE 1 (continued)

Source	Dates	Age/Grade	Type of measure
Stevenson et al.	1979-1981	Kindergarten	Letter and word recognition comprehension
		Grade 1 Grade 5	Cognitive Tasks (coding spatial relations, perceptual speed auditory memory, serial memory for words, serial memory for numbers, verbal spatial representation, verbal memory, vocabulary, general information)
			Reading (sight reading of vocabulary, reading of textual material, comprehension of text)
			Mathematics (concept skills, computation, word problems)
Hess/Azuma	1972-1977	3 years 8 months	Concept Familiarity Index Peabody Picture Vocabulary Test
		4	Block Sort Task Referential Communication
		5	School Readiness Test
		6	School Readiness Test, IQ
		11 (Japan)	WISC-R (Japan) Achievement ratings by teachers in school subjects (Japan)
		12 (U.S.)	Iowa Test of Basic Skills (U.S.) Achievement ratings by teachers in reading and mathematics
Lynn	1975	6-16 years	WISC-R IQ

FIGURE 1

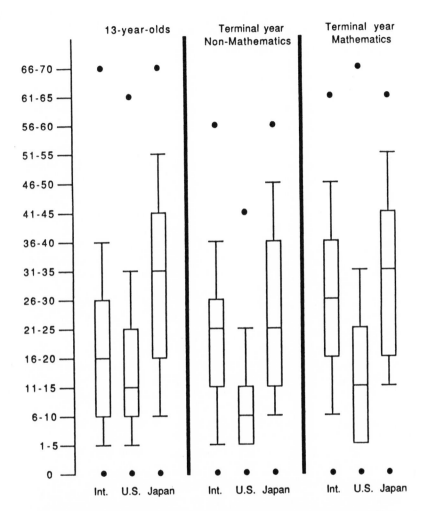

Approximate box and whisker plots of the distribution of performance in Japan, U.S., and internationally from the First International Mathematics Study. The sources of the data are tables 1.1, 1.3, and 1.4 from Husen (1976, vol. II, 24-27). These scores have been corrected for guessing. The "box and whisker" plots designate the approximate 10th (bottom of lower inverted "T"), 25th (bottom of rectangle), 50th (solid line through rectangle), 75th (top of rectangle), and 90th (top of upper "T") percentiles of the score distributions. The single dots at the bottom and top of each distribution set the full range of scores.

every comparison with U.S. students, there was no contest. Given these results, there is little wonder that FIMS provoked so much attention in the United States.

IEA Six Subjects Survey of Science Achievement

The Science Achievement Study (Comber and Keeves 1973) from the IEA Six Subjects Survey produced data on science performance and other characteristics from students, teachers, and school officials from nineteen countries including Japan and the United States. The pattern of exceptional performance that Japan exhibited in the IEA Science Study mirrors the earlier performance on the First International Mathematics Study. Both overall and by subtest, younger *and* older populations performed well. However, the phenomena of large variance as well as high mean scores that occurred for all three samples in FIMS occurred only with the fourteen-year-old Japanese sample. Contrary to certain stereotypes, then, Japanese performance is not particularly homogeneous (at least in the lower and upper secondary years). At the same time, however, in terms of absolute performance levels, the weakest Japanese students did well compared with students from other countries, and many more Japanese students did exceptionally well.

There are hints in the performance data at the subtest level that contradict another stereotype among Japanese students. There has been speculation that Japanese teaching methods and schooling in general tend to emphasize memorization, perhaps to the detriment of other psychologically defined categories of cognitive knowledge. But, compared with their performance on items measuring "Understanding and Higher Processes," Japanese students did relatively poorly on information items. There is simply no evidence in this study (or from FIMS as well) to support a narrow cognitive emphasis of Japanese schooling and its consequences.

Finally, expectations about the disparity in performance between the sexes in Japan were supported by the science data. There were roughly two females for every male scoring in the bottom 20 percent of pupils and almost three males for every female scoring in the top 20 percent. But these differences were not unusually large, in most cases, compared with most other countries. Moreover, compared with other countries, Japanese girls did quite well, ranking either second or third on all subtests at age ten (after

Japanese boys) and fourth or fifth at age fourteen (after Japanese boys and Hungarian boys and girls).

In nearly every other participating country, then, the performance of the typical Japanese girl would be viewed as exceptional. Yet, there are undoubtedly many Japanese girls relegated to lower status opportunities and institutions who would be among the mathematics and science elites in other countries. Once again, socialization and differential opportunities appear to be better explanations than differential ability for the sex differences.

In summary, the reading of the two IEA sponsored studies considered thus far indicates that, if anything, contemporary popular accounts of exceptional Japanese performance based on IEA data understate their findings. Yes, differences existed, and they were large virtually everywhere. What these studies do not address is whether Japan's elevated performance pattern persists to the present, whether non-IEA data corroborate the results, and whether Japan's superior achievement would be exhibited by younger groups and in other subject areas besides mathematics and science.

The Second International Mathematics Study

Data from the IEA Second International Mathematics Study (SIMS) do address the issue of whether superior Japanese performance still persists, at least in the area of mathematics (Chang and Ruzicka 1985; Garden 1985; McKnight, Crosswhite, Dossey, Kifer, Swafford, Travers, and Cooney 1987; National Institute for Educational Research 1981, 1982, 1983; Travers 1985; Travers and McKnight 1985; Wolfe 1983; and other reports in progress). However, two caveats are in order before examining selected data from this study. First, the Second International Mathematics Study was a much more complex undertaking than its IEA predecessors. The focus was more on issues and topics of interest to mathematics educators than had been the case with FIMS (which was more strongly influenced by comparative educators). This orientation led to an emphasis on teaching and learning in mathematics classrooms, and classes become the targeted sampling units.

Twenty-four countries participated in some facet of SIMS, either at the early secondary level (eighth grade in most countries, seventh grade in Japan) or the last year of secondary school (only those students taking a full year of college preparatory mathematics). Eight countries, including both Japan and the United States, conducted a longitudinal version of the study for the early secondary school population (population A), wherein students were tested prior to and following a year of mathematics instruction and their teachers completed extensive questionnaires describing their teaching practices. The United States also conducted a longitudinal study for the terminal mathematics student population (population B).

The evidence from the SIMS suggests that:

> In terms of absolute levels, Japan's exceptional performance in mathematics (and presumably science) has persisted through the period spanned by the IEA studies (basically 1964-82). Its students do well essentially across the board.

> In terms of a single year of instruction, Japanese students exhibit substantial growth on topics emphasized in the Japanese curriculum.

> The trend in performance from FIMS to SIMS is decidedly positive for students in the final year of secondary school but more mixed at the population A level (seventh grade). On the other hand, this group was probably a year younger in SIMS than the younger population of students from FIMS.

> Gender differences in performance are generally inconsequential in population A but markedly favor boys in population B.

> As in virtually every country, demographic differences in performances do occur. Certain of these differences (region, academic orientation of the school) are fairly standard while others (national or comparatively poor private schools' scores) are consequences unique to the Japanese educational milieu.

Beneath the surface of the results are intriguing glimmers of some special attributes of the Japanese system. Reports prepared by the National Institute for Education Research (NIER 1981, 1982a, 1982b) contain tables that examine performance from a variety of angles, sometimes in microscopic detail. A few examples follow:

> In Japan, high performance items (students averaged greater than 80 percent correct) come from all the major content areas, and for virtually every item, both teachers and students report high opportunity-to-learn (OTL) with much of the learning in areas other than algebra and geometry occurring in prior years.

> The commonalities among the test items that might account for high Japanese performance are evidently not because of their emphasis on computational material. Rather, most of these items appear to represent concepts that involve teachable algorithms and rules, whether verbally or nonverbally presented. Symbolic versus pictorial or graphic presentations seem not to matter nor does the number of steps entailed in applying the algorithm. Apparently, if Japanese students have been taught how to approach a specific type of problem, *regardless of modality and representation*, most learn how to solve it.

> There were items that were relatively difficult for Japanese students. Typically, they represent topics Japanese students were not taught. Where there is clear indication of little OTL (for example square roots, Pythagorean theorem, transformational geometry), performance is low.

> There were a large number of items for which Japanese teachers underestimated performance for both populations. However, there were only four items where teachers substantially overestimated performance.

> The limited text provided in the English translation of the Japanese summary report expresses some concerns with student performance in geometry and for higher-level processes. There is also some concern that performance levels for verbal items might be lagging behind those for computational items.

One comes away from the Japanese report with a perception of detailed self-criticism in the interest of shoring up weak spots. Whether this is simply a matter of style or the reflection of sincere concerns that mathematics training might be deteriorating in some way cannot be ascertained from the materials in hand. One would think, however, that this type of introspective inquiry into status and progress would help to maintain what by international standards is a highly effective educational system in the area of mathematics.

What is clear is that the quality of mathematics and science training is a long-term, continuing focus of the Japanese educational system. Reports on a 1956 nationwide survey of mathematics achievement (Ministry of Education 1958) and a 1957 nationwide survey of science achievement (Ministry of Education 1959) preceded the American awakening of concern for mathematical and scientific training fostered by Sputnik. The surveys also predate the IEA studies as well as the origination of the American national assessment program. Given Japan's preeminence on international studies, one might do well to mirror their long-term commitment and continuing introspection.

The Harnisch-Sato Study of High School Mathematics

Most of the evidence on the performance of Japanese students at the secondary level has been derived from the IEA studies. Recently, however, mathematics performance data that tend to corroborate the IEA findings were collected from students in Japan (primarily Tokyo and its surrounding communities) and in Illinois as part of a collaborative study between Nippon Electric Company (NEC) and the University of Illinois. The results of the study are most readily accessible in Harnisch and Sato (1983) and Harnisch, Walberg, Tsai, Sato, and Fyans (1986).

In this study the achievement results are reported only for the total mathematics scores. In some reports, a performance is broken down by age levels and by the number of items answered correctly by the top 1, 5, 10, 25, 50, and 75 percent of the relevant age groups. Overall, Japanese students averaged 39.6 out of 60 items correct, roughly double the number correct for Illinois students. When these performance differences are examined by selected variables taken from the background questionnaires (Harnisch and Sato 1983, table 1, p. 179; Harnisch et al. 1986, table 1), other patterns emerge:

> The gap between Japanese and U.S. performance increased with age, going from less than 18 points for fifteen-year-olds to more than 26 points for the seventeen and older group.

> For all three age groups, performance differences were greatest at the low end of the score distributions (25th percentile) and least for the top 1 percent of the age groups.

> Japanese males averaged almost six more items correct than females while the gender difference in mean scores for the United States was less than 1 point.

> Students who claimed that they read additional books just about every day in Japan averaged more than 5 points higher than students who hardly read additional books at all. In the U.S. the difference between these two groups was less than 2 points. In contrast, reading self-evaluations yielded larger differences in the United States than in Japan.

It would have been useful to know more about the students sampled in Japan and about performance differences on more refined content classifications as in the IEA studies. Nevertheless, there is nothing in the results from the Harnisch-Sato study that contradicts the general pattern of a substantial Japanese performance advantage found in the IEA studies.

Stevenson et al.

With the single exception of the IEA science data for ten-year-olds, all the results cited have been for secondary school students. The most extensive comparative study of achievement differences between Japanese and the United States elementary school students has been conducted by Harold Stevenson and his colleagues and collaborators from Japan and Taiwan. The study was conducted from 1979 through 1981 on samples of students from kindergarten, first and fifth grade classrooms in presumably comparable cities in Japan (Sendai), Taiwan (Taipei), and the United States (Minneapolis). Stevenson and his colleagues have continued and extended their research in recent years (see Chapter 4).

The evidence from this study can be summarized as follows:

1) Contrary to the results from Makita's (1968) teacher survey, Stevenson et al.'s data (1982) offer little support for the hypothesis that reading disabilities are less prevalent in Japan than in the

United States. At the fifth grade level, 8 percent of the Japanese students and 3 percent of the American students fell more than two grades behind in their reading level. Using a combined criteria of falling in the lowest 10 percent of the distribution of reading scores and having average cognitive task scores more than 1 standard deviation below the mean, 5.4 percent of the Japanese students and 6.3 percent of the U.S. students would be classified as reading disabled using both verbal and performance tasks. The corresponding figures when only verbal tasks are used were 8.3 percent and 7.9 percent, while the figures for performance tasks only were 6.3 percent and 7.1 percent.

2) Contrary to Lynn's (1982) assertion of the cognitive superiority of Japanese children to American children, Stevenson et al. (1985) found no overall differences in total scores on the cognitive ability tasks. If anything, the results somewhat favored the United States at kindergarten and first grade levels.

3) The superior mathematics performance of Japanese students found in other studies occurred here as well (Stevenson, Lee, and Stigler 1986 and Stigler et al. 1982). The differences between Japan and the United States were similar for kindergarten and first grade but increased dramatically by grade five. According to Stevenson et al., of the top 100 scores at grade one, 15 were American while there was only 1 American child in the top 100 at grade five. Among the lowest 100 scores at each grade, there were 58 American children at grade one and 67 at grade five (corresponding figures for Japan are not reported). Differences at the classroom level were also substantial. The lowest scoring Japanese class at the first grade fell at about the midpoint of the distribution for United States classrooms; at the fifth grade, the lowest scoring Japanese class performed better than the highest scoring American class. These patterns held up when individual items (or items classified by computation versus story problems) were examined.

The results from Stevenson et al.'s work challenge assertions that Japanese performance is substantially higher than in the United States on virtually all measures of cognitive functioning. Here, again, we find Japanese strength in mathematics (along with evidence of broader, greater, and earlier coverage of mathematical concepts and skills). But the data regarding cognitive abilities and reading performance is more balanced, with a slight advantage to the United States overall. The inclusion of Taiwanese results raises additional questions about Japanese superiority across cognitive measures.

Whether the absence of broad-based performance differences accurately reflects population differences among countries is hard to determine. The United States sample certainly underrepresents the ethnic, social, cultural, and regional diversity of the country, most likely in ways that would raise American performance levels. At the same time, the Japanese and United States samples in this study are probably more comparable than those used in the IEA surveys; comparisons among countries are more likely to be based on children coming from comparable home circumstances. The United States sample might lead to an underestimate of the prevalence of reading disabilities and overestimate its reading and mathematics achievement. The biases introduced by the sample selection in Japan are less clear but presumably are along the same lines.

The other major limitation of this study holds for any attempt at cross-cultural comparisons. The transferability of cognitive tasks across cultures is difficult at best. Transfer is likely to be easiest in the area of mathematics, where Japanese students shine, and most difficult in the area of reading. The limitations in the mathematics tests constructed by Stevenson et al. have to do with their relevance to each country's curriculum; the problem was less severe in Japan because its students were taught more topics earlier (and apparently better). Possible problems with the interpretability of the cognitive ability tasks results have to do with their comparative familiarity across cultures; American students are likely to have prior familiarity with similar tasks while Japanese students typically are not administered such tests.

The difficulties in constructing comparable reading measures are thoroughly documented by Stevenson et al. (1982). The methods they employed reflect the state of the art and the psychometric properties of the resulting instruments are generally quite good. Moreover, there is no evidence to suggest that the reading measures were less fair in Japan than in the United States.

In summary, then, the evidence presented by Stevenson and his colleagues challenges some notions about Japanese performance (lower incidence of reading disabilities, higher levels of cognitive functioning) and reinforces others (superior mathematics performance). While their samples were not nationally representative and their test tasks may have suffered from inherent limitations in cross-cultural transferability, Stevenson and his colleagues do provide results that cast doubts on the universality of exceptional Japanese performance.

Hess, Azuma, et al.

The collaboration of Robert Hess and Hiroshi Azuma in parallel studies of cognitive socialization and development represents the only major comparative longitudinal data base besides the IEA SIMS study (key references are Hess et al. 1985). In addition, this study is the only source of cognitive data from the elementary school years outside of the Stevenson et al. study and the IEA science data and the only source with preschool data from both Japan and the United States. Data collection for the study started with children aged three years eight months in 1972 and continued through age eleven in Japan and age twelve in the United States.

The difficulty of conducting cross-cultural, longitudinal research on cognitive development is clearly illustrated by the collaborative effort of Hess and Azuma. The kind of detailed examinations of maternal behaviors and family influences of interest caused them to restrict sample sizes to manageable numbers and the locales to those easily reached over time by participating researchers. While it was relatively straightforward to use common protocols for observations and interviews, most of the cognitive tasks had to be adapted to unique conditions in the participating countries. To a certain degree, comparability could only be assumed and not explicitly determined. Stevenson and his colleagues went to greater efforts to ensure comparability of their measures, but their data collection began at about the time that Hess and Azuma's ended. Moreover, the purposes of the two studies differed in ways that placed greater emphasis on test development in the Stevenson et al. project.

Despite its limitations, there are hints of intriguing differences between cognitive development patterns between Japan and the U.S. Hess and Azuma's reports (Hess et al. 1985) stress the role of the mother in cognitive socialization and cross-cultural differences in that role. They find differences between Japan and the United States in maternal teaching styles, strategies of behavior control, expectations for mastery of developmental skills, and causal attributions for performance; moreover, these maternal characteristics are related to school readiness and later cognitive performance, but differ across countries. Perhaps, then, the Hess and Azuma investigations' major contribution to this review is to remind the researcher about cross-country differences in the ways in which the foundation for cognitive performance is established through family influences on behavior and development.

Lynn

The work of Richard Lynn is the main source of comparative data on Japanese and American intelligence. Lynn's work is largely derived from standardizations of the major intelligence tests used in the United States (versions of the Wechsler and Stanford-Binet).

In 1977, Lynn reviewed the data from the available standardizations of the Wechsler tests in Japan (unaltered subtests for the WISC (standardized in 1951 on 1,071 children aged 5.0-15.11), WAIS (mid-1950's for 35- to 44-year-olds), and the WPPSI (late 1960s for children ages 4, 5, and 6)). Converting these subtest results to mean IQs (actually performance IQs since all verbal subtests were altered during translation), he obtained eighteen separate estimates of mean Japanese IQ. All estimates were higher than the American scores, with a mean difference across age groups of 3.1 points (about .20 standard deviations) for the WISC and 3.8 and 11.7 points for the WAIS and WPPSI, respectively.

Lynn (1977, 70) acknowledged two caveats with regard to these differences. First, Japanese sampling methods may have systematically biased scores in favor of more intelligent groups within their population. Second, the subtests for which differences were most pronounced were largely measures of spatial ability. Nevertheless, Lynn concluded that the evidence supported an interpretation that the Japanese had "the highest mean IQ ever recorded for a national population" (1977, 70). He then proceeded to cast doubt on the plausibility of environmental explanations for the difference and, by inference, claimed that genetic factors were the most plausible source of the Japanese-American difference.

In 1982 Lynn extended his IQ analyses to include the 1975 standardization of the WISC-R in Japan. The estimate of mean Japanese IQ from this sample was 111, roughly .70 standard deviations higher than the American norm value of 100. Given his earlier work, this new estimate led Lynn to conclude that "mean

Japanese IQ has been rising relative to the American during the twentieth century" (1982, 222). Further, by pooling across the data, he concluded that there was a significant secular trend in favor of the Japanese of about 7 points per generation, which Lynn attributed to improvements in health and nutrition rather than to changes in the genetic structures of the population or to education. Lynn went on to extrapolate his estimates to derive comparative estimates of the percentage of the population with IQs higher than 130; this comparison further highlighted the purported superiority of the Japanese. Based on these results, Lynn concluded that, "Since intelligence is a determinant of economic success...the Japanese IQ advantage may have been a significant factor in Japan's high rate of economic growth in the post-World War II period" (1982, 223).

While his 1977 paper apparently provoked little reaction, the 1982 paper, appearing in *Nature* with the title "IQ in Japan and the United States Shows a Growing Disparity," certainly did. *Nature* later published four comments (Anderson 1982, Flynn 1983, Stevenson and Azuma 1983, and Vining 1983) along with Lynn's rejoinder (1983). The major points of the critique were that:

> Lynn's contentions failed to take into account differences in the American norming population between standardizations and increases in performance over time (Flynn 1983). The recent American standardization had a more representative ethnic mixture, which meant that Japanese scores were no longer being compared to those of white Americans. Moreover, the average American IQs increased by 7.86 points over roughly the same period of time when ethnic mixture was held constant.

> Taking additional subtests into account in deriving Japanese IQ estimates shrinks the estimate. When combined with other disparities already mentioned, Flynn (1983) concluded that the 1975 estimate was closer to 107 than to Lynn's figure of 111.

> While estimates of the Japanese mean IQ are higher, the variances were significantly lower which would considerably shrink the estimated disparity in the percentage of high IQs (Flynn 1983 and Vining 1983).

> The WISC-R standardization sample in Japan lacked representativeness and was not comparable with that from the

United States (Stevenson and Azuma 1983). Unlike the American standardization, the occupation of the head of household and urban/rural residence were not used in selecting the Japanese sample. Given the extensive evidence regarding the relationship between socioeconomic status and student performance on cognitive tasks (including studies of Japanese samples; IEA; Hess and Azuma) and of urban-rural differences in performance (again, Japanese data from the IEA studies exhibit this difference), these omissions are likely to be consequential.

> The schools used in the Japanese standardization considerably overrepresented urban areas (Stevenson and Azuma 1983). Ninety-two percent of the Japanese classrooms sampled were from cities with a population greater than 50,000, although only 64 percent of the Japanese population resides in this type of setting. No sampled classes were from villages and small towns where 24 percent of the Japanese population live. The consequence of the Japanese sampling method was a bias favoring higher socioeconomic status and urban residency.

> The reliance on strictly performance subtests in IQ calculations is inappropriate (Hess and Azuma 1983).

In his reply to the critics, Lynn (1983) softened several of the assertions from his earlier article and attempted to take into account several of their concerns. Once the adjustments suggested by Flynn, Stevenson, and Azuma were all taken into account, however, Lynn still estimated a Japanese IQ mean of 104.4, which he judged to be significantly higher than the IQ of white Americans.

What the above means in the final analysis is hard to say. Clearly, Lynn lost some of his caution, and dispassion, between 1977 and 1982. Moreover, in response to criticisms, he backed away from his assertions of "increasing disparity" and the high IQ differences. What is left is what Lynn would view as a replicable 4 point mean IQ difference between Japanese and Americans, based on performance tasks only.

If the kinds of selective sampling evidenced in the Japanese WISC-R standardization occurred in the other Wechsler standardizations and caused the typical kinds of biases associated with socioeconomic conditions and community type, then all the differences are suspect. The available evidence and documentation do not show what differences in measured IQ really exist between the two countries. Neither can the economic implications be interpreted as Lynn tried to do.

Cognitive Evidence--What's There, What's Missing

Earlier, eight questions that guided the probes into existing evidence bearing on the popular belief that Japanese students exhibit superior academic performance when compared with the United States were delineated. The purpose was to see whether this belief could withstand a detailed scrutiny of the primary empirical studies. The possibility of the secondary interpretations of Japan's supposed performance advantage being misinterpretations, misstatements, overstatements, or overgeneralizations were analyzed.

Seven separate studies with extensive empirical data about the cognitive characteristics of Japanese students that also contained comparable information about American students were examined in detail. Looking across the seven studies, there is substantial evidence from multiple sources to support the judgment of exceptional mathematics achievement in Japan as measured by conventional paper-and-pencil objective tests. The mathematics performance advantage for Japan relative to the United States starts early and increases during secondary school. This finding has stood up over time and across the topics covered within the Japanese curriculum, which the evidence suggests is substantially more comprehensive in coverage at any given age level than the typical U.S. curriculum. There are mathematical topics for which the Japanese students have not performed well; however, these topics tend not to have been part of the Japanese curriculum by the time of testing.

Once one ventures outside the area of mathematics (and to some degree science), information becomes sparse and the evidence spotty. Comparative data at the secondary level on Japanese performance in reading, literature, social studies, writing, foreign language, or other nonquantitative content areas were not available. The little data available from studies conducted in the elementary school years (essentially from the Stevenson et al. study and from the Hess and Azuma collaboration) do not exhibit any distinctive Japanese performance and may actually favor U.S. students, once mathematics and science performance are excluded. Evidence in the realm of cognitive abilities also lends little support to the judgments that Japanese students are exceptional (outside of spatial abilities perhaps). Also the data purporting to demonstrate superior Japanese mean IQ appear to be seriously flawed at worst, and questionable at best.

The evidence regarding differential performance for identifiable subgroups within Japan appears to be consistent, but again is available almost exclusively in the areas of mathematics and science. Variability in Japanese mathematics and science performance is apparently smaller than that in the United States during the elementary school years but is greater for secondary school samples. However, when combined with the exceptionally high Japanese mean performance, low scoring Japanese students do well relative to students from other countries. Differences in performance are also associated with socioeconomic status variables and locale of residence (urban, town, rural), in much the same way as in the United States. The limited data on differences between public and private school students (primarily from SIMS) do not point to general advantages for private schooling.

Finally, there is evidence of gender differences in mathematics and science performance, especially for upper secondary students, but the differences are not large relative to differences found in other countries. In fact, Japanese girls outperform the boys from virtually every other country participating in the IEA studies. None of the studies reviewed provided any insights into ethnic group differences in Japanese performance.

Noncognitive and Behavioral Characteristics

The domain of noncognitive characteristics of interest here include self-concept, locus of control, aspirations, expectations, and values (self-responsibility, self-criticism, group responsibility, loyalty, and perseverance). The proposed list of behavioral characteristics includes coping behaviors, task orientation, group functioning, productivity, motivation, and creativity.

However, the search for comparable literature on noncognitive and behavioral characteristics of Japanese students yielded very little empirical data on most attributes. The choices about how to proceed, then, were limited. This chapter is based, therefore, on the empirical data found and also cites statements from secondary sources that lack empirical documentation. By doing this, however, there is a risk, as in the cognitive characteristics review, of providing an imbalanced picture of actual circumstances regarding noncognitive and behavioral attributes. Moreover, the inferences are likely to be more strained than for the cognitive data.

The cross-cultural transportability of American conceptions of noncognitive attributes and behaviors to Japanese society and culture might be even more problematic than in the cognitive domain. The American penchant for "psychologizing" about individual attributes and behavior may not mesh well with the Japanese collective sense of personal and social responsibility or the Japanese agenda for the study of human behavior. Some of the difficulties are evident in Lewis' study (see Chapter 7).

New Data Sources: Noncognitive

In addition to the studies that were considered in the examination of cognitive characteristics, two other comparative studies that gathered survey data on the attributes are central to this part of the analysis.

HS&B in Japan

In 1980, the Japan Youth Research Institute conducted a partial replication of the High School and Beyond (HS&B) Study, initiated in the United States by the National Center for Education Statistics. Questionnaire data were gathered in Japan from a sample of 7,239 high school seniors drawn from 46 schools. In contrast, HS&B collected both questionnaire and cognitive test data from a probability sample of roughly 30,000 sophomores and 28,000 seniors from approximately 1,000 public and private schools in the United States.

World Youth Survey Number Three

In 1983 the Youth Development Headquarters of the prime minister's office in Japan conducted the third in a series of World Youth Surveys (WYS). The stated purpose of the WYS was "to determine the major problems confronting young people in Japan, to help work out future policies for young people, and to obtain basic data that is necessary to promote mutual understanding between the youth in Japan and in foreign countries" (Youth Development

Headquarters 1984, 1). Eleven countries, including Japan and the United States, participated in this survey of young people aged eighteen through twenty-four. In Japan 1,021 interviews were obtained by the Nippon Research Center, Ltd., using a stratified, two-stage random sample; 1,134 interviews were obtained in the United States by the Gallup Organization, Inc., using a replicated probability sample.

Information about Specific Attributes

The attributes to be considered cluster roughly into two groups. The first set includes measures that reflect beliefs, interests, attitudes, and feelings. Data regarding a variety of behavioral characteristics constitute the second set.

Self-Concept

Despite the substantial body of American literature involving judgments of one's value and abilities along a number of dimensions (primarily called self-concept or self-esteem), data on the self-concept of Japanese students are limited. Fetters et al. (1983, table 6) reports the percentage of high school seniors that agreed with the three statements on self-esteem and another question about ability, in Japan, to enter college, or, in the United States, to complete college.

Japanese responses to the questions about worth and self-satisfaction were much less positive than the Americans'; less than 33 percent of the Japanese students agreed with three statements while more than 80 percent of the U.S. students responded positively. On the question, "At times, I think I'm no good," there was a higher percentage of negative response for Japanese, especially for females (71 percent of the Japanese females agreeing in contrast to 49 percent for Japanese males, and 51 percent and 41 percent for U.S. females and males, respectively). The question about college showed a similar Japan-U.S. pattern with over 80 percent of the U.S. seniors judging themselves able to complete college, while less than 40 percent of the Japanese stated that they had the ability to enter college (since the dropout rate from college is negligible in Japan, entering is essentially tantamount to completing college).

If the Japanese results had come from a typically American sample, there might be cause for considerable concern. The responses to most self-concept questionnaires from U.S. samples are typically skewed with substantially more positive than negative replies, except in clinical samples.

This tendency toward self-critical judgment by Japanese is apparently not an isolated event but rather a consistent pattern. Japanese students in the Harnisch and Sato study (Harnisch and Sato 1983 and Harnisch et al. 1986) had more negative reading self-evaluations than Illinois students. In their report on student opinions, attitudes, and preferences from SIMS, Kifer and Robitaille (1989) found that despite their high cognitive scores, Japanese students from both populations were more likely than students from other countries to consider school mathematics to be hard and to have low opinions of their performance in mathematics.

These patterns of responses are attributed to distinctive cultural tendencies in socialization regarding appropriate expressions about self-judgment. Within Japanese society, humility is valued as an essential ingredient of interpersonal harmony, while overconfidence and public expression of beliefs that might reflect negatively on others are discouraged. American society, on the other hand, places a higher premium on self-confidence and self-assurance, and its competitive tendencies afford greater tolerance for and encouragement of public expression of one's capabilities.

What this means in terms of "true" differences in the distribution of self-concept between Japanese and American students is unclear. Japanese students, as a group, may be overly self-critical, professing greater concerns about their worth and abilities than they truly believe. On the other hand, their self-opinions might also reflect realistic reactions to the tightly connected system of secondary and postsecondary educational stratification. In contrast, the responses of U.S. students are more likely to reflect overconfidence and weaker societal linkages between school performance, opportunities, and self-esteem.

Locus of Control and Attributions

This category of attributes deals with the tendency to judge whether the factors responsible for individual actions and performance are under one's personal control (internal) or not (external). Current emphasis in applications of the locus of control construct in academic contexts is on an individual's causal attributions for his or her success or failure. Attributions to personal ability and effort are viewed as internal (but vary on other dimensions in Weiner's (1976) theory), while those to task difficulty, luck, and fate are considered to be external factors beyond the control of the individual. Among the internal factors, effort is considered to be a changeable behavior while ability (or aptitude) is seen as a more stable personal characteristic.

The evidence from Japanese-U.S. comparisons with respect to locus of control and causal attributions for success and failure is mixed, seemingly varying across time and age group considered. On a scale intended to measure "the extent to which man is perceived as having effective control of and mastery over his environment" that was used in the FIMS (Husen 1967), Japan exhibited high means (ranked first or second among the countries) and low standard deviations, while means in the United States were much lower (close to the bottom ranking) and the scores more variable at all three population levels. On the whole, then, Japanese students were more likely than students from other countries to feel that mankind has control over its own fate, while American students were more likely to view mankind as helpless in the face of forces at work in the world.

The remaining studies focus on the relative prevalence of ability, effort, luck, and task difficulty in causal attributions regarding success and achievement. During the follow-up phase of the Hess and Azuma study (the Japanese students were in the fifth grade while the Americans were in the sixth grade), both students and their parents were asked about their attributions for low performance in mathematics (Hess et al. 1985 and Holloway et al. nd). Both Japanese children and mothers were less likely to attribute poor performance to lack of ability and training in school and more likely to attribute it to lack of effort than American children and their mothers. American children were also more likely than Japanese children to blame poor performance on bad luck. At an earlier phase of the study (when the children were four), Japanese mothers were more likely to emphasize children's natural abilities (effort and ability were not separated in this part of the study) and less likely to emphasize parental encouragement as reasons for their children's future success in school. The investigators interpreted their results as supportive of the Japanese belief in individual responsibility for and control over success; that is, that internal changeable factors such as effort are more important than either internal stable factors (ability) or external factors (luck, task difficulty, quality of teaching).

The pattern from the Hess and Azuma study is evident, but to a lesser extent, in students' success and failure attributions regarding test-taking in the Harnisch and Sato study (Harnisch and Sato 1983, table 1). Although effort was the most frequently chosen reason for either success or failure in both countries, Japanese students were less likely to attribute success to ability and more likely to attribute it to luck or task difficulty than U.S. students. Effort was a more likely attribution, and task difficulty a less likely one, for failure in the Japanese sample. The Harnisch-Sato results for the success condition seem to reflect a mixture of two Japanese attributes: humility and assuming individual responsibility. The failure results more neatly match other evidence from the internal-external control paradigm applied in academic contexts.

The report on the WYS (Youth Development Headquarters 1984) states that personal effort and abilities were ranked as the first and second choices in Japan and most other countries as reasons for success in school. Apparently luck or fate was a more popular choice in Japan, and good education a less popular one, than in many countries.

The results from the HS&B comparison (Fetters et al. 1983) with respect to locus of control appear to be at odds with those found elsewhere. While only a quarter of Japanese seniors agreed that "good luck is more important than hard work for success," this percentage was more than twice as large as that for American seniors. Moreover, Japanese students were less likely to agree that "what happens is my own doing" (59 percent versus 77 percent for the United States). Finally, the statement "Plans hardly ever work out" provoked a remarkably higher percentage of agreement in Japan (74 percent versus 23 percent in the United States).

The HS&B reversal of the pattern wherein the Japanese appear to place greater emphasis on effort and personal responsibility than comparable American samples is puzzling. The timing of the HS&B survey may have been a factor in Japan; if the survey were conducted late in the senior year, Japanese students may have been at a point of maximum stress (or maximum disappointment) with respect to pending or completed university examinations. Such an interpretation would also fit with the more negative self-evaluations regarding self-esteem and ability to enter college.

On the other hand, the data from HS&B on self-esteem and locus of control may reflect a recent undertone of general dissatisfaction and unrest among Japanese youth at this sharply demarcated juncture in their educational system. The tight coupling between educational performance and occupational opportunities places substantial pressure on this age group. The limited data from the 1983 administration of the WYS also contained some indications of comparative dissatisfaction in Japan--lower ratings of satisfaction with home life, somewhat lower satisfaction with school life, and apparently markedly higher dissatisfaction with life at work (the trends from the previous survey were also toward decreasing satisfaction). This may be the result of growing frustrations with the sustained dependence on the family and limits on social relations with peers accompanied by a dampening of the willingness of Japan's "old adolescents" to take the long-range view when juxtaposed with perceptions of the independence and freedoms enjoyed by their American peers (Rohlen (1983) describes circumstances that might foster such reactions).

Another explanation for the confusion surrounding locus of control and causal attributions for Japanese in the academic domain is that the area of academic pursuits may be anomalous with respect to Japanese control-relevant behavior in other areas. In a recent comprehensive review, Weisz, Rothbaum, and Blackburn (1984, with comments from two eminent Japanese psychologists, Hiroshi Azuma and Hideo Kojima) identify two general paths to a feeling of control, and contrast Japanese and American perspectives and practices in child rearing, socialization, religion and philosophy, work, and psychotherapy. According to Weisz et al., Americans emphasize and highly value *primary* control, whereby individuals are rewarded for influencing existing realities. Japanese, on the other hand, place greater emphasis on *secondary* control, whereby individuals receive "rewards by accommodating to existing realities and maximizing satisfaction or goodness of fit with things as they are" (Weisz et al. 1984, 955).

Weisz et al. report that of the five studies they found comparing locus of control, the Japanese scored as significantly more influenced by external forces than Americans in all of them: Japanese were more likely to see fate and luck as influential, perceive themselves as less able to alter others' opinion of them, view the world as a capricious place where people do not always produce the outcomes they deserve, and believe that individuals can have only limited effectiveness acting alone.

In their discussion, Weisz et al. repeatedly point to the emphasis Japanese place on maintaining harmony and on alignment with and obligation to family and group (friendship, work group) members. The apparent inconsistency they cite in the academic domain (Weisz et al. 1984, 960) is seen as an extension of an individual's commitment to enhancing the family's standing, which Weisz et al. see as a form of secondary control.

The two Japanese commentators (Azuma and Kojima) on the Weisz et al. review express appreciation for the perceptive and generally sensitive portrayal of Japanese control strategies. Nevertheless, their comments highlight the difficulty of applying a distinctively American primary/secondary dichotomy to the Japanese culture. Azuma points to the need to focus on the nuances in secondary control (using the Weisz et al. scheme) in Japan. Kojima suggests that between-country differences in the nature of socially accepted modes of primary control deserve more consideration and that certain relations classified as secondary in American culture are better perceived as primary in Japan.

This discussion serves as an appropriate reminder that one's perception of a cultural attribute depends on the cultural perspective from which one operates, the structural paradigm one invokes, and the aspects of behavior one considers. Otherwise, one is likely to misconstrue the descriptive evidence which, depending on vantage point, highlights either the internal or external facets of control exhibited by the Japanese.

Toward School and Subject Matter

The IEA studies are the primary sources of information about school-related attitudes. In the First International Mathematics Study, Japanese students ranked either first or second among countries in terms of their attitudes toward school and school learning; the attitudes of U.S. students were typically much less positive, placing them at or near the bottom internationally. On questions related to interest in mathematics, the picture was more mixed. Japanese thirteen-year-olds and terminal year non-mathematics students were above the international means for their respective populations, but terminal year mathematics students were slightly below the international means. The average interest scores for U.S. students were higher than for Japanese thirteen-year-olds and terminal year mathematics students.

The cross-country comparisons from the IEA Science Study also indicate that Japanese attitudes toward schooling tended to be positive. Their means on the "like school" scale at both age ten and fourteen ranked second among the developed countries (the United

States was third). Science interest and activities scores for Japanese ten-year-olds were the highest internationally (the United States ranked third) while the corresponding scores for fourteen-year-olds were closer to the international median (sixth versus fourth in the United States).

No general school attitude questions were included in the SIMS. Kifer and Robitaille (1989) report that the Japanese students at both population levels ranked lowest on the "mathematics in school" scale (indicating a greater dislike for the topics that were universally part of the mathematics curriculum than students from other countries) and on the "mathematics and myself" scale (containing items on willingness to persevere in mathematics, self-perceptions of mathematics performance, and intentions to pursue the study of mathematics).

Both the WYS and the HS&B surveys report evidence of negative attitudes toward school by Japanese students. As mentioned earlier, Japanese students had a somewhat lower percentage that indicated school satisfaction than in most other countries. Their reasons for dissatisfaction (poor teaching, inappropriate vocational and educational counseling, inadequate facilities and equipment) were the same as in other countries.

In HS&B, Japanese students were substantially less likely than American students to rate all aspects of schooling considered (physical plant, library, quality of academic instruction, reputation in community, fairness of discipline, school spirit) as good or excellent. In most cases, the percentage of positive ratings was three times higher in the United States. Japanese students were also more likely than U.S. students to believe that their school should have placed more emphasis on basic academic subjects and did not offer enough practical work experience, but were less likely to believe that the school should have placed more emphasis on vocational and technical programs. Japanese students were more likely to agree, however, that their school provided continuing education and employment counseling.

The most recent evidence (from the early 1980s) suggests that the attitudes of Japanese students were more negative than in the 1960s and 1970s and also were more negative than the attitudes of presumably comparable American groups. This may be a reaction to the tremendous academic pressures on Japanese secondary school students, who choose to express their bitterness in a manner that has no impact on their academic standing.

Educational Expectations

That the pressures are greater on Japanese students than American students completing secondary school is quite clear. Evidence from both the WYS and HS&B surveys and from Rohlen (1983, 1986) point to the higher educational aspirations for Japanese students. They ranked highest on the WYS. On the HS&B survey, approximately 10 percent more Japanese students aspired to finish college or graduate school than U.S. students expecting to achieve these levels of education. The pattern was reversed for females. These trends represent a departure of sorts from the earlier data on educational expectations taken from the IEA surveys; Japanese fourteen-year-olds in the science study actually had a mean expectation two years lower than the U.S. mean and ranked only sixth (although the data from certain countries were questionable).

The pressure to go to the right university is substantial. Japanese students rarely change universities or fields of study. There is also a strong correlation between job opportunities and the university one attends. Since Japanese tend to change jobs and companies less often during their careers than Americans, the decision point at the end of secondary school has lifelong consequences for Japanese students. Rohlen (1983, 1986) vividly depicts the growing presence of *ronin*, or students who fail to get into the university of their choice on the first try, but who choose to study and retake the examination rather than choose another university or seek employment. There is simply no comparable point in the American educational system where the stakes are so high. Under such conditions, there is little wonder that Japanese secondary school graduates are more likely to experience frustrated ambitions and express their frustration through their survey responses.

Other Attitudes

Details of attitudes outside the academic domain are sparse (Fetters et al. 1983, Rohlen 1983, and Youth Development Headquarters 1984). For the most part, the response patterns within the studies are consistent with expectations based on popular accounts of Japanese society and culture or with other evidence reviewed here. For example, Rohlen's friendship results show systematic differences across high schools that appear to be associated with the school's academic status. The Fetters et al. survey found substantially greater emphasis on job security and permanence than on beginning income in the Japanese sample, as expected, while U.S. students tended to rate the two as equally important. In the WYS, the Japanese were less likely than Americans to choose "to live as I like" as an aim in life, but more likely to choose "to get rich." There were perhaps fewer curious results than for the other noncognitive attributes considered.

A Sample of Behavior

The information on the behavioral characteristics of Japanese students is spotty in most areas. A substantial body of evidence has accumulated about the amount of time Japanese students spend on academic pursuits outside of regular school hours. Several sources (Comber and Keeves 1973, Fetters et al. 1983, Husen 1967, and Rohlen, 1983, 1986) report that Japanese students spend more than twice as many hours per day doing homework than American students; they also tend to take more courses and more advanced courses in school and are absent less often. Moreover, the United States (and apparently other countries) have nothing comparable to the Japanese *juku* or *yobiko* cram schools offering supplementary schooling. Rohlen (1983) cites figures indicating that well over one-half of Tokyo's students beyond the fourth grade (over 25 percent nationwide, according to his 1986 paper) attend one of these schools or have a private tutor. Coupled with the longer regular school year, longer school week, and the special vacation schools attended by many Japanese youth, there is clearly much more time devoted to academic matters with a consequential payoff described in earlier sections.

Skipping to the opposite end of the spectrum, Rohlen (1983) reviews the data on juvenile delinquency patterns in Japan. While differences in reporting systems introduce certain obstacles to cross-cultural comparisons, he nevertheless points to substantially lower crime rates among Japanese youth than for American teenagers. Rohlen cites statistics indicating an increase in juvenile crime during the 1970s but points out that the increase occurred primarily for lower secondary school students. He also provides data that indicate a correlation between delinquency rates and school rank (defined by university examination results).

Critics of Japan's high-pressure educational system often point to youth suicide rates as a negative consequence of the system. Rohlen's examination of the data is again most useful for our purposes (Cummings (1980) also discusses the suicide issue). He points out that the World Health Organization figures indicate that the Japanese suicide rate for the fifteen to twenty-four age group peaked in the mid-1950s, dropped dramatically by the late 1950s and stayed low for males through the early 1970s (female rates remained high). Considering data from a number of sources, Rohlen concludes that examination pressures and poor academic performance are major causes for suicides among persons under twenty in Japan, more so than would be the case in other countries.

Time use outside of school is another area of apparently marked difference between Japanese and American youth. Fewer Japanese students hold part-time jobs or spend considerable amounts of leisure time with their friends outside their homes (either on dates or other socializing: Fetters et al. 1983 and Rohlen 1983). They are more likely to spend time at home with their families and concentrate on their studies.

There is extensive literature on the distinctions in family relations and child rearing practices between Japan and the United States. Rohlen (1983) and Cummings (1980), to a lesser extent, portray the close bonding and interdependencies established between child and parents (especially the mother) early on and maintained until young adulthood (see also references in Weisz et al. 1984). The Hess and Azuma collaboration provides a wealth of data on the contrasting patterns of developmental socialization as practiced in Japan and the United States (reported in the papers already cited; Hess et al. 1985 provides a comprehensive summary of the major distinctions). For example, they found that Japanese mothers encourage compliance, politeness, and emotional maturity at an earlier age, while U.S. mothers expect social skills with peers and verbal assertiveness at an earlier age. According to Hess and Azuma, Japanese mothers are more concerned with orienting the child toward proper behavior with adults while U.S. mothers are more concerned with effective peer behavior. They also point out differences in maternal teaching styles.

Creativity

Creativity is difficult to examine. Even within a culture, conceptions of what creativity involves and how it is demonstrated vary considerably. Moreover, regardless of the choice of conception, there is little empirical evidence about Japanese creativity, most of which appears in a few interpretive summaries (Schiller and Walberg 1982 and Torrance 1980).

Discussions of Japanese creativity revolve around definitional differences and cultural stereotypes. From an American perspective, creativity is often viewed as the ability to diverge from normative thought and knowledge--demonstrating novel ways of looking at phenomena, going beyond what is known, being able to perceive or generate unique facets of concrete objects and abstract ideas. The alleged Japanese penchant for accumulation of facts and information, attention to details, and emphasis on applied problem solving (as reflected in a supposed scientific focus on adapting and improving existing technology as opposed to the pursuits of abstract theory and invention) causes one stream of American opinion to view the Japanese as not being creative compared with Americans. Others (such as Torrance and Walberg) point to Japan's leadership in inventions and patents, the reverence and respect accorded to its artists (in literature, drama, music, dance, art), and its high levels of literacy and musical talent, all signs of a highly and broadly creative society and culture.

The divergence of opinion about Japanese creativity seems to have the aura of a squabble about "scoring rules." The reading of the information about Japanese schooling is that it attempts to turn the novel into the familiar through broad curricular coverage, emphasis on problem solving across a wide array of applications, and extensive purposive practice. If this characterization is accurate, then by one group's scoring system few Japanese get points for creativity, because it is harder to diverge (in a positive direction) from their higher norm. Japan's collective, purposive approach to the world of knowledge, thought, and behavior works against them when judged by the typically American scoring rules.

How one views Japanese creativity seems to depend more on what one perceives to be the consequences of differences in cultural choices, and this, in turn, depends on what is being valued. A country's economic prosperity, intellectual climate, and quality of everyday life have all been attributed to the creativity (and intelligence) of its people. It seems that Japan and the United States are countries whose distinctive cultures pursue different creative routes to achieving similar but not absolutely congruent goals. Using one country's criteria to evaluate an attribute such as creativity in the other results in invidious comparisons that are more likely to mislead than illuminate.

Summary of Noncognitive Evidence: Perplexing Patterns

At the outset of the discussion of the empirical evidence on noncognitive and behavioral characteristics of Japanese students, some misgivings about whether an adequate portrayal was possible were expected. The cultures of Japan and America reverberate in strong and complex ways upon the attitudes and behavior of their respective youth populations. The likelihood of being able to accurately depict, through the filter of American psychological theories and paradigms, what Japanese youth believe seems remote.

Thus, it was no surprise that the picture unveiled through the various articles was sometimes puzzling. Do Japanese students have lower self-esteem than American students, or is this culturally proscribed modesty and humility? Do they consider themselves internally controlled masters of their destiny through their willingness to persist and commit the necessary effort for success, or are external control mechanisms a more compelling force in their lives? Have their school-related attitudes really turned more negative over time or is this merely adolescent flailing at a convenient target? Is their willingness to sacrifice for family and for future success still strong, or is it crumbling under exhausting and lengthening academic pressures? If attitudes are changing, can behaviors be far behind?

When peculiarly American perspectives are applied to the evidence in hand, it is perplexing. Most Americans cannot even conceive of living and behaving according to the Japanese code of conduct; they would probably find it too confining. It works the other way, as well, for most Japanese, used to a society with scarce physical resources that must be compensated for by maximizing human resources. They cannot fathom squandering physical and human resources in the haphazard American manner.

The Role of Culture in Educational Achievement in Japan

The basic focus in this section is on Japanese culture as an aspect of the context in which Japanese education functions. In each case, the authors of the articles surveyed have suggested that the products of the Japanese educational system achieve higher than world standards due to cultural factors. In addition, there are articles that challenge the notion that Japan's educational system is superior and produces overachievers.

Literature Related to Cultural Factors
Influencing Student Charactericstics

In much of the literature on Japan's social and economic successes, the writers refer to Japan's unique culture as a major factor. The writings of these Japanese and Western scholars convey a subtle sense that Japan's successes are, perhaps, culture specific and could not really be duplicated in any other society.

Tsukada

Tsukada's (1984) work provides a useful introduction to this perspective. In his comparison of the Japanese and American experience, three aspects of considerable difference are noted. The first aspect is the historical and cultural tendency toward centralization, or, as the writer puts it, "...the public sector plays a monopolizing role in Japan..." (Tsukada 1984, 12), in contrast to the vigorous role of the private sector in the United States.

A second major sociocultural difference relates to the varying sex roles for females with respect to higher education. According to Tsukuda, "In Japan, females tended to be enrolled in junior colleges whereas females in the United States became equal to males, or even started exceeding males in the enrollment rate in four-year institutions in the United States" (1984, 12).

Finally, Tsukuda notes the historical increase in the number of higher education institutions in Japan as compared with the United States. Unlike the elementary and secondary sector referred to above and dominated by public controls, the private sector has played an important role in higher education; again, this is a phenomenon peculiar to Japan (Tsukuda 1984, 12).

Tsukuda concludes from an analysis of the statistical data produced in Japanese and American governmental reports that although Japan and the United States are similar to each other in terms of enrollment rate, expenditure for education, and the suicide rate, they are not similar in terms of the female position in higher education, the role of the private sector in education, and the rate of juvenile delinquency. The notion that the two nations are socially and culturally unique is a pervasive aspect of his analysis.

Cummings

Against this more or less factual description of Japanese and American education, three studies provide an interesting "perceptual" profile of the two systems. William Cummings, in "Japanese Images of American Education" (1984) notes that "Japan has been looking at American education much longer than America has been looking at Japanese education, and Japan has far more information" (1984, 1). He discusses four classes of observers of American education in Japan and their approach in conveying to the Japanese public their perceptions of American education: "Ministry of Education observers focus on aspects of finance, enrollments, and administration. Professors comment on the quality of academic life in the United States. Parents and students focus on events in the classroom and community. And politicians seem most aware of the American disease of drugs, violence, and sex" (Cummings 1984, 11). The view is invariably one-dimensional depending on the interest group doing the viewing.

What emerges from Cummings' study is the cultural difference involved in interpreting a complex phenomenon such as "education." On the one hand, "...American education was seen as expressive, individualistic, opulent, and creative; on the other as undisciplined, wasteful, and hedonistic" (Cummings 1984, 11). Generally speaking, Cummings concludes that the Japanese currently view American education in a negative light due perhaps to cultural tendencies, but more likely due to current political and economic successes.

Ichikawa

Americans have also had a history of "discovering" and perceiving Japan and Japanese education. Ichikawa (1984) traces three stages of American perceptions of Japanese society and education: from the Occupation to the renewal of the U.S.-Japan Security Treaty of 1960 (based on the U.S. belief that Japan was in need of radical educational reform to democratize the system); the 1960s-1970s (U.S. admiration of Japan's economic growth); and the 1980s (Japan becomes an economic rival and the educational system is given great credit) (Ichikawa 1984, 2-3).

Ichikawa notes how American perceptions of Japanese education have become more accurate, statistically more informed, and generally more rigorous than in the past. Moreover, these

American scholars have informed Japanese educators and stimulated various reforms.

However, several caveats are in order, due to a lack of understanding of Japanese culture. First, American scholars are hampered by limited sources of information since "most of the visiting specialists depend for information mainly on publications in English, or Japanese people with communicative competence in foreign languages" (Ichikawa 1984, 18). Second, visiting specialists rely on secondhand information rather than comprehensive surveys. Third, even if newspapers and other media are surveyed, this too can bias the foreign observer since journalism, according to Japanese culture, is commercial by nature and tends to "report sensationally" rather than objectively on educational news items (Ichikawa 1984, 19). Finally, intellectuals tend to be antigovernment and, therefore, overly critical of educational policy and practice. This is a cultural trait and not necessarily objectively accurate. Overall, Ichikawa concludes that the differences in Japanese and American culture are such that most attempts by American scholars to correctly interpret Japanese educational practices are compromised from the beginning. What emerges from American efforts to comment intelligently on Japanese education are biased, ill-informed, and culturally irrelevant interpretations of Japan's educational policies and practices over the past thirty years.

Kobayashi

Somewhat related to this line of thought is Kobayashi's (1984) study on tradition, modernization, and education in Japan, which debunks many of the stereotypes held by most writers who seek to explain Japan's success economically and educationally. Kobayashi acknowledges the many successes that the Japanese have achieved and the creative ways they have maintained aspects of their traditional culture in the face of rapid modernization (Kobayashi 1984, 98-100). But he introduces an ecological, theoretical construct against which to discuss differences in American and Japanese pedagogy. What is perceived as rote learning by American observers in fact is part of a complex, group interaction process inherent in Japanese culture: "This 'rote' is not really repetition since, from the practitioner's point of view, each 'repetition' is regarded as always containing learning something new, such as minuscule modifications in writing the kanji [Chinese characters] each time one does it..." (Kobayashi 1984, 110).

The thrust of Kobayashi's argument is that contrary to many thinkers in the West, tradition and modernity are not mutually exclusive. In fact, aspects of Japanese tradition may contribute to their success in education:

> Thus, rote and imitation practices deemed outmoded by new scientific theories of teaching-learning which entered education in Europe and America during the time of the industrial revolution, are still maintained in the teaching-learning of traditional arts in a nation considered the most modern and industrial in Asia. Planners in developing countries sometimes argue that "tradition" prevents modernization, but this doctrine is too simplistic, as the case of contemporary Japan illustrates (Kobayashi 1984, 113).

Shimahara

A final article in this section analyzes the college entrance examination (CEE) in Japan. The CEE has long been recognized as a major shaper of both elementary and secondary school experiences. Shimahara (1978) argues that the manner in which it is administered and the nature of the kind of pressures it exerts on students is unique to Japan. He views the CEE as "...an institutionalized practice compatible with the group orientation in Japanese society..." (Shimahara 1978, 265).

While being critical of the current CEE practice in Japan, he nevertheless notes how, due to the uniqueness of Japanese culture, it does serve several important functions:

> It serves as a sorting device to assign students to certain groups in Japanese society;

> It contributes to the political stability of Japanese society;

> The drilling associated with the CEE helps instill basic knowledge at both the elementary and secondary levels (as well as disciplined behavior);

> It has created an entire industry of tutoring and this has not only created employment for thousands of people but also additional educational experiences for most Japanese children; and

> CEE promotes an achievement orientation from an early age (Shimahara 1978, 262).

Shimahara believes the system should be changed due to the extraordinary pressures placed on students, but he and others who have studied the CEE in Japan recognize it as being imbedded in the deeper culture of the society and, therefore, not easily adopted by other cultures nor easily discarded.

Critique

All of the studies referred to above have in various ways lauded the Japanese system of education. But another body of literature exists that challenges the foundation of the positive perception of Japanese education. In fact, these studies range from the mildly critical to those that morbidly suggest that Japanese education is in a state of absolute decline. In light of the exuberant praise for Japanese education on the one hand, or reluctant admiration on the other, it is worthwhile to examine the critical literature on Japanese education to place in perspective the current debate on Japanese student achievement as it compares with the record in other nations.

Western Critiques

The studies in this category emanate from both Western and Japanese scholars. White (1984) provides an interesting tour through the Japanese educational system, a system she acknowledges produces superior educated products. However, she details the costs involved in achieving the educational successes so positively noted in the literature referred to above. The stress placed upon students by parents and society to achieve has created what some psychotherapists refer to as "school phobia" (White 1984, 99).

Other signs of trouble are cited by White. She reports on the relatively new "battered teacher" and "battered parent" syndrome. Problems in identifying superior intellect are noted and attributed to the fact that the Japanese do not track students in the manner that American schools do. "The superbright may indeed be disadvantaged" (White 1984, 100). She also admits to the stifling of creativity in Japanese schools, but insists that creativity is engendered in a different way than in the United States.

On the whole, White's critique is mild and tempered by her conclusion: "We should see Japan as establishing a new standard, not as a model to be emulated" (White 1984, 101). In her view, Japan is coping with its problems better than we are with ours.

More along the lines of popular stereotyping of Japan and its educational system (and problems) is the article by Rosenberg (1983). Rosenberg states: "...a visit to a Japanese campus is like a trip backward in time to a long forgotten day when authority was respected without questions and traditional values reigned...In Japan, achievement is all that counts...There are signs that Japan is paying a heavy price for the failure of its schools to foster the development of independence and creativity" (Rosenberg 1983, 47, 48, 52). The tone of this article is that Japan succeeds but at an enormous cost.

Tobin (1984) summarizes some of the critical literature on Japanese education in an effort to demonstrate that American critiques of Japanese education are "...sometimes right, sometimes wrong, and always self-serving" (Tobin 1984, 6). He notes that many writers idealize American education while being harshly realistic when discussing Japanese education. He maintains that much of the critical literature on Japanese education is culture-bound, narrowly focused (on such sensational topics as "examination hell," teenage suicide, and school violence), concentrated on the top 5 percent of the student cohort, and "...tell us much more about our problems, our values, and about how we view our lives, than they tell us about Japan" (Tobin 1983, 19). Finally, he asserts that the American critiques almost always lack data upon which to base their wide-ranging assumptions about Japan's educational problems.

Japanese Critiques

By way of contrast, Japanese commentators on their own educational system are much harsher and more critical. Although their critiques range from mild to highly critical, their tone is much less forgiving than that of their American counterparts.

As Japan entered the 1980s, several governmental studies and conferences were held to assess the strengths and weaknesses of the entire Japanese educational system. These reassessments are summarized in Kobayashi (1980). The problems of the 1960s and 1970s (lack of quality in teaching, overexpansion of the educational system, what Ronald Dore called the "Diploma Disease," student alienation and unrest) have endured into the 1980s according to Kobayashi. Major tasks for this decade will be to create more flexibility in the system as a whole, to further diversify higher education, to internationalize higher education in particular but the entire system in general, and generally to improve the quality of the educational experiences of Japanese students (Kobayashi 1980, 242-44). To accomplish these tasks, Kobayashi suggests that a fundamental reform of Japanese education will have to be undertaken.

Amano (1984) provides a similar, more detailed reassessment of the Japanese educational "crisis" but distinguishes between a crisis "created" by politicians and one that is rooted in the structure of Japanese society (Amano 1984, 3). At the secondary level, the most critical problem for Japan is the "selectiveness of admission under the universalized secondary school system" (Amano 1984, 6). The rise of prestigious private prep schools, the declining prestige of vocational schools, and the increasing competition of the general public high school have created a host of problems for educators, students, and parents alike. The pace of competition has not slackened over the years and in fact has increased. Japanese secondary education has become more hierarchical, and this has resulted in a rigid curriculum, inequities, and psychological pressure (Amano 1984, 12).

These problems are reflected as well at the higher educational level. Here problems center on increasingly difficult placement of graduates, low quality of undergraduate education, and the underdevelopment of graduate education (Amano 1984, 18-19). Universities are also not responding to the needs of adult learners and the notion of "lifelong learning" has not developed well in Japan.

Amano concludes that higher education is the "weakest and most problematic part of the Japanese educational system" (Amano 1984, 21). His critique continues as he focuses attention on "examination hell" and the dysfunctional outcomes of this selection process. His discussion concludes with a criticism of "overstructurization" of Japanese society in general and education in particular. As the society becomes more differentiated, less equitable, and the success function attributed to schools becomes more rigid, the greatest problem facing Japanese education in the future will be "the crisis of aspiration originating from an overstructurization of society" as increasing numbers of Japanese youth opt out of the system and "are not willing to join the competition" (Amano 1984, 31-32).

A more specific focus on "examination hell" is provided by Iga (1981). His study demonstrates how this system of examinations, while producing high achievement results and economic successes, creates enormous social and individual stress often resulting in suicide. He notes how a combination of family pressures (overly strict family environment), the examination system, weak ego, and Japanese views of life, death, and suicide all contribute to this particular outcome of Japan's urge to achieve (Iga 1981, 26-29). Iga neither judges nor condemns this situation but simply concludes: "It may be said that suicide is a more or less institutionalized adjustment mechanism in Japan" (Iga 1981, 29).

A more ominous note is taken in the last article in this section by Kitamura (1984). He states that education as a whole in Japan is in a state of decline: financially, in terms of enrollments, and public trust. The number of dropouts has increased dramatically at the primary and secondary levels, absences are on the increase, as is school violence (Kitamura 1984, 1-6). Another source of evidence for Japan's declining educational system is the increase in volume of criticism from abroad, particularly from the United States. Japanese educators are particularly sensitive to foreign criticism, and in fact some reforms have been stimulated by this criticism. Finally, the need to develop a more "student-centered" educational system is also identified as a much needed reform for Japanese higher education (Kitamura 1984, 34). The system from top to bottom is undergoing major changes according to Kitamura and critical reforms will be necessary to reverse this state of "decline."

Conclusion

The evidence on the cognitive and noncognitive characteristics of Japanese students and the prevailing wisdom regarding cultural influences on these characteristics have been recounted. Throughout, the account has been dictated by the empirical data and the inferences its gatherers have made based upon them. Now, from an inherently American perspective, the "armchair" explanations for cognitive performance data from the Japanese are offered, in particular the mathematics and science results and the virtual absence of evidence elsewhere.

The reasoning, strongly influenced by data from the various IEA studies, Stevenson and his colleagues, and books by Rohlen (1983) and to some degree, Cummings (1980), is as follows:

> Start with a society that is concerned about making the most of its human resources and respects and appreciates education and educators;

> Add a cooperative relationship between the private sector and the government that is committed to developing, through education, the whole person-citizen who has a command of mathematical and scientific knowledge deemed as essential to economic productivity and progress;

> Ensure that both the home and the school support these goals;

> Offer a curriculum (nationally) that emphasizes the development of algorithmic reasoning across a wide range of topics, concepts and skills;

> Provide extensive practice in a broad array of applications;

> Train prospective teachers extensively in both content and in pedagogical strategies designed to enhance algorithmic reasoning and applied problem solving skills;

> Develop comprehensive curriculum guides; and

> Offer inservice activities that reinforce this orientation.

Japanese education in mathematics (and perhaps in other subjects as well) does a good job of making the novel familiar. Most students become adept at "figuring out what the problem is," recognizing the algorithms that are applicable from among those that they have committed firmly to memory, and then applying the algorithm accurately. Japanese students cover a lot of material in school and spend a good deal of time in what some might view to be drill-and-practice work, but there seems to be a clear purpose in approaching instruction in this way. Presumably, through practice, the routine aspects of algorithmic operations become automated, requiring less time and thought and thereby shifting the mental exercise to one of problem recognition. Experience with a wide array of content and problem types simplifies the problem solving task because the student is more likely to have seen a similar problem before. Moreover, there is continuity over the years in applying the system; the student is unlikely to find dramatic shifts in instructional strategy from one year to the next.

In trying to understand why there was so little performance information outside the areas of mathematics and science, several related explanations surfaced. First, there are known difficulties in attempting to transfer language-oriented tasks across cultures. What are the English language equivalents to Japanese characters? How does one control for passage across languages in reading comprehension, social studies, and literature? These concerns have plagued the IEA studies over the years even when countries shared at least a common alphabet. The difficulties one has to surmount are foreboding, as Stevenson and his colleagues clearly portray.

A second possible explanation has to do with wise investment of resources. Whether it is true or not, the Japanese believe that human capital in the areas of mathematics and science is important to their economic prosperity. Therefore, they are willing to invest in efforts that help them document the state of knowledge in these areas and how their students are doing comparatively. While learning is important in other areas also to produce the well-educated and well-rounded citizen, it is not the focus of concern for economic development. Moreover, it is harder to examine performance in areas other than mathematics and science comparatively. Therefore the thinking is to concentrate and invest resources in what is most important.

The other side of the coin is that one should "put one's best foot forward" in public. Most Japanese educators, and business and government leaders, are proud of the image derived from their country's performance in international comparisons of educational achievement. It reflects well on the society as a whole and apparently impresses business and government leadership in other countries. Yet, outside of the mathematical and scientific areas, the emphasis in Japanese schooling might be sufficiently distinctive from that in Western Europe and the United States to make it more difficult to reflect the accomplishments of Japanese students.

Coupled with the difficulty of developing culturally fair tests in content areas that are heavily language dominated, the Japanese question the investment of effort while still risking the possibility of conveying a misleading impression about the quality of Japanese schooling outside of mathematics and science.

What is distinctive about curricula in Japanese schools (from an American perspective) in areas other than mathematics and science? Several features of the curricula stand out. First, while it is widely known that students in Japan spend more time in school during a year than U.S. students, it is less well-known that this additional time is spread among more subjects for more years than in the typical U.S. curriculum. According to international studies and various other reports, Japanese students take nine subjects through the end of the lower secondary school compared with six subjects in the United States. English, music, art, and moral education are part of every student's course of study until the upper secondary level (tenth grade).

Second, coursework in all areas is more systematic, comprehensive, and uniform than in the United States. Music is a case in point. According to Abdoo (1984), Japanese music education covers a combination of music history, theory, conducting, instrumental and choral performance, and reading and writing of music at progressively more complex levels through the ninth grade; both Western and traditional Japanese music are studied. Abdoo claims that by the time of graduation from lower secondary school, almost every person can read music and has the basic historical and theoretical tools to enjoy it. Coursework in social studies, humanities, literature, and the arts also appears to be broad-based with heavy doses of Western culture and thought. Rohlen (1983) notes that "social science textbooks encourage the development of a high level of competence and sophistication both in the facts of civics, history, and geography and in the principles of economics. Most high school students can understand economic and social policy,... grasp the interplay of domestic and external factors" (Rohlen 1983, 256).

A third feature worth noting is the nature of the learning rather than its content as one progresses through the secondary school years. There appears to be an emphasis on what might be termed convergent (as opposed to divergent) thinking skills. Instructional emphasis is heavily oriented toward mastery of facts, attention to details, and developing the skill to apply information and theory to solving problems. This orientation is dictated, at least in part, by the importance of the examination system (both for upper secondary school and university eligibility), which typically emphasizes objective, selection questions (multiple choice, short answer) and excludes production questions (essays and written composition).

Rohlen (1983, 93-101) presents examples of questions from university exams that, in his view, epitomize the thrust of Japanese curriculum in secondary schools. In one question, students are asked to fill in fifteen blanks appearing in a long passage on ancient Greek thought, choosing their answers from a list of forty names, places, dates, eras, and schools of philosophy. The subject matter of the passage, so central to an understanding of the history of Western thought, is not likely to be part of the schooling of American students until their early university years, if at all. Even then, there would probably be less focus on the mastery of facts and details and more on what Greek philosophy has to say about independence of thought and rationality. The same sort of emphasis is seen in exam questions taken from other areas outside of mathematics and science.

In an attempt to portray the focus of instruction in Japan, especially during the secondary school years, the appropriateness of Japan's emphasis on memorization of facts and attention to detail is not questioned. The same point holds for the attempts to explain the reasons for Japanese performance in mathematics and science and the limited availability of comparative evidence in other areas. It would be the height of cultural arrogance to view Japanese society and schooling from a narrowly American perspective. The activities and actions that characterize Japanese education, the characteristics of its citizens, and the choice of information to collect about them, are dictated by values, purposes, and needs of their society and culture, not by ours. If a difference in interests and emphases causes data about their characteristics to be noncomparable to U.S. data (the standardization of the WISC-R in Japan is a case in point, as is the general indifference to providing information about occupational status), this limitation should be viewed as an inherent feature of cross-cultural comparison rather than a shortcoming or an evasion of the issues that the data might help Americans address.

References

Abdoo, F.B. 1984. "Music Education in Japan." *Music Educator's Journal* 70:6, 52-56. (EJ293970)

Amano, I. 1984. "The Socio-Political Background of Educational Crisis in Japan." Paper presented at the East-West Center Conference on Learning from Each Other.

Anderson, A.M. 1982. "The Great Japanese IQ Increase." *Nature* 279, 180-81.

Burstein, L., and J. Hawkins. 1986. *Analysis of Cognitive, Non-Cognitive and Behavioral Characteristics of Students in Japan.* Washington, D.C.: National Institute of Education

Burstein, L., ed. (In press). *The IEA Study of Mathematics III: Student Growth and Classroom Processes in Lower Secondary Schools.* Oxford: Pergamon Press.

Chang, L., and J. Ruzicka. 1985. *Second International Mathematics Study United States Technical Report I: Item Level Achievement Data Eighth and Twelfth Grades.* Champaign, IL: Stipes Publishing Co.

Comber, L.C., and J.P. Keeves. 1973. *Science Achievement in Nineteen Countries.* New York: John Wiley & Sons.

Cummings, W. 1980. *Education and Equality in Japan.* Princeton, NJ: Princeton University Press.

-----. 1984. "Japanese Images of American Education." Paper presented at the East-West Center Conference on Learning from Each Other.

Fetters, W.B., F.A. Owings, L.E. Suter, and R.T. Takai. 1983. "Schooling Experiences in Japan and the U.S.: A Cross-National Comparison of High School Students." Presented at the 1983 Annual Meeting of the American Educational Research Association, Montreal, Canada.

Flynn, J.R. 1983. "Now the Great Augmentation of the American IQ." *Nature* 301, 655.

Garden, R. 1985. *Second IEA Mathematics Study: Sampling Report.* Washington, D.C.: Center for Education Statistics.

Haberman, C. 1985. "Japan's School System Fails to Pass a Hard Nosed Test." *The New York Times*, June 12, p. F1.

Harnisch, D.L., and T. Sato. 1983. "Differences in Educational Influences and Achievement in Mathematics for Secondary Students in Japan and the United States." Paper presented at the ICMI-JSME Regional Conference on Mathematical Education, Tokyo.

Harnisch, D.L., H.J. Walberg, S.L. Tsai, T. Sato, and L.J. Fyans, Jr. 1986. "Mathematics Productivity in Japan and Illinois." In *Evaluation in Education: International Progress.*

Hess, R.D., K. Kashiwaga, S. Nagano, K. Miyake, G. Hatano, H. Azuma, W.P. Dickson, S. Holloway, G. Price, and T. McDevitt. 1985. "Family Influences on School Readiness and Achievement in Japan and the United States: An Overview of Longitudinal Study." In H. Stevenson, H. Azuma, and K. Hakuta, eds., *Child Development and Education in Japan*, Freeman Publishers.

Holloway, S.D., K. Kashiwagi, R. Hess, and H. Azuma. nd. "Causal Attributes by Japanese and American Mothers and Children about Performance in Mathematics."

Husen, T., ed. 1967. *International Study of Achievement in Mathematics: A Comparison of Twelve Countries*, vols. 1 and 2. New York: John Wiley & Sons.

Ichikawa, S. 1984. "American Perceptions of Japanese Education." Paper presented at the East-West Center Conference on Learning from Each Other.

Iga, M. 1981. "Suicide of Japanese Youth." *Suicide and Life-Threatening Behavior* 11:1, 17-30.

Kifer, E., and D. Robitaille. 1989. "Attitudes, Preferences, and Opinions." In D.F. Robitaille and R.A. Garden, eds., *The IEA Study of Mathematics II: Contests and Outcomes of School Mathematics.* Oxford: Pergamon Press, pp. 178-208.

Kitamura, K. 1984. "Education in a State of Decline in Japan?" Paper presented at the East-West Center Conference on Learning from Each Other.

Kobayashi, T. 1980. "Into the 1980's: The Japan Case." *Comparative Education* 16:3, 237-44.

Kobayashi, V.N. 1984. "Tradition, Modernization, Education: The Case of Japan." *Journal of Ethnic Studies* 12:3, 95-118.

Lerner, B. 1982. "American Education: How Are We Doing?" *The Public Interest* 69, 59-82.

Lynn, R. 1977. "The Intelligence of the Japanese." *Bulletin for British Psychological Society* 30, 69-72.

-----. 1982. "IQ in Japan and the United States Shows a Growing Disparity." *Nature* 297, 222-23.

-----. 1983. Untitled (Lynn replies). *Nature* 306, 292.

Makita, K. 1968. "The Rarity of Reading Disability in Japanese Children." *American Journal of Orthopsychiatry* 38, 599-613.

McKnight, C., F. Crosswhite, J. Dossey, E. Kifer, J. Swafford, K. Travers, and T. Cooney. 1987. *The Underachieving Curriculum: Assessing U.S. School Mathematics from an International Perspective.* Champaign, IL: Stipes Publishing Co.

Ministry of Education. 1958. *Mathematics Achievement Test in Japan: The 1956 Nation-Wide Survey.* Tokyo: Monbusho.

-----. 1959. *Mathematics Achievement Test in Japan: The 1957 Nation-Wide Survey.* Tokyo: Monbusho.

National Institute for Educational Research. 1981. *Mathematics Achievement of Secondary School Students. Second International Mathematics Study, National Report of Japan: Vol. I (Tables and Figures)*. K. Ishizaka, trans. Tokyo: National Institute for Educational Research.

-----. 1982a. *Mathematics Achievement of Secondary School Students, Second International Mathematics Study, National Report of Japan: Vol. II (Tables and Figures)*. K. Ishizaka, trans. Tokyo: National Institute for Educational Research.

-----. 1982b. *Mathematics Achievement of Secondary School Students, Second International Mathematics Study, National Report of Japan: Vol. III (Tables and Figures)*. K. Ishizaka, trans. Tokyo: National Institute for Educational Research.

Robitaille, D.F., and R.A. Garden. 1989. *The IEA Study of Mathematics II: Contexts and Outcomes of School Mathematics*. London: Pergamon Press.

Rohlen, T.P. 1983. *Japan's High Schools*. Berkeley: University of California Press.

-----. 1986. "Japanese Education: If They Can Do It, Should We?" *The American Scholar*, winter, 29-43.

Rosenberg, N.S. 1983. "Education in Japan: A Study in Contrasts." *Independent School* 42:3, 47-53.

Schiller, D., and H.J. Walberg. 1982. "Japan: The Learning Society." *Educational Leadership* 39:6, 411-12.

Shimahara, N.K. 1978. "Socialization for College Entrance Examinations in Japan." *Comparative Education* 14:3, 253-66.

Stevenson, H.W., and H. Azuma. 1983. "IQ in Japan and the United States." *Nature* 306, 291-92.

Stevenson, H.W., H. Azuma, and K. Hakuta, eds. 1985. *Child Development and Education in Japan*. Freeman Publishers.

Stevenson, H.W., S. Lee, and J.W. Stigler. 1986. "Mathematics Achievement of Chinese, Japanese, and American Children." *Science* 231, 693-99.

Stevenson, H.W., S. Lee, J. Stigler, and G.W. Lucker. 1984. "Family Variables and Reading: A Study of Mothers of Poor and Average Readers in Japan, Taiwan, and the United States." *Journal of Learning Disabilities* 17:3, 150-56.

Stevenson, H.W., J.W. Stigler, G.W. Lucker, and S. Lee. 1982. "Reading Disabilities: The Case of Chinese, Japanese, and English." *Child Development* 53, 1164-81.

Stevenson, H.W., J.W. Stigler, S. Lee, and G.W. Lucker. 1985. "Cognitive Performance and Academic Achievement of Japanese, Chinese, and American Children." *Child Development* 56, 718-34.

Stevenson, H.W., J.W. Stigler, G.W. Lucker, S. Lee, C. Hsu, and K. Kitamura. 1986. "Classroom Behavior and Achievement of Japanese, Chinese and American Children." In R. Glaser, ed., *Advances on Instructional Psychology*. Hillsdale, NJ: L. Erlbaum Associates.

Stigler, J.W., S. Lee, G.W. Lucker, and H.W. Stevenson. 1982. "Curriculum and Achievement in Mathematics: A Study of Elementary School Children in Japan, Taiwan, and the United States." *Journal of Educational Psychology* 74:3, 315-22.

Tobin, J.J. 1984. "American Images of Japanese Secondary and Higher Education." Paper presented at East-West Center Conference on Learning from Each Other.

Torrance, E.P. 1980. "Lessons about Giftedness and Creativity from a Nation of 115 Million Overachievers." *Gifted Child Quarterly* 24:1, 10-14.

Travers, K.J. 1985. "The Second IEA Mathematics Study in the United States: Some Personal Reflections." Conference on Statistical Standards for International Assessment of

Student Achievement in Science and Mathematics. Washington, D.C.: National Academy of Sciences.

-----, and C.C. McKnight. 1985. "Mathematics Achievement in U.S. Schools: Preliminary Findings from the Second IEA Mathematics Study." *Phi Delta Kappan*, February, 407-13.

-----, and I. Wesbury, eds. 1989. *The IEA Study of Mathematics I: Analysis of Mathematics Curricula*. Oxford, England: Pergamon Press.

Tsukada, M. 1984. "A Factual Overview of Education in Japan and the United States." Paper presented at the East-West Conference on Learning from Each Other.

Vining, D.R. 1983. "Mean IQ Differences in Japan and the United States." *Nature* 301, 738.

Weiner, B. 1976. "An Attributional Approach for Education Psychology." In L.S. Shulman, ed., *Review of Research in Education* 4, 179-209.

Weisz, J.R., F.M. Rothbaum, and T.C. Blackburn. 1984. "Standing Out and Standing In, the Psychology of Control in America and Japan." *American Psychologist* 39:9, 955-69.

White, M.I. 1984. "Japanese Education: How Do They Do It?" *Public Interest* 76, 87-101.

Wolfe, R.G. 1983. "*Processing of Selected Longitudinal Data Files, Second Study of Mathematics*. Technical Report No. 1. Toronto, Canada: Ontario Institute for the Study of Education.

Youth Development Headquarters. 1984. *The Japanese Youth: In Comparison with the Youth of the World*. Tokyo: Youth Development Headquarters.

CHAPTER 7

CREATIVITY IN JAPANESE EDUCATION

Catherine C. Lewis
University of California, San Francisco
and
Developmental Studies Center, San Ramon

This chapter addresses the relationship between education and creativity in Japan, and is divided into three major parts. The first section addresses the definition and measurement of creativity. The second section reviews evidence on the factors that promote or inhibit the development of creativity. The third section discusses Japanese education in light of the theory and research reviewed in parts one and two.

Definition and Measurement of Creativity

Introduction: Creativity and Western Views of Japan

> I discuss the subject of creativity with considerable hesitation, for it represents an area in which psychologists generally whether they be angels or not, have feared to tread (Guilford 1968, 77).

> The term creativity is used with something approaching gay abandon...(Nicholls 1972).

> Definitions of creativity range all the way from the notion that creativity is simple problem solving to conceiving it as the full realization and expression of all of an individual's unique potentialities (MacKinnon 1970).

Creativity research has targeted three major issues: the creative process, the creative product, and the creative person. Assumptions about the causes of creativity influence the choice of outcomes and research methods. For example, researchers who assume that creativity is a stable trait of individuals may use personality tests to identify the aspects of childrearing which influence creativity. On the other hand, researchers who hypothesize that creativity is a product of certain situations such as brainstorming may scrutinize differences between Japan and the United States in the ways groups solve problems.

MacKinnon (1970) wrote, "One would be ill advised to seek to choose from among these several meanings the best single definition of creativity, since creativity properly carries all of these meanings and many more besides. Creativity is, indeed, a multifaceted phenomenon." Following the spirit of MacKinnon's advice, this chapter will focus broadly on the many facets of personality, product, and process that have been called "creativity."

The impact of Japanese social and educational practices on creativity has been a subject of intense discussion. While some observers portray Japanese society as rich in creative accomplishments in the arts and industry (for example, Torrance 1980 and Vogel 1979; see page 229 on societal indicators of creativity), others posit an inability to conceive original ideas as a critical failing of Japanese society. Variations in definitions of creativity may partially account for this disparity. At least four different senses of creativity seem to inform Western writings on Japan.

Originality

Novelty, the capacity to produce new ideas or new combinations of existing ideas, is an issue frequently discussed with regard to Japan. The notion that Japanese success is built on the skillful adaptation of ideas that originated outside Japan is frequently repeated, and frequently disputed. The factors in Japanese education that may facilitate or inhibit the tendency to produce novel ideas or solutions will be discussed.

Deviation from the Group

In discussion on the issue of creativity with American and Japanese researchers, conformity and uniformity are frequently mentioned as indices of lack of creativity in Japan. For example, the tendency of school children to arrange desk contents in a uniform way and the tendency of Japanese adults to order the same dish when eating as a group in a restaurant were both offered as examples of lack of creativity. Whether or not conformity in behavior is predictive of low originality (that is, low production of novel ideas), the two appear to be linked in the minds of many observers.

Self-Expression

Self-expression, including aesthetic and emotional expression, is a third sense in which researchers use the word "creativity." This aspect of creativity often overlaps with originality, but may also be distinct. For example, children's creative writing may not be original, in the strict sense of novel ideas, but may be thought valuable for the experience it gives in awakening or developing expression of aesthetic impulses.

Achievement

Some writings on Japan equate creativity with high achievement (for example, Torrance 1980). This is not surprising in view of the common linking of the two aspects of behavior. For example, "gifted" and "talented" are often combined for educational purposes, virtuosity is studied as an aspect of creativity, and so forth. While psychologists may continue to debate the relationship between creativity, achievement, and intelligence (for example, Crockenberg 1972, Cronbach 1970, and Nicholls 1972), there is evidence that at least some measures of creativity are independent of measured intelligence (Wallach and Kogan 1965). However, most models of creativity include attention both to intelligence and to achievement. Intelligence is sometimes posited as a necessary but not sufficient condition for creativity. However, many researchers do not believe that there is a simple relationship between creativity and intelligence (for example, Guilford 1981); that relationship probably depends greatly on the nature of the creative domain in question. Achievement is frequently used as a measure of creativity and also as a means of assessing motivation toward creative accomplishment (for example, MacKinnon 1968 and Walberg 1969). Particularly if real-life societal indicators of creativity are compared, rather than specially derived IQ-independent or achievement-independent measures, it is likely that indices of creativity will also measure, to a greater or lesser extent, achievement and intelligence.

While there may be many other senses of creativity, concern with originality, achievement, distinctiveness from the group, and self-expression appear to characterize much of the Western interest in creativity in Japan. Of the four aspects of creativity outlined above, originality would seem to have the most obvious relationship to scientific progress and economic benefit. However, very little is known about the interconnections, if any, among the four aspects of creativity. It is possible that a high degree of originality may be dependent on a social or educational climate that tolerates substantial diversity of behavior and deemphasizes individual conformity. It is equally possible that originality and social conformity are quite independent. This review includes evidence on all four aspects of creativity. It is important to keep in mind the distinction among these aspects and the lack of evidence regarding possible interconnections.

Measurement of Creativity

Reviews of creativity research reveal diverse approaches to the measurement of creativity and suggest that this diversity has been a major stumbling block in the progress of creativity research (see, for example, Amabile 1982). Major approaches to the measurement of creativity include the following:

Creativity Tests

A common approach to the measurement of creativity, particularly during childhood, has been the use of standardized tests. These tests are reviewed in standard reference works on assessment (for example, Buros 1974, Cronbach 1970, and Goodwin and Driscoll 1982) as well as by creativity researchers (for example, Amabile 1982). One of the most widely used batteries is the Torrance Tests of Creativity (Torrance 1962). Subtests measure both verbal and artistic creativity, and include tasks such as thinking of many different uses for a common object, and writing stories on unusual topics (for example, the dog that does not bark). The scoring of the test takes into account the number, variety, statistical infrequency, and degree of development of the ideas generated. The Torrance Tests are typical of many creativity tests in form, content, administration, and scoring.

The relationship between performance on creativity tests and production of creative products is not clear (see reviews by Amabile 1982 and Cronbach 1970). In particular, conceptual definitions of the creative product suggest that it must not only be novel, but also be appropriate or useful. Standardized tests measure novelty more readily than appropriateness, which, Amabile argues, is best measured by consensual judgments of experts within a given field. Cronbach (1970) presents evidence that one test of creativity, the Remote Associates Test, does show impressive validity with real-world indicators of creativity, including patents, scientific productivity, research grants, and rated creativity.

A second problem with creativity tests is that they are designed to assess the variance in creativity due to personality traits, and not that portion due to environmental influences. In looking at creativity in Japan, the influences of both personality and environment (for example, how tasks are structured or rewarded) will be considered.

Societal Indicators

A second approach to the measurement of creativity is societal indicators. For example, Japan's high number of inventions and patents, high number of novels published yearly, and the nature of the trade imbalance between the United States and Japan have all been cited as evidence of Japanese innovation and creativity (Seward 1977, Torrance 1980, and Vogel 1979). While such indicators have obvious appeal, they may also have shortcomings. For example, the use of patent rate as a form of Japanese intercompany competition may inflate Japan's patent rate relative to the United States; the nature of the trade imbalance may be influenced by trade barriers; per capita newspaper reading rates may mask reading of very different materials; and so forth. While this review will cite relevant indicators wherever possible, their limitations should be kept in mind.

Consensual Assessment

A third approach to measuring creativity is to have creative products rated by multiple experts in the field, resulting in reliable, subjective judgments (Amabile 1982). For example, by using this technique, artists and art teachers rating the creativity of children's collages showed very high inter-rater reliabilities (.77 to .88). This would seem to be a promising technique for cross-cultural research. For example, the creativity of product innovations or of children's science projects could be evaluated by a group of experts in the relevant field.

Influences on Creative Behavior

This section briefly identifies and discusses factors that have been demonstrated or posited to influence creativity. As noted above, the definition of creativity is broad and includes the creative personality, process, and product. Both the evidence on the factors which influence creativity and the evidence on the Japanese situation are spare. This section might better be read as a catalogue of hypotheses than as a review of established findings. It should be noted that this discussion of influences on creativity is based on *Western* theory and empirical research.

What are the factors that inhibit or promote creative performance? After a brief review of the evidence on childrearing and creativity, Amabile's (1983) model of the components of creative performance will be presented. Amabile's model identifies three major components of creative performance: domain-relevant skills (for example, knowledge of nuclear physics); creativity-relevant skills (for example, breaking a perceptual set, suspending judgment); and task motivation (for example, attitudes towards the task).

Influences of Parenting Styles on Creativity

Perusing any library or bookstore section on childrearing suggests that creativity can be fostered through appropriate early childrearing. Titles such as *Guiding Your Child to a More Creative Life* abound. Research on the childrearing antecedents of creativity is limited. Much of the existing research investigates the two dimensions of parent behavior which are at the core of much developmental psychology research: warmth and control. A 1982 review by Rejskind concludes that there is mixed evidence regarding parent warmth and children's creativity, but much firmer evidence regarding parent control styles and children's creativity. Control refers to a dimension of adult behavior which ranges from high control or restrictiveness, at one end, to high autonomy-granting or independence at the other. While the eighteen studies reviewed by Rejskind (1982) employed a wide variety of measures of control and of creativity, the overall pattern of results suggests a clear and positive, if not always strong relationship between parent auton-omy-granting and children's creativity. The notion that the individual can actualize creative potential only if given psychological freedom, or only if possessing the freedom to explore unconscious impulses, has also been at the root of many psychoanalytic and phe-nomenological theories of creativity (for example, Hacker 1965).

Domain-Related Skills

An essential prerequisite for creativity, according to most accounts, is thorough mastery of the skills and knowledge of the domain of creative endeavor. Amabile (1983) calls this set of pre-requisites "domain-relevant skills," and identifies subcategories such as knowledge, talent, and technical skills. Such domain-relevant skills might include, for example, detailed knowledge about the properties of various chemical compounds, advanced proficiency on a musical instrument, or the ability to imagine a three-dimensional structure from a two-dimensional drawing. Most theorists propose that task-related skills are the product both of innate abilities and of education and experience.

There is a popular notion that too much knowledge of a given subject matter reduces creativity. (This is sometimes humor-ously referred to as the "immaculate perception" notion of creativ-ity.) Amabile's summary of evidence suggests just the contrary: "an increase in domain-related skills can only lead to an increase in creativity, provided that the domain-relevant information is orga-nized appropriately" (Amabile 1983, 364). By "appropriately," Am-abile means knowledge that is organized according to general prin-ciples, rather than as specific, narrowly applicable collections of facts. As seen below, the issue of appropriate organization of knowl-edge is a key issue with respect to the acquisition of knowledge for Japanese entrance examinations.

Creativity-Related Skills

The preceding section discussed the acquisition of basic skills related to a particular domain of endeavor: for example, musical techniques or information about chemical properties. This section discusses more general creativity skills that cut across various do-mains of creative endeavor. These skills might be thought of as the "something extra" which distinguishes creative performance from performance which is merely highly competent. Amabile's (1983) conceptual framework identifies three categories of creativity-related skills. These include a cognitive style appropriate to creative problem solving, conscious or unconscious knowledge of the strategies for generating novel ideas, and a work style conducive to creative achievement.

Cognitive Style Appropriate to Creative Problem Solving: Amabile (1983) includes in this category such aspects of cognitive style as breaking out of a perceptual set (for example, envisioning an unusual use of an object); keeping response options open (for example, approaching a canvas without a definite plan for a painting); generating ideas while suspending evaluative judgments; remembering accurately; critically examining one's own problem-solving process; and using broad organizational categories that forge relations between apparently diverse bits of information. An additional aspect of cognitive style important to creativity may be "problem finding." Research suggests that one difference between highly creative and less creative individuals is that creative people notice problems where others do not (Guilford 1968). As MacKinnon wrote:

> The creative process starts always with the seeing or sensing of a problem. The roots of creativeness lie in one's becoming aware that something is wrong, or lacking, or mysterious. One of the salient traits of a truly creative person is that he sees problems where others don't....(MacKinnon 1973, 20).

Knowledge of the Strategies for Generating Novel Ideas: The second category of creativity-related skills identified by Amabile (1983) is knowledge, either intuitive or explicit, of strategies for generating novel ideas. These include such strategies as "when all else fails, try something counterintuitive" (Newell, Shaw, and Simon 1962); or the use of case studies or paradoxical incidents to generate hypotheses (McGuire 1973).

Work Style Conducive to Creativity: In this category, Amabile (1983) includes such elements of work style as the ability to concentrate efforts for long periods of time, and such personality characteristics such as perseverance in the face of frustration, absence of conformity in thinking, and low dependence on social approval.

Although Amabile (1983) reviews considerable research linking the three categories of creativity-relevant skills described above with creative achievement, current research is far from definitive in several respects. First, most creativity-related skills have been studied only for one or a very limited range of creative domains. They may or may not be helpful in other areas. For example, suspending evaluative judgment in order to brainstorm may aid in generating new ideas for product development, but may prove unhelpful or even distracting and detrimental to creative problem solving in theoretical physics. In fact, quite different skills may be needed for creativity in different domains, or even during different phases of a single creative endeavor (Nicholls 1972). For example, problem finding may demand skills antithetical to those required for problem solving.

A second problem is the as yet unestablished cross-cultural validity of the creativity-related skills identified by American research. Although much has been written regarding the personality characteristics, such as low social conformity, that facilitate creative achievement (for example, MacKinnon 1968 and Stein and Heinze 1960), these personality characteristics may differ across cultures. For example, an anecdote reported by Ouchi (1981) suggests that different social conditions may promote creativity in Japan and the United States. An American company's program to solicit productivity improvement suggestions from Japanese employees was a dismal failure as long as rewards were offered for individuals' suggestions; a switch to group rewards for group suggestions stimulated a flood of new ideas from employees. Employees explained to an American manager that they were embarrassed to suggest ideas as individuals because "production improvements come from watching others." Although it is common for Americans to think of creativity as the result of individual maverick genius, research by Ouchi (1981) suggests that highly successful and innovative American companies are likely to show a strong emphasis on shared group responsibility and other features typical of large Japanese corporations.

Motivation

Motivation is the third component of Amabile's model, after task-related and creativity-related skills. Amabile calls motivation "the most important determinant of the difference between what a person can do and what he or she will do" (Amabile 1983, 366).

Researchers have been particularly interested in the impact on creativity of intrinsic versus extrinsic motivation. Intrinsic motivation is the desire to engage in an activity because of properties of the activity itself (for example, enjoyment of tinkering in the laboratory). In contrast, extrinsic motivation is the desire to engage in an activity because of extrinsic rewards (for example, money, grades, praise). Intrinsic motivation is a product of both personality and situation. For example, people differ in the extent to which they intrinsically enjoy tinkering in a laboratory. Situations differ in the extent to which external rewards are offered for tinkering.

One of the most intriguing findings of intrinsic motivation research is that, under certain conditions, salient extrinsic rewards for engaging in an activity may undermine an individual's intrinsic motivation to engage in that activity. For example, by promising children rewards for coloring pictures with magic markers, researchers actually reduced children's subsequent coloring (when rewards were no longer given) (Lepper, Greene, and Nisbett 1973). Similar decrements in performance were not seen among children who were not rewarded or who were rewarded incidentally (that is, not promised the reward as a condition of participation). How can the negative impact of a promised reward be explained? The children promised a reward may have come to perceive themselves as coloring only in order to receive the reward, and this self-perception may have decreased their subsequent interest in coloring when not rewarded. The promised rewards may also have focused children's attention on the rewards, reducing their attention to and enjoyment of the process of coloring.

Several studies directly link extrinsic motivation to decreased creativity. Amabile (1979) found that anticipation of external evaluation reduced the creativity of children's art work. Amabile (1985) also found that questions focusing creative writers' attention on the extrinsic reasons for writing reduced the creativity of poems written; questions focusing on intrinsic reasons for writing increased the creativity of poems written. Decrements in creativity when a reward is offered for performance have been shown by other researchers for other age groups as well (for example, Kruglanski, Friedman, and Zeevi 1971).

Diverse evidence also suggests that anticipated rewards may prompt individuals to alter their problem-solving styles. They may attempt easier problems, be less efficient in information acquisition, make more errors and stereotypical responses, achieve less "incidental" learning, and be more answer-oriented and less logical

(Condry 1977 and Maehr and Stallings 1972). Children's creativity may be greater under gamelike than under testlike conditions (Dentler and Mackler 1964).

Like reward, other practices such as surveillance or evaluation which direct attention to the extrinsic aspects of tasks may undermine intrinsic motivation. For example, children's intrinsic motivation to engage in a task can be undermined by surveillance alone (Lepper and Greene 1975). With a reduction in intrinsic motivation may come reduced attention to the process of tasks, including reduced creativity. For example, the ability to "break mental set" when an entirely new problem approach is necessary is undermined by offering a reward, although performance on more routine, difficult problems is not (McGraw and McCullers 1979).

It is important to recognize the boundaries of the negative impact of rewards. Amabile's (1983) review of the impact of reward on creativity suggests that rewards are not detrimental to intrinsic motivation in all circumstances. For example, if reward is perceived as an exchange for services offered (as in the case of salary), or as an incidental "plus" by an individual who is already highly intrinsically motivated (for example, a scientist who wins a Nobel Prize), it may not have the power to affect self-perception and task attitude. It is possible that systems of early childrearing and education that foster intrinsic motivation may create individuals who are relatively immune to the detrimental effects of extrinsic rewards. The interaction between personality and social institutions may mean that a given social institution (for example, the examination system) could have quite different effects if exported to a different society. Hypothetically, it is possible that examination-oriented education could operate in Japan without undermining intrinsic motivation because of a strong early educational emphasis on intrinsic enjoyment of education. However, that same examination-oriented education could have devastating consequences for U.S. students. It should be emphasized, however, that this mere speculation is meant to illustrate the possible interactions between personality and social institutions.

Research on eminent creative individuals in various fields also suggests a strong role of intrinsic motivation in creative achievement. Self-initiated, task-oriented striving is a distinguishing characteristic of creative scientists, as well as of creative writers (Barron 1963 and Chambers 1964). Creative architects, compared to their less creative peers, tend to be guided by self-generated standards of excellence rather than by conformity to professional standards (MacKinnon 1962, 1968). It has been suggested that motivation plays a major part in the repetition of "thought trials" necessary to arrive at a new idea: "The number of trials necessary to arrive at a new construction is commonly so great that without something of a fascination for the subject one grows weary of the task. This is the emotional condition of originality of mind in any department" (Bain, cited by Campbell 1960, 385).

An aspect of creativity widely cited in subjective accounts of the creative process, but neglected by most researchers, is the desire for self-expression. The creative act may represent a means for "coming to grips with ideas and emotions of great significance, ones that cannot be articulated and mastered through ordinary conversational language" (Gardner 1982, 90). Isadora Duncan is quoted as saying, "If I could say it, I wouldn't have to dance it." Although the impact on creativity of educational strategies that promote self-expression has not been systematically studied, encouraging children's expression of emotion through various artistic media has been a central feature of many programs designed to stimulate children's creative development (Maynard 1973 and Torrance 1962).

Japan: Influences on Creativity

This section reviews evidence on the factors which may promote or inhibit creativity in Japan. The evidence is organized in sections which correspond to those in the previous section: parental styles which foster creativity; development of task-related skills; development of creativity-related skills; and motivation.

Evidence on Japanese Parental Styles

Evidence reviewed in the previous part suggests that low restrictiveness by parents is related to high creativity in children. Evidence from diverse sources suggests that, at least through early elementary school, Japanese parents fall at the very low end of the continuum of restrictiveness (Benedict 1946, Hara and Wagatsuma 1974, Lewis 1984, Peak 1987, and Vogel 1963). Japanese mothers tend to avoid making explicit demands on their children and do not enforce rules when children resist. *Amae*, sometimes translated as "indulgence," has been described as the centerpin of Japanese early childrearing (Doi 1973). The early childhood years in Japan may well be a time of freedom unparalleled in the life of an American child (Benedict 1946). While evidence on Japanese childrearing during middle childhood and the adolescent years is somewhat more sparse than for the early years, anthropological accounts do not suggest any sharp discontinuity in childrearing. It has been suggested that, at least traditionally, parents transfer much responsibility for the more unpleasant parts of childrearing, such as restrictions and punishment, to other social institutions, perhaps including the school (Benedict 1946, Hara and Wagatsuma 1974, and Singleton and Singleton 1984).

The American studies of parenting styles related to children's creativity do not, for the most part, identify the specific behaviors related to high creativity in children. Nevertheless, on the level of global dimensions such as restrictiveness vs. autonomy-granting, Japanese childrearing during the early years does appear to approximate the situation of low restrictiveness, which empirical work and theory suggest is a key condition for the development of creative potential.

Japanese Education: The Acquisition of Task-Related Skills

Japanese Achievement in Skill Acquisition

Diverse sources suggest that the Japanese educational system is excellent, perhaps even the best in the world, in imparting knowledge and skills in a number of subject matters. Best known are the high scores of Japanese youth on international tests of science and mathematics (Comber and Keeves 1973, Walberg 1986, and Walberg, Tsai, and Harnisch 1984). Recent comparisons of mathematics achievement among Japanese, Taiwanese, and American first and fifth graders demonstrate that Japanese children exceed American children in mathematics achievement as early as the first grade, and that this difference is not attributable to differences in innate cognitive abilities (Stigler, Lee, Lucker, and Stevenson 1982). Nor is the difference likely to be accounted for by differences in the mathematics curriculum in the two countries, since achievement differences appear even for concepts which have been taught in both countries. Rather, the researchers point to such factors as amount of time spent in mathematics instruction, children's attentiveness to instruction, and time spent on homework as possible keys to the cross-national differences in achievement.

Less publicized, but equally impressive, are Japanese achievements in reading. The Japanese literacy rate of 99 percent (Woronoff 1983) is particularly noteworthy since the Japanese language has two syllabaries, each with 46 letters, 1,850 required ideographs (some very complicated, with twenty or more strokes), and 1,000 or more additional characters necessary for a high degree of literacy. Furthermore, most ideographs have multiple pronunciations.

Japanese school achievements in music, art, and physical education are also noteworthy. For example, all Japanese learn to read music and play several musical instruments. Cummings (1980) provides a further discussion of Japanese achievements in nonacademic subjects.

Memorization and Creativity

The preceding litany of Japanese accomplishments could be extended considerably (see Cummings 1980, Torrance 1980, and Vogel 1979). It appears that Japanese education provides a high level of training not only in academic subjects, but also in nonacademic and aesthetic pursuits. But does the nature of this training facilitate subsequent creative achievement in the humanities, mathematics, science, and the arts? As noted above, thorough knowledge of a given domain is essential to creative achievement in the domain. But certain types of learning, particularly emphasis on general principles, are likely to facilitate creativity. Other types of learning, including rote memorization and learning which deemphasizes meaning, may not facilitate creativity. One well-known cognitive psychologist asserts: "the more we concentrate on...heavily contextualized (specific) concepts and propositions, the less capacity we will have available to learn general principles and questions that crosscut different areas and perspectives" (Wickelgren 1979, 382).

Does Japanese education emphasize rote memorization or meaningful integration of concepts? While the answer to this question is a matter of some debate (for example, Sayeki and Miyake 1983 and White 1987), several generalizations may be drawn from existing research. First, early and primary education probably emphasize general principles and thinking skills more than does secondary education, which may emphasize memorization more strongly.

Second, there is probably a major difference in the teaching of thinking versus memorization between what we might call

Japan's official and "shadow" school systems. Public and private schools comprise the official school system; *juku* (after-school schools) including exam preparation schools ("cram" schools) comprise Japan's shadow school system. Nearly one-half of Japanese ninth grade students, and as many as 30 percent of sixth grade students and a substantial number of high school students attend after-school schools (*juku*) designed to improve performance on junior high, high school, or college entrance examinations (Leestma, August, George, and Peak 1987). (This figure does not include *juku* that focus on nonexam subjects such as calligraphy, music, swimming, or English conversation.) Accounts of Japanese "examination hell" and the stresses it places upon children, families, and teachers can be found in many English-language sources (Cummings 1980; Cummings, Amano, and Kitamura 1979; Rohlen 1983; Vogel 1963; Vogel 1979; and Woronoff 1983). Two potential effects of the examination system on creativity should be noted. One, the impact of the examination system on students' subsequent motivation to learn, will be discussed in the section on motivation and creativity. The second is the impact of examination preparation on students' ways of thinking and integrating information; this issue will be discussed here.

What sorts of memorization and thinking skills are required by university entrance exams? Rohlen writes:

> Emphasis is on mastery of facts, control over details, and practiced skill in the application of mathematical and scientific principles. As most anyone with experience in exam taking realizes, some forms of learning and knowledge can be tested with precision and some are measured inadequately by the inherent nature of virtually any question answer approach. Science and math fit the short-answer mode comfortably, humanities and social science do not (Rohlen 1983, 95).

The example below reproduces Rohlen's translation of an item from the 1974 entrance examination of Kobe University:

> Select the appropriate answer for each numbered blank space from the list that follows the passage below. Fill in the dates directly.

The philosophy that arose in ancient Greece
had an enormous influence on subsequent human
thought. The earliest forms, (1)_____ philosophy,
arose in the (2)_____century in the (3)_____ region. Liberating itself from the mythological
approach to natural phenomena, this philosophy
aimed to explain the fundamentals of nature in a
rational manner. (4)_____, who explained the
origin of things to be water, and (5)_____, who
treated the basis of matter mathematically, were
representative scholars of the age. Following the
war with (6)_____, democratic government was
implemented with Athens as its focal point, and a
school of teachers, the (7)_____, arose to give instructions to citizens in the arts of public debate.
This development began the division of philosophy
into component fields. As can be seen in the famous
phrase, "Humans have many ways of measuring
things," of (8)_____, the existence of absolute
causality was denied by the assertion of subjective
understanding. (9)_____ offered counter-argu-
ments to this in his teaching. Known for his special
questioning of students as a way of teaching them to
understand the truth, he was misunderstood by his
society and sentenced to death. One of his students,
(10)_____, recorded his words and also bequeathed
to the world a theory of idealism and a treatise on
political utopia, and another student, (11)_____,
drew together and synthesized all of existing Greek
philosophy, for which he is now regarded as the figure representative of Greek learning at its zenith. In
the latter half of the (12)_____ century, Hellenism
arose, and, reflecting the decline of the democratic
independent city-state, philosophy shifted from being
primarily part of the education of a democratic citi-
zenry to being part of the tendency to seek psychological solace and contentment. The (13)_____
school, which explained matters in terms of pleasure
and pain, and the (14)_____ school, which sought
to eliminate appetites, were characteristic of the age.
Both subsequently spread to the aristocracy of ancient Rome, where Emperor (15)_____, who wrote

his confessions, and the philosopher (16)_____
were representative figures.

a. Academia	u. Attica
b. Aristedes	v. Aristotle
c. Aristophenes	w. Archimedes
d. Antonius Pius	x. Ionia
e. Euripides	y. Epicurean
f. Cicero	z. Xenophon
g. Chrysippus	aa. Enlightenment
h. Constantine	bb. Natural Philosophy
i. Natural law	cc. Absolutism
j. Existentialism	dd. Stoic
k. Seneca	ee. Socrates
l. Sophists	ff. Thales
m. Solon	gg. Hadrian
n. Dorian	hh. Phaedrus
o. Pythagoras	ii. Protagoras
p. Plato	jj. Persia
q. Hesiod	kk. Polybius
r. Peloponnesus	ll. Marcus Aurelius
s. Macedonia	mm. Laconian
t. Mycenae	

Answers: (1) i, (2) 6th B.C., (3) x, (4) ee [sic], (5) o,
(6) ii [sic], (7) l, (8) hh [sic], (9) ee, (10) p, (11) v,
(12) 4th B.C., (13) y, (14) dd, (15) kk [sic], (16) k
(Rohlen 1983, 96-97).

[Editor's note: The correct answers to questions 4,
6, 8, and 15 are, respectively, ff, jj, ii, and ll.]

This item dramatically demonstrates the degree of factual
knowledge demanded by entrance examinations; Greek history
comprises only a fraction of the material which must be mastered
by students. The sheer volume of material to be mastered means
that classroom teachers jeopardize students' entrance examination
performance by "wasting" time discussing the meaning, implications, or relevance of material presented. Rohlen writes that:

The emphasis of Japanese education is on disciplined apprenticeship in which, through arduous study, basic knowledge is memorized. The student is trained first to be a patient, persistent worker, a good listener, one preoccupied with details and correctness of form. Unlike many of their American counterparts, they do not learn a glibness that has little foundation in knowledge. But Japanese students learn to keep their thoughts largely to themselves, even as their minds mature (Rohlen 1983, 269-70).

What is the impact on creativity of this "disciplined apprenticeship"? Does the experience of memorizing large bodies of factual information obviate, or even undermine, skills of critical thinking and the ability to forge conceptual links? One possibility is that these skills are learned equally well in Japan, but are not openly demonstrated in the Japanese high school. A second possibility is that these skills are learned somewhat later in Japan. A third possibility is that the centering of education on memorization results in lasting deficits in critical and analytic thinking skills. Although no data are available on the influence of examination-oriented memorization on analytic skills, Walberg et al.'s (1986) analysis of data obtained by the International Association for the Evaluation of Educational Achievement provides some evidence on Japanese children's analytic skills in mathematics. Japanese ten- and fourteen-year-olds outperformed students in compulsory school in other countries not only on items requiring information, but also, and by a greater margin, on subsections tapping understanding, application, and higher processes such as hypothesis formation. These subsections tap the most creative aspects of mathematics.

The connection between knowledge and analytic skills in Japanese mathematics proficiency underlines the considerable psychological research and theory that links expertise or creativity in a domain with detailed and accessible knowledge of the domain. Walberg (1986) reviews evidence from Simon (1978 and 1981), Newell and Simon (1972), and others suggesting that experts differ from novices in science, chess, and some other fields in having more information in permanent memory, being able to bring it into conscious memory rapidly, and having items of information elaborately linked so that information can be retrieved by alternate links if certain links are lost. Newell et al. write: "there is a high correlation between creativity (at least in the sciences) and proficiency in the more routine intellective tasks that are commonly used to measure intelligence" (Newell, Shaw, and Simon 1962, 145).

Walberg's findings and the psychological research and theory in the area raise the possibility that the herculean efforts of memorization which are the heart of Japanese secondary (and perhaps late primary) education may not be harmful, or may even be beneficial, in the development of creatively functioning experts. However, two shortcomings of current knowledge should be noted. First, psychological theory and research suggest that memorization of large quantities of factual information would be beneficial only to the extent that it is meaningfully organized, using crosscutting conceptual principles, rather than specific tricks of memory. For example, let us consider two ways of memorizing the functions of the various muscles in the body. One student memorizes the function of each muscle in the body by visualizing the particular movement which could not be conducted without that muscle. A second student devises a clever acronym linking muscle names and function names. The first student, who memorizes using meaningful associations, may set up a much more enduring and creatively enabling knowledge network than the second student. If examination preparation focuses on use of memory "tricks," an interesting question is whether these strategies can be discarded, and strategies that may better facilitate conceptual integration and creativity adopted, in adulthood.

A second unanswered question is the impact of examination-centered education on creativity in the nonsciences. The theories and research that link creativity to greater and more accessible information and to proficiency on routine intellectual tasks are concerned with scientific creativity. It is possible that the skills which facilitate creative endeavor in the social sciences and humanities differ from those described for the natural sciences, and that the impact of the examination system may be particularly detrimental to creativity in these "softer" areas. This is a hypothesis that remains to be tested.

Screening by the Examination System: Impact on Creativity

An additional impact of the examination system on creativity may be to screen out of higher education, or screen out of the more competitive institutions of higher learning, individuals with certain creative abilities who do not "test well." Examples might be individuals with highly discrepant quantitative and verbal abilities, individuals who are intensely interested in one area of subject matter but not in others, and individuals with creative skills not tapped by the entrance examinations either to academic or performing arts schools (for example, creative writers, debaters, individuals with a genius for diplomacy or politics). MacKinnon reports that creative architects, in comparison to their less creative peers, tend to achieve high grades only in the courses which interest them: "...creative persons share, then, the fundamental characteristic of not being particularly interested in achieving in situations which demand conforming behavior but, rather, are strongly motivated to achieve in situations that demand independence in thought and action...."(MacKinnon 1968, 152).

Practice, Mastery, and Creativity: The Japanese View

Although "examination hell" is a recent phenomenon in Japanese society, learning through persistence and repetition is not. Many traditional Japanese arts and trades emphasize learning by repeated practice (rather than by explanation or experimentation) and by mastery of set forms (with only minor innovations after many years of study) (Rohlen 1976 and Singleton and Singleton 1984). As Rohlen points out, in Japanese aesthetic pursuits, freedom is an end product of years of devotion to mastery of established forms, not a prerequisite for artistic expression. Herrigel, a student of Japanese archery, eloquently makes this point:

> Far from wishing to waken the artist in the pupil prematurely, the teacher considers it his first task to make him a skilled artisan with sovereign control of his craft. The pupil follows out his intention with untiring industry. As though he had no higher aspirations he bows under his burden with a kind of obtuse devotion, only to discover in the course of years that forms which he perfectly masters no longer oppress but liberate. He grows daily more capable of following any inspiration without technical effort, and also of letting inspiration come to him through meticulous observation. The hand that guides the brush has already caught and executed what floated before the mind at the same moment as the mind began to form it, and in the end the pupil

no longer knows which of the two--mind or hand--
was responsible for the work (Herrigel 1953, 60).

What all of this suggests is that repetitive tasks and imita-
tion of set forms may have a very different relationship to creative
endeavor in Japan than in the United States. Nevertheless, many
Japanese arts have produced internationally recognized creative
products and individual practitioners.

Mastery of established forms through repetitive practice is
more than simply a pedagogical technique; it is the path to self-cul-
tivation (Rohlen 1976 and Singleton and Singleton 1984). Practicing
calligraphy or piano is not simply acquiring a skill; it is a form of
spiritual self-improvement. The Suzuki method for teaching violin is
known in the United States mainly for its ability to produce extraordinary musical accomplishment in the very young; yet, the
avowed goals of the program are not to train musicians, but to cultivate "sensitivity, service to others, and nobility of character"
(Taniuchi (Peak) 1986). As Taniuchi (Peak) notes, when the Suzuki
method is practiced in the United States, the spiritual components
are often lost, and the pragmatic goal of producing skilled musicians
becomes paramount. Practice, self-improvement, and creative
achievement are linked in Japanese pedagogy. Anthropologist
Thomas Rohlen reports being told by his teacher of Japanese
painting: "All of your academic work which has integrity will pay
off in your art" (Rohlen, personal communication, 1985).

In view of the intense social criticism contemporary
Japanese direct at the examination system (Cummings, Amano,
and Kitamura 1979), it would be naive to regard examination-oriented education as a natural outgrowth of mastery-oriented traditional teaching styles. Nevertheless, the parallels between mastery
of examination of information and mastery of skills in traditional
arts do exist. In the traditional arts, repetitive practice and memorization of set forms is compatible with creative achievement. While
the intellectual domain may differ from the artistic in the conditions
that nurture creative accomplishments, the possibility of creative intellectual accomplishments through emphasis on memorization and
mastery of factual information cannot be discarded.

Mastery of Forms and Creativity: Gardner's Theory

Gardner's (1982) theory of creativity in children provides an
interesting perspective on Japanese training in basic skills. Gardner

seeks to explain the transition from the "golden age of creativity" during the preschool years to the "literal stage" of early elementary school, when children whose speech and drawings had formerly qualified them as poets and artists suddenly "limit their graphic efforts to the faithful copying of forms about them" (Gardner 1982, 88). Unlike educators who vilify the school system for robbing children of their creativity, Gardner views the literal stage as a crucial phase of development: the time for mastering rules. He posits that quite different educational strategies may foster creativity during the preschool years and during the later "literal phase" of elementary school:

> During the natural artistry of the preschool years, active intervention is unnecessary; simply equipping children with materials (paints or xylophones) and exposing them to works (stories or drawings) suffices. But with the onset of school and the preoccupation with rules and convention, the environment must assume a more active role. This is a time when children crave knowledge of how to do things: they want to know how to play an arpeggio, render a drawing of a building in perspective, or write a mystery (or even a parody of Sherlock Holmes). Accordingly, teachers willing to instruct and models of how to do things become crucial.
>
> Indeed, I suspect that there exists a kind of "sensitive period" during the years preceding adolescence. The future artist needs to acquire skills at a rapid rate so that by adolescence he is already accomplished in his craft. If he is, he can then withstand the rise in critical powers of his adolescent years and still conclude, "I'm not that bad" (Gardner 1982, 89-90).

Many Japanese educators suggest that creativity is fostered by mastery of basics during elementary school. Some psychological theory draws the same conclusion.

Creativity as a Japanese Cultural Value

Several sources of evidence suggest that Japan and the United States may differ in the cultural value placed upon creativity. As discussed above, creativity in the Japanese arts is achieved through repetition and mastery of prescribed forms. Deviation from the prescribed forms is a mistake, not creativity, unless one has already achieved mastery by devoting to the art the many years necessary to attain the status of expert. Self-expression and originality, in and of themselves, may not be valued as highly in Japan as in the United States (LeVine and White 1986, Rohlen 1976, and Singleton and Singleton 1984). For example, Azuma and Kashiwagi's (1987) investigation of Japanese concepts of the intelligent person found originality to be a relatively unimportant component of concepts of intelligence. Nor does originality predict academic success in Japan to the extent that it does in the United States (Kashiwagi et al. 1984). Longitudinal evidence on the predictors of school achievement in the United States and Japan reveals that originality at age four predicts school achievement at age eleven to twelve in the United States but not in Japan. In contrast, persistence at age four predicts later school achievement in Japan but not in the United States. These findings suggest that originality in the United States, and persistence in Japan, enable children to succeed in their respective educational systems. Other data from the same study suggest that Japanese mothers emphasize conformity to social standards, while U.S. mothers emphasize verbal self-assertiveness, as developmental tasks during the preschool years (Azuma, Kashiwagi, and Hess 1981).

Observations of Japanese elementary schools by Peak (1985) and Lewis (1987) suggest that enforcement of uniform standards of behavior may extend to different domains within Japanese classrooms more than within U.S. classrooms. For example, classroom charts demonstrate the correct configuration for storing study materials in one's desk; detailed school procedures dictate the number of pencils and handkerchiefs which each child must bring to school daily (and scheduled self-evaluations of compliance occur); and children practice washing their hands, opening their desks, and storing their belongings until they achieve a uniform standard of performance. While Americans tend to view such cultivation of uniformity as antithetical to individual expression and creativity, these practices coexist with an emphasis on self-expression in academic subjects as well as in art and music, and with encouragement of energetic, noisy, and even rowdy behavior during some academic activities. Thus, early elementary education in Japan emphasizes some practices Americans associate with creativity (including self-expression and originality) while it emphasizes disciplined mastery

of prescribed forms in areas such as hygiene, decorum, and neat-
ness. Disciplined mastery and rowdy self-expression may not be
contradictory educational goals; Japanese children may learn that
both types of behavior are appropriate, depending on the setting
(Peak 1987).

Creativity-Related Skills

Recognizing Problems: An Aspect of Creativity

> We hear a great deal about the "divine discontent" of
> the creative person. It is said that Thomas A. Edison
> frequently admonished his workers with the com-
> ment, "There must be a better way. Go and find it."
> The uncreative, in contrast, are often willing to set-
> tle for half-way measures and tolerably successful
> solutions to problems (Guilford 1968, 107).

The foregoing suggests that complacency is the enemy of
creativity. Problem finding may be a creativity-related skill in which
Japanese excel. A common feature of accounts of successful
Japanese product development is the Japanese recognition and solution of minor problems not recognized by other researchers. For example, the varistor (voltage-dependent resistor) is a device invented
in Japan that prevents minute variations in voltage from causing
instabilities on the television screen. Uchihashi suggests that the
Japanese developed the varistor because they were not content to
ignore the miniscule instabilities of the television screen, and "felt
driven to spare no effort in investigating the cause of such instabil-
ity" (Uchihashi 1983, 16). Thus, they recognized and pursued a
problem that others did not. Uchihashi attributes to the varistor the
continued product competitiveness of Japanese television sets in foreign markets, despite their loss of cost competitiveness.
　　An unwillingness to be satisfied with current levels of performance may be a characteristic that cuts across many aspects of
Japanese performance. For example, studies reveal that Japanese
children report lower levels of satisfaction with themselves than do
United States or European children (Kashiwagi 1983). While this
finding may be attributable to some extent to cultural differences in
modesty or in response style, Kashiwagi argues convincingly that it
also reflects different internal standards of comparison; Japanese

children may choose as a reference point a higher standard of behavior. Nagano links the academic achievement of Japanese children to their feelings of low self-esteem: "As they feel incomplete they keep on trying to understand and memorize.... They are anxious to learn anything because of a sense of incompleteness or immaturity" (Nagano 1986, 2). Speculatively, it is interesting to ask whether a child's choice of stringent standards of comparison may be related to standards chosen by classroom teachers or to other cultural traditions. Self-criticism and self-reflection are encouraged by teachers as early as first grade (Lewis 1989). In many traditional Japanese arts, years of devoted study are necessary even to graduate from the status of novice. Speculatively, the tendency to choose a high standard of comparison, and to search for problems in one's performance, maybe a creativity-related skill which is highly developed in Japan.

Self-Expression in Japanese Education

Does the Japanese educational system promote self-expression by students? Rohlen's (1983) account suggests that encouragement of expression of emotions through regular academic activities is not a prominent feature of high schools, but that nonacademic activities, including club activities, sometimes permit a degree of self-expression which would go beyond the bounds of propriety in the United States. Observations of Japanese elementary schools suggest that self-expression is an integral part of the curriculum in many areas (Lewis 1989). For example, first graders were observed in wild, free-form dancing to rock'n'roll music; in acting out music and stories with their bodies; in animated discussion of their "treasures" during a reading lesson about a boy's treasures; and in recalling at great length the smells, feelings, and sights of potato-digging in a composition. In arithmetic classes focused on measurement, children gleefully devised such activities as lying on the floor to measure it in body lengths and standing on each others' shoulders to create an object taller than the teacher. E.P. Torrance, a major proponent of educational strategies that foster self-expression, was deeply impressed with creative expressiveness he witnessed in Japanese preschools (Torrance 1980).

Tolerance for Rejection of Conventional Thinking

Western accounts of creativity suggest that the creative person or product is unconventional. Included in Newell, Shaw, and Simon's definition of creative problem solving is that "the thinking is unconventional, in a sense that it requires modification or rejection of previously accepted ideas" (Newell, Shaw, and Simon 1962, 65). This definition suggests that a climate hostile to the "rejection of previously accepted ideas" might also be a climate hostile to creativity. Japanese classrooms at the secondary level may focus on memorization of accepted ideas, rather than on creating a climate that permits their rejection. The extent to which Japanese classrooms support or stifle unconventional thinking, and the long-term implications for creativity, are not known. Rohlen's (1983) account suggests that the busy high school curriculum simply may not include time for indulging in departures from conventional thinking in quest of creativity. Other accounts suggest that Japanese elementary education demands behavioral conformity by students in areas which United States schools might consider personal, such as behavior when children are out of school, hygiene at home and school, and so forth.

Whether these demands for behavioral conformity are accompanied by demands for intellectual conformity is not known. The Ministry of Education's control over textbook content has received sharp criticism as a force undermining the creativity and life of classroom activity (Horio 1988). In one textbook approval incident which received notoriety, the Ministry of Education failed to approve a well-respected work of literature because of certain unapproved sound effects (syllables which expressed the sounds of nature). The ensuing debate focused on whether the ministry had the right to identify certain syllables, but not others, as correct expressions of natural sounds such as the movement of a stream. Rohlen's comments on Japanese textbooks also suggest a self-censorship of potentially controversial material:

> Although high school textbooks do not actually carry the strong imprint of official government attitudes, they have been purged of materials potentially critical of the government's position. And in order to appeal to teachers and avoid the scorn of the union, textbooks avoid topics and style offensive to the left. They are thus characterized by a bland neutrality on

key social and political issues....Authors also differ in
the way they add touches of salt or pepper to subjects, but all avoid stronger spices (Rohlen 1983,
249).

Intolerance of divergent ideas may also be bred by the examination system. As Rohlen (1983) observed, unusual or provoca-
tive interpretations of historical events are irrelevant to students
who are preparing for examinations on factual content. That
examination preparation may put intellectual blinders on children,
making them unwilling to entertain divergent, creative thoughts,
has long been a concern to Japanese intellectuals. In the 1960s, es-
sayist Hajime Yamashita made famous the child whose answer was
marked wrong because, in response to the question "When snow
melts, what does it become?" she said, "Spring."

Despite the possible impact of examinations in reducing tolerance for divergent thinking, observations of elementary education
in Japan suggest that Japanese teachers recognize a variety of children's approaches to mathematics and science problems (Easley and
Easley 1981 and Lewis 1989). It is not yet known to what extent
the stereotype of Japanese as uncreative may stem from highly
visible conformities in behavior (similar clothing or group choice of
the same meals) and to what extent Japanese education actually
may foster intolerance for divergent thinking in the intellectual
domain.

Japanese Education and the Development of Intrinsic Motivation

Use of Rewards in Japanese Classrooms

Accounts of Japanese early childrearing, preschool education, and early elementary education all suggest that Japanese parents and teachers go to great lengths to help children develop a
sense of internal control over both schoolwork and discipline. For
example, the popular Suzuki method of teaching violin to young
children focuses on techniques for building children's interest in music. These include having the child watch the mother's violin classes
for months before the child is offered an opportunity to play, allowing the child to play violin only for short times when intensely interested, terminating each practice session before the child loses interest, and so forth (Taniuchi (Peak) 1986). Nursery school teachers

also use management techniques and disciplinary strategies likely to foster a child's own desire to follow rules. For example, children "themselves" decide what the classroom rules will be; teachers' responses to misbehavior suggest not that offending children have willfully misbehaved but that they have "forgotten" or not "understood" the rules; much of the monitoring and enforcement of rules is left to the children themselves (Lewis 1984).

The literature review in the previous section suggests that external rewards and evaluation can undermine children's intrinsic motivation and creativity. Rewards and grades are not a noticeable part of early elementary education in Japan. For example, recent observations of fifteen first grade classrooms in Tokyo public elementary schools revealed that none of the teachers used what American teachers often call motivators (stars, prizes, rewards) for either behavioral or academic achievements. One progress chart for songs mastered on a small wind-keyboard instrument, the pianica, was observed, and several classrooms had charts on which children had themselves identified and charted progress on individual goals ("learning to write Chinese characters," "finishing all my lunch," "playing outside without fighting").

Pedagogical techniques during the early elementary school years also emphasize stimulating and fostering children's intrinsic interest in subject matter. A remarkable feature of the official Course of Study for Elementary Schools in Japan is the extent to which attitude, rather than simply performance, is the target of pedagogy. For example, goals include helping children "develop an attitude of willingness to express what they think about" and helping children "experience the pleasure of intimacy...[with]...living things in their surroundings" (Ministry of Education 1983, 4, 56). Observations of Japanese elementary schools suggest that these objectives are realized in practice with activities that mobilize children's interest (Cummings 1980, Easley and Easley 1981, and Lewis 1989). Attention to process as well as performance is a striking emphasis of Japanese preschool and early elementary education. Understanding, not compliance, is the first goal of discipline (Lewis 1984). Enjoyment of subject matter often assumes as much importance as mastery itself (Lewis 1989 and White 1987). High internal motivation to work among Japanese is also suggested by an international poll which asked youth in eleven countries "Why do you think man works?" Japanese were least likely among the young of the eleven nations to choose the instrumental response "to earn money"; a large percentage chose the response "to find self-fulfill-ment" (cited in Cummings 1980).

A second emphasis of Japanese elementary school education is on drill, repetition, and mastery of basics, such as arithmetic and writing (Lewis 1989). Teachers often gear the pace to the average or slower student, and efforts to keep the brighter students from being bored are not as apparent as they might be in the United States (Cummings 1980). One effect of the repetitive drill and rela-tively slow pace may be to teach children that academic work re-quires persistence, but that, with persistence, one can succeed.

Although available research suggests that conditions in the preschool and early elementary school may foster intrinsic moti-vation, curiosity, and enjoyment of the process of learning, sec-ondary school education appears to focus more heavily on an exter-nal reason for learning: entrance examinations. One Japanese educational researcher has suggested that docility, not curiosity, facilitates learning in the exam-centered system (Nagano 1986).

That preparation for examinations can undermine subse-quent motivation is suggested by no less an intellect than Albert Einstein, who wrote that the process of "cram[ming] all this stuff into one's mind" for a physics examination was so unpleasant that afterward he could not bring himself to consider scientific problems for an entire year (Schilpp 1949). Einstein wrote:

> It is, in fact, nothing short of a miracle that the modern methods of instruction have not yet entirely strangled the holy curiosity of inquiry; for this deli-cate little plant, aside from stimulation, stands mainly in need of freedom; without this it goes to wreck and ruin without fail (Schilpp 1949, 17).

Although the ability of external rewards, surveillance, and evaluation to undermine intrinsic motivation and creativity has been demonstrated in well-controlled studies (see above and reviews by Amabile 1983 and Condry 1977), the societal implications of an exam-system such as Japan's have not been researched. We do not know whether any impact on intrinsic motivation and creativity, if it exists, would be short-lived or permanent; whether it would ex-tend to the full range of an individual's creative endeavors or a nar-row domain of academic activities; whether the examination system places all individuals equally at risk or particularly affects those with initially low intrinsic motivation. An impressive feature of psychological research on intrinsic motivation is that seemingly trivial manipulations, such as being promised a gold seal or filling out a questionnaire on extrinsic rewards, can substantially undermine creativity. The major impact of these small, one-time interventions suggests that the impact of a major force such as the entrance examination could be dramatic indeed.

Arenas of Creativity Neglected by Research

This section briefly notes several arenas of creativity which have received little systematic attention from researchers of Japanese culture. Further research in these areas would provide a more complete picture of the ways creativity should be studied in Japan.

Innovation in Business and Industry

Increasingly, writings suggest that Japanese industry is not only a skillful adaptor, and that Japanese companies have shown considerable creativity in their innovations (Gregory 1984, Ishii 1983, and Uchihashi 1983). Some researchers link Japanese creativity to motivation and persistence on the part of workers (Peters and Waterman 1982 and Uchihashi 1983). Creativity of industrial or business innovation might be an excellent target for investigation by the technique of expert consensual judgment described above (Amabile 1982).

Creativity in the Sciences

Aiso et al. (1985) provide evidence that the proportion of United States papers presented to two international societies of electronics researchers has declined dramatically, while the proportion presented by Japanese researchers has increased dramatically. While indices such as papers and scientific honors have obvious shortcomings, scientific achievement might be well suited to study by consensual judgment (Amabile 1982). In addition, interviews with the large number of scientists who have conducted research in both Japan and the United States might provide valuable insights into the factors that inhibit or promote creative endeavor in the two countries.

The Arts

The continued popularity of the traditional art forms in Japan and the emergence of new art forms suggest that the arts are an area of continued vitality (Kobayashi 1990). Once again, expert consensual judgment of Japanese accomplishment in this area might round out the understanding of creativity in Japanese society.

Interpersonal and Social Creativity

Some aspects of creativity in Japanese society may not be captured in the categories of creative endeavor, such as art and science, typically studied in the United States. Ingenuity in reasoning about the needs, feelings, and perspectives of others might be considered a form of creativity. A common thread in many accounts of successful Japanese business products is thoughtful reasoning about the needs of the consumer. For example, Japanese companies developed the first watches with alarms which automatically signal prayer time to Moslem wearers. As Vogel (1979) has noted, Japanese companies gather a great amount and high quality of information about the countries where they operate. An ability to anticipate the needs of others (even if their lifestyles differ from the Japanese as widely as that of devout Moslems) is an aspect of creative behavior worthy of study. There is evidence that learning to recognize and anticipate the needs and perspectives of others is a feature of early Japanese education (Lewis 1984).

Summary

As the foregoing pages suggest, English-language research on creativity in Japan is sparse. Basic research does suggest some tentative conclusions about the facets of Japanese education which may encourage or inhibit creativity. These are summarized below.

Mastery of Basic Skills

Substantial psychological research suggests that mastery of basic skills in a subject matter area is an essential prerequisite for creativity. Fluency with the basic subject matter separates creative from noncreative individuals. There is ample evidence, from international tests, that Japanese education does an exceptionally good job of teaching basic skills in mathematics and science; evidence on literacy and accounts of Japanese schooling suggest that language, art, and music skills are also widespread and of a high level. Ethnographic evidence also suggests that drill and mastery of established forms is an integral part of traditional Japanese learning in the arts, and that creativity is considered to be a product of disciplined submission to established forms, rather than a prerequisite for artistic endeavor. It is unclear, however, whether students' memorization for examinations provides an informational base for later creativity; some psychological research suggests that rote memorization (in contrast to integration of information by meaningful principles) does not facilitate creativity.

Creativity-Related Skills

Some evidence suggests that originality may be differently valued in the United States and Japan. For example, originality may help a child succeed in school in the United States but not Japan, and may be a more central part of the concept of intelligence in the United States than in Japan. Observations of Japanese schools suggest that original thinking, self-expression, and expression of feelings through aesthetic pursuits are all fostered in the Japanese elementary school. These qualities are less apparent in Japanese secondary school teaching, but may be fostered in school-sponsored, nonacademic activities. The system of entrance examinations in Japan may screen out students with creative abilities who do not also test well. For example, children with discrepant verbal and quantitative abilities and talents in domains not tested (for example, leadership) may not enter higher education, or may enter higher educational institutions lower in prestige, from which it is harder to advance to key societal roles. Problem finding (noticing a problem where others do not) may be a creativity-related skill in which Japanese excel. This skill may be linked to a tendency to be unsatisfied with current levels of performance, or to choose a high standard of comparison.

Motivation

Motivation is another area in which Japan may excel. Elementary and preschool education in particular are designed to promote children's intrinsic motivation to engage in work, avoid external rewards and punishments that might undermine children's intrinsic motivation, and foster children's commitment to rules and procedures that allow the classroom to function well as a learning environment. However, researchers need to investigate the possible role of the examination system as an external force which may undermine students' interest in the intrinsic rewards of learning. Some Japanese educators and policymakers view Japanese postsecondary education as of low caliber compared with primary and secondary education and compared with other countries (National Council on Educational Reform 1986); this is often attributed to the negative impact of the examination system on students' motivation.

New Approaches to Understanding and Measuring Creativity in Japan

Some aspects of creativity in Japan may not be captured by the categories of creativity typically studied in the United States. For example, Japanese creativity may show up in areas such as modifying Western technology and developing products responsive to the needs of users.

Summary of Factors Which May Promote or Inhibit Creativity

Although the knowledge regarding the determinants of creativity and regarding Japanese education is quite limited, the following probable influences on creative development in Japan can be tentatively identified:

Factors Which May Promote Creativity

1) Early childrearing is not restrictive.

2) Preschool and elementary school education appear to promote conceptual integration of material, self-expression, and enjoyment of the intrinsic rewards of both academic and aesthetic pursuits.

3) Extrinsic rewards, such as grades and motivators, which might undermine intrinsic motivation, do not appear to be widely used during elementary school.

4) A high level of training in basic skills is achieved in major academic subjects, and probably in other subjects (art, music) as well.

Factors Which May Inhibit Creativity

1) Examinations may provide a powerful external incentive that undermines intrinsic motivation; low intrinsic motivation is in turn related to low creativity.

2) Examination-oriented memorization may encourage use of memory strategies that focus on trivial aspects of information, rather than on crosscutting conceptual principles. The latter type of memorization strategy is more likely to facilitate creativity.

3) Demands for behavioral conformity and low valuation of originality may socialize Japanese children away from original approaches to schoolwork.

4) The examination system may screen out creative individuals whose interests or abilities are uneven across domains or whose particular creative abilities are not the target of testing.

References

Aiso, H., J. Baba, H. Inose, J. Morizono, S. Okamura, T. Okoshi, M. Uenohara, and H. Yamaguchi. 1985. "Japanese National Attitudes with Regard to Electronics and Communication." Paper presented to the First U.S.-Japan Conference on High Technology and the International Environment, Santa Barbara, CA.

Amabile, T. 1979. "Effects of External Evaluation of Artistic Creativity." *Journal of Personality and Social Psychology* 37, 221-33.

-----. 1982. "Social Psychology of Creativity: A Consensual Assessment Technique." *Journal of Personality and Social Psychology* 45, 997-1013.

-----. 1983. "The Social Psychology of Creativity: A Componential Conceptualization." *Journal of Personality and Social Psychology* 45, 357-76.

-----. 1985. "Motivation and Creativity: Effects of Motivational Orientation on Creative Writers." *Journal of Personality and Social Psychology* 48, 393-99.

Azuma, H., and K. Kashiwagi. 1987. "Descriptors for an Intelligent Person: A Japanese Study." *Japanese Psychological Research* 29, 17-26.

Azuma, H., K. Kashiwagi, and R.D. Hess. 1981. *Hahaoya no taido/kodo to kodomo no chiteki hattatsu.* Tokyo: Tokyo University Press.

Barron, F. 1963. *Creativity and Psychological Health.* Princeton, NJ: Van Nostrand.

Benedict, R. 1946. *The Chrysanthemum and the Sword.* New York: Signet.

Buros, O.K., ed. 1974. *Tests in Print.* Highland Park, NJ: Gryphon Press.

Campbell, D.T. 1960. "Blind Variation and Selective Retention in Creative Thought as in Other Knowledge Processes." *Psychological Review* 67, 380-400.

Chambers, J. 1964. "Relating Personality and Biographical Factors to Scientific Creativity." *Psychological Monographs* 78 (7, whole no. 584).

Comber, L.C., and J.P. Keeves. 1973. *Science Education in Nineteen Countries.* New York: John Wiley.

Condry, J. 1977. "Enemies of Exploration: Self-Initiated vs. Other-Initiated Learning." *Journal of Personality and Social Psychology* 35, 459-77.

Crockenberg, S. 1972. "Creativity Tests: A Boon or Boondoggle for Education?" *Review of Educational Research* 42, 27-45.

Cronbach, L. 1970. *Essentials of Psychological Testing.* New York: Harper & Row.

Cummings, W. 1980. *Education and Equality in Japan.* Princeton, NJ: Princeton University Press.

-----, I. Amano, and K. Kitamura, eds. 1979. *Changes in the Japanese University.* New York: Praeger.

Dentler, R.A., and B. Mackler. 1964. "Originality: Some Social and Personal Determinants." *Behavioral Science* 9, 1-7.

Doi, T. 1973. *The Anatomy of Dependence.* Tokyo: Kodansha International.

Easley, J., and E. Easley. 1981. *Kitaemono School as an Environment in Which Children Study Mathematics Themselves.* Unpublished report, University of Illinois, Bureau of Educational Research, Champaign, IL.

Gardner, H. 1982. *Art, Mind, and Brain.* New York: Basic Books.

Goodwin, W.L., and L.A. Driscoll. 1982. *Handbook for Measurement and Evaluation in Early Childhood Education.* San Francisco: Jossey-Bass.

Gregory, G. 1984. *Japanese Electronics Technology: Enterprise and Innovation.* Tokyo: Japan Times, Inc.

Guilford, J. 1968. *Intelligence, Creativity, and Their Educational Implications.* San Diego: Knapp.

-----. 1981. "Factors That Aid and Hinder Creativity." In J.D. Gowan et al., eds., *Creativity: Its Educational Implications*, pp. 59-71. Dubuque, IA: Kendall/Hunt Publishing Co.

Hacker, F.J. 1965. "Creative Possibilities for a Consideration of Creativity." In H. Anderson, ed., *Creativity in Childhood and Adolescence*. Palo Alto, CA: Science and Behavior Books.

Hara, H., and H. Wagatsuma. 1974. *Shitsuke*. Tokyo: Kobundo.

Herrigel, E. 1953. *Zen in the Art of Archery*. London: Routledge and Kegan Paul.

Horio, T. 1988. *Educational Thought and Ideology in Modern Japan*. Tokyo: University of Tokyo Press.

Ishii, T. 1983. "Sustaining a Lead in High Technology." In T. Ishii, K. Uchihashi, S. Yamamoto, S. Kimura, and M. Moritani, eds., *A Look at Japanese Technological Development*, pp. 5-12. Tokyo: Foreign Press Center.

-----, K. Uchihashi, S. Yamamoto, S. Kimura, and M. Moritani, eds. 1983. *A Look at Japanese Technological Development*. Tokyo: Foreign Press Center.

Kashiwagi, K. 1983. "Another Perspective on Japanese Self-Concept." Paper presented at the Conference on Child Development in Japan and the United States, Center for Advanced Study in the Behavioral Sciences, Stanford, CA.

-----, H. Azuma, K. Miyake, S. Nagano, R.D. Hess, and S.D. Holloway. 1984. "Japan-U.S. Comparative Study on Early Maternal Influences upon Cognitive Development: A Follow-Up Study." *Japanese Psychological Research* 26, 82-92.

Kobayashi, V. 1990. "Ecological Perspectives on Kyoyo and Aesthetic Quality: Japan and America." *Senri Ethnological Studies* 28, 83-90.

Kruglanski, A., I. Friedman, and G. Zeevi. 1971. "The Effects of Extrinsic Incentives on Some Qualitative Aspects of Task Performance." *Journal of Personality* 39U, 606-17.

Leestma, R., R.L. August, B. George, and L. Peak. 1987. *Japanese Education Today*. Washington, D.C.: U.S. Government Printing Office.

Lepper, M., and D. Greene. 1975. "Turning Play into Work: Effects of Adult Surveillance and Extrinsic Rewards on Children's Intrinsic Motivation." *Journal of Personality and Social Psychology* 31, 479-86.

Lepper, M., D. Greene, and R. Nisbett. 1973. "Undermining Children's Intrinsic Interest with Extrinsic Rewards: A Test of the 'Overjustification' Hypothesis." *Journal of Personality and Social Psychology* 28, 129-37.

LeVine, R.A., and M.I. White. 1986. *Human Conditions: The Cultural Basis of Educational Development*. New York: Routledge and Kegan Paul.

Lewis, C. 1984. "Cooperation and Control in Japanese Nursery Schools." *Comparative Education Review* 28, 69-84.

-----. 1989. "From Indulgence to Internalization: Social Control in the Early School Years." *Journal of Japanese Studies* 15, 139-57.

Lewis, H. and D. Allison. 1982. *The Real World War*. New York: Coward, McCann, and Geohegan.

Lunstedt, S., and E.W. Colglazier. 1982. *Managing Innovation*. New York: Pergamon.

MacKinnon, D.W. 1962. "The Personality Correlates of Creativity: A Study of American Architects." In G.S. Nielsen, ed., *Proceedings of the XIV International Congress of Applied Psychology* (Vol. 2), pp. 11-39. Copenhagen, Denmark: Munksgaard.

-----. 1968. "Educating for Creativity: A Modern Myth?" In P. Heist, ed., *The Creative College Student: An Unmet Challenge*. San Francisco: Jossey-Bass.

-----. 1970. "Creativity: A Multifaceted Phenomenon." In J.D. Roslansky, ed., *Creativity*. New York: Fleet Academic Editions.

Maehr, M.L., and W.M. Stallings. 1972. "Freedom from External Evaluation." *Child Development* 43U, 177-85.

Maynard, F. 1973. *Guiding Your Child to a More Creative Life*. Garden City, NY: Doubleday.

McGraw, K., and J. McCullers. 1979. "Evidence of a Detrimental Effect of Extrinsic Incentive on Breaking a Mental Set." *Journal of Experimental Social Psychology* 15, 285-94.

McGuire, W. 1973. "The Yin and Yang of Progress in Social Psychology: Seven Koans." *Journal of Personality and Social Psychology* 26, 446-56.

Ministry of Education. 1983. *Course of Study for Elementary Schools in Japan*. Tokyo: Monbusho.

Nagano, S. 1983. "Docility and Lack of Assertiveness: Possible Causes of Academic Success of Japanese Children." Paper presented to the Conference on Child Development in Japanese and American Societies, Center for Advanced Study in the Behaviorial Sciences, Stanford, CA.

National Council on Education Reform. 1986. *First Report on Educational Reform*. Tokyo: Government of Japan.

Newell, A., and H. Simon. 1972. *Human Problem Solving*. Englewood Cliffs, NJ: Prentice-Hall.

Newell, A., J.C. Shaw, and H.A. Simon. 1962. "The Process of Creative Thinking." In H.E. Gruber, G. Terrell, A. Newell, H. Simon, and M. Wertheimer, eds., *Contemporary Approaches to Creative Thinking*. New York: Atherton Press.

Nicholls, J. 1972. "Creativity in the Person Who Will Never Produce Anything Original and Useful: The Concept of Creativity as a Normally Distributed Trait." *American Psychologist* 27, 517-27.

Ouchi, W. 1981. *Theory Z: How American Business Can Meet the Japanese Challenge.* Menlo Park, CA: Addison-Wesley.

Peak, L. 1985. "Management of Classroom Discipline and the Role of the Classroom Teacher." Paper prepared for the U.S. Study of Education in Japan, U.S. Department of Education.

-----. 1987. *Learning to Go to School in Japan: The Transition from Home to Preschool Life.* Unpublished doctoral dissertation, Harvard University, Cambridge, MA.

Peters, T.J., and R.H. Waterman. 1982. *In Search of Excellence.* New York: Harper and Row.

Rejskind, F.G. 1982. "Autonomy and Creativity in Children." *Journal of Creative Behavior* 16, 58-67.

Rohlen, T.P. 1976. "The Promise of Adulthood in Japanese Spiritualism." *Daedalus* , 125-43.

-----. 1983. *Japan's High Schools.* Berkeley: University of California Press.

Sayeki, Y., and N. Miyake. 1983. "From Transmission to Participation: How to Overcome the Negative Side-Effects of Schooling." Paper presented to the Conference on Child Development in Japanese and American Societies, Center for Advanced Study in the Behavioral Sciences, Stanford, CA.

Schilpp, P. 1949. *Albert Einstein: Philosopher-Scientist.* Evanston, IL: Library of Living Philosophers.

Seward, J. 1977. *The Japanese.* Tokyo: Lotus Press.

Simon, H. 1978. "Information-Processing Theory of Human Problem Solving." In W.K. Estes, ed. *Handbook of Learning and Cognitive Processes: Vol. 5. Human Information Processing.* Hillsdale, NJ: Erlbaum.

-----. 1981. *The Sciences of the Artificial.* Cambridge, MA: MIT Press.

Singleton, J. 1989. "Japanese Folkcraft Pottery Apprenticeship: Cultural Patterns of an Education Institution." In M.W. Coy, ed., *Apprenticeship: From Theory to Method and Back Again.* Albany: SUNY Press.

Stein, M., and S.J. Heinz. 1960. *Creativity and the Individual.* Glencoe, IL: Free Press of Glencoe.

Stevenson, H., H. Azuma, and K. Hakuta, eds. 1986. *Kodomo: Child Development and Education in Japan.* San Francisco: Freeman.

Stevenson, H., J. Stigler, W. Lucker, and S. Lee. 1982. "Reading Disabilities: The Case of Chinese, Japanese, and English." *Child Development* 53, 1164-81.

Stigler, J.W., S.Y. Lee, G.W. Lucker, and H.W. Stevenson. 1982. "Curriculum and Achievement in Mathematics: A Study of Elementary School Children in Japan, Taiwan, and the United States." *Journal of Educational Psychology* 74, 315-22.

Taniuchi (Peak), L. 1986. "Cultural Continuity in an Educational Institution: A Case Study of the Suzuki Method of Music Instruction." In M.I. White and S. Pollak, eds., *The Cultural Transition: Human Experience and Social Transformation in the Third World and Japan,* pp. 113-40. Boston: Routledge and Kegan Paul.

Torrance, E.P. 1962. *Guiding Creative Talent.* Englewood Cliffs, NJ: Prentice-Hall.

-----. 1965. *Rewarding Creative Behavior: Experiments in Classroom Creativity.* Englewood Cliffs, NJ: Prentice-Hall.

-----. 1980. "Lessons about Giftedness and Creativity from a Nation of 115 Million Overachievers." *Gifted Child Quarterly* 24, 10-14.

Uchihashi, K. 1983. "Making the Most of Masterly Expertise." In T. Ishii et al., eds., *A Look at Japanese Technological Development*, pp. 13-20. Tokyo: Foreign Press Center.

Vogel, E.F. 1963. *Japan's New Middle Class*. Berkeley: University of California Press.

-----. 1979. *Japan as Number One*. New York: Harper.

Walberg, H.J. 1969. "A Portrait of the Artist and Scientist as Young Men." *Exceptional Children*, 5-11.

-----. 1986. "Science and Mathematics Learning in Japanese and U.S. Schools." In H. Stevenson, H. Azuma, and K. Hakuta, eds., *Kodomo: Child Development in Japan*. San Francisco: Freeman.

-----, D.L. Harnisch, and S.L. Tsai. 1986. "Elementary School Mathematics Productivity in Twelve Countries." *British Educational Research Journal* 12, 237-48.

Wallach, M.A., and N. Kogan. 1965. *Modes of Thinking in Young Children*. New York: Holt, Rinehart & Winston.

White, M. 1987. *The Japanese Educational Challenge: A Commitment to Children*. New York: The Free Press.

White, M.I., and L. Taniuchi (Peak). 1981. "The Anatomy of the *Hara*: Japanese Self in Society." Unpublished paper from the Bernard Van Leer Project, School of Education, Harvard University, Cambridge, MA.

Wickelgren, W. 1979. *Cognitive Psychology*. Englewood Cliffs, NJ: Prentice-Hall.

Woronoff, J. 1983. *Japan: The Coming Crisis*. Tokyo: Lotus Press.

CHAPTER 8

YOBIKO: PREP SCHOOLS FOR COLLEGE ENTRANCE IN JAPAN

Robert L. August
U.S. Department of Education and the Library of Congress

The views and ideas expressed in this chapter are those of the author and do not necessarily reflect the position or policy of the U. S. Department of Education or of the Library of Congress.

Introduction

Importance of University Degree and University Exams

There is strong and pervasive emphasis on one's academic background in Japan. *Japanese Education Today* concluded:

> The education credential, not the individual talent, determines initial employment with the more prestigious companies and remains a major consideration in any employment...In Japan, one's university largely determines one's prospects for the best careers and jobs. Career patterns of various universities are widely known, and institutions are informally ranked according to the success of their graduates in securing prestigious employment (Leestma, August, George, and Peak 1987, 44).

Consequently, students are keenly aware of the difference that graduation from a particular university can make in their lives. Success on the entrance examinations for college--for certain schools in particular--takes on a special significance for Japanese students.[1] These college entrance examinations are extremely important, because subsequent graduation, virtually automatic, from the institutions to which these tests permit access is still such a major determinant of the level of career and employment success in Japan, especially for those students who aspire to work in upper echelon corporations or in the Japanese civil service.

College Entrance and Examinations

In theory, besides the entrance examination, entrance requirements also include the official high school record and an interview. In reality, it is seldom more than the entrance examination that carries any weight in other than the most borderline of admissions cases. Although it is true that there are also alternate ways to enter some institutions (particularly junior colleges)--via recommendation for example--and that the number of students gaining admission through alternative or special procedures has been rising, the numbers of such students entering the national or the local public universities remains minuscule.[2]

Part of the problem of understanding the entrance system in Japan is that there is such a bewildering number and variety of examinations. The system of college entrance examinations in Japan is tiered, and the examinations depend not only on which university one is aiming for, but also on which particular department or course one elects to enter.

Basically, many Japanese students take two sets of college entrance examinations: a national level qualifying test for national and local public universities, and a university entrance examination for the school(s) they hope to enter, whether public or private.

Joint First Stage Achievement Test

The closest thing Japan has to a uniform national college admissions test is the Joint First Stage Achievement Test, which was initially adopted for use in 1979. Currently, all national colleges, all local public colleges, and one private college, a total of 132 schools, administer this test. The number of students now taking this test annually has reached almost 370,000. Taken toward the end of January, the Joint First Stage Test is then followed by a second examination given in early March by the university to which the student is applying. Students applying to private colleges take only one examination. This is administered by the college the student wishes to enter and is usually taken in late February. The department that the student hopes to enter defines the areas and subject matter of the examination for each university, whether public or private. In 1990 a new test was introduced, the National Center for University Entrance Examination Test, and initially sixteen private colleges chose to participate.

The Joint First Stage Test is based on the Course of Study for Upper Secondary Schools, and all Japanese high school students are, in theory, expected to have covered the appropriate curriculum. The test, therefore, has a certain uniform applicability to all students. However, questions have been raised in Japan about the ability of all teachers and classes to cover the material thoroughly, or for the students to actually master the material in school, even if all the items on the course of study are covered. There are also questions concerning the test process itself. Primary emphasis in the Joint First Stage Achievement Test is on factual recall. Questions also include reading comprehension based on short passages, interpreting graphs or charts, or both. There are also questions that require interpretation of longer, narrative passages where the student must demonstrate other abilities besides rapid recall of occasionally arcane facts. These types of questions are also found on the university tests, as are short essay questions.

The University Level Examination

The university test is more reflective of the character of the individual school, and is theoretically designed to identify students who are suitable for the education provided by that school and its respective departments. While the universities administer the tests, the matrix of required and elective subjects tested may differ from department to department within the same university, reflecting departmental requirements. In addition, both the format and content of tests in some subjects vary from school to school, and can vary considerably.

Competition

An increase in the number of applicants seeking to take the Joint First Stage Test has resulted in an increased gap between prospective students and openings and in increased pressure on all students. In 1987, the ratio of those applying to take the Joint First Stage Achievement Test to first year openings at the national universities was about four to one, a slightly higher ratio than in recent years. Other recent figures for the university level examinations for and entrance to national and local public universities are shown in Table 1. The ratio of university level test takers to entrants in national and public universities is about three to one.

With such large numbers of examination takers and prospective entrants, the public universities have even had to restrict the number of students they can permit to take the university level examination, and so the Joint First Stage Examination is being used as a kind of first filter, where those with scores below a certain point will not even be permitted to sit for the second exam. If students miscalculate in choosing their targets, there is a heavy price to pay. Further complicating the examination picture are some potentially significant changes introduced in the administration and format of the Joint First Stage Achievement Test in January, 1987.

Previously, the examinations for the national universities were arranged in such a way as to permit a student to sit for the examination of only one national university. In 1987, the calendar was modified, permitting students to sit for two national examinations, but forcing them to choose their prospective schools before the scores on the Joint First Stage Test were known. Both of these decisions have implications for further intensifying the competition for college entrance. Since students with excellent ability now have the opportunity to sit for two examinations, both of which they can theoretically pass, a degree of competition is introduced where it may not have been present before.[3]

Competition for the most desirable private universities is also quite keen. At least one major *yobiko*, Kawaijuku, was forecasting a much greater degree of difficulty in entrance to the better private universities in large urban areas. While such forecasting is also self-serving to a degree, it is clear that the competition for college entrance is also going to heat up.

Demographic trends in the college-age group will also contribute to entrance pressures, as well. The population of eighteen-year-olds will peak in about 1992, and the Ministry of Education is trying to meet its stated goal of keeping the ratio of cohort to new admissions at a level on a par with 1983, but will fall short at the current rate of expansion (Ministry of Education 1984, 64-65). Table 2 shows the expansion of four-year colleges and universities since 1960.

Competition is even more pronounced at the actual university and departmental entrance level due to the fact that many students apply to more than one school. Some applicant/entrant ratios are quite high. Amano (1986) suggests that each applicant applies

TABLE 1

National and Local Public University Examination Takers and Entrants, 1983, 1984

National Universities			
Year	Examination takers	Successful applicants	Actual enrollment
1983	240,158	94,069	87,605
1984	232,355	94,195	87,343
Local Public Universities			
1983	54,723	15,852	11,176
1984	51,320	16,415	11,042

SOURCE: National Center for University Entrance Examination 1984, 22.

TABLE 2

Growth of Higher Education in Japan Since 1960

Year	Number of Universities			
	Total	National	Local Public	Private
1960	245	72	33	140
1965	317	73	35	209
1970	382	75	33	274
1975	420	81	34	305
1980	446	93	34	319
1985	460	95	34	331

SOURCE: Monbusho 1985, 71.

to three schools. Figures published in 1987 suggest some departments have much higher ratios.[4]

Thus, there are at least three factors serving to intensify the competition in university admissions. First, college education is now virtually universally recognized as very important, both because of underlying social emphasis, and particularly due to the weight placed on university credentials by many major employers. Competition is severe and is reflected in the very high application rates for entrance to particular schools and their departments. These numbers can vary widely from school to school and department to department, however.

The second factor has been the relative lack of growth in recent years of the number of entrance slots in the national and local public universities.

The third is the complex and demanding nature of the series of entrance exams themselves, the new changes, and the strategy that one must employ in deciding on appropriate goals and schools.

Since general knowledge and ability, high school record, and other factors all take a back seat to examination scores, the pressures for a student to employ stratagems to improve a score even slightly are enormous.

Ronin

Obviously, many students cannot compete successfully on the examinations, and yet desire a college education and degree from a particular school. Because entrance examinations are given during only one short period annually, a student who is unsuccessful must either wait to take the examinations again the following year or give up the hope of entrance to a school of choice or perhaps even give up the hope of a college education entirely. Many such students in Japan elect to spend their first postsecondary year in study, preparing to take the university entrance examinations again the following spring. This group of aspiring college students, all of them by definition high school graduates and virtually all of them unsuccessful on their first try at entrance to the school of their choice, makes up that segment of the population of young people in Japan known as *ronin*.

The term literally means "wave men," referring to the masterless samurai of the premodern period who no longer had a lord to whom they owed allegiance and who were "tossed about" old Japan,

adrift. The word today has retained at least some of its archaic
spirit and flavor. The students are "between roles" in a sense, and
are casting about for a place to anchor. The term also has a bit of
the samurai stoicism about it. In popular myth, samurai *ronin* were
undaunted by hardship, were good fighters, and were often loners,
who persevered at all costs. These students too are dedicated, sin-
gle-minded, disciplined, and tough (some of them, anyway). If some
of these failed entrants wonder about their future, few of them are
truly aimless wanderers.

This group of students, indeed this phenomenon of a young
person spending an additional year between high school and college
preparing for examinations, has become so pervasive in Japanese
society that the secondary education structure is sometimes referred
to as a 3-3-1 system, with the "1" indicating the extra year of post-
high school study. Though this "*ronin* year" has become part of the
folklore and ethos of modern Japan, many of the *ronin* have concrete plans for the future, for study, and for success on the examinations. Very often at the center of these plans is a particular private Japanese institution, the *yobiko*, which many believe, and
which the *yobiko* claim, will actively and effectively aid the student
in the quest for success.

The percentage of *applications* to four-year universities and
colleges submitted by students who graduated high school at least
one year prior to applying has been rising steadily, from only 12
percent of the applicant pool in 1967 to about 30 percent in 1984
(Central Council on Education 1972, 89). The percentage of actual
entering freshman who have spent a year between high school
graduation and college entrance was about 35 percent in 1984
(Monbusho 1984, 100-101). Figures for the more competitive colleges can be considerably higher, and it is not uncommon for a student to take the exam for his or her desired school twice or even
three times (Amano 1986, 39).

For example, at Hosei University in 1984, applications
submitted by *ronin* and by new graduates of high school were
roughly 50 percent each, but *ronin* entrants outnumbered the successful current graduating high school entrants 70 percent to 30
percent. The same pattern repeated itself in 1985 (*Nyugaku shiken
shirizu: Hosei Daigaku* 1986, 30-34). Amano (1986, 39) tells us that
at Tokyo University more than half of the freshman class is composed of *ronin*. Table 3 shows the increases in first-year enrollments
and applications at various classes of universities.

Yobiko

The *yobiko* are specialized private schools dedicated to preparing their students for success on college entrance examinations. Many of the larger *yobiko*, frequently those with branches scattered throughout Japan, are extremely sophisticated with elaborate programs and well-developed curricula that have been designed for, and that are geared to, the specific subject requirements and the examination style of particular universities. *Yobiko* facilities and physical plants are often first-rate and replete with the latest in high technology educational equipment, often in stark, if not ironic, contrast to the spartan physical surroundings of so many of the schools which the students are trying to enter.

It is important to remember that the *yobiko* themselves are part of a much larger "examination industry" in Japan. The prime components of this industry are involved in the collection and dissemination of examination and college entrance information; the publication and sale of study and tutorial materials, examination guides, and the like; the related phenomenon of the preparation, administration, and scoring of practice entrance examinations; and classroom schooling.

Most of the schools in this industry are called *juku*, and many are involved in academic instruction, examination preparation, or both, usually for elementary or junior high school students preparing for entrance examinations to high school (or, sometimes, to private junior high school). High school is not compulsory in Japan, and an entrance examination is required. Some *juku* also tutor senior high school students who are studying in preparation for the eventual college entrance examinations, as do many *yobiko*. There are also academic *juku* that avowedly pursue other aims as well, even some that disregard examination preparation entirely. Academic *juku* vary greatly in philosophy, ownership and scale of operation, ranging from multibranch nationwide chains to one-man, one-room schools[5] (Leestma et al. 1987, 11). The subject of much debate and considerable criticism in Japan, they are pervasive in Japanese society.[6]

The *yobiko* are the upward extension of the *juku* system, but have a single focus--preparing students to pass university entrance examinations. With few exceptions they are not concerned, as many *juku* are, with academic enrichment or remedial education.[7]

The *yobiko* concentrate on preparing their students for qualifying successfully on the entrance examinations for college by providing instruction in the subjects tested as well as offering various important information and support services. The *yobiko* develop and administer model examinations against which students can chart progress, estimate chances of gaining admission to particular institutions, and become familiar with the various styles and formats of examinations and different types of questions as distinct from the subject content. A student can pick and choose from the examinations offered by various *yobiko* and need not restrict his testing practice to one school or to the school in which he may be enrolled. These practice examinations are given frequently during the year and are also open regularly on a fee basis to the general student public. The latter is often the means by which students first come to a particular *yobiko*. Many of the large *yobiko* also maintain sophisticated data banks and information-gathering operations that collect and maintain data on the content and results of both practice examinations and actual university and Joint First Stage entrance examinations. Practice tests are designed by the *yobiko* (especially true of the large schools), or by a number of the commercial publishing houses that specialize in such tests. Some smaller or regional *yobiko* affiliate with one of the larger schools in order to have access to and administer the tests created by certain *yobiko*.

The *yobiko* use the results to assemble a comparative database and to measure their students' progress. *Yobiko* also use these tests as a basis on which to periodically reorganize the composition of their classes. Students take examinations to build familiarity with the form and content of such tests and to assess their own progress.

One of the most important things which the data on test results do is provide information to the students on where they stand relative to the other national practice test takers in the race for entrance to particular schools. Results from many previous years' Joint First Stage Achievement and various university examinations are also available. Thus, the student and the school know how much improvement is still needed, as well as the strengths and weaknesses of a candidate in the various subject areas and examination question types. The data also help clarify the relative degree of difficulty of entrance to each university. The data services area in general is literally equal in significance to instruction itself.[8]

For example, because Joint First Stage Test scores are not reported to the students directly, students have to calculate their scores themselves after the answers to the examinations are made public. They report the results obtained from this after-the-fact self-scoring to those *yobiko* that process the data on a nationwide basis. The *yobiko* then make the information on scores available publicly. This information is important and helps the students decide where to apply and how to prepare for the university level examination.[9]

Yobiko also publish a wide variety of books and study aids which they sell through subsidiaries. Textbooks the schools create for the exclusive use of their own students are a big drawing card for the *yobiko*, since they are often prepared by teachers and staff intimately familiar with the entrance examinations and are based on indepth data acquisition and analysis. These books are not usually available in exactly the same form in the commercial book stores.

The number of *yobiko* has remained relatively constant over the last decade, at around 200 schools. There are *yobiko* in each prefecture, and local *yobiko* are often geared to preparing students for admissions to local or prefectural universities. However, the system itself is often characterized as being dominated by the *san dai juku*, or the "big three *juku*," none of which is really a *juku* in the sense that *juku* are conceptualized by most Japanese[10] (see note 6).

The *yobiko* student population (*ronin* and high school students) has grown over the last two decades, from about 118,000 in 1966, peaking at about 225,000 in 1980, then falling to about 200,000 where it hovered for most of the 1980s.

Programs

Ronin *Programs*

Ronin *yobiko* students generally enroll in programs that are designed for a full year's full-time study. There are, however, a host of after school and Saturday programs--both year-long and shorter-term--which attract students from the general *ronin* population, from other *yobiko*, and from high school. Besides these programs, some *yobiko* permit, and indeed encourage, high school students as well as their own students to enroll in additional special courses or lecture programs of varying duration. These special lecture series are in addition to the students' normal course load at *yobiko*.

Full-time *yobiko* programs are generally year-long and heavily, though not exclusively, academically oriented. They are characterized by a daily regimen of lectures in various subjects, as well as by practical exercises and frequent testing. The object of the program is to insure successful entrance into a university of the student's choice, and full-time programs, especially, include a large dose of advice and counseling on that subject in addition to regular lessons.

Part-time *yobiko* programs come in many forms, but perhaps the most common is the subject lectures series, a program usually of two or three semesters' duration. On a trimester basis, for example, this would consist of a ten- or twelve-week series of lectures, one lecture or perhaps two per week for the length of the series, with all of the lectures being on one subject. These lectures are frequently held in the late afternoon or on Saturdays, which permits attendance by both high school students and other *ronin* in addition to students of the *yobiko* who have finished their regular daily lessons. Short-term, vacation, and intensive preexamination courses, lasting two to three weeks, can cover individual, or in some cases, even all examination subjects, as well as examination-taking techniques.

High School Programs

Yobiko programs for high school students take two main forms: 1) general supplementary lessons and examination preparation which can include such things as the subject lectures above--concentrating on one or more subjects of the curriculum--or 2) one-, two-, and three-year structured after-school/Saturday programs, covering all the examination subjects. These programs aim to have high schoolers qualify on the college entrance examinations on their first try, a theme heard with increasing frequency.

What Yobiko Do; Reasons for Attendance

Students attend *yobiko* chiefly to improve their chances for successful entrance. *Yobiko* have excellent advertising and public relations operations by which they successfully promote themselves, but it is also true that they 1) can be highly specialized (local *yobiko* that concentrate on particular regional or local universities can target their lessons and prepare students very effectively); 2) provide good data services, for which there is a real need; and 3) can point to statistics that suggest that given the high percentage of *ronin* entrants to particular schools, the chances of gaining admission to a university of choice are better as a *ronin* than as a high school senior.[11]

Just how effective the *yobiko* really are is difficult to assess. The *yobiko* keep detailed records but use different ways to report success. For example, *yobiko* track the practice-test takers and know with some accuracy which successful entrants to which schools and departments had the advantage of practicing on one or another of their tests, or who profited from enrollment in one of their programs. Some *yobiko* report both types as their students. Thus, the widely advertised success ratios of the different *yobiko* are not reported on a uniform statistical basis. Data, at least from the "big three," support the idea that it is advantageous to attend a *yobiko* program. Table 4 shows *ronin* and new high school graduate entrants to three types of Japanese universities. The figures show that in 1984 successful *ronin* accounted for 34.8 percent of all new daytime enrollments in four-year institutions. *Ronin* accounted for 41.5 percent of new entrants in the national universities, 42.5 percent in the local public universities, and 32.6 percent in the private universities.

A number of factors influence the student's selection of a *yobiko*. The image that the school has succeeded in creating and projecting, its history, location, and reputation all play a part. There is a saying about the big three *yobiko* to the effect that "Yoyogi has the students, Sundai has the teachers, and Kawai has the desks." In fact, Kawai asked its students why they had chosen the school, and found 37 percent selected Kawai because of its success history, and 21 percent because Kawai was perceived to be especially effective in preparing students for the entrance examinations of the schools in which the students were interested. Other reasons were: 17 percent because it was easy to commute to, 12 percent because their friends attended, and 5 percent because of Kawai's "high class" image (*Kawaijuku daigaku jukena* 1986, 14).

There is considerable variation in *yobiko* size, location, and orientation. Many of the schools have a long history and a local reputation of some standing. Various schools still focus on individual institutions or classes of institutions.

The attraction of many *yobiko*, especially the regional or local affiliates of one of the big national *yobiko* chains, lies in their reputation for and experience in preparing students for the examinations of local or regional universities, as well as for those of the best-known national schools.

TABLE 3

Trends in Applications and Enrollments in Japanese Universities Since 1965

Year	First-Year Enrollments (daytime and evening)				Applications	
	National	Local Public	Private	Total	High School Seniors	Ronin
1965	54,681	9,130	186,106	249,917	300,231	94,959
1970	64,519	10,215	258,303	333,037	360,175	178,686
1975	75,479	10,673	337,790	423,942	457,363	182,857
1980	84,731	10,848	316,858	412,437	452,065	184,899
1984	87,569	11,114	317,319	416,002	470,463	204,018

SOURCE: Monbusho 1985, 61, 84.

TABLE 4

Ronin and Non-Ronin Entrants to Universities 1983-1984

University Type	Entrants (daytime only)		Percent Ronin
	Total	Ronin	
Total			
1983	391,570	127,135	32.4
1984	387,517	135,219	34.8
National			
1983	85,887	31,552	36.7
1984	86,682	35,607	41.5
Local Public			
1983	10,564	4,007	37.9
1984	10,488	4,462	42.5
Private			
1883	295,119	91,576	31.0
1984	291,347	95,150	32.6

SOURCE: Monbusho 1984, 108-15.

The *yobiko* themselves are active advertisers and persuasive recruiters. In addition, their various practice examinations and data services bring them in touch with a majority of college-bound youth, with the result that the names of some of these schools have become household words over the last twenty years. Interestingly enough, cost does not seem to be a major factor in selecting a *yobiko*, once one has decided to attend[12] (see section on costs, pp. 291-92).

Students, successful *ronin* especially, often give credit to particular *yobiko* and teachers in assisting them in their study. A whole body of testimonial literature of the "How I Got Into the University" sort abounds, and students do read both books and articles on the subject. The advice is dispensed by the successful student or, not infrequently, by a mother; is detailed; and includes study tips, names of reference books and study guides, and sometimes specific recommendations about *yobiko*.

For example, a one-year *ronin* who successfully entered the medical department of a national university in Shikoku writes:

> For that year I enrolled in the Sundai *yobiko* course taught in Kyoto. All of the lessons were fantastic. Since I praise Sundai so much, some of you readers probably must think I am an agent for the school, but since the lessons were truly outstanding, that's the way it has to be. If you attend one of their classes you will soon understand why I say this (Mizuno 1987, 121).

Another student, a one-year *ronin* who got into a national university in Nagoya, wrote,

> Well, I attended Yoyogi Zeminaru in Nagoya, and they are absolutely determined not to be outdone by Kawai, whose home base is Nagoya, so they expended tremendous effort in that regard...(Kojima 1987, 48).

Entrance and Class Formation

Entrance requirements for *yobiko* vary due to school size, location, desired class, and applicant pool, among other reasons. Even within the same institution, requirements for entrance to a *yobiko* may vary if the school has several branches, particularly when separated by some distance. Generally speaking there are two types of entrance--general admissions and selected entrance. General admission classes are usually open to all applicants on a first come/first served basis, while selected admissions classes require a qualifying entrance examination. Selected admissions classes are often aimed at preparing for the examinations of universities where competition is greatest. Some *yobiko* and special programs have few minimum requirements for admission, and a number of programs have none at all.[13] Once admitted to a *yobiko* the student may also take a placement examination. These tests, like many given throughout the examination industry, are used in class formation and also serve several other related functions.

First, they ensure that each class has students of about the same general level of academic ability, a proposition that runs counter to the prevailing principle and practice in most Japanese schools in the official system. This is important since despite the individual nature of some of the year's study in pursuit of college admission, the classroom hours will be spent as a group. It is, therefore, important that the students be able to keep up and, at the other extreme, not be easily frustrated by material too far below their present level of attainment.

Second, accurately assessing student ability at entrance to *yobiko* has several advantages for the student directly and, over the longer term, for the school as well. If students are placed in classes geared to achieving attainable goals, the students will likely have a better chance to succeed in their endeavors, and the school's reputation for placement of its students will ultimately be enhanced. Class formation based on ability means that the students in all the classes know exactly how much they have to improve their scores in order to become competitive. Of course a higher initial level of class ability means more ground can be covered in the year. The assumption is that the more advanced a student is, the better the chance of passing the examinations.

Third, such entrance tests, by indicating relative strengths and weaknesses in academic areas, provide a better picture of exactly where additional work is needed and assist the school both in accurately assigning texts and courses and in recommending strategies to the students.

Finally, the tests are part of a baseline, which together with the results obtained on periodic practice college entrance examinations, is used to measure progress and provides a yardstick against which goals of study can be reassessed periodically.

When a particular segment of the school year or major unit of the curriculum is completed, students in *yobiko* are often re-grouped into classes based on their school progress to that point, on the improvement of their scores in the practice examinations, or on performance in another class formation test.[14]

Facilities

Basic *yobiko* facilities consist of the physical plant and equipment that one might associate with schooling: buildings and classrooms (more like lecture halls in many cases) with their desks and chairs, and study rooms. There are also those *yobiko* that have laboratories, libraries, dormitories, gymnasiums, and cafeterias. *Yobiko* also offer extensive support services, less tangible than the physical plant, but equally as important in the *yobiko* system.

In the realm of data and information services, the *yobiko* provide current information on school entrance, test scores, and standings. They provide counseling, particularly in the area of col-lege selection and entrance, and often personal advice as well. *Yobiko* may also have homeroom advisors who meet regularly with the students. In short, the *yobiko* have a generally holistic approach to the year-long study program and to examination success. They try to back up this philosophy wherever possible with concrete sup-port services, hardware, and education personnel.

Courses and Curriculum

Since subject content and test format can vary from school to school and department to department, *yobiko* make a point of designing their curricula primarily to address the demands of the examinations, not only in terms of the required mastery of general and specific levels of subject and information content, but also in the domains of format and question types. In addition, they stress test-ing experience and test-taking techniques. Though sometimes char-acterized as devoting the most attention to the latter, it is largely not the case, and it is a mistake to ignore the actual transmission of basic information that also occurs.

Kawaijuku, a Nagoya-based nationwide *yobiko*, has twenty schools, including branches and affiliates, with specialized curricula geared to various admissions programs. However, not all Kawai schools offer the full range of programs for all universities. At its schools in the Tokyo area, Kawai has two specialized courses for entrance to Tokyo University, two for Kyoto University, one for Hitotsubashi University, a general university premedical course, two special national and local public university courses, three different Waseda University programs, and two for Keio University, as well as a general program for students in the performing and other arts.

While certain elements of these Kawai study programs are the same as the courses at many *yobiko*, particularly because of the wide use of the Joint First Stage Achievement Test, *yobiko* programs and study still maintain a strong individual and sometimes regional flavor, due to the influence of the individual university second stage entrance examinations, students' geographic preferences, and the history and location of the *yobiko* themselves.

In its schools in the Nagoya region where Kawai has its home base, Kawai offers courses similar to those listed above, in addition to programs for Nanzan University and Nagoya University, schools with a strong regional reputation. Sapporo Yobigakuin in Hokkaido has similar general programs, but emphasizes its courses for the main regional universities there.

The programs at other *yobiko* are similar, and the pattern of offering separate general courses for preparation for the national, public, and private universities, as well as specific courses for particular institutions, is generally repeated throughout the *yobiko* system.

Not all of the formal curriculum is specifically information oriented. In essay questions, which are typical of the second stage examinations, a student must be able to express ideas clearly. Although students have studied composition throughout their school life, this writing ability has not necessarily been mastered. Accordingly, in preparing for essay questions, *yobiko* place considerable emphasis on the ability to organize ideas and on structuring a written argument.

In addition to subject content, the curriculum tends to emphasize different aspects of study at different times during the school year. At Kawai for example, the curriculum is segmented in oughly the following manner. During the spring and early summer the most attention is paid to basic knowledge acquisition. Despite considerable attention to placing students of similar ability levels together when classes are formed, the students still have different knowledge bases, and this period is used to bring everyone up to speed, particularly to ensure that basic subject information is taught. Midsummer brings attention to identifying the areas where the students remain weak. After class reorganizations in early fall, greater emphasis is placed on individual and specialized study. In the weeks just prior to the examinations themselves there is increased emphasis on test questions and test techniques, with orientation tailored to the entrance examinations of the different target schools. *Yobiko* frequently shift into high gear for study during the last three months preceding examinations.

Large parts of the *yobiko* curriculum are not devoted to rote memorization of facts, but to problem solving and to developing the ability to apply what one has learned. Analytical ability, the ability to think through a problem and adopt a strategy for solution is an important part of the examination, and, consequently, part of the curriculum designed to deal with the tests. Comprehension and logic, as well as a deep reservoir of factual knowledge, are all required. Thus, rote memorization, examination-taking techniques, logic, analysis, writing, and problem-solving ability can and do exist side by side in these institutions.[15]

Some *yobiko* attempt to broaden the student's intellectual and cultural horizons, both in the narrow sense of providing information that might be useful in an examination, particularly in an essay question, and in the broader sense of widening the student's outlook and perspective in general, through exposure to nonacademic activities in addition to formal instruction.

That is, these activities constitute an unwritten curriculum of sorts at *yobiko*, one that evolves through a series of school events and activities, as well as through formal studies, and one that at first glance may seem to have no direct applicability to entrance examinations. Clearly *yobiko* believe that these activities can pay dividends not only on the examinations in the near term, but over a much longer time as well. Many of the *yobiko* recognize the serendipity inherent in the pursuit of learning and knowledge and encourage their students accordingly (see calendar section, pp. 292-300).

Over the year-long course of study, a student who enrolls in a general program preparing for entrance to a national or local public university can expect to spend close to 1,000 hours in the classroom, and often more. Table 5 shows a composite of an annual schedule for a program oriented to general admission to a science department of a national university.

Practice testing also makes up an important part of the formal curriculum. *Yobiko* students, as well as many who are not enrolled, will take a five-hour major practice test of one kind or another on a number of the Sundays on which these are offered throughout the school year. Tests are very important, and most students avail themselves of the opportunity to sit for several of the various types of practice examinations.[16]

Most *yobiko* rely heavily on a lecture method of instruction. Classes tend to be large, and enrollments of between 100 to 200 students per class are not unusual. Some classes and classrooms are large enough to require that lecturers use lapel or hand-held microphones in order for all students to hear and to insure that enthusiastic teachers can avoid shouting themselves hoarse.

At Kawaijuku students take two forty-five-minute lectures back-to-back, for a total of ninety minutes in a subject with the same teacher at one time. At other schools, the duration varies depending on the program, but classes usually run from 80 to 100 minutes. At Kensu Gakkan for example, in a part-time, year-long *ronin* program arranged for afternoon, early evening, and Saturdays, sessions run between two and a half and three hours per day.

The term lecture should not be taken to mean a professor droning on at the front of the class while sleepy-eyed students struggle to maintain consciousness at the rear of the classroom. *Yobiko* lectures are lively. Lecturers are active and make energetic presentations, constantly using the blackboard to illustrate their remarks, solve problems, and make various points. The blackboard (or boards) cover the entire front of the room and sometimes one side as well, and by the end of class they are often completely filled. There are few, if any, inattentive students. Lessons are predominantly textbook centered, and frequently focus around the texts that the *yobiko* itself has prepared.

The *yobiko* say that some subjects, such as English, are covered too quickly in high school for the students to absorb, but that in step by step *yobiko* instruction, even a single year's instruction can be structured so that students really learn the material (Kawaijuku (Tokyo), interview, January 27, 1987).[17]

Kawai management says that students become *ronin* because they fall behind. Therefore, Kawaijuku and other *yobiko*

TABLE 5

Number of Class Hours per Week for a One-Year *Yobiko* Program for Entry to a National University Science Department, by Subject

Subject	Hours*	Subject	Hours*
English		Japanese	
General	2	Modern Language	2
Explication	2	Classical	2
Grammar	2	Classical (Chinese Style)	2
Composition	2		
Mathematics		Required Electives	
General	2	Two courses from the following	
Basic analysis	2	Physics	4
Algebra and geometry	2	Chemistry	4
Probability and statistics	1	Biology	4
Differential calculus	2	Electives	
and integral calculus		Social science	2
		Other	2

*Class hours are forty-five minutes long.

NOTE: Example based on *Kawaijuku daigaku jukenka* 1986, 42-43.

increasingly emphasize enrollment of high school students. They want to get the students younger, before the information gaps become unmanageable, so they can set up a program to ensure high school students succeed on their first try at the examinations. Qualification on the first try is especially emphasized by *yobiko* and *juku* trying to attract the high school population.[18]

Following up on the theme that high schools cover too much material too rapidly, Kawaijuku contends that they (the *yobiko* in general) cannot be content with just giving their students what they did not get in school. Students have to learn *how* to study, not just be exhorted *to* study.

Study suggestions range from the obvious, such as "work on one subject at a time," "devote specific periods of concentrated effort to one theme," "take notes," or "create a study routine," to the less obvious, such as "learn by doing something with your hands": *draw* the chart, *graph* the problem, or *write* the list.[19] Setting both long-term and short-term goals and sticking to them is emphasized. Sunyu *Yobiko* urges its students to review all of their high school textbooks thoroughly, since the *basic* information they contain is fundamental to the Joint First Stage Test.

Textbooks and Publications

The schools, especially the larger schools, have constructed elaborate curricula, and their publications generally, and textbooks specifically, are designed to cover the material and to be used as an integral part of the classroom lectures.

Textbooks and study guides fall into two categories: those produced for use by the schools' enrolled students only and not available for sale or distribution outside of the school, and those created for sale outside of the school and available in the commercial bookstores. Fees for texts for school use are usually included in tuition (see below). The style and format of the books are similar to that of books used in Japanese public schools. Textbooks are supplemented with numerous handouts, worksheets with practice problems, and mimeographed items of various sorts. There are also composition papers turned in to the instructors who correct and annotate them and return them to the students. This extensive written exchange of comments and critiques by teachers is an important feedback mechanism. Some schools conduct seminars on how to get ready for essay questions, and there are *yobiko* correspondence courses devoted solely to improving one's ability to deal with essay questions or other examination subjects.

The quality of the texts, as well as the thoroughness with which they cover the curriculum and anticipated test contents, is a source of great pride for the *yobiko* and plays no small role in enhancing the reputation of the school and its faculty.

Depending on the *yobiko* and the program in which a student enrolls, there may be a wide choice of textbooks available. Kawai boasts it can choose the most appropriate books for each of its students, once they are placed, from a possible list of over 100.[20] The texts are *not*, like the commercial materials, designed to be used by the student independently. Their use is predicated on integration with the school's lectures. Extensive preparation is recommended and students are exhorted to prepare fully for the next week's lecture in each subject. Kawai says that adequate preparation for the program takes a full week.

A second category of *yobiko* publication is material prepared for sale outside of school. Commercial items are published by affiliated or subsidiary corporations, but not by the *yobiko* themselves.[21] *Yobiko* books, coupled with the hundreds of similar items available from independent publishers, give students an enormous choice of study aids. High school students and *ronin* alike, whether enrolled in *yobiko* or not, avail themselves of these kinds of study aids.

Commercial books tend to be problem oriented or specialized test materials, such as *English at Tokyo University*, or *Keio University's Examinations: The Last Five Years*. General study guides and examination books for the Joint First Stage Achievement Test abound. Prices are generally modest: prices from $3.50 to $6.50 were not uncommon in 1987.

Throughout the year, but particularly in the November to March period, the bookstores are overrun with anxious students eagerly seeking the latest supplementary text--the one which may hold the magical key to success. Every corner bookstore in Japan carries at least some of these, and the large bookstores give over entire departments and sometimes whole floors to them. *Yobiko* affiliation and the origin of the texts are displayed prominently.

Many of these books are published in series, so that students can obtain books of a similar format and style covering many or most of the universities and subjects in which they are interested, particularly if there is a preference for a particular publisher or for one *yobiko*'s authors over another's.[22]

A third category of *yobiko* publication is the house organ. These have a wider audience than the school's student body and are sometimes part of the school's public relations program. Tabloid newspaper publications, broadsides, and journals are the general formats. Some are distributed free or for only the most nominal of fees; others are more expensive and require an actual subscription. The latter, particularly those major publications concerned with entrance examination data or with nationwide analysis of practice test results, are important sources of information for students.

The circulations of the publications vary. A *yobiko* with only one school building in Tokyo may issue 15,000, while a national chain may print more than 200,000 per issue. There is at least one with a press run over one million.[23] Some of the schools issue more than one such publication. Frequency varies. Some school newspaper types appear weekly, others quarterly or after major examinations.

The content of these publications is largely devoted to information about entrance processes and changes in university testing practices and emphases, study tips, or suggestions for lifestyle or even eating habits.[24] Narratives, testimonials, and advice from students, entrants, and teachers also appear.

Teachers

Though most *yobiko* still employ both full-time and part-time teachers, the mainstay, increasingly so, of the *yobiko* are those teachers now engaged full time in *yobiko* instruction. This distinction between classes of faculty is important because the degree to which a *yobiko* maintains a full-time teaching staff is an indicator of the dedication and commitment of the school and of those whose livelihood depends on their teaching ability and that of their colleagues (not to mention on the efforts of their students). It also serves as a barometer of the economic health and strength of the institution and is symbolic of the dedication of the institution to the goals it espouses and of the success of the institution in placing students.

This is by no means to say that those who teach part time are in any way inferior. Some are so popular and so inspiring that they can and easily do work as free agents. They are in great demand, traveling around the country, lecturing at several schools each week (*Za yobiko* 1986, 39). Nonetheless, of the 102 best teachers selected in a recent poll, 90 percent were full-time teachers of the *yobiko* with which they were affiliated.[25] Many teachers in both categories are present or former college teachers.[26] The schools accommodate teachers with a variety of backgrounds and teaching styles, but teachers are also expected to comply with the schools' own teaching practices.

It has sometimes been said that the best qualified *yobiko* teachers are often those who have come into *yobiko* teaching from another profession. Apart from the tongue-in-cheek nature of this remark, *yobiko* operators themselves suggest that besides being a teacher a *yobiko* faculty member also has to be an actor, a performer, a doctor, and a fortuneteller, among other things (Kawaijuku (Nagoya), interview, February 28, 1986; *Za yobiko* 1986, 39).

Other than good salaries, *yobiko* teachers seem also drawn to these schools because they find teaching at *yobiko* attractive. It has been suggested that the opportunity to teach truly motivated students was very important to many teachers who were discouraged by university teaching and attendance practices, so much so that they were willing to give up the prestige and title that so often accompany university teaching in Japan, but which has not yet accrued to teachers at *yobiko* despite some dramatic changes in public perception (*Za yobiko* 1986, 19).

The number of hours taught by *yobiko* teachers varies, but at Kawai teachers often teach twelve to eighteen hours per week. Good teachers can get from 30,000 to 50,000 yen (between $200 and $300) for each ninety minutes of instruction. On an annual basis, this salary at the lower end of the range is about 7 million yen (about $46,000) and at the higher end of the range can equal the salary level of a professional baseball player in Japan.[27]

Some *yobiko* have a formalized system of after-class teacher consultations, individual discussions of problem areas with the students in the teachers' room. At other *yobiko*, teachers provide after-class advice and information on a more informal basis or sometimes in a special (formal or informal) seminar organized for that purpose.[28] Other *yobiko* employ graduate students from public and private colleges who keep office hours and provide information on both course material and on college entrance.

Most *yobiko* also provide their students with several other channels for obtaining information and advice, both on personal and academic matters. Frequently, there are class advisors or home-room teachers who meet with students (and sometimes parents) regularly to discuss such issues as school selection, academic progress, and personal problems. These meetings can be a scheduled part of the weekly curriculum. At Kensu Gakkan, for example, conferences on school selection and counseling sessions are regularly held for parents. The school also issues a journal for parents which it publishes five times a year.

Providing formal information on school selection is another function of the *yobiko*. Besides using their own range of publications to disseminate the latest information to students in an effort to keep them current with what is happening in various universities, the schools frequently invite representatives of various private colleges to come to the *yobiko* and make presentations. They discuss a whole range of issues, from entrance procedures to employment prospects for graduates. The *yobiko* also maintain information files, databases, pamphlet collections, and reading materials on the various colleges and on college entrance, which the students are encouraged to consult.

Cost

Yobiko costs are as varied as the number of schools and programs. Both full-time and half-time attendance at *yobiko* usually require formal admission to the *yobiko* for which there is an admission fee. Such fees are common in many Japanese educational institutions. The fees can be equal to a hefty percentage of the first year's tuition. This fee is required of all new *yobiko* students. If a *yobiko ronin* had been previously enrolled in a high school program at the *yobiko* (for which he had paid an admission fee), the *ronin* admission fee would usually be waived. Once a student is admitted, the costs will vary depending upon which classes are taken. It is fair to say that school-related expenses for a full-time year at *yobiko* can amount to roughly 500,000 yen. Though the registration and fees for a full year at a good private college can be well over this figure, costs at a national or public university, though slightly less, are quite similar to it. Thus, a *ronin yobiko* student in a full-time program is often paying about the same amount of money it would cost to enroll for the freshman year at a university.

The *yobiko* also make provisions for helping students finance these costs, and a number of loan programs (with the accompanying service charges or other fees) are available to ease the short-term financial burden. Some of the schools also offer scholarship programs with which they hope to attract particularly able students who will ultimately add to the school's prestige and record of success.[29]

Table 6 shows something of the range and basic costs for six types of programs. For comparison, some first-year costs for college are also shown.

Daily Schedule/Daily Life

Lessons at Kawai begin at 8:45 a.m. and end at 4:15 p.m., and everyone is off for lunch from 12 to 1. Each week, at least one period (forty-five minutes) is given over to tutors, who serve more as advisors. A representative schedule for students preparing for entry into a science department of a national university is illustrated in Table 7.

Morning classes at Kawai are largely given over to the required subjects on the examinations, while afternoons are devoted to the elective subjects and to materials or areas for particular tests such as the Joint First Stage Achievement Test or specific second stage tests. At many *yobiko*, laboratory courses are also included. The feeling is that one cannot master the curriculum of the science course (particularly chemistry) or pass the written tests without them.

Sunday and Monday are free days at Kawai, but Sunday is frequently examination day for the entire *yobiko* (and *juku*) industry, and most of the important practice tests are scheduled for Sunday.

Kensu Gakkan's afternoon/evening and Saturday program has a different sort of schedule, but manages in its six days of instruction to offer courses in all of the major required and elective areas.

Annual Calendar

Although a study orientation is essential, a *ronin* does not spend the entire year relentlessly poring over the books. Yoyogi Zeminaru's slogan is "every day a decisive battle," but as the editors of *Za yobiko* (1986) point out, there is a limit. The schools realize that it is important for the students to get away from the

TABLE 6

Sample Costs in Selected *Yobiko* Programs and First-Year University Programs in Japan 1985

(in yen)

Program	Total	Admission Fee	Tuition
Full-Time *Yobiko* Preparing for Tokyo or Kyoto University (N)	495,000	85,000	410,000
Tokyo University (N)	450,000	150,000	300,000
General *Yobiko* Course for Waseda or Keio (P)	475,000	85,000	390,000
Keio University (P)	625,000 and up	220,000	390,000 and up
Waseda University (P)	773,000 and up	Varies	400,000 and up
General *Yobiko* Course for National University	470,000	85,000	385,000
National University	450,000	150,000	300,000
General *Yobiko* Course Private University	450,000	85,000	365,000
Private University	400,000 and up	Varies	400,000
Part-Time *Yobiko* One Subject Five Hours per Week	67,000 plus	4,000	63,000
Two-Hour Test Seminar	102,000		+39,000
Intensive Six-Day per Week, After-School High School Program	172,000	22,000	150,000

P=Private N=National

SOURCE: *Kawaijuku daigaku jukenka* 1986, *Kensu Gakkan '86: gogobu sogoka* (Kensu Gakkan 1986 afternoon general program), *Zenkoku daigaku juken yoran* 1985, and Monbusho 1985.

TABLE 7

Representative Weekly Schedule at Kawai

Hour	Tuesday Subject	Wednesday Subject	Thursday Subject	Friday Subject	Saturday Subject
1	Modern	Mathematics	English	Math	English
2	Japanese	Mathematics	composition	Math	grammar
3	English	English	Differential	Classical	Math
4	English	English	and integral	Japanese	Math
			calculus		
	Lunch				
5	Chemistry	Chemistry	Classical	Physics	Geography
6	Chemistry	for exam	Japanese	for exam	for exam
7	Probability	Free	Math for	Chemistry lab	Physics
8	& statistics	Advisor	exam	Chemistry lab	Physics

SOURCE: Based on *Senbatsu kokkoritsu sogo rikei* (Selected Admissions Course for Science Departments, National and Public Universities) in *Kawaijuku daigaku jukenka* 1986.

constant pressure, and they frequently repeat this theme and encourage their students to relax periodically. For example, summer advice from students who have been through the Kawai program deals with more than study habits:

> 1) Get up early in the morning and study while it is cool.
> 2) Thoroughly review the basic texts.
> 3) Take a day off each week--it is good for life rhythm, it is a good way to ward off summer doldrums and fatigue.
> 4) When you feel like playing, do so.
> 5) Don't complain about the heat or that it's difficult.

(*Kawaijuku Daigaku Jukena* 1986, 17)

A suggestion for autumn as stress mounts, is to make sure to deal with it by doing something like engaging in sports activities or even by complaining, but in any case be sure to dissipate the stress (*Kawaijuku daigaku jukena* 1986, 19). "You have got to get exercise, be youthful, have friends, otherwise you are not a *yobiko* student" (*Za yobiko* 1986, 46). It seems the message is you must work hard, but it is important to play, too.[30] Perhaps the best way to see something of the balance that *yobiko* try to strike is to look at an abbreviated annual calendar.

At Kawai there are basically three semesters, and a fourth, shorter, session before examinations, but the courses and the set schedules are subject to change during the final phase especially. The periods are April-July, July-August, and a final series of classes starting in September and running through the examination period.

APRIL:

> *1) Creation of a study plan for the year (starting with the results of the basic ability test)*
> *2) Deciding on target schools (there will be no improvement without goals)*
> 3) Class formation test
> *4) School entrance ceremony*
> 5) All-Japan *yobiko* practice examination

6) Homeroom class convocation

MAY:

7) Establishment of the learning pace
8) Personal consultations
9) First all-Japan Joint First Stage practice test
10) Parents' meeting
11) Progress test
12) Academic enrichment program

JUNE:

13) Summer period planning
14) Sports meet
15) Enrichment program
16) First all-Japan reading and interpretation test

JULY:

17) Strengthening the academic base
18) Parents' meeting (includes the students)
19) End of basic lessons
20) Class re-formation test
21) Private university entrance examination guidance
22) First all-Japan private university and junior college
     practice test

AUGUST:

23) Dealing with weak subjects
24) Japan Alps camp-out convocation
25) Distribution of student ranking list
26) Summer session lectures (several series)
27) Second all-Japan Joint First Stage practice test
28) First open practice exam for major national universities

SEPTEMBER:

29) Review of the year-long study plan (review of all learn-
     ing thus far, evaluation of plan for qualifying)

30) Announcement of the third trimester class, distribution of textbooks
31) Second all-Japan reading and interpretation practice

OCTOBER:

32) Commencement of study focusing on specific schools
33) Ball games competition
34) Second all-Japan private university and junior college practice examination
35) Distribution of application forms for the Joint First Stage Achievement Test
36) Individual consultations
37) Guidance for public and national university entrance examinations
38) Third all-Japan Joint First Stage practice test

NOVEMBER:

39) Winter-term planning
40) Third all-Japan reading and interpretation practice test
41) Health examination
42) Second open practice exam for major national and private universities

DECEMBER:

43) End of third trimester classes
44) Second practice test for Waseda and Keio, etc.
45) General conclusion of studies
46) Final decision on what schools to apply to
47) Parents' meeting (includes the students)
48) Fourth all-Japan Joint First Stage Achievement practice test, distribution of application forms for the universities
49) Fourth all-Japan reading and interpretation practice test
50) Winter lecture series (several series)

JANUARY:

    51) Final study before examinations
    52) Planning for a tactical improvement in strong areas
    53) All-*Yobiko*-Association practice examination
    54) Personal computer consultation (data services)
    55) Listings of individual achievements posted
    56) Special series for public/private universities
    57) Consultations on the second stage examinations
    58) The Joint First Stage Achievement Test

FEBRUARY:

    59) Study strategy for second stage examinations
    60) End of special final series for second examinations
    61) Lectures immediately preceding examinations
    62) Private university entrance examinations

MARCH:

    63) National and public university second stage exams
    64) Examination-takers festival
    65) Congratulatory celebration for qualifiers

    Let us examine this calendar briefly, with special reference
to the italicized items.
    In April the schools get off to a fast start by focusing on
goals (2), undertaking early homeroom and student counseling (6),
and having a school entrance ceremony (4). This ceremony is important in the Japanese cultural context, and is found throughout
schooling and in Japanese society at large. It symbolically welcomes
the newcomer to the group and formalizes his or her association
with the endeavor.[31]
    May brings a nationwide practice test and early data on
student standing (9), as well as a meeting with parents (10). In
June there is a sports meet (14) in which all students participate.
This event, too, is typical of those held in regular schooling: it builds
camaraderie, reinforces the solidarity of the group, and strengthens
identity with the school. July brings another formal meeting with
parents and students (18).

The class re-formation test (20) is representative of the constant reevaluation of progress and the assessment of possibilities that occur in tandem with frequent counseling. The summer group encampment (24) in the Japan Alps is also typical of those events that solidify group associations and of those that provide an opportunity for learning outside of usual channels. This short trip to a natural spot is also quite typical of the kind of events one finds in both the business and school worlds. There are other similar events, such as the ball games day (33) in October.

November brings a health examination (41). Various *yobiko* provide different levels of attention to health issues, some even to the point of offering health instruction.[32] The examination-takers' festival (64) and the congratulatory celebration for new university entrants (65) are the final two purely nonacademic functions. Both serve to let off steam and confirm one's association with the larger enterprise.

The calendar clearly reveals that there is not only an academic schedule, but also a yearly schedule of prescribed activities unrelated to the purely academic study routines. The latter falls nicely into a pattern also seen in Japanese schooling in general.

In addition, the *yobiko*, especially the larger schools, have a number of other cultural and social activities which are conducted throughout the year as tension and stress relievers, and as genuine cultural activities designed to broaden student outlooks and deepen appreciation of learning and culture beyond school study. Depending on the school, the events can be quite similar to many of those listed in the calendar above, but can also include such things as a New Year's festival, or a summer faculty/student baseball match (where students are encouraged to "break out of their slump, and smack their pressures off into left field").[33] Other events have included concerts, lectures, and symposia of all kinds.

One might correctly ask why a *yobiko*, given the rather narrow focus, would be interested in investing students' time, or its own money and facilities, in such activities, especially when these activities do not seem to be related to its basic mission.

Yobiko sponsor such events for various reasons. First, the schools believe that these things contribute (even if indirectly) to exam success (that is, they help produce effective results), and second, they understand that a school must have more than mere physical plant and equipment in order to be perceived as a school. The environment must include social and cultural activities, as these are deemed important for schooling as well. Students and parents have expectations about what a school is, and what kinds of things schools in Japan do aside from formal instruction, which the *yobiko* must address. *Yobiko* need such activities in part to fulfill those expectations. Another aspect of the rationale has to do with the fierce competition that exists between the enterprises themselves. They take the *yobiko* beyond mere focus on the exams and broaden the scope and perception of the institution from cram school to whole environment. They suggest that the school has more to offer.

Summary

It is undeniable that almost all the things the *yobiko* do can be seen as subordinate to the goal of success on the examinations. Yet, everything contributes to the reputation and commercial success of the schools. Many of the activities reflect a broader concern with intellectual life and a view that examination success is not all there is; such success must include more than mere exam preparation. In some of the schools, there is a deeper concern with a longer term view of learning and culture, and this may be a reflection of a deeper cultural predilection toward the education of the "whole man." This is evidenced in the health orientation, the calendar, the learning philosophy, counseling mechanisms, and the pedagogy. Mind (spiritual health) and body (physical health), a broad view of learning, as well as factual knowledge, are all required. Without one of these elements something important is missing. In Japanese terms learning without one of these elements would be an incomplete experience, if not a contradiction in the basic philosophical sense.

Though the goal is to pass the examinations--and to this end any number of cramming techniques, or examination-taking strategies, can contribute to a higher score--one cannot really do well on the examinations without a substantial knowledge base to handle questions one has not encountered before. This is especially true of the university-level examinations whose range is very broad, where essay questions appear, and where the depth of information and detail required can be considerable. The *yobiko* seem to be effective in providing at least some portion of the prospective college population in Japan with the requisite base of knowledge and skills.

At the same time, *yobiko* do at least a credible job of aiding students in attaining the goals that have been set, if the rising percentage of new entrants who have had the *ronin* experience is any indicator.

The *yobiko* have often been branded "cram schools," with all of the attendant negative connotations cramming entails. To a degree this criticism may be justified, especially if applied to the narrowest definition, or to those special crash programs that exist. But in the larger context, as we have seen, cramming is by no means all that is occurring at the better *yobiko*.

Yobiko are a response to the societal emphasis on academic credentials, a hierarchical distinction in the status of various institutions of higher learning, and a predilection of both employers and the government ministries to prefer graduates of particular schools. All contribute to the rush of young people banging on the doors of particular universities. As long as the social basis of this pressure remains intact, it is unlikely that students will alter their aspirations downward, when there exists a mechanism by which they have a chance to enter the school of their choice.

As one Kawaijuku advertisement in a weekly magazine (at the bottom of a page of an article listing which high schools in Japan were the best at getting their students into top universities) suggested, students could enroll at Kawai to "get in where you want to go, not merely where you can qualify."

Both teachers and students suggest that *yobiko* are filling a social as well as educational niche and that a distinct "*yobiko* culture" is emerging. In the suggestion of this *yobiko* culture and in the broadening scope of *yobiko* activities, one gets a clue to where the *yobiko* are headed in the future.

The *yobiko* have begun to branch out into other education areas besides examination preparation for college entrance, and their future may lie in other than their traditional sphere of operation.[34] They are already active at other educational levels, such as high school. Adult education and lifelong learning seem natural extensions, as do overseas and distance education. Whether the *yobiko* will ever become mainstream education institutions is unclear--and, at present, they operate for very specific purposes--but, they do so in a way that defines them as distinctly Japanese institutions and that will likely ease future transitions into other fields of education.

Notes

1. Among the schools perceived to be most prestigious are Tokyo and Kyoto Universities (national) and Keio and Waseda Universities (private). Year after year, though departmental rankings vary, these schools place at or near the top of the list of those institutions most difficult to enter. National universities are public institutions.

2. In 1985 about 3,700 such students entered a national or local public university, about 3 to 4 percent of entrants. Amano suggests that entrance by recommendation in *private* universities accounts for perhaps 20 percent of entrants. Many of these were graduates of the institutions' affiliated secondary schools. See Leestma et al. 1987, 50-51. For junior colleges, admission by recommendation is about 60 percent.

3. In point of fact this is what happened in the spring of 1987. Of the 3,738 students who passed examinations for two national universities, 1,513 qualified on both the Tokyo University and Kyoto university examination. Reported in *Sandei Mainichi*, April 5, 1987.

4. In an extreme case, at the City University of Science and Technology of Tokyo, there were 10,115 applicants for 180 openings in 1987, a ratio of 56.2 to 1. Ratios of 15 or 20 to 1, depending on the department, are not uncommon at many private universities. This and other figures reported in *Asahi Shimbun*, January 25-February 3, 1987.

5. For a brief summary see Leestma et al. 1987, 11-14, and Rohlen 1980, 207-42.

6. The distinctions between the two types of schools, *juku* and *yobiko*, are becoming blurred. To the Japanese, *juku* often connote an elementary or secondary school oriented organization, while *yobiko* are associated with concentration on college entrance. In fact, many *yobiko* have programs for high school students and some *juku*, which are not *yobiko*, have programs tutoring high school students for college entrance examinations. *Ronin* are almost exclusively identified with *yobiko*.

7. In *yobiko* with programs for high school students as well as for *ronin* there are, of course, those with remedial and tutorial/enrichment orientations. There are also *ronin* programs emphasizing intensive basic instruction, but still aiming to qualify the student by the end of the year.

8. A recent editorial in a major Japanese newspaper suggested that there is a real need in Japan for a fair and better system of information dissemination, particularly in the area of guidance in college selection and entrance, and suggested that the private sector and the government work together to study the creation of such a mechanism. "*Kosei na shingaku joho kikan o*" [Create a fair mechanism for provision of information on advancement to higher education] *Asahi Shimbun*, January 18, 1987, p. 5.

9. Self-scoring was theoretically going to be brought to an end by the new test calendar of 1987, but students continue to use this system and report scores to the *yobiko*.

10. The big three are Yoyogi Zeminaru, Kawaijuku, and Sundai Yobigakko.

11. Statistics for Tokyo university show that one-year *ronin* account for a little over 40 percent of entrants in most departments and students who have a second year or more as *ronin* account for about 10 percent of new entrants. Entrance by third year *ronin* is very small.

12. *Yobiko* cannot price their clientele out of the market and there are 200,000-plus students enrolled. The authors of *Za yobiko* intimate that a *yobiko* has to be careful not to underprice the market much (otherwise it might be regarded as having less to offer). For more on costs, see pages 291-92.

13. In a year-long special lecture series at Sundai, for example, admission is accomplished merely by registering for the course, the only caveat being that once fully subscribed (200-300 students), further admissions would close. Thus the only requirement was early registration, and current Sundai students receive preference.

14. In *yobiko* these class reformations are only periodic, but particularly in some of the more aggressive *juku* at lower grade levels, they occur with somewhat more frequency.

15. One wonders if the tendency to view Japanese formal schooling through the prism of examination-taking and to see its instructional emphasis on memorization as paramount, has resulted in overlooking a much richer pedagogy and classroom experience that may actually exist in regular schools as well as in *yobiko*.

16. There are also examinations that first- and second-year high school students are encouraged to take. This testing allows a database to be compiled for comparison with ultimate actual college entrance. It gives these high school students an opportunity to check their scores against those of their peers and those of successful students who preceded them.

17. Among the subjects held to be most important in the examinations is English, but it is also a subject where instruction in Japanese secondary schools has been criticized. See Leestma et al. 1987, 36.

18. This is also an effective business strategy.

19. There is a pun in the original Japanese. Study without one's hands is *te-nuki* (literally with hands removed) but *tenuki* is an expression which means carelessness, or that something important has been omitted.

20. Kawai's regular three-year course for high school students has more than fifty textbooks (including some on tests).

21. A school corporation may not publish commercial books directly.

22. Some of the series on entrance to and examinations of particular schools are quite large, numbering in the hundreds of volumes annually, though no one student buys more than a few--for the universities he/she hopes to enter.

23. Kawai's *Eikan Mezashite* [Laurels of Victory], for example.

24. Advice on food habits (not merely "meals you can fix in ten minutes") is actually a very interesting cultural artifact, since it suggests that there are certain correct foods for the study situation. Of course the message is also that one has to "eat right" to be healthy, and that soundness of body (health) and spirit are important for a student.

25. Faculty at *yobiko* with high school programs may teach both levels of students, although there are those who specialize in one level or another. Based on data from *Za yobiko* 1986, 266-82.

26. Faculty members at national or public universities (who are civil servants) may not teach at *yobiko*.

27. Average private sector wages for males in Japan in 1985 were 3.99 million yen per year. A forty-year-old head teacher in Japanese public schools earned between 5.3 and 5.8 million yen (depending on allowances). See *Japan 1985: An International Comparison*, Tokyo: Keizai Koho Center, p. 72 for wages and Leestma et al. 1987, 19 for teachers' salaries. Also see *Za yobiko* 1986, 39.

28. Formal seminars will be fee based.

29. The phenomenon of scholarship assistance to *juku* students has also been the topic of recent attention. See, for example, the *Asahi Shimbun*, March 29, 1986.

30. This has an interesting relationship to the fact that many of the better students, even in junior high school, also belong to athletic clubs. See Leestma et al. 1987, 36.

31. See also Leestma et al. 1987, 26.

32. See also the comment under food habits on page 291, and note 24, above.

33. At Sunyu *Yobiko*, for example.

34. Sundai has founded a high school--a giant extension of high school *yobiko* programs--and is looking at other areas. Other schools are already active at several education levels.

References

Amano, I. 1986. "Educational Crisis in Japan." In W.K. Cummings et al., eds., *Educational Policies in Crisis*. New York: Praeger.

Central Council on Education. 1972. *Basic Guidelines for the Reform of Education*. Tokyo: Ministry of Education.

Kawaijuku daigaku jukenka [Kawaijuku University Entrance Course]. 1986. Nagoya: Kawaijuku.

Kensu Gakkan '86: gogobu sogoka [Kensu Gakkan 1986 afternoon general program]. 1986. Tokyo: Kensu Gakkan.

Kojima, T. 1987. "Mumeiko o nagekuna, watakushi wa soritsu 6 nen no koko kara nankan toppashita" [Don't cry that your high school is not famous; I got in from a school founded only 6 years ago]. In *Watakushi no kokkoritsu daigaku gokaku sakusen* [My strategy for qualifying at the national and local public universities]. Tokyo: E-ru Shuppansha.

Leestma, R., R. August, B. George, and L. Peak. 1987. *Japanese Education Today*. Washington, DC: U.S. Government Printing Office.

Ministry of Education. 1984. *Higher Education in Japan*. Tokyo: Monbusho

Mizuno, T. 1987. "Eigo no shoronbun taisaku ga gappi no kagi da" [English language short essay questions are the key to passing or failing]. In *Watakushi no kokkoritsu daigaku gokaku sakusen* [My strategy for qualifying at the national and local public universities]. Tokyo: E-ru Shuppansha.

Monbusho. 1984. *Gakko kihon chosa hokokusho* [Basic school survey]. Tokyo: Monbusho.

-----. 1985. *Monbu tokei yoran* [Abstract of education statistics]. Tokyo: Monbusho.

National Center for University Entrance Examination. 1984. Exam. Tokyo: National Center for University Entrance Examination.

Nyugaku shiken shirizu: Hosei Daigaku [College entrance examination guide: Hosei University]. 1986. Tokyo: Kyogakusha.

Rohlen, T.P. 1980. "The Juku: An Exploratory Essay." *Journal of Japanese Studies* 6:2, 207-42.

Za yobiko. 1986. Tokyo: Daisan shokan.

Zenkoku daigaku juken yoran [Japanese university entrance examination handbook]. 1985. Tokyo: Kojunsha.

CHAPTER 9

EDUCATION AND LABOR SKILLS IN POSTWAR JAPAN

Koji Taira
University of Illinois at Urbana-Champaign

and

Solomon B. Levine
University of Wisconsin-Madison

For a major, perhaps overwhelming, proportion of the working population, formal education in Japan since the 1950s has played a crucial but indirect role in forming and acquiring skills in paid employment. Educational level appears to have been a highly significant factor for recruitment, assignment to training opportunities, compensation and promotion, and retirement. Probably of greater importance in developing labor skills has been direct on-the-job experience. Yet, the significance of on-the-job experience is likely to change as formal education becomes increasingly relevant for direct acquisition of work skills.

Levels of Educational Attainment

In recent decades, the percentages of the employed population of Japan by final level of formal education have been as follows (Management and Coordination Agency 1984, 63):

	Compulsory education (9 years)	Secondary education (12 years)	Higher education (14 or more years)
1960	68.7	23.0	6.6
1970	54.9	33.1	10.6
1980	38.4	42.9	17.5

The percentage of working people with higher education (including technical school beyond high school, two-year junior college, four-year university, and graduate school) shown above appears low by standards one would associate with Japan's reputation as a country of high quality human resources. In comparison, in 1980, 18.8 percent of the U.S. population twenty-five years old or older had received four or more years of college education. If people with one to three years of college education are added, this raises the percentage of people with higher education in the United States to more than 30 percent (U.S. Department of Commerce 1985, 134).

The college enrollment rate in Japan increased rapidly in the 1950s and 1960s. It peaked at 38.6 percent in 1976. In the 1980s, this high college enrollment rate has not yet been reflected fully in the composition of the labor force by education. Given time, however, as older, less educated members of the labor force retire, the proportion with higher education will converge on the college enrollment rate, which, despite slight decreases after 1976, still remains high at more than 35 percent.[1]

Table 1 presents the 1980 data on enrollment, graduation, and employment for three levels of education: compulsory (9 years), secondary (+3 years), and higher (+2 or more years). If the enrollment structure of 1980 continues, the distribution of Japan's adult population by terminal level of education by the early 2000s will be substantially like what is shown in Table 1, column B in parentheses. Nearly 40 percent of the future adult population will have had a college education of two or more years, and almost 95 percent will have completed twelfth grade (high school). This would be a remarkable achievement, considering the optional nature of high school education in Japan.

Table 1 also shows the distribution of the March graduates who found jobs by May 1, 1980, by level of education. (Graduation was in March, and the Ministry of Education survey was conducted on May 1, 1980). The relationship between columns A and B roughly indicates how the structure of the working-age population translates into that of the employed labor force, by level of education. The two structures are similar. The employment ratio (that is, the ratio of the graduates employed by May 1 to the March graduates minus those who have moved on to the next higher stage of education) is highest for college graduates (two or more years of college) and lowest for high school graduates.

TABLE 1

**Distribution of Graduates of March 1980, by Terminal Level of Education
Attained and by Employment Ratio as of May 1, 1980**

Level of education	(A) All graduates (in thousands)	(B) Employed by May 1, 1980 (in thousands)	(C) Employed ratio (B/A) (%)
1. Compulsory education completed	1,723		
2. Advanced to high school	1,623		
3. Compulsory terminal (=1-2)	100 (6.2)[3]	67 (6.1)[3]	67.0
4. High school completed	1,399		
5. Advanced to college	466		
6. High school terminal (=4-5)	953 (59.1)[3]	600 (54.5)[3]	63.0
7. Junior college graduates[1]	178		
8. University graduates[2]	379		
9. Two or more years of college (=7-8)	557 (34.6)[3]	433 (39.3)[3]	77.7
10. All graduates excluding those advanced to next stage (=3+6+9)	1,610 (100.0)[3]	1,100 (100.0)[3]	75.3

[1] Two years above high school. Includes graduates of five-year technical colleges that admit students finishing nine years of compulsory education. The entering students of these colleges are counted in "Advanced to high school."

[2] Four years above high school. Implicitly includes those who enroll in and later graduate from graduate school.

[3] Figures for rows 3, 6, and 9 under columns (A) and (B) are also expressed as percentages of those for row 10.

SOURCE: Ministry of Education 1985b, 28-37.

For some years, Japan has stabilized the enrollment structure by level of education. The college enrollment rate peaked at 38.6 percent in 1976. Subsequently, it has been decreasing (35.6 percent in 1984). The high school enrollment rate peaked at 94.3 percent in 1981 and tapered off. Thus, in the late 1980s, young Japanese in the labor force are distributed by terminal level of education as follows: about 6 percent with compulsory education, 56 to 59 percent with high school, and 35 to 38 percent with college. Provided the school enrollment structure by level of education remains stable, this will be the structure of the entire labor force by level of education a generation later.

Interestingly, the peaking of the college enrollment rate in 1976 and its subsequent decline occurred in close parallel to the end of Japan's "miracle growth" in 1973-75 and its transition to lower growth at rates half as high. This apparent correlation between slowdown in economic growth and stabilization of enrollment in higher education is a product of complex relationships between economic growth and demand for education (Kaneko 1984). One can think of two kinds of demand for education: as a consumption good and as an investment in human capital. By enriching households, economic growth enables them to buy more goods and services, education being one of the services households want to buy (Iwauchi et al. 1985, 119-20). On the other hand, by requiring more sophisticated technology, a growth economy also needs higher quality human resources to go with the technological changes.

Table 2 shows recent calculations of rates of return on investment in college education for male employees in manufacturing firms. Interest rates on one-year time deposits are also noted for comparison. This table shows a declining trend in the rate of return on investment in college education. (According to Umetani 1980, the declining trend started in the early 1950s). Compared with the interest rates on savings, college education may have been a sound investment earlier but has of late lost its attractiveness.[2] One may generally suppose that in Japan, firms' demands for college graduates largely determine households' demands for college education. Subsequent pages will describe how firms' demands for labor, schools' and colleges' supplies of education, and households' preferences for different levels and kinds of education are interrelated in ways basically consistent with how the labor market is expected to work as an allocative mechanism for human resources.

TABLE 2

Rates of Return on Investment in University Education for Male Employees in Manufacturing, by Size of Enterprise, Selected Years: 1966-80 (percent)

Size of enterprise*	1966	1970	1976	1978	1980
Total	8.2	7.5	6.4	5.7	5.2
10-99	9.0	7.9	6.5	5.7	5.1
100-999	5.0	5.9	4.9	4.4	4.0
1,000 or more	4.5	4.9	4.6	4.3	3.9
Interest rates on one-year time deposits	5.7	6.0	6.75	4.5	7.5

* By number of employees.

SOURCES: Ministry of Labor 1981, 142. Interest rates are from the Bank of Japan, various years.

Recruitment of School Leavers

Japan's alleged "lifetime employment system" requires that the new recruits come directly out of school or college with no interval of employment or unemployment. The required articulation between school and work results from a period of careful mutual search by employers and students during the last school year. As explained later, recruitment is heavily regulated by law and closely supervised by the Ministry of Labor. It takes the employer more than a year to employ new graduates.

To illustrate the recruitment of high school graduates, the typical employer formulates hiring plans in January-April for a share in the March graduates of the following year (for detailed accounts, see Clark 1979, Rohlen 1974, and Tsuchiya 1978). In May, the employer explains the plans to the Public Employment Stabilization Office (PESO) in the area. In June, the employer fills out the officially prescribed recruitment forms with details of his plans. By this time, the employer has targeted certain high schools for visits by his recruiters. These schools tend to be the alma maters of the current employees. In July, the completed recruitment forms are submitted to the PESO for approval. The forms approved by the PESO are copied and mailed to the targeted schools. Recruiters are then ready to visit the schools. However, the law prohibits the recruiters from meeting students individually. This is to prevent unfair pressures that recruiters might bring on the youths, whose knowledge of the world and whose skills to handle employment contracts are still immature. The recruiters only explain their plans to the school placement officers and groups of students. Individual students, however, can visit companies on their own for informational purposes.

In August, the employer sends out notices on hiring tests, dates, places, and so forth to the school placement officers. In September, the placement officers and students file applications for taking the tests. In October, the tests are administered. Letters of reference usually are also required. The results are speedily communicated to the students, placement officers, and PESOs. The successful ones are now prospective employees. In November, the prospective employees and their guardians are asked to sign tentative agreements to accept the employment offers.

After this, the employer's worry is usually how to keep the prospective employees from changing their minds during the next four months before they are formally employed in April of the following year. The employer uses the preemployment period for educating the prospective employees through intensive information sessions and occasional interviews. In April, new employees are formally admitted to the firm at a grand rite of passage in which all the important company officials and the new employees' parents and relatives participate. At this point, the youths who were students a week or so before acquire a totally new status as responsible citizens (*shakaijin*) and company employees (*kaishajin*), or so it is perceived by everyone concerned.

This recruitment process also applies to college seniors with minor schedule variations. A major difference is that college seniors are assumed to be fully grown individuals capable of undertaking legally binding business transactions on their own behalf. They are free to do whatever they want in search of jobs, while employers are free to seek them out individually with employment offers, including checking with professors, relatives, and friends of applicants. Although the formal "employment entrance examinations" are administered on November 1, an intensive mutual search by companies and students during the preceding months will have pretty well determined successful candidates for employment by then. Under the circumstances, the tests are a mere formality, used as a step toward employment contracts with the applicants the company has already informally decided to hire (Matsuura 1978).

How early companies want to start looking for potential employees at colleges depends on the strength of the demand for high level manpower. When the demand is tight, companies even scramble for college students in their third year! Colleges are rated by companies, while companies are rated by students and their placement counselors. Students at highly rated colleges have no difficulty in getting offers from better rated companies. In this way, better human resources are first allocated to better organizations. Excellent companies and prestigious universities are thus directly linked in their labor market functions (demand and supply). If one desires a career in an excellent company, one first has to be admitted to a prestigious university. Thus, labor market competition is transformed into college entrance competition.

On May 1, the Ministry of Education surveys how the March graduates have fared in their transition to a new stage of life. Table 3 shows the results of the May 1 surveys for recent years. By May 1, nearly 40 percent of the high school graduates of March 1984 had found jobs. In addition, nearly 30 percent of the graduates had gone on to college, while about 25 percent were enrolled at nonformal miscellaneous or specialized schools (run or supervised by the Ministry of Education) or at the public vocational training centers (run by the Ministry of Labor) for further training and education. Only about 5 percent of high school graduates were in the nonactive category (neither working nor going to school--and usually not counted as unemployed). It appears then that youth make an orderly transition to a new stage of life after high school with a minimum of delay and uncertainty.

The lower part of Table 3 shows that on May 1 nearly 85 percent of the March college graduates were employed or doing graduate work, leaving about 15 percent in nonactive or unknown statuses. Some of these nonactive graduates may have been unemployed in the sense that they were still looking for work. On the whole, however, it is remarkable that within a little over a month of graduation, the placement rates of new graduates were as high as shown in Table 3.

Further comments on Table 3 are called for. The college enrollment rates among high school graduates (column 2) show a part of the declining trend after the peak of 1976. In parallel, one observes a rising trend in the enrollment rates for miscellaneous (*kakushu*) or specialized (*senshu*) schools and public vocational training centers (column 3). (Prior to 1980, these schoolgoers and trainees were included in the nonactive category.) These schools and centers are outside the regular educational track and often enroll the youngsters who are said to be less bright than the regular-track students. Some have failed to advance to high school, and some have flunked college entrance examinations. The miscellaneous schools enroll students by course and educate them in the enrolled course commonly for a year or two. Since 1975, better organized miscellaneous schools have been upgraded as specialized schools and have been strengthened as post-high school institutions of vocational or general education.[3]

In 1984, new entrants into four-year colleges, two-year junior colleges, and specialized schools were respectively 416,000; 181,223; and 156,001 (counting only those high school graduates who entered these institutions immediately after graduation). Both the nonformal miscellaneous and specialized schools can also enroll younger people with compulsory education into lower-grade curricula. College graduates and adults are also admitted; they can pick up useful skills at these schools.

The courses offered by the specialized and miscellaneous schools are diverse. The top five courses by enrollment size at the

TABLE 3

Percentage Distribution of March High School and College Graduates by Path Chosen, as of May 1 of Each Year: 1980-84

Year	Advanced to college or graduate school [1]	Enrolled in nonformal school or training [2]	Employed [3]	Nonactive	Deceased or unknown
High school graduates (total = 100)					
1980	31.9	20.2	41.6	6.2	0.1
1981	31.4	21.2	41.8	5.4	0.2
1982	30.9	22.0	41.6	5.3	0.2
1983	30.1	24.2	40.2	5.2	0.3
1984	29.6	25.1	39.8	5.2	0.3
Colleges graduates (total = 100)					
1980	4.4	-	76.7	9.6	9.3
1981	4.6	-	77.6	9.5	8.3
1982	5.0	-	78.3	9.4	7.3
1983	5.3	-	78.0	9.8	6.9
1984	5.7	-	78.5	9.2	6.5

[1] Includes those expected to work while going to school.

[2] Means "miscellaneous" and "specialized" schools under the Ministry of Education as well as public vocational training centers of the Ministry of Labor.

[3] Does not include working students among high school graduates, but includes medical interns among college graduates.

SOURCE: Ministry of Education 1985b, 58-59, 88-89.

specialized schools in 1983 were, in descending order: 1) nursing, 2) tailoring, 3) preparation for entrance examinations, 4) cooking, and 5) information processing. These courses accounted for 48 percent of total enrollment. At the miscellaneous schools, preparatory courses were most popular, alone accounting for 35 percent of total enrollment. Thanks in part to preparatory courses at the specialized or miscellaneous schools, about a third of every year's college entrants come from the ranks of repeaters (ronin) who failed at the first try. The schools offering the prep courses (yobiko) are often profitable private enterprises. Whether the returns on college education justify the stiff tuition and fees for the prep courses is certainly a good question in view of the declining trend in the rate of return on investment in college education. Nevertheless, it is interesting that the demand for improved chances to pass college entrance examinations has called forth a commercial supply of training to help attain that objective. This is an example of how the training market responds to the demand of the labor market.

The public vocational training centers are run by the Ministry of Labor (MOL). They might just as well be called schools. But the peculiarly Japanese taste for status differentiation denies the application of the "school" title to these centers, reserving it only for educational institutions under the jurisdiction of the Ministry of Education (MOE). Thus, the MOL training centers suffer from lower status, even though they are perfectly capable of offering vocational training comparable to the vocational education offered by various MOE schools. Training at the public vocational training centers is offered to youth and adults alike. A variety of courses cater to the needs of different kinds of trainees. Recent graduates of compulsory education or high school enroll in basic courses which, aside from their emphasis on practice, look much like those offered at MOE schools. In Table 3, the basic trainees, fresh out of high school, are counted together with enrollees at miscellaneous and specialized schools. The adult trainees are treated to different kinds of training, according to their vocational objectives. Some need training for the purpose of acquiring national trade certificates (see below). Some want to acquire new skills to change jobs. In recent years, the basic trainees have been a minority of all trainees at the MOL training centers. On the average, the basic trainees number about 60,000 and adult trainees about 140,000 (Ishikawa 1981 and Umetani 1980).

Education and Occupation: A Sequential Narrowing of Choices

At two points in a person's earlier life, serious decisions have to be made, with implications for the person's occupational future (Bowman 1981). First, at the end of the nine-year compulsory education, a person chooses between high school enrollment and labor force entry. If the high school path is chosen, further thoughts have to be given to school types (public or private, day or night, regular or technical, on-campus or correspondence) and curriculum types (general or vocational). The decision on the school and curriculum types at this point also constrains choices at the end of the three-year high school education. Second, at this point, the choice is between college enrollment and labor force entry. There are two types of college: two-year junior college and four-year university. Night and correspondence courses as well as miscellaneous schools are also available. The outcome of the second choice is usually implied in that of the first choice: for example, advancement to a four-year university almost requires prior enrollment in the general curriculum at a regular high school. One unique choice that can be made at the end of compulsory education is enrollment in a five-year technical college (*koto senmon gakko*) which combines the equivalent of a high school and a two-year junior college.

An unusual rigidity exists in the Japanese school system, although some flexibility has been introduced recently: credits are largely nontransferable between schools or colleges as well as between curricula within schools or between departments within colleges. Once a path is chosen, one has to follow it to the end. There is no way to shift to another path, short of starting all over again, when the first choice is later felt to be a mistake. The difficulty of course changes in school mirrors the difficulty of career change. Such difficulties tend to generate a firm determination to stick it out with the first choice till the end of the world. A high degree of personal commitment to the first choice, be it school, course, or employer, results.

As soon as compulsory education is over, gender begins to play a differentiating role with respect to the educational paths that boys and girls are encouraged to pursue. At high school, boys and girls balance roughly equally in enrollment, but the sex ratio varies widely among vocational courses. At the college level, the junior college is more than 90 percent female, the university largely male, and the graduate school predominantly male. Those who enter the labor force also experience different sex ratios in different occupations and industries.

Table 4 shows the 1984 distribution of all high school students by curriculum. A little over 70 percent of all students are enrolled in the general curriculum. This curriculum is essential for college entrance later, although a large proportion of aspirants is destined to fail at the entrance examinations for the colleges of their first choice. For those enrolled in vocational curricula, high school is practically their terminal education.

Unusually bright students enrolled in these curricula may succeed in advancing to the four-year university. But if the university is the goal, no sensible youngster should enroll in vocational curricula in the first place. The differences in the sex composition of students enrolled in vocational curricula follow a predictable pattern: boys dominate vocations likely to need physical strength such as agriculture, fisheries, and industry, while girls dominate, and often monopolize, business, home management, and nursing.

In recent years, 94 percent of boys and girls who finish compulsory education advance to high school. This leaves only 6 percent for labor force entry. In the 1950s, most new labor force entrants were fifteen-year-old boys and girls who had just finished compulsory education. Company training programs then were organized with these recruits in mind. Now, entry into the labor force with only compulsory education is regarded as almost anomalous. Companies have already readjusted their new employee training programs with high school and college graduates in mind.

Table 5 shows what happened to the high school graduates of March, 1984, as they branched out into college, employment, nonformal schooling, and other pursuits. Although the sexes seem balanced in the group of high school graduates going on to college, for the most part, men go to four-year universities and women to two-year junior colleges. Sex also steers female high school graduates into occupations generally considered suitable for women: clerical work, sales, and services. Male graduates largely become blue collar workers (skilled craftsmen, production operators, and laborers). A tiny percentage of high school graduates (3 percent) become "professional, technical." (One only wonders what "professional, technical" standards these jobs employ.)

About a third of the high school graduates advance to college (see Table 3). Table 6 shows the 1984 distribution of three levels of college students by field of specialization, together with sex ratios by level and field. Many four-year universities offer all or most of

TABLE 4

Number of High School Students and Percent Who Are Women by Curriculum: 1984

	Number of students	Percent women
Total enrollment	4,885,913	49.6
General curriculum	3,487,047	51.0
Vocational curriculum	1,398,866	46.1
Agriculture	152,769	31.3
Fishery	16,237	11.1
Industry	465,979	3.7
Business	563,181	70.8
Home Management	138,256	97.6
Nursing	26,587	99.8
Others	25,857	48.3

SOURCE: Ministry of Education 1985b, 54-55.

TABLE 5

Distribution of High School Graduates, by Path Chosen and by Sex: 1984

Path chosen	Number of graduates	Percent women
Total	1,482,312	50.4
Advanced to college	439,250	55.4
Four-year university	266,810	31.1
Two-year junior college	168,107	93.8
Other types of college	4,333	61.8
Enrolled in nonformal school or training[1]	372,669	40.6
Employed[2]	607,237	53.8
Professional, technical	18,574	53.0
Clerical	173,238	86.5
Sales	110,150	55.9
Craftsmen, production process workers, laborers	202,828	39.9
Services	61,131	67.4
Others	41,316	15.3
Nonactive	77,574	48.6
Deceased or unknown	2,694	45.6

[1] Means "miscellaneous" and "specialized" schools under the Ministry of Education and the public vocational training centers of the Ministry of Labor.

[2] Includes working students enrolled in college.

SOURCE: Ministry of Education 1985b, 54-55. The statistics of the employed are supplemented by Ministry of Education 1985a.

TABLE 6

Number of College Students and Percent Who are Women, by Level and Field: 1984

Field	Number of students			Percent women		
	Junior college	University	Graduate school	Junior college	University	Graduate school
Total	377,107	1,734,080	65,692	90.0	23.4	13.7
Humanities	83,642	245,489	8,762	98.0	58.6	31.0
Social Science	36,379	675,501	6,681	68.8	8.9	15.2
Science	—[1]	58,446	6,846	—[1]	21.9	7.8
Engineering	19,961	342,456	21,091	15.4	2.6	1.7
Agriculture	4,110	59,777	5,834	20.3	14.4	13.2
Health Care	20,072	117,071	10,385	88.5	32.6	9.8
Merchant Marine	0	1,539	59	0	3.5	0
Home Management	100,558	31,948	349	99.9	99.2	93.7
Education	82,870	134,711	3,939	99.2	51.5	29.6
Fine Arts	19,160	45,133	1,320	93.4	63.9	45.1
Others	10,355[2]	22,009	426	98.2[2]	27.4	16.2

[1] No entry for science.

[2] Includes enrollment in general education (*kyoyo*).

SOURCE: Ministry of Education 1985b, 74-77.

the fields appearing in the table. But two-year junior colleges generally have small enrollments and can offer only a narrow range of
subjects. Indeed, 75 percent of junior colleges operate on the basis of
a single curriculum (*gakka*), such as English literature, music, or
painting (Tomita 1984). A junior college can be started on a small
scale with a few hundred students enrolled in a few selected
courses. Private enterprise plays a much larger role in establishing
and operating junior colleges: more than 80 percent of approximately five hundred junior colleges are private.

Private enterprise in Japanese higher education is generally
substantial. Even among four-year universities, a little more than
70 percent of them are private and depend mainly on revenues from
tuition and fees. Many of them are in financial difficulties and are
subsidized by the Ministry of Education. The graduates of these
universities are not as prized by large excellent companies as graduates of state or public universities. This generates a squeeze on the
rate of return on college education for the students of large
metropolitan private universities: costs are high, but employment
opportunities after graduation are inferior.

The question of comparable worth has not arisen yet in
Japan. But the tradition which steers women to two years of college
education and men to four or more years is a convenient way of
preempting the question. With such a clear differential in the
amount of education between men and women, lower pay for
women would appear all too certain. As recently as 1985, Japan
passed a watered-down law (with no clearcut enforcement requirements or penalties on violations except an appeal mechanism) concerning equalization of employment opportunities for men and
women. In the course of the debate on this legislation, the Japanese
made it clear that they did not want a straightforward *equality* of
employment opportunity, but considered it desirable to move in that
direction by progressive *equalization*, acknowledging that the current situation was one of inequality. Thus, the title of the law is
Koyo kikai kinto ho, in which the well-chosen word is *kinto*
(balancing and equalizing), not *equality*.

At least nearly a quarter of the four-year university student
body is female. But, again, female university students tend to enroll
in "women's courses": humanities, home management, education,
and fine arts. Very few women enroll in the social sciences and engineering, the fields which are most desirable for successful careers
in large private companies. Graduate school is male dominated almost to the same extent that junior colleges are female dominated.

Table 7 shows various levels of college graduates in different socioeconomic statuses as of May 1, 1984. A majority of the graduates from each level joined the labor force, and more than 95 percent are professional, technical, clerical, and sales workers. The number of blue collar workers is minuscule. Despite great increases in their supply, graduates still can avoid blue collar jobs without risking unemployment. This may imply that the changes in the economy create higher grade jobs as fast as the supply of college graduates increases. Or it may largely be a matter of widely shared perceptions: for example, even intrinsically blue collar jobs that college graduates do should not be considered blue collar. Nearly a third of junior college graduates obtained professional and technical jobs. Even high school graduates, the number of which is much smaller in proportion, got such jobs. But "professional" sounds a little too grandiose for what one can do immediately after high school or junior college. In Japan, therefore, persons with such diverse educational qualifications as high school, two years or four years of college, or years of graduate work can be bundled together and called professional and technical workers. The suspected "status inflation" implied in the generous use of the classification technical worker (*gijutsusha*) may be seen in the curriculum backgrounds of the workers so classified. For example, although 41 percent of the technical workers recruited from junior colleges in 1984 had engineering backgrounds, other curricula like social studies and education also supplied as many technical workers as engineering did (Ministry of Education 1985, 84). The picture becomes more credible with respect to the technical workers who are graduates of four-year universities or holders of graduate degrees. Of the technical workers who are university graduates, 77 percent came from the engineering programs. Of technical workers who hold graduate degrees (master's or doctor's), 80 percent took their degrees in engineering. Nevertheless, the role of nonengineering backgrounds as sources of technical workers is still substantial--20 percent or more. This mixture of technical workers in Japanese occupational statistics cautions against a hasty conclusion that Japan produces the largest number of engineers in the world.

In relation to employment, the college graduates to watch are the men in clerical and sales work. These categories for college graduates reflect the initial training and testing stages of managerial candidates. It is generally assumed that all male graduates of four-year colleges should eventually attain at least middle-level managerial positions. With the increase in the number of college graduates, this assumption becomes less and less tenable. In 1970, 37 percent of fifty to fifty-four-year-old men with college degrees were managers and executives. In 1979, this proportion was down to about 30 percent (Ministry of Labor 1981, 109). This decline was due in large part to the proportionately greater increase in the number of men with a college education in that age group over the years. The supply of managerial positions increased by a different logic from that by which the supply of college-educated people increases. In recent years, the discrepancy between the two (relative shortage of managerial posts) has become an acute management problem. Companies have been looking for ways to match promotions with the available managerial positions without hurting or demoralizing those not promoted. One solution has been to create staff specialists outside the line hierarchy with pay and prestige comparable to what their peers promoted to managerial positions enjoy.

If specialists are qualified for managerial positions, this implies that a company is hoarding an excess supply of managerial resources. This excess dampens the rise in managerial compensation, just as unemployment in the labor market dampens wage increases. Indeed, between 1965 and 1981, in establishments employing five hundred or more employees, the average salary of nonmanagerial personnel in the age group of forty to forty-three years rose from 52 percent to 70 percent of the average salary of the division manager. The differentials among managerial levels also narrowed (Ministry of Labor 1981, 137). As the ranks of eligible and actual managers swell, as the better educated, younger employees grow older, the resources for managerial compensation must be spread thin over larger numbers of educated employees over forty. The Japanese employment system thus embraces a peculiar logic of comparable worth among the college-educated men and at the same time reduces the rate of return on college education. This may be lauded as an aspect of greater industrial democracy, but probably cannot continue for long. Sooner or later differential pay and privileges will be demanded by individuals who believe in their superior worth. The companies also may have to turn their attention to the problem of underutilization and undercompensation of superior abilities. This may require some new philosophy which, for example, condones the notion of the survival of the fittest in career competition and which implies a move away from the view of a company as one big family. As college education becomes commonplace, the educated increasingly find themselves caught in a fierce labor market competition

TABLE 7

Number of 1984 College Graduates and Percent Who are Women, by Path Chosen After Graduation: 1984

Field	Number of students			Percent women		
	Junior college	University	Graduate school	Junior college	University	Graduate school
Total	170,041	365,315	22,583	92.8	24.6	11.7
Advanced to next stage	4,684	20,992	3,118	70.2	12.1	13.5
Employed*	134,463	285,443	15,360	93.3	29.3	7.4
Professional/ Technical	42,300	115,330	14,151	91.9	27.6	7.0
Technical	6,366	66,677	8,626	60.6	9.5	2.0
Educational	14,351	33,714	2,746	98.8	51.8	16.9
Health Care	8,741	7,241	1,401	94.3	59.0	12.5
Others	12,842	7,698	1,378	98.2	49.1	12.7
Managerial/ Administrative	191	682	42	72.2	7.3	9.5
Clerical	77,489	95,056	597	97.8	27.6	14.4
Sales	8,541	63,304	107	84.6	7.6	12.1
Craftsmen, production, process workers, laborers	2,150	901	15	1.7	7.7	0.0
Services	1,832	3,327	122	91.8	27.5	6.6
Others	1,960	6,843	326	87.1	10.3	9.8
Nonactive	25,045	34,164	2,772	95.4	48.9	28.0
Deceased or unknown	5,849	24,716	1,333	86.6	26.7	24.2

*Includes working students.

SOURCE: Ministry of Education 1985b, 74-77, 94-97. The statistics of the employed are supplemented by Ministry of Education 1985a.

under an excess supply of labor--a condition which only a short while before they might have thought was the lot of the uneducated, but not theirs.

Skill Acquisition in Employment

Once Japanese employees begin paid work, the process of learning and applying work skills becomes diverse. Opportunities to develop skills range from unconscious and unplanned experience to highly organized, educational programs off and on the job. While Japanese industry has long had training-within-enterprise institutions, no single pattern of skill acquisition appears to predominate (Levine and Kawada 1980). However, it is safe to say that wage and salary earners learn most of their new or improved job skills informally within the employing organizations and at workplaces (Umetani 1980, 94). While little is known about the extent of the informal training process, probably the great bulk of occupations performed by the great bulk of employees requires only a few weeks or months to master. For most jobs, little formal training is required.

In the small fraction of the labor force that actually undergoes formal training after entering work careers, more is offered for managerial than nonmanagerial personnel, for male employees than female employees, for younger workers than older workers, for the more educated than the less educated, for recruits brought in directly from school graduation than midterm recruits, and for those who already have received training than those who have not. While in 1977 half or more of all firms employing at least thirty workers had some type of formal training program (basic and advanced skills, general knowledge, supervisory), they provided the training to only about 5 percent of all employees. Apparently, most widespread were short-term (ten to thirty days) basic training courses for new school leavers. Even then, two-thirds of the new recruits from school received no training at all in taking up their jobs (Umetani 1980, 89, 92). This depiction of formal training in Japan seems far removed from that frequently portrayed in the popular media.

Whether training is formal or informal, Koike (1984) has systematically described the process of skill formation on the shop floor in Japan. Rejecting the primacy of cultural influences (groupism, work ethic, acceptance of authority), he attributes the strong drive of Japanese workers for skill acquisition and improved efficiency to the rationality of attaining employment security and increased rewards. The chief mechanism for this behavior, he contends, lies in the structure of skill-enhancing work opportunities available to Japanese workers and the method for teaching skills. While formal educational level bears on both this structure and learning opportunity, there is nothing like actual experience with new jobs and work tasks for getting ahead.

Koike finds that in many major enterprises in Japan, work is layered into a large number of progressively sequenced tasks that permit an employee, properly instructed, to move continuously from one task to another, always adding to his stock of skill and ability. In comparing Japanese and American industries, he holds that, despite similar technology, typically the Japanese work structure affords more of these opportunities, both horizontally and vertically, than in the United States. Thus, with continued experience in a single firm (and often only in a single workshop, department, or division, but with opportunities for transfer), the mature Japanese employee acquires a broader and deeper stock of skills than his American counterpart. Although this hypothesis cries for much more systematic research, it seems to conform to characteristics attributed to older (over thirty or thirty-five years of age) skilled workers in Japan who are members of core worker teams in major firms and organizations.

Moreover, such progressive learning, Koike claims, tends to minimize training costs to the firm in comparison with the process of acquiring skill in moving from one enterprise to another, or hiring graduates of outside vocational training institutions. To capture the benefits of "internal" skill improvement, the employing enterprise offers inducements to the worker in the form of employment security, wage advances, fringe benefits, and promotions. This fortifies the labor market internal to the firm.[4]

The other side of this coin is the instructional method, most of which is informal. In Japan, as management of large-scale operations began to learn on a major scale in the 1920s (Levine and Kawada 1980), skill learning was best achieved by attaching new, young recruits to experienced older workers who transmitted their knowledge to the recruits on the job. Even though they might perform the same tasks and together face the challenge of new processes and technologies, the senior worker--partly as the result of his broader mastering of related jobs through experience and partly because of his teaching function--would be rewarded considerably more. Also, the senior would receive promotions and be ranked higher.

Thus, it became an important practice to both workers and managers alike for technical knowledge to flow from the experienced to the inexperienced at work. Such work teams change dynamically as the older workers retire, younger workers move up to middle age, and unskilled recruits enter at the bottom. All members of a team secure their employment as long as they keep on learning new skills that are handed down from senior to junior.

However ad hoc it may appear to be, for large scale firms such a skill acquisition strategy probably proved more effective than attempting to rely on high cost vocational training to emerge within the formal education system or await the development of well-defined craft apprenticeships. On the other hand, small and medium firms apparently have had neither the technological possibilities nor enough experienced senior employees to provide the internal training of large firms. Thus, they have been more likely to seek skills from the external labor market, specialized and miscellaneous schools, and public vocational training programs.

In large enterprises, managers and employees rely upon formal training programs only to a minor degree--contrary to popular impression. At best, formal training is utilized only when the objective cannot be achieved informally on the job or within the enterprise. However, should the internal structuring of skill formation opportunities become difficult, as may well become the case with microelectronic and other high technologies, the established pattern of informal training could crumble. Under such circumstances, one would expect Japan to depend more directly on formal education and external work experience for skill formation.

Employment Tenures and Skills

Certain characteristics seem to differentiate Japanese industrial employment from other countries, at least in the large-scale sector, and are often believed responsible for skill development. These include: 1) relatively long job tenures of workers in a single company and even in one workshop; 2) highly interactive personal relationships within continuing work teams; and 3) a strong degree of homogeneity in attitudes, values, and other characteristics among work team members. Such factors are believed to be especially reinforcing for employee skill learning, although there is a problem of ascertaining cause and effect. Unfortunately, except for a limited set of case studies (mostly by non-Japanese scholars, such as Clark 1979, Cole 1979, Dore 1973, Marsh and Mannari 1976, and Rohlen 1974) there are few systematic, cross-national comparisons of 2) and 3) despite oft-repeated assertions and anecdotes about them.

However, in recent years, considerable quantitative evidence has been accumulated about the duration of jobs in Japan to confirm that, even if lifetime employment is a myth, relatively long tenures are not. Length of employment with a single firm in postwar Japan had to remain speculative for many years simply because many enterprises and job openings only came into existence after Japan's high growth rate began in the 1950s. Now that three decades have passed since the early assertions about lifetime employment, and thanks to detailed labor market surveys regularly conducted by Japanese government agencies (especially the Ministry of Labor and the Prime Minister's Office), expert analysts are now able to examine the actual record systematically.[5] Full agreement is lacking among these analyses. While all concur that only a minority of paid employees in Japan during the past thirty years has experienced lifetime employment (in a single firm), they disagree over the proportion and distribution of the employee labor force that have had long tenures, such as twenty or more years with one employer, and over the results of statistical comparisons with other countries, particularly the United States. The discrepancies may be attributed, at least in part, to differing methodological approaches, too intricate to treat here.

For example, Sterling (1984) finds a much larger proportion of "middle-length" jobs (five to twenty years) in Japan than in the United States, not long enough to qualify as the idealized lifetime employment of model (standard) workers (almost exclusively male) in the large scale enterprises (one thousand workers or more). In fact, Sterling concludes that jobs of thirty years' duration or more, which would be more akin to that ideal, are more frequent in the United States (30 percent) than in Japan (2.2 percent). A major difference between the United States and Japan is not so much the length of tenure but the timing of long-term tenures during the work careers of employees. In Japan, they tend to occur at earlier ages, usually beginning soon after school graduation, while in the United States they tend to start after the worker experiences several different jobs and employers in the external labor market.

Also, according to a recent OECD study (1984) comparing eleven countries for various years in the 1970s and 1980s, Japan led all the others in distribution of job tenure and average number of years in the current job for male workers. In this analysis, Japan had the largest proportion of male workers who had completed 20 years or more on the same job. The figure for Japan was 21.9 percent in 1982, and the next closest, Luxembourg, 18.8 percent in 1972. The United States ranked eighth with 9.9 percent in 1983, and Australia was lowest with 6.8 percent in 1981. The data showed Japan at the top in average job duration for both males and females with 11.7 years. Luxembourg again ranked second with 9.9 years, the United States ninth with 7.2 years, and Australia last with 6.3 years. For males only, Japan led the group with 13.5 years (the United States was ninth with 8.4 years). Even for females, Japan topped all the others with 8.8 years (the United States was tied for seventh with 5.6 years and the Netherlands was last with 3.7 years). These averages, as one would expect, are influenced considerably by the proportion of workers in current jobs not exceeding one year in duration. Only about one-tenth of the Japanese workers occupy such jobs, whereas about three times as many do so in the United States, Australia, and Canada. Further, the OECD study projected the distribution of eventual tenure of jobs currently held. Japan again led with an average of 23 years, while Australia at the bottom averaged less than 13 years. Likewise, 28.1 percent of all American workers eventually would have 20 years or more in the same job, while more than 43 percent would be in jobs lasting 10 years or more.[6]

On the basis of survey and panel data, Tachibanaki (1984) also found that, while a preponderance of both Japanese male and female workers, in all age categories and job tenure groups, reported a desire in 1979 to remain with their present firm (or job), the data on actual tenures do not show fulfillment of these desires. His statistical analysis concludes that only about 10 percent of male workers and less than 2 percent of female workers over the age of forty-five have never changed jobs. Thus, there seem to be few pure lifetime employees who remain with one enterprise from school to retirement. Such completely immobile workers are scarce and tend to be limited to the males with higher formal education who hold white collar jobs in the larger firms. Most Japanese workers will make several changes in employers during their work careers. According to Tachibanaki, almost 42 percent of the panelists interviewed had switched employers three times or more in their careers up to 1979, while about 27 percent had changed at least once. Even more frequent changes seem to take place among workers with less formal education, in lower occupational levels and employed in smaller firms.

On the other hand, Hashimoto and Raisian (1985), using still another mode of econometric analysis, concluded that indeed there is longer job tenure, especially for males, in Japan compared with the United States, not only in large-scale but also in small-scale firms, although that may not have been the case only a few years previously. Comparing official survey data from 1962 and 1977 for Japan and from 1973 and 1978 for the United States, they found that average job tenures in Japan were indeed less than in America two decades ago, but then went ahead more recently. Yet, even in this transition, by the time the average male worker reached the fifty-five to sixty-four age category, he had almost five (4.91) jobs (or employers), whereas his counterpart in the United States held nearly eleven (10.95). In both countries, the average male worker is mobile when young, holding about half the jobs by his mid or late twenties, that is, within about a decade after beginning a career. (The other half occur over the ensuing three or four decades.) Both countries show a similar slowdown in job changing after twenty-five to thirty years of age. Indeed, the two even out in the fifty-five to sixty-four age range.

What the Hashimoto and Raisian data for the late 1970s further clarify is that for each size class of enterprise, job tenures of five or more years are held by a larger percentage of Japanese male workers than by their American counterparts. If that is indeed the case, then it follows that taking advantage of skill acquisition opportunities--through education and training beyond school graduation either on or off the job, formal or informal--has been more likely in Japan than America, regardless of company size, at least for work specific to employing organizations.

These findings lend credence to Koike's hypothesis that Japanese employers provide on the average more learning and training opportunities for their workers than do employers in other countries, especially at earlier stages of work careers. This seems to be the result both of job duration and actual investment in training. What is unclear, however, is whether average tenures, ranging from 7.0 to 13.5 years for males, provide enough of a difference to result in substantially different opportunities for training and skill acquisition.[7] The question is further clouded when skill acquisition and learning is primarily an informal process on the job. With lower turnover rates for shorter-duration jobs in Japan than elsewhere, one might logically expect Japanese employers to make training opportunities more available to their younger workers in comparison with other countries. On the other hand, turnover rates in other countries are no higher for their older workers than in Japan. Therefore, one might expect increased skill acquisition for such older workers compared with the Japanese case where, with mandatory retirement between fifty-five and sixty years of age, learning opportunities frequently seem to come to an abrupt halt. In addition, it is not well-known whether mobile workers, moving from firm to firm, learn more or fewer skills during their early years than those who remain with a single employer.

Certainly, the newer studies utilize much fuller and up-to-date data than ever before. They provide an improved perspective on the relative importance of lifetime employment in several countries, especially Japan and the United States. Remaining in doubt, however, is whether Japan has a decisive edge in this regard for skill formation, as has often been claimed. Still in need of further research is whether lengthier tenures make a vital difference for skill acquisition, either of the specific or general variety.

High Level Professions and Skilled Craft Occupation

Another indicator of skill level in industrial societies is the proportion of the population engaged in high level professions and craft occupations. High level is defined as requiring at least fourteen to sixteen years of formal education or the equivalent in experience and other training. Crafts also require an extended period of preparation under a master. Both usually require official licensing or degrees.

An earlier study (Levine and Kawada 1980, 70-77) estimated the ratios for the rise of the professions in Japan since the Meiji Era. The study included elementary and secondary school teachers, scientists and engineers, physicians and dentists, nurses, and licensed pharmacists. For all these, measured by number per 10,000 population, Japan's ratios had come up to other advanced industrialized countries by the 1960s or 1970s. As seen in Table 8, most attained their current levels, or close to them, by the late 1970s. Since then they have only inched upward and appear to be leveling off.

In many industrialized countries, specific crafts of skilled manual trades and occupations are explicitly encouraged because of their recognized contribution to industrial productivity and work

TABLE 8

**Number of Persons per 10,000 Population Engaged in
High Level Professions in Japan: Selected Years, 1940-82**

Profession	1940	1950	1960	1970	1975	1980	1982
Teachers (elementary and secondary)	39.6	71.8	74.5	76.9	87.6	100.3	103.5
Scientists and engineers	14.2	30.9	42.3	80.1	113.3	n.a.	n.a.
Physicians and dentists	12.4	12.4	14.6	15.2	17.6	21.0	22.6
Nurses	19.2	15.6	19.9	26.5	35.5	47.6	54.1
Licensed pharmacists	4.4	5.5	6.5	7.7	9.4	11.6	12.4

SOURCES: Levine and Kawada 1980, 71; *Japan Statistical Yearbook* 1979, 1984.

quality. Japan has long had official programs for 1) licensing instructors to teach such trades and occupations, and 2) testing and certifying those who intend to enter or are already engaged in those trades and occupations. Instructor training goes back at least to the 1930s (Ishikawa 1981), but it was not until enactment of the 1958 Vocational Training Law that Japan first placed training and licensing of qualified instructors under the joint jurisdiction of the Ministry of Labor and the prefectures. The Ministry's Institute of Vocational Training, begun in 1961 under this act, has since administered these programs. By 1979, it had granted more than 733,000 instructor licenses with the largest numbers in the construction crafts, auto mechanics, and machine shop work (Ishikawa 1981, 14). Most instructors received licenses based on experience rather than through training courses and qualifying examinations and were acitvely engaged in their trades although presumably available for teaching.

A national system of skilled trade testing and certification also was begun in 1959. Under the 1958 law, the Ministry of Labor designates the trades for testing and certification. The number of trades so designated grew from an original 5 to 102 by 1979 (Ishikawa 1981, 16). Within these, various skill grades, usually related to years of work experience, educational background, and degree of difficulty, also have been established. Tests include practical and theoretical materials.

From 1959 to 1979 almost two million applications for skill testing were received by the Ministry of Labor or prefectural governments (Ishikawa 1981, 16). Successful applicants numbered more than 1.175 million, the largest number of whom where construction craftsmen and machinists. Certification, of course, does not guarantee a job, but it is often helpful in securing employment, receiving wage increases or bonuses, or obtaining promotions. Many employers, especially in smaller firms, seem to encourage their workers to take the tests and give additional tests themselves.

Under the law, a central, nationwide organization with regional branches promotes the taking of tests, designates trades to be tested, and determines test content and standards. A large annual affair in Japan is the national skill competition in the certified trades, from which winners are selected to represent Japan in the International Training Competition (Skill Olympics). The Ministry of Labor awards prizes in all these events (Ishikawa 1981, 17).

The Challenge of a Changing Labor Force

Despite efforts in Japan to assure an adequate flow of skilled personnel, the emphasis in training has been largely upon the younger workers of the labor force. Substantial groups appear cut off from skill training opportunities, notably older male workers (usually beyond fifty to fifty-five years of age), and an assortment of part-time and nonregular workers, a large bulk of whom are women. These groups are growing faster than the labor force itself, so that without changes there is an eventual threat of deskilling.

Especially problematic are older employees, many of whom already have had long years of work experience. With a dramatic demographic shift occurring in present-day Japan, several critical policy questions face government, employers, and unions regarding employment opportunities for the swelling numbers of senior workers. (By 1983 almost 39 percent of males and about 16 percent of females over sixty-five participated in the Japanese labor force, compared with less than 18 percent and 8 percent, respectively, in the United States.) A commonplace solution at the company level has been to raise retirement ages gradually from fifty-five to sixty by leveling off earnings at an earlier age or encouraging separations from companies prior to mandatory retirement. By itself this approach does not enhance adaptation to new jobs.

Another frequent solution, although not necessarily confined to older workers, has been to transfer employees from one enterprise to another, often on an indefinite loan basis, on the theory that such transferred workers remain members of their original companies and eventually will return to them. In these cases, skills acquired in one enterprise are believed to be equally useful elsewhere. However, relatively little is known about what actually happens to skills in such transfers, although a high degree of cooperation among companies has taken place in the areas of personnel management and human resource development for these workers (Amaya 1983, 11-12).

More promising in this regard is that more and more large-scale enterprises have launched career planning programs for regular employees, especially at the managerial levels. Related to these are conscious efforts to redesign work itself to permit improved employee adaptation to jobs, as well as to tap latent skills and abilities. On the other hand, as personnel and training costs have mounted, managements often have turned to labor-saving robotization and to less costly overseas production, making career planning in Japan all the more urgent.

While various experiments are underway in Japan for providing productive employment opportunities for aging workers, and laws have been adopted to encourage companies to retain older employees (and the handicapped, also), Japan has yet to make a shift in training patterns and practices for this group comparable to what occurred in the past thirty years as the educational level of young recruits rose dramatically. This remains a major challenge for the future.

The educational content in the Japanese labor force continues to rise as the more educated, younger people are added to it every year and as less educated, older workers retire. When the ratio of college graduates is equalized in time for all age groups as a result of the stabilized enrollment among youth, the problems of unemployment and underemployment of older educated people, women as well as men, are bound to rise. Managerial positions will become relatively scarce. Training opportunities within enterprise will decline.

A solution that commands widespread attention is professionalization of work that older educated people, males and females, can do, through greater specialization. The objective is to enable them to be individually independent with dignity, supported by their own professional practices. Professions, certifiable by the national government, are multiplying, giving rise to all kinds of specialists and consultants inside and outside companies.

Much of the agonizing problem in Japanese education and employment today arises from the tyranny of unilinear thinking and its institutional reinforcement. The respected life course for a man (though not for a woman) has been the regular progression in education in the 6-3-3-4 sequence (elementary school, junior high school (compulsory through this), high school, and college) and, after a successful entry into the employ of a major company, the scheduled rise, as if on an escalator, through ranks to retire as an official of the company. This is the model path, put on a single string of time. At major junctures of this path, there are examinations to pass. A person's merits are thus constantly evaluated. A person's worth and social prestige are then judged by the degree of consistency of his life course with this model path, although as Plath (1983) points out there are important exceptions. The education system and the employment practices of the government and major companies apparently enforce the model path with special kinds of reward and punishment systems (recruitment fresh out of school or college, lifetime employment, *nenko* wages, and *teinen* retirement).

But a great majority of Japanese men, and virtually all working women, now fail to get on this model path of education and employment. They are failures, although they are ordinary people. Those put on the model path constitute the elite, the meritocrats. The wonder of it all is that this particular system of elite formation and perpetuation evokes so little resentment anywhere in Japan. The labor market is the major mechanism by which the nonelite populace tries to settle with the second, third, and n-th best outside the model path. In these circumstances, one would expect a rising demand for self-help education and new training opportunities outside of enterprises to cope with the rigidities of the unilinear system, especially when the demographic and technological structures face enormous modification.

Notes

1. Japan's college enrollment rate is defined as the ratio of all new college students in a given year to all boys and girls who completed nine-year compulsory education three years earlier.

2. The calculations for Table 2 show the standard formula that equates the present value of all future earnings of college graduates over and above the earnings of high school graduates to the present value of foregone earnings and direct educational expenses of college years.

3. The specialized school, to qualify for its name, is required by the Ministry of Education to offer at least a year-long curriculum with eight hundred or more hours of instruction per year (Ministry of Education 1980, 207).

4. Koike also notes that because the knowledge of skills and operations held within the team is often more than possessed by management and engineering personnel, team leaders may enjoy considerable autonomy and have discretion to assign and rotate tasks among team members. Because of the close interpersonal relationships which develop, rotation usually occurs on an egalitarian basis, and equal participation for all members of the team becomes well-established. (Formalized QC circles easily emerge in these

circumstances.) It is no wonder that wage rates and benefits in Japan have been heavily based on length-of-service and level of formal education rather than specific jobs. In the large firms, where the job skills can become broad and deep through experience within the enterprise itself, the treatment of regular, or standard, blue collar workers becomes similar to that for white collar employees (Koike calls this "white collarization").

5. Prominent among recent studies in English are Levine 1983, Sterling 1984, OECD 1984, Tachibanaki 1984, and Hashimoto and Raisian 1985.

6. These estimates support the long-established finding for most countries that show that the longer workers are already in jobs, the more likely they will stay longer than will short-termers. Thus, since early job leaving is less frequent in Japan than the other countries, the average tenures are bound to be lengthier, but not necessarily of the lifetime variety.

7. Much the same questions may be raised for *expected* average tenures and distributions of tenures. The conventional wisdom is that they do, but actually the answer remains unsettled.

References

Amaya, T. 1983. *Human Resource Development in Industry* (Japan Industrial Relations Series No. 10). Tokyo: The Japan Institute of Labour.

Bank of Japan. 1960, 1970, 1980. *Keizai tokei nenpo* [Annual Economic Report]. Tokyo: Bank of Japan.

Bowman, M. J. 1981. *Educational Choice and Labor Markets in Japan*. Chicago: The University of Chicago Press.

Clark, R. 1979. *The Japanese Company*. New Haven: Yale University Press.

Cole, R. 1979. *Work, Mobility, and Participation: A Comparative Study of American and Japanese Industry*. Berkeley: University of California Press.

Dore, R. 1973. *British Factory-Japanese Factory: The Origins of National Diversity in Industrial Relations*. Berkeley: University of California Press.

Hashimoto, M., and J. Raisian. 1985. "Employment Tenure and Earnings Profiles in Japan and the United States." *American Economic Review* 75:4, 721-35.

Ishikawa, T. 1981. *Vocational Training* (Japanese Industrial Relations Series No. 7). Tokyo: The Japan Institute of Labour.

Iwauchi, R., et al., eds. 1985. *Kyoiku to shakai* [Education and society]. Tokyo: Gakubunsha.

Japan Statistical Yearbook. 1979, 1984. Tokyo: Office of the Prime Minister.

Kaneko, M. 1984. "Rise and Fall of Educational Expansion." Paper presented at the 29th Comparative and International Education Society Conference, Houston, Texas.

Koike, K. 1984. "Skill Formation Systems in the U.S. and Japan: A Comparative Study." In M. Aoki, ed., *The Economic Analysis of the Japanese Firm*, pp. 47-75. Amsterdam, the Netherlands: Elsevier Science.

Levine, S. 1983. "Careers and Mobility in Japan's Labor Markets." In D. W. Plath, ed., *Work and Lifecourse in Japan*, pp. 18-33. Albany, NY: State University of New York Press.

-----, and H. Kawada. 1980. *Human Resources in Japanese Industrial Development*. Princeton, NJ: Princeton University Press.

Management and Coordination Agency (MCA). 1984. *Kyoiku kara mita nihon no jinko* [Japanese population as seen from education]. Tokyo: Nihon Tokei Kyokai.

Marsh, R. M., and H. Mannari. 1976. *Modernization and the Japanese Factory*. Princeton, NJ: Princeton University Press.

Matsuura, T. 1978. *Shushoku* [Occupational entry]. Tokyo: Nihon Keizai Shinbunsha.

Ministry of Education (MOE). 1980. *Wagakuni no kyoiku suijun* [Our country's level of education]. Tokyo: The Ministry of Finance Press.

-----. 1985a. *Gakko kihon chosa* [Basic school survey]. Tokyo: Monbusho.

-----. 1985b. *Monbu tokei yoran* [Abstracts of education statistics]. Tokyo: Daiichi Hoki Shuppan KK.

Ministry of Labor (MOL). 1981. *Rodo hakusho* [White paper on labor]. Tokyo: Ministry of Labor.

Organization for Economic Cooperation and Development (OECD). 1984. "The Importance of Long-Term Job Attachment in OECD Countries." *OECD Employment Outlook*, September, 55-68.

Plath, D. W. 1983. *Work and Lifecourse in Japan*. Albany, NY: State University of New York Press.

Rohlen, T. 1974. *For Harmony and Strength: Japanese White-Collar Organization in Anthropological Perspective*. Berkeley: University of California Press.

Sterling, W. 1984. "Patterns of Job Duration in Japan and the United States" (mimeo).

Tachibanaki, T. 1984. "Labor Mobility and Job Tenure." In M. Aoki, ed., *The Economic Analysis of the Japanese Firm*, pp. 77-102. Amsterdam, the Netherlands: Elsevier Science.

Tomita, K. 1984. *Monbukei tanki daigaku no saihen katei ni kansuru kenkyu* [An inquiry into the reorganization of the Ministry of Education's junior colleges]. Sagamihara, Kanagawa: Research and Development Center, Institute of Vocational Training.

Tsuchiya, H. 1978. *Saiyo no jitsumu* [Hiring in practice]. Tokyo: Nihon Keizai Shinbunsha.

Umetani, S. 1980. *Vocational Training in Japan*. Hamburg: Institut fur Asienkunde.

U.S. Department of Commerce, Bureau of the Census. 1985. *Statistical Abstract of the United States*. Washington, DC: Government Printing Office.

CHAPTER 10

FURTHER RESEARCH: NEEDS, POSSIBILITIES, AND PERSPECTIVES

Robert Leestma
U.S. Department of Education

The views and ideas expressed in this chapter are those of the author and do not necessarily reflect the position or policy of the U.S. Department of Education.

Introduction

There has been considerable progress in the West's understanding of education in Japan. In addition to much basic information from Japanese sources, many significant contributions have been made by scholars from the United States as well as some from Britain, France, and various other OECD countries. The general characteristics, structure, functioning, cultural context, and values involved in most major aspects of the education system are now fairly well identified, at least in broad outline, and much of the detail has been sketched in. This volume and its predecessor in the U.S. Study of Education in Japan make their own contributions to reliable research and synthesis.

But our knowledge and understanding are hardly complete. Apart from knowledge gaps in matters not yet addressed or research evidence not readily available, there are many areas of uncertainty because much of the accessible evidence leaves something to be desired. Several of the generalizations widely publicized in English rest on weak scholarly foundations--or on none at all.

The small team that produced *Japanese Education Today* (Leestma, August, George, and Peak 1987), the first volume of the U.S. Study, completed that general audience report with a sense of genuine accomplishment. But the feeling was tempered by a strong concern about the adequacy of the field's existing research base. That concern was the genesis of this chapter.

Virtually none of the space available here is used for re-
peating information contained in the earlier report. The assumption
is that readers are familiar with the content and conclusions of
Japanese Education Today, hereafter Leestma et al. 1987. Nor is
there duplication of research ideas contained elsewhere in this
volume.

Most of the chapter is devoted to identifying important topics, issues, and questions about Japanese education that need research attention. Related aspects and ideas will occur to many readers. The matters for inquiry are introduced by some underlying concerns, including reasons why more is not yet known, an overview of
chapter contents, and an indication of priorities. The research topics, questions, and issues are followed by a discussion of some research considerations and approaches and an identification of research opportunities with special potential. The final section summarizes the importance of increasing communication and cooperation with Japanese researchers, notes the likely consequences of
securing more good evidence, and concludes with some personal perspectives on education and change in Japan.

While primarily a call for needed research, this chapter is
also a general appeal for cooperation in sharing information about
sources and data useful to the research community at large. Thus
whatever solid information is brought to light as a result of questions or concerns presented here will be welcome in the common
cause of understanding education in Japan.

Background

Fact or Fancy

In *Japanese Education Today*, we did our best within what
turned out to be severe time constraints to take an objective look at
Japanese education and report the results in an unvarnished fashion. Some myths or persistent misconceptions were exposed and
cleared up along the way. These included the facts about the 240-
day school year (Leestma et al. 1987, 10), the high school completion rate (p. 7), the multifaceted nature and significance of *juku* (pp.
11-14), the high school admission process (p. 38), the actual state of
affairs about the presumed widespread mastery of foreign languages (p. 36), and the suicide issue (p. 45).

The more one probes the growing body of literature, pursues discussions with sophisticated scholars of Japanese education and culture, and reflects on what is believed or alleged to be "known," the more it becomes apparent that it is time to reexamine several other aspects of "common knowledge" about Japanese education, as well as to explore important areas where we know we don't know. Indeed, in the former category one begins to suspect that some measure of demythologizing may prove warranted on various fronts that usually have not been subjected to close inspection, at least not recently.

Among prime candidates for verification, conceivable revision, or possibly being put to rest are claims of equality of opportunity for all throughout elementary and secondary education, claims of universal literacy, and the much publicized assertion that the average Japanese high school graduate is educationally equivalent to the average American college graduate. (The last is a guaranteed attention-grabber, to be sure, but whether it would hold up to critical examination remains to be demonstrated.) Other examples of major areas ripe for careful scrutiny include the quality of teacher education and the extent, causes, and consequences of student disaffection with school at the secondary level.

Why More Is Not Yet Known

In the United States, the largest single Western source of research on Japanese education, attention to the subject continues to proliferate in the professional literature as well as in the mass media. However, the increase in activity is not producing a proportionate gain in knowledge and insight. The reasons include the seemingly endless recycling of basic misconceptions (e.g., all or most Japanese children must take examinations to enter first grade) despite established knowledge to the contrary, ignorance or misunderstanding of cultural values and context, ethnocentric misinterpretation of education terminology and scenes that appear familiar and clear on the surface, and, of course, the formidable language barrier.

Much of the literature in English on Japanese education contains more than its share of misconception, oversimplification, old data, misleading anecdotes, and dubious impressionistic interpretation. Use of Japanese language sources is infrequent, usually limited in amount, and sometimes seriously outdated at time of citation. Journalistic approaches outnumber scholarly efforts, and, while the former category accounts for most of the offenses, the misinformation that occurs in the professional literature is far from insignificant and helps fuel the former.

A special problem is the small number of American scholars (or other non-Japanese) capable of working insightfully in the Japanese language and cultural milieu--and the very small number of these who have chosen to apply their special capabilities to matters of education. The problem is compounded because few of the best American specialists on Japanese education pursue the subject full-time or on a continuing basis, and the generation of specialists that emerged from the Occupation period is passing from the scene. Further, the school field work in some of the finest studies by the subsequent generation of scholars (Cummings 1980 and Rohlen 1983, for example) is now fifteen years old, and the number of foreign scholars of any nationality who have developed productive collaborative relationships with Japanese researchers of education is not large.

At least until very recently, the total number of American scholars conducting primary research on Japanese education who were producing without a likely serious language or cultural handicap directly or indirectly (without appropriate Japanese collaborators, if not personally fluent in Japanese) did not appear to exceed a dozen or so individuals.[1] The number would seem smaller still in other Western countries. Because so much of education in Japan is at one with society and culture, because of the great differences between Japanese culture and familiar Western models, because the language barrier is so great, and because of Japanese society's relative inaccessibility to foreigners, few nonspeakers and nonreaders of Japanese are likely to make major research contributions on most topics single-handedly.

The latest problem to emerge affects all categories of researchers--it is the high cost of conducting research in Japan now because of the painful reality of the currency exchange rate. And brief stays pose serious problems of their own, particularly for researchers new to Japan.

It should be noted at the outset that not all of the questions raised in the pages that follow are unexplored. Something is known about various items and quite a bit about many, at least by Japanese scholars, as indicated later. Indeed, sufficient information in Japanese might well be available on a considerable number of the topics, particularly those not dealt with in the first volume.

Unfortunately, relatively little of the body of Japanese research literature is available in English, and time constraints limited what could be searched in Japanese. However, we located enough to know that much more good material on various topics remains waiting to be tapped.[2] But some of the questions of interest to Americans probably have not yet been addressed by Japanese scholars. This usually would be because such topics have not been seen as significant or necessary in the Japanese context or, in some cases, because they are considered too sensitive for one reason or another.[3]

The upshot of all the foregoing factors is that researchers not proficient in the Japanese language are overly dependent upon a very limited number of usually narrowly focused (though appropriate to the original task), small-scale, good studies--and some not so good--reported in English. However, it should be noted that on some matters important scholarly work in English and Japanese is in process or about to begin (see, for example, note 5).

Overview

This chapter presents the nagging questions we were left with as the first U.S. report went to press, along with additional ones not addressed there and some that emerged later in the course of reflecting further on Japanese education. The list is put forward neither as a complete research agenda on any count nor as a partial agenda in finished form. Rather, it is a selection of various things believed worth knowing or verifying--along with some related concerns, puzzlements, ideas, and approaches--to help round out a basic understanding of contemporary Japanese education.

The sequence of topics in the study's first volume is followed to some extent, but certain basic issues of interest to many are taken up at the outset. Other items are placed or grouped as they are for reasons of emphasis or to encourage their consideration in a particular context.

The thrust of the chapter is on education matters per se during the years of formal schooling, rather than on fundamental studies of other aspects of Japanese society and culture, including child development, adolescence, and adult and continuing education. For the most part, history also receives less attention than some might wish. Important though these and other such dimensions are, for the most part they lie outside this chapter's brief. More to the point, at least at the present stage of intercultural understanding, there exists a much larger and firmer base of specialized scholarship on relevant Japanese history, culture, and on both traditional and modern society than there is on Japanese education. (To be sure, much more work is needed, especially on cultural change now in process, particularly on matters affecting youth in general and adolescents in particular.) The availability--and informed use--of this solid knowledge base in the humanities and social sciences makes it easier for serious students of Japanese education to do significant work in appropriate context.

Some of the matters addressed are basic questions in any indepth examination of an education system in cultural context (still a surprisingly uncommon research undertaking), while others may break new ground in exploring the relationship of school and society in Japan. Some deal with recalibration of familiar baselines, with obtaining actual data on or otherwise verifying aspects usually taken for granted ("everybody knows"), or with updating basic information to see if circumstances have changed and new patterns are emerging. (In many respects, the times and youth are indeed a-changing, but are the schools and teachers?) A few items explore genuine terra incognita and may suggest development of new indicators. And a few are clearly speculative. In most cases, the research need includes going beyond development of an accurate description of what is to try to determine why things are as they are.

While a number of the questions raised represent fairly straightforward research tasks that should yield readily to those with suitable skills, several will be quite difficult in the best of hands, and some are extremely sensitive (the education situation of minorities in Japan, for example). Questionnaires that only skim the surface, other quick and superficial data gathering (particularly through foreign ethnocentric filters), and monolingual approaches in English aren't likely to produce much of value.

Whether a project is simple or complex, surmounting the barriers of language and culture cannot be taken for granted. Research instruments which are translated into Japanese from English or other languages should have the accuracy of all items and instructions verified by independent back translation and corrected as necessary before data collection is undertaken. Foreign interviewers need to be knowledgeable about and sensitive to Japanese social conventions and language usage in dealing with strangers. It can be very difficult, especially in a single, brief session, to elicit the real views of subjects or sources, particularly if those views are contrary to what the interviewer is perceived to believe or want.

In many instances, the complexity of the problem requires interdisciplinary research. And some matters won't yield to a fragmented approach; they must be dealt with as organic wholes in appropriate context (a caveat as applicable for some education research in the United States as in the study of education in other countries).

Several of the questions posed in this chapter reflect predominantly American concerns, values, and perspectives. Others will be of at least equal interest to Japanese educators and, on occasion, perhaps of greater value. Some, like the development of mutual understanding through school programs, are natural prospects for cooperative effort with qualified Japanese collaborators.

Various items have related dimensions in the American context and would seem particularly suitable for comparative treatment. In some cases, more work will need to be done in one or the other country before valid comparisons can be undertaken. (We don't yet know the answers to some of the questions for the United States.) Sometimes the comparative dimension is mentioned, more often it is not, on the assumption that readers are in a better position to make their own determination of cross-cultural possibilities.

The allure of comparative studies seems especially strong for helping achieve a better understanding of the interaction of home, school, and society in human development, of the nature and process of effective education, and of the dynamics of change in cultural context. Enhanced understanding and insight about these and other matters hold promising potential for helping improve American education. The potential includes an enlarged sense of what is possible for children to learn at various developmental stages, at least under Japanese circumstances, knowledge of new alternatives, fresh perspectives on present problems, and other forms of stimulus and assistance.

Research Priorities

Given the large number of research needs identified and the wide range of topics involved, several of the specialists on Japanese education who reviewed the chapter in draft felt that some indication of priorities would be helpful. The writer was persuaded to share a personal perspective on the matter, but obviously others interested in the field might well settle on different priorities. In any event, what follows reflects essentially one person's judgment on some central concerns and critical knowledge gaps that need careful, systematic attention if we are to reach a more complete understanding of education in Japan--in Japanese education's own terms as well as for such ideas and insights as the Japanese experience might hold for strengthening American education.

Equality of Opportunity

> Current extent of equality of opportunity, especially in relation to socioeconomic class and to children who are different.

Family Involvement

> Nature and extent of family involvement and investment in education, including supplementary out-of-school assistance, particularly beyond the compulsory school period.

Teaching and Learning

> Teacher quality.

> Content and effectiveness of preservice education of teachers.

> Student achievement in subjects other than science and mathematics.

> Noncognitive learning--attitudes and values, especially with regard to individualism, egalitarianism, intercultural understanding, and democracy.

> Problems of slow learners, low achievers, and student alienation from school, especially in secondary education.

> Case studies of teachers and students in action: the dynamics of teaching and learning in all curriculum areas at every elementary and secondary grade level.

Curriculum

> Content, methods, and effectiveness of efforts aimed at moral education and character development, including integration of the academic and nonacademic aspects of the school program.

> International objectives and content in elementary and secondary curricula, in high school and university entrance examinations, and in preservice teacher education programs; international interests, knowledge, attitudes, and perceptions of students and teachers.

> Japan-United States comparative studies of education objectives, efforts, achievements, and trade-offs between and among goals and values involving conformity, cooperation, group cohesion, social harmony, individual development, and creativity.

School Culture

> Studies of classrooms within the ethos of their respective schools and of schools as total entities in community context.

Higher Education

> Nature and extent of Ministry of Education control over higher education, particularly the private sector, and ministry interest and efforts regarding reform.

> More valid and reliable measures of the quality and productivity of university undergraduate education--representative national samples of what is taught and how, and of what is learned.

> To the extent undergraduate education is as weak as generally represented, why does Japan ask and accept so little?

Education Change

> Process of experimentation and change in Japanese education, including parental involvement in the change process.

> Results of the reports and recommendations of the National Council on Educational Reform.

Research Information and Design Considerations

In addition to the foregoing topics, priority attention is also indicated for three areas having wide utility for research purposes:

1) Improving awareness of and access to research sources and literature on Japanese education, particularly material in the Japanese language (see recent development at end of note 2);

2) Determining extent of variability in Japanese education; and

3) Developing criteria for selection of representative national samples in the various education sectors, fields, and topics.

Context and Caveat

It should be emphasized that the research topics and priorities set forth in this chapter are essentially complementary to and should be considered in the context of the U.S. Study's first report, *Japanese Education Today*. There are diverse questions of related significance not dealt with in either place, largely because they concern topics and fields that lie beyond the Department of Education's purview, but within the domain of other agencies. For example, the quality of science, engineering, and technology programs in Japanese higher education are matters attended to by the National Science Foundation.

Some Basic Issues

Equality of Opportunity

Given a) the direct relationship between the academic ranking of high schools and the success of their graduates on university entrance examinations, b) the close relationship between university credentials and preferred employment, and c) the continuing impact of university entrance examinations on most precollegiate education, up-to-date studies of sufficient scope and depth are needed to determine the actual status of and extent of government commitment to equality of opportunity, particularly beyond compulsory education. The basic question: to what extent do socioeconomic class differences affect education outcomes at all levels, particularly access to advantages in the examination and admission process at upper secondary and university levels?

Public Funding and Public/Private School Cost Comparisons

Because of a strong legal basis, longstanding policy commitments, and substantial central government funding, public financial support of compulsory education is believed to be fairly uniform throughout Japan. However, the data commonly used to support the view that the variance is no greater than 20 percent among school districts are now twenty years old. It is time for an up-to-date analysis of 1) the extent to which financial support is equally available to schools throughout the nation for the compulsory education period, and 2) the national variations in per-pupil expenditure for public and private upper secondary schools, and the correlation with secondary school rankings as determined by the success of graduates on university entrance examinations.

Private Advantage

It is well established that Japanese parents go to great lengths, including considerable financial sacrifice, to help ensure educational success for their children. Indeed, as Rohlen points out, "No other country in the world comes close in the percentage of their populations involved in buying private educational advantage" (Rohlen 1980, 238). Increasingly, there are indications that beyond elementary education the children of affluent families have a significant advantage in the competition for admission to the most prestigious upper secondary schools and universities because of the ability to afford the higher costs of selected private secondary schools, family tutors, and the best *juku* and *yobiko*--all of which bear on the probability of success in crucial entrance examinations.

To what extent do those who are successful in gaining admittance to the highest status upper secondary and postsecondary institutions have the advantage of *juku*, tutors, *yobiko*, or other special assistance and at what total cost? What is the relationship to family income? Just how much equality of educational opportunity exists beyond elementary school, and how does it relate to decreasing or increasing socioeconomic mobility in contemporary Japanese society? To the extent economic barriers to purchasing supplementary education for competitive advantage are a reality for a significant proportion of elementary school graduates, how aware is the general public of the extent of the situation, how is social cohesion being affected, and how strong is public pressure for increasing equality of opportunity?

Quality of Instruction

While school financing is usually assumed to be more or less equalized throughout the country (to be determined), school facilities are believed to be generally comparable, and textbooks are selected from the same Ministry of Education-approved list, what is the status of equality of instruction? Are there significant variations in teacher quality among prefectures and municipalities? Between public and private secondary schools of the same type? Between rural and urban areas? What contribution does NHK educational broadcasting make to equalize the quality of instruction throughout Japan?

Children Who Are Different

The cumulative research on Japanese culture by scholars from diverse fields has established well enough the enormous emphasis placed on conformity to established norms and values, and the costs and penalties for those who are different or behave differently. The Japanese school system reflects its society. To be different is to be disadvantaged.

Careful studies are needed to explore this phenomenon in all of its categories and complexities. "Different" children would include those of the few ethnic and/or cultural minority groups, those with physical and/or mental handicaps, and those whose principal difference is a strong individualistic, nonconformist personality. In Japan, children who have lived and studied abroad are also considered different, and clearly in a negative rather than a positive sense. Disadvantaged status has been acquired through resident exposure to a foreign culture.

It should be noted that some of these domains of difference, especially where ethnic and cultural minorities are concerned, involve some of the most sensitive issues in Japanese education. For example, consider the education situation confronting the Korean minority. Given the deep-seated and pervasive Japanese prejudice against Koreans in Japan, how do students of Korean heritage fare in regular Japanese high schools? How effective in education terms alone are the special high schools for Korean residents that are af- filiated with either *Mindan* or *Soren*? On what basis do students of Korean heritage decide to attend these schools rather than regular Japanese high schools--and how does this choice affect their subse- quent life chances? Such matters require special sophistication for meaningful research with constructive results. They are not suitable research topics for ethnocentric, monolingual Westerners.

The field of education for the handicapped illustrates some of the kinds of studies needed about children who are different, begin- ning in this case with a comprehensive description of special provi- sions for education of the physically and mentally handicapped. Are adjustments made in the usual pedagogical premise that effort is more important than ability? Is more individual assistance given to handicapped children? To what extent are concepts of main- streaming and individual development plans involved? What special training do teachers of the handicapped receive? To what extent is public secondary education available to handicapped students? Some of these questions--concerning individual assistance and special teacher training, for example--are equally valid for children from ethnic and/or cultural minority groups. Some information on such questions is available in English, but much more in Japanese.

Children who have lived and studied abroad face special problems upon return (Leestma et al. 1987, 33) and represent a unique challenge to an education system based on uniformity and conformity. The system makes special provision for helping such students purge themselves of foreign influences and academic defi- ciencies that are at odds with Japanese norms. Systematic, up-to- date studies are needed of the problems of returning students and the present status of the reentry programs, as well as of the Min- istry of Education's cumulative experience with the various special efforts to facilitate readjustment to the Japanese educational and cultural milieu. Where feasible, study samples should be adequate in size and representativeness to permit conclusions about the re- lationship of reentry problems to such variables as student gender, duration and level of schooling abroad, country where foreign expe- rience took place, and school type and level to which student returned.

Specifically, what problems do returning students face, and how do the special classes and programs go about their tasks of resocialization and bringing students up to speed academically? What changes in approach, if any, have occurred since the first such special arrangements were established? What changes, if any,

are evident from the relevant recommendations of the National
Council on Educational Reform? How are teachers selected for these
programs, what orientation do they receive, and how is experience
with returnees shared among participating teachers in the many
schools approved to offer such programs?

How many children have experienced the special reentry
programs since they were first established? What does recent
Japanese research show about any problems with and the effectiveness of such remedial efforts from the system's point of view? From
the viewpoint of the students and parents involved--at the time and
subsequently, say, five and ten years later?

Related studies are needed of the readjustment experience of
students who resume their education in regular Japanese schools directly rather than through any of the special programs. Companion
studies are indicated of the initial attitudes of classmates of the returning students, particularly in regular schools. Are peer group attitudes strongly and uniformly negative toward a student returning
from abroad, or is there some measure of individual curiosity, for
example, about the unusual experience the returning student has
had and any new views acquired? Does peer group reaction to returning students differ at different school levels? An important, up-
to-date contribution on several aspects of the subject of Japanese
students returning from abroad and "reverse culture shock" has just
been provided by Goodman (1990), who appears to be the first to
detect some emerging recognition in Japan that returnees are a national asset rather than a liability.

Concept of Failure, Grading System, and Motivation

With promotion from grade to grade being essentially automatic and not dependent upon academic achievement (except for the
sorting into different senior high schools at grade ten), what is the
concept of failure in Japanese education, especially during the compulsory school period? How do teachers evaluate whether a student
is putting forth sufficient effort or doing less than his or her best?
How does the marking system reflect student performance and
teacher judgment up to the time of entry to senior high school? How
do teachers endeavor to maintain student motivation, particularly
on the part of children with learning difficulties who fall further behind as they progress through the grades, and how well do they
succeed? (Holloway (1988) provides an insightful summary and

analysis of recent work on concepts of effort and ability in Japan and the United States. Of particular value is the exploration of how home and school environments in Japan help develop and maintain student orientation to effort and motivation.)

Does the concept of failure change in upper secondary education? If so, are there differences between regular academic programs and vocational programs in the concept or its application? Is there any change in how the marking system reflects student performance and teacher judgment? Exactly what academic standards must be met for high school graduation? Is there a minimum level of scholastic competency required or is regular attendance, compliant behavior, and some measure of effort sufficient?

How extensively do Japanese senior high school teachers endeavor to maintain the motivation of students who are not performing well academically and may have fallen hopelessly behind so far as prospects for university entrance are concerned? Or do teachers simply accept the slow learners and those who essentially have opted out of serious study and let them coast through to graduation in exchange for not being a disruptive force in school (a bargain hardly unknown in American education)?

How many children are held back each year at each grade level, what are the reasons for nonpromotion, and what are the effects--psychologically, socially, and academically--on children who have to repeat a grade in Japan?

Literacy

One of the strongest perceptions foreigners hold of Japanese society and education is that of universal literacy, that there is no illiteracy in Japan. There is no doubt that Japan reflects a high level of literacy by any reasonable standard--or that literacy rate is strongly affected by the definition and assessment process employed. In light of recent reliable evidence that a sizeable number of Japanese children have severe reading problems (Stevenson, Azuma, and Hakuta 1986, 225-26, 233) and given the pervasive social promotion policy through high school graduation, it is time to determine the actual level of proficiency in reading and writing of high school seniors and recent graduates, as well as of the 12 percent of the age cohort that do not complete high school.

System Characteristics

Centralization and Standardization

Roles of and Interaction Among Levels of Authority

Certainly by comparison with the situation in the United States, the Japanese education system at the elementary and secondary levels is highly centralized and standardized. But there isn't complete uniformity, and there is some measure of give and take. A comprehensive analysis is needed of centralization and decentralization of authority for education in Japan, and of the extent and dynamics of formal and informal interaction between the various levels of authority, from the Ministry of Education down to the individual school. What is negotiable and how is consensus developed on these matters?

Governance and Management

How do prefectural and municipal boards of education and education offices work, and how do prefectural governors, municipal mayors, and education superintendents go about their governance and management responsibilities for education? What role does the Japan Teachers Union play? These matters are common knowledge to Japanese concerned with education, but little is known about them in the United States. (Rohlen 1983 provides a useful introduction, and some up-to-date firsthand information is likely to be provided in due course by various alumni of the Japan Exchange and Teaching Program described later in the section entitled, "Research Opportunities with Special Potential.")

Variation in Schools and Instruction

A careful study is indicated of the nature and range of variation within and between prefectures and municipalities. Nationwide, how much variation is there in instructional methodology in Japanese elementary schools? How much variability in goals, curriculum coverage, and methodology exists between and among secondary schools of different types and status levels? Any significant difference between rural and urban areas? Between public and private sectors? (Rohlen stands virtually alone with regard to sophisticated analysis of the upper secondary sector.)

High School Equivalence Credential

The Japanese system contains provision for a credential equivalent to graduation from high school. What is involved in qualifying for the credential, how many students seek and secure it, and what are the reasons and characteristics of the students who avail themselves of this route? How does the market value of this credential compare with that of a conventional high school diploma from the different categories and rankings of upper secondary schools? How useful is the equivalence credential for university admission purposes? For admission to other categories of postsecondary institutions? (Much is known about all of this in Japan.)

Finance and Costs

Institutional

What are the specific sources and total amounts of public and private funds for the Japanese education system, including higher education? To what extent and how does the national government influence local taxation and spending for education?

Family

It is clear that most Japanese families make a sizeable investment of time and money in the elementary and secondary education of their children--for preschool attendance, supplementary study materials and furnishings, *juku* and/or private tutors, high school tuition, and the like. Much useful information on household expenditure for education is available in Japanese. More of it needs to become accessible in English, including information on rural/urban differences.

What proportion of the annual income of a representative family with school age children is devoted to investment in education at the preschool, elementary, junior high, and senior high school levels, and how does this compare with the education expenditures of a comparable family in the United States? Related studies of the amount of parental time devoted to education support services for school age children at the various levels would be of considerable value.

Studies of family expenditures for education at the postsecondary level are also needed for representative students and institutions, including *ronin* costs (Leestma et al. 1987, 45) for the university category. And better data are needed on the share of costs contributed by students who earn part of their higher education expenses by teaching in *juku* or through other employment.

Textbooks

More information is needed on the criteria and decision-making process involved in elementary and secondary textbook approval by the Ministry of Education and for textbook selection by local authorities from the ministry's approved list. Among the basic questions: What range of alternative views or approaches is permitted in each of the subject areas at the elementary and secondary levels? How does the ministry harmonize the universities' entrance examination needs with precollegiate curriculum requirements and syllabus contents--or is the sequence the reverse? On what basis do local authorities make their selections from among the options available on the ministry's approved list? How much say do teachers have in selecting the books they use?

Given the central importance of textbooks and their direct relationship to university entrance examinations, what do textbooks reveal about Japanese society's view of itself, the Japanese concept of citizenship, and Japan's role in the world?

Some excellent recent work has been done on comparing Japanese and American textbooks in mathematics (see Chapter 4 in this volume by Stevenson and Bartsch) and a good beginning has been made in social studies *(In Search of Mutual Understanding* 1981).[4] Comparable studies are needed for basic and supplementary instructional materials in the other elementary and secondary education curriculum areas common to the two countries.

Attached and Alternative schools

Attached Schools

A number of public and private universities, including several in the top rank, maintain associated elementary and secondary schools, so-called attached schools. How do they differ from the best free-standing public and private schools in the same prefecture? Are the attached schools experimental in any sense, or merely captive feeder schools which provide an inside track to their host universities? What is the relationship of such schools to the parent university's teacher education program?

How much latitude for experimentation do schools attached to national universities have, and how much of it do they use? Are the schools attached to the most prestigious institutions considered "lighthouse" schools in any sense--are they expected to provide national or regional leadership to mainstream Japanese education? What guarantee of university entrance do they provide to their own or comparable institutions?

Alternative Schools

A very small number of Japanese schools, mainly at the upper secondary level, are significantly different from the norm. Most, if not all, are private. Some are "progressive" in the American sense of the term. Little is known about them in the West, and quite possibly they may not be widely known in Japan. How many at what levels are there, and what is their nature, origin, and history? What are the characteristics of the students and parents, and how do they differ from the norm in Japanese education? What led the parents to prefer these uncommon schools, with the attendant risks concerning status, university admission, and subsequent employment opportunities and career prospects for the children who attend?

How do the schools' curriculum, faculty, and methodology differ from that found in the typical Japanese school at the same level? How do students, teachers, and parents evaluate the nontraditional education being experienced? How do the students fare on university entrance examinations? How do the career paths of graduates compare with those of the same age group who graduate from conventional schools? How are these schools perceived by the mainstream education establishment, and what influence, if any, do these schools have on traditional Japanese schools?

Education Profession

This broad field is multifaceted and complex. Important research questions abound. Many deal with matters of universal concern, others are particular to Japan. Rural/urban and public/private comparisons should be explored. Much information on various items is available in Japanese. A number are the subject of international research in process or about to be undertaken. Some of the issues are being approached in promising collaborative fashion.[5] The following are among the natural priorities for early attention.

Characteristics of Personnel

Socioeconomic Origins

From what socioeconomic strata within Japanese society do school teachers and principals come? Are there significant differences at the preschool, elementary, and secondary school levels?

Career Choice

What are the major factors that influenced the decision of individuals now in service to become career educators? Has the pattern changed over the past five, ten, or twenty years (see Leestma et al. 1987, 15)?

Qualifications

Much is made in the literature, and in praise of Japanese education generally, about there being five applicants for every teaching position. It would be interesting to pin down just how firm that figure is--do applicants apply for more than one vacancy? If so, what is the actual net ratio?

More importantly, how does the academic standing of the applicants for teaching positions and the ranking of the institutions they attended compare with those of other graduates of the same year, particularly with the same majors, who did not seek teaching positions? How do those hired to teach compare with those who entered other occupations?

Mobility

How much nationwide mobility do members of the profession exhibit from the time and place of their preservice training and initial employment through the balance of their careers? To what extent are teachers educated in their home prefectures? Do prefectures recruit nationwide? How common is it for teachers to move from one prefecture to another during their careers? Do principals and head teachers exhibit different mobility patterns than regular teachers? Are vacancy lists readily available nationally? Are promotions to higher status positions normally limited to members of the profession within the same prefecture? To what extent do career professionals in education spend their entire career in the prefecture where initially employed?

Satisfaction and Dissatisfaction

What are the major sources of satisfaction and dissatisfaction that education professionals report in their respective roles and careers?

Current View of Profession

What do teachers and principals think about the criticism they have received in recent years--how fair is it, how helpful? What changes in education do teachers and principals believe are most needed? If they were entering or completing university today, would they again prepare for teaching, and, upon graduation, would they make the same career choice for teaching?

Career Retention and Departure

What is the rate of teacher turnover, and what proportion lasts how long? Why do teachers leave the profession before retirement and what is their subsequent employment? How is the lifetime employment provision met when school enrollments in an area decline at a faster rate than teacher retirement?

Status

An up-to-date study is needed that compares the prestige of the various roles in the education profession with roles in other professions and occupations, along with an analysis of any changes in status from earlier surveys. How has the hue and cry for education reform over the past decade and the public criticism of schools and educators affected the status of teachers and principals?

Teacher Education and Socialization

Preservice Education

Content: The content of preservice preparation of teachers, particularly the professional education portion, is a basic education issue worldwide. For Japan we know the number of credit hours required and the names of subjects and fields, but neither the actual content nor the articulation between work in the disciplines and in pedagogy. What concepts, principles, facts, and methods are actually contained and/or employed in courses categorized as professional education, particularly the foundation courses?

For example, what pedagogical theory is promulgated: what is taught about the nature of the child, child development, individual differences, learning theory, study skills, discipline, the role of the school, the role of the teacher, and the theory and practice of motivation? What are prospective teachers taught about learning disabilities and how to deal with them? About delinquency and how to handle it? What is the preparation for teaching moral education and character development, especially with the latitude classroom teachers are given in this area? What are prospective teachers taught about instructional methodology, including the potential, role, and use of the new technologies? What attention is given to developing professional collegiality, collective responsibility for school effectiveness, and a commitment to lifelong learning--for teachers as well as students?

How is the content and methodology of professional education preparation determined by policymakers and by certification and institutional authorities? What is the Ministry of Education's role and how much national standardization is promulgated by the ministry? How are standards maintained in the preservice education of pre-elementary school teachers--given that most preschool teachers are prepared in junior colleges, the great majority of which are private? How much and what kind of feedback do preservice programs receive on their graduates from the prefectures and schools that first employ them, and to what extent is this information used in program modification? Given the apparently slight involvement of preservice training institutions and faculty in inservice education, what are the principal sources of leadership for improving teacher education in Japan?

What national variation is there in formation of the knowledge, skill, and value base that determines what teachers will do when they begin teaching? What comparisons can be made on the foregoing factors with preservice teacher education in the United States? The focus should be on the programs of those institutions that produce the bulk of the graduates who actually go into teaching.

Faculty: What are the training, experience, and methods of instruction employed by the education faculty engaged in preservice preparation of teachers? How much knowledge and understanding do they have of other countries' education concepts and practices that differ from their own, and how much of this do they share with their students? How do Japanese teacher educators compare with their counterparts in teacher education in the United States?

Results: If undergraduate higher education is as weak as generally believed, how strong is teacher education? What depth of knowledge do prospective teachers have in their major fields and in professional education matters? What do they know about other approaches to education--teacher roles and practices abroad? Upon completion of their preservice preparation, what knowledge and skill do they command in the art and science of teaching and learning? What does preservice education do to prepare teachers to deal with slow learners and those with other kinds of learning problems? How adequate do new teachers find their preservice preparation? Does their evaluation differ from that rendered by their head teachers and principals and, if so, how?

Among the aspects that merit specific attention are the contributions of teacher education to children's liking for school and the early development of student self-discipline. One of the characteristics and special achievements of Japanese education at the elementary school level is the positive attitude pupils have toward education--children *like* school, and this makes its own important contribution to academic performance. What does preservice education (and, later, inservice education) contribute to this process?

One of the most fascinating aspects of Japanese child development and education is how the extensively indulged and self-indulgent Japanese preschool child metamorphoses into the disciplined first grader. While much is known about the general socialization process involved, including what the teacher does, less is known about the details of how preschool and first grade teachers learn to bring about this remarkable transformation with such apparent consistency and success. What stems from the teacher's own school and general cultural experience and what is the result of teacher education programs?

What aspects of beginning teachers' philosophy, perspectives, and job performance can be traced to their preservice professional education, and what aspects to their prior experiences as students, teaching as they were taught, and/or as family members whose attitudes toward education were influenced by their parents? What can be attributed to the small amount of practice teaching experience? To the informal or hidden curriculum of the teacher education program? In short, what difference does the preservice program make?

Institutional Status: What categories and rankings of institutions and what specific institutions prepare the largest numbers of graduates who achieve employment as teachers and go on to a career in the education profession? Do the preservice programs of the major suppliers differ significantly from those of other institutions, or is it overall institutional prestige that gives them their market edge and leadership?

Are there teacher education programs with status in their own right, independent of that of their parent institutions? What weight do prefectural teacher selection authorities give to teacher education programs independent of the national ranking of the institutions of which they are a part?

Inservice Education

Inservice training and the professional support system for teachers on the job are among the strong suits of Japanese education. What do teachers, head teachers, and principals see as desirable next steps in improving the scope and effectiveness of inservice education for professional development? What is involved in the new internship program for beginning teachers that is scheduled to start in the spring of 1989?

What does inservice education do to improve the ability of teachers to provide special assistance to slow learners and those with other kinds of learning problems?

With regard to the three graduate education universities established by the Ministry of Education (Leestma et al. 1987, 17), specifically what do their programs aim to accomplish, how do they go about it, and what impact are they having on the school system and teacher education generally?

Teacher Policies and Practices

Employment

What criteria are used by selection authorities to choose the one teacher from among five applicants, and how do these authorities explain the basis of their decisions? Specifically, what is the content of the prefectural written examinations and how is it determined (Leestma et al. 1987, 17)? How does the content differ from tests taken by the applicants during their preservice university programs? Are there special cram schools or classes to help applicants prepare? What qualities do the selection authorities look for in the personal interviews? How much weight is given to the ability to communicate with and inspire children, and on what basis are these abilities estimated? How much variation is there among prefectures in selection examinations, policies, and practices? How does the teacher selection process work in private schools?

Private Schools

Is there much movement back and forth between the public and private sectors in secondary education? Is the principle of lifetime employment operative in private schools? What are the relative advantages and disadvantages of a career in private schools in comparison with a career in public schools?

Rotation

What criteria determine how frequently rotation occurs and who goes where? Is rotation always or usually within the same commuting area or do teachers have to change their place of residence? Do all teachers, including head teachers, rotate and with about the same frequency? Does seniority play any role in assignments? Do teachers have any say in where or when their next assignment will be? Are principals also subject to rotation? Does seniority play any role in their assignments? Do rotation policies differ at the three school levels? What variations in rotation policy exist among the prefectures?

Career Patterns and Relationships

Detailed case studies are needed of career paths and personal and institutional networks. How are teachers and those in other roles evaluated and how does the process of professional advancement work? Is geographic mobility a significant factor in career advancement? What linkages exist between and among the faculties of teacher education institutions and the hiring, placement, and/or promotion authorities who determine an education professional's career development? To what extent are assignments and promotion decisions based on networks and reciprocal obligations--personal and/or institutional--and to what extent on objective factors and demonstrated performance? Related studies of career professional staff within municipal and prefecture education offices and the Ministry of Education bureaucracy would also be of value. What are the similarities and differences in the career paths and decisions of educators in Japan with those of their counterparts in the United States?

During the past ten years, is there any evidence of increased opportunity for women and minorities to become head teachers and principals, particularly in secondary schools? To become high level officials within the Ministry of Education?

Inappropriate Conduct

What constitutes unacceptable teacher behavior during the school day? After hours on personal time? How is such behavior handled by school authorities--who deals directly with the offending teacher, and what sanctions are applied to what infractions?

Teachers in Action

We need comprehensive case studies of representative teachers at work in their various roles, particularly in the classroom, in their various moral education and character development efforts, and in the nature and extent of their personal bonds with students. Studies are needed at the various grade levels and in all the different subjects and school-related activities, and in the different kinds of schools.[6] The following are among the aspects that warrant specific attention:

Special Assistance to Individuals

With regard to any individual attention rendered to secondary school students within the school framework, how does the amount of assistance given to those with serious learning problems compare with that given to those who are university bound and making good progress in the preparatory program?

Student Behavior and Discipline

Despite the general perception foreigners have of Japanese children as docile and highly disciplined, in elementary school and sometimes in junior high there is at times a surprising amount of boisterous behavior in class by various children, sometimes related to the specific learning task at hand, but sometimes not. Even in the latter case such behavior often seems ignored by the teacher; a different threshold is operative than in most American education. What constitutes unacceptable behavior in class and elsewhere on school grounds--where does the teacher draw the line and on what basis at the three school levels--and what corrective measures are used in dealing with problem behavior at different school levels? How strictly and severely are rules enforced? Does corporal punishment exist, and if so to what extent? Is it valued, discouraged, or forbidden?

School-Home Relations

At each of the three school levels, what is the nature and extent of teacher contact with parents during the school year: number, duration, and content of discussions? To what extent is the home visitation seriously substantive and to what extent ritual?

Vacation Periods

What proportion of their time do teachers at elementary, junior high, and senior high school levels devote to school responsibilities during the periods between trimesters?

Class Size and Total Work Load

Comparative studies at elementary, junior high, and senior high school levels in Japan and the United States of class size and total annual workload, including time spent after school hours and between semesters, would be of great interest in both countries.

Leadership

Good case studies are needed of the roles and careers of principals and head teachers. Much information is available in Japanese, but more data are needed in English on such aspects as motivation for seeking and/or undertaking these two key leadership roles, process of selection, position responsibilities, methods of operation, relationship to each other, criteria for evaluation, and sources of job satisfaction and dissatisfaction. How do individuals in the two roles work together? For example, how much guidance is the principal expected to provide to the head teacher, and what are the relative roles of the two school leaders in the evaluation of teachers and *tannin*? Several of the foregoing questions also would be applicable in developing a fuller understanding of the roles of grade level head teachers, *tannin* (Leestma et al. 1987, 34), and *shido shuji* (p. 17).

Of special importance would be research on how teachers work together and determination of the extent to which the faculty runs the school. The leadership contributions of union representatives need to be included.

Student Attitudes, Learning Problems, and Alienation

Formation and Change of Attitudes and
Expectations About Education

Japanese children typically enter first grade with a sense of great excitement and sometimes awe about their new status and role. From the child's point of view, how does the reality of the first grade experience compare with his or her expectations? How do the initial attitudes and expectations change as the child progresses through the grades? When, why, how, and for what proportion of the age cohort do the initial strong positive feelings about school give way to negative reactions, intellectual and emotional disengagement from learning, troublemaking, and/or a lapse into mere attendance for those who persist to graduation? Formation and change of attitudes and expectations about formal schooling clearly offer fertile ground for international comparative studies.

Slow Learners and Low Achievers

Ochikobore--children struggling academically and seriously behind in their studies--are known to be more than a few in number and a source of serious public concern in Japan. What are the specific dimensions of the problem--the nature and extent by grade level and subject area? What proportion of the high school graduating class is seriously behind in one or more basic subjects and skills; what proportions are how far behind in what subjects and skills?

Self-Concept

How is the development of self-concept related to academic achievement? What factors besides academic achievement do Japanese students identify as being significant in shaping their views of themselves, of their relative status in their age group, and of their future? How does fate fit into the picture? What is the effect on self-concept of failure to gain admission to a fairly prestigious high school? At what stages of schooling do significant portions of the cohort plateau in their aspirations and expectations for the future? How do occupational aspirations of secondary school students change over time?

Alienation, Opt-Outs, and Dropouts

It is increasingly apparent that all is not well in secondary education, particularly in upper secondary education (although lower secondary has received disproportionate public attention, largely because of the *ijime* problem; see Leestma et al. 1987, 37). Given the strong thrust of the required curriculum toward preparation for rigorous university entrance examinations, a growing number of students fall behind, many increasingly so, as the age group progresses toward graduation. Many not in the academic track lose interest for other reasons. Some balk at going to school, but most of the alienated students remain in school and graduate. They opt out of serious study, but persist in passive, disinterested, or sometimes even disruptive attendance.

Much more information is needed about the size of the group turned off by the education system, the causes and evolution of their difficulties and disenchantment, the dimensions of the "school refusal" syndrome, the effect of the continuing presence of those who stay in school upon the rest of the student body (including any relationship to *ijime*) and how the alienation problem has developed over the past ten to twenty years. Has there been or is there planned any significant liberalization of rules for student conduct and discipline? How do those who stay in school cope psychologically with the monotony and drudgery of an academic grind outside their interest and/or beyond their capability? Comparative studies are needed of those enrolled in academic programs and those in vocational programs and schools, as well as of those in high schools of the same type but of different status. Any rural/urban and public/private differentials need to be explored further.

Other matters for inquiry include the proportion of alienated youth that leaves school after completion of compulsory education and the proportion that stays in and coasts until graduation, the correlation of student delinquency rates with academic ranking of schools, and the reasons students give for disaffection with school. The parental and teacher dimensions need related attention--to what extent do the parents of alienated students share their offsprings' dissatisfaction with the system? What do students, teachers, and parents believe are feasible solutions to alienation and dropout problems?

More information about student dropouts is needed. Is the rate continuing to increase? If so, why? What proportion of those who drop out before high school graduation do so for reasons of alienation or deep discouragement, and what proportion leave because they believe they can more effectively prepare for university entrance examinations through other means, including tutors, *yobiko*, and/or self-study? What proportion of the dropouts who do not gain admission to any postsecondary institution subsequently acquire high school graduation status, either by returning to finish school or through attainment of the equivalence credential?

Curriculum, Instruction, and Achievement

Student Achievement

Largely as a result of studies during the past twenty years by the International Association for the Evaluation of Educational Achievement (IEA), there are good data and comparative analyses of science and mathematics education in Japan and the United States (as well as for other countries). Comparable attention to the rest of the basic curriculum is needed, particularly for any insights that might be gleaned from Japanese experience on the achievement possible in other school subjects. In music, for example, what level of vocal and instrumental proficiency does the average student actually reach by the end of compulsory schooling?

Social studies would seem to be an area of special importance. How thoroughly and how effectively does each country handle its own history, geography, and civic education? (For the United States, see, for example, Ravitch and Finn 1987, and the recent survey of geographic knowledge in nine major countries, including Japan and the United States, conducted by the Gallup Organization for the National Geographic Society, 1988.) How thoroughly and how effectively does each country come to grips with its relationship to the other and with international relations generally in an increasingly interdependent world?

Ability Grouping

What is the actual current status of ability grouping in upper secondary education? Is there an increasing or decreasing trend? What is teacher, student, and parental reaction to ability grouping in secondary education?

Cost of University Entrance Examinations

To what extent does the dominant emphasis on preparation for university entrance examinations, particularly at the senior high school level, distort or unbalance student learning and the learning process? Apart from the psychic costs of competitive pressures and effect on self-concept, what are students not exposed to and what learning skills are not mastered?

How satisfied are the parents, students, teachers, and employers with the education of the noncollege-bound student majority?

Conformity, Cooperation, and Creativity

One of the dominant foreign perceptions of Japanese education is that cultural norms and objectives regarding conformity,
group cohesion, and social harmony are achieved at the expense of
individual development and creativity. To the extent valid and reliable measures of such matters can be developed, what would they
reveal in a comparison of American and Japanese children?

Moral Education and Character Development

Given the latitude teachers have in achieving objectives in
this curriculum area, especially at the secondary school level, what
methods are considered the most effective, and what are the principal variations in content and approach? How do teachers share their
experiences with each other? Does variation in approach within a
school dilute or enhance the impact of moral education? What are
student reactions to moral education: how important do students
think the subject area is, how seriously do they take it, and how
much does the instruction and guidance actually shape their behavior in and out of school?

Nonacademic Aspects and the Holistic Approach to Education

A comprehensive analysis, grade by grade and cumulative
for a school, is needed of the nonacademic aspects of the school's
program: food service and school cleanup activities, class and all-
school trips, sports days, cultural festivals, and the like. Then, a
more complete picture is needed of exactly how the various nonacademic aspects are related to the academic aspects in the system's
holistic approach to moral education and character development, to
development of group identity, teamwork, and school spirit, and to
shaping student behavior generally. Duke's work, *The Japanese
School* (1986), provides an informative introduction to this broad
area of inquiry.

Foreign Language Skills

Is there movement toward requiring proficiency in spoken English (or in any other foreign language) on university entrance examinations in the near future? If so, how will the capability for teaching conversational English (or other language) be provided in secondary education, and how will student proficiency be tested and evaluated? How effective is the Japan Exchange and Teaching Program (see below) in improving English language instruction?

Education Media and Technologies

To what extent does Japanese education employ the full range of audiovisual media, methods, materials, and education technologies, particularly beyond the elementary school level?

Regarding educational broadcasting, it would be interesting to review the latest developments of NHK's radio and television programming for schools: production planning, program content, coordination with curriculum, school utilization, student and teacher attitudes about available programs and their use, and evidence of effectiveness. (Much information is available in Japanese and some in English.) Research on the last two aspects could be of particular value.

Beyond the NHK dimensions, how much additional technology is used in Japanese elementary and secondary education (in foreign language teaching, for example) and in higher education (apart from the University of the Air)? Given the intrinsic potential and demonstrated effectiveness of various technologies for educational purposes, and given Japan's outstanding capabilities in the design and production of technologies useful in education, how much classroom use is made now of, say, personal computers, VCRs, videodiscs, interactive video, and CD ROMs? If the use remains as slight as previously, what are the reasons for not exploiting what would seem like a natural national advantage? With respect to the future, what are the Ministry of Education's plans for the *TRON*-based personal computers developed through the Center for Educational Computing for school use, and what are the implications for education change?

Internationalizing Japanese Education

In several major reports and much public rhetoric, the Japanese education reform movement places special emphasis on "internationalizing" Japanese education. However, with the major exception of the recently established Japan Exchange and Teaching Program described later in this chapter, there does not appear to have been much actual change yet by education authorities in opening up the culture of the school. The evidence includes the at least initial ostracism of many of the students returning from residence and study abroad because of differences acquired in the course of their foreign experience, and the nonutilization by schools of this unique, high potential human resource for expanding international understanding in and through the peer group and the education system.

What is the current status of international objectives, rationale, and content in the curriculum at various school levels? To what concepts, facts, and attitudes are Japanese students exposed and with what results? What are their interests, knowledge, attitudes, and perceptions about other countries and other peoples? What is the international content of the entrance examinations for upper secondary school and for university entrance? What are the current and planned dimensions of the international student exchange effort at each education level? What comparisons can be made with the international education opportunities, experiences, achievements, and characteristics of American students? An interesting introduction to the Japanese situation is provided by Ehara (1989).

What are the founding purposes and distinguishing characteristics of the new international high school to be established in 1989 by the Tokyo local government? Are there any other signs of action toward "internationalization," particularly the use of students with firsthand knowledge of other cultures through residence and study abroad?

How effective are the innovative youth exchange programs, such as "The Ship for World Youth," sponsored by the Management and Coordination Agency? How widespread and effective are special events sponsored by Japanese businesses, communities, and grass roots organizations to bring foreign students and townspeople together, such as "Japan Tent" in Ishikawa Prefecture in the summer of 1988? What are the scope and importance of the various exchange efforts sponsored by the Japanese nonprofit education sector, such as the new foundation, Japan Education Exchange-BABA Foundation?

More than a decade ago, this writer identified areas of research needed to help determine status, needs, and priorities in the international dimensions of American education (Leestma 1979). They remain valid today. Most are equally applicable to Japanese education. Comparative studies of such aspects as those indicated below could illuminate how well the current generation of students is being prepared (by teachers with what sort of qualifications and perspectives[7]) for meeting the challenge of international understanding, not only between Japan and the United States, but with other countries around the world in an age of growing interdependence:

1) Studies of what students are now being taught about the world in schools (as distinct from what they know from all sources), both public and private, and how well they are learning, with suitable attention to global perspectives.

2) Studies of school practices that improve international understanding, including educational exchange programs.

3) Studies of intercultural attitude formation and change and the role of the school therein.

4) Studies of the international content and orientation of television programs watched by students.

5) Studies of the international knowledge, attitudes, and perceptions of teachers now in service.

6) Studies of what prospective elementary and secondary school teachers are now being taught about the world and about related effective educational practices during the course of their preparation for teaching.

7) Studies of the effectiveness of international educational exchange programs for teachers, including both exchange teaching and short-term seminars and workshops abroad, for inservice, preservice, or both, as appropriate.

8) Longitudinal studies of the development and modification of the international interests, knowledge, attitudes, and perceptions of individuals over the full span of their compulsory schooling period, through secondary and postsecondary education, and on into their adult lives.

9) Parallel studies in the education systems of other countries. Of particular interest would be data on the knowledge, attitudes, and perceptions of students and teachers about Americans and the United States.

10) International cooperative studies of ethnocentrism and prejudice among children, including the development of national stereotypes and the role of the school therein (summarized from Leestma 1979, xv-xvi).

In higher education, there clearly are related needs for up-to-date national surveys of the international interests, knowledge, attitudes, and perceptions of students and faculty in the various kinds of postsecondary institutions, particularly in the emerging era of "internationalization" (see note 7).

Juku and *Yobiko*

Academic Effectiveness

One of the significant contributions of the first volume of the U.S. Study of Education in Japan was laying out the symbiotic relationship between *juku* and the regular school system, particularly the role of *juku* in providing remedial assistance for students who have fallen behind and the supplementary instruction needed by many students to enable them to keep pace. It would be interesting to have case studies of representative national samples of students paired by socioeconomic status and class standing before *juku* participation was begun by one member of the pair. The findings might help better assess the effects of *juku* experience for remedial and supplementary purposes. Related studies could focus on the entrance examination preparation effects of *juku* and *yobiko*.

Participation Patterns in Upper Secondary School

Once a student enters high school and thus knows generally where he or she stands academically in the age cohort, what are the implications for further *juku* attendance? On a nationwide basis, what are *juku* and *yobiko* participation patterns in grades ten through twelve? What subjects are studied by what proportion of students at each grade level? What proportion of *juku* participants are not serious about seeking university admission? Are there significant differences in participation rates and patterns between students from public and from private schools? From rural and urban areas? How does participation by grade and subject correlate with prior, concurrent, and subsequent academic achievement in school and with success on university entrance examinations? (There is much data in Japanese for the compulsory school years, but apparently less for the upper secondary period.)

Yobiko, Ronin, and University Freshmen

Nationwide, what portion of each year's total number of university freshmen have studied at *yobiko* while in grade twelve, after grade twelve, and before taking entrance examinations, or have been *ronin*? How many and which universities account for the bulk of *ronin* experience? Have there been any changes in the list during the past decade? Are any trends apparent or emerging? How essential do entering freshmen, universities, and the Ministry of Education think *yobiko* preparation is? Data on several of these questions are available in Japanese, but relatively little is readily available in English.

Vocational and Technical Education

This section benefits from some useful recent work from Great Britain. Dore and Sako (1987), in particular, show the great difference that language proficiency and historical and cultural expertise can make in understanding education in a societal context. The study also illustrates productive, cross-national collaboration. Some of the work's special comparative education value is summarized in an introductory section, "Common Assumptions About

Vocational Training Which Japan Brings Into Question" (Dore and
Sako 1987, vii-ix).

Student Characteristics

Generally speaking, the characteristics of students entering
vocational education programs in Japan and in the United States
appear to be broadly similar--a perception that needs more specific
verification--although the Japanese students have the advantage of
a strong, basic foundation from nine coherent years of well-balanced
compulsory education. It would be interesting to know more specifically how the level of academic ability of students in the various
kinds of vocational education programs and schools in Japan compares with that of Japanese students enrolled in other kinds of
programs and schools, and how it varies by geographic region.

Program Results

How effective are the existing Japanese vocational education
programs at the upper secondary school level in the different categories of institutions: regular and vocational secondary schools, special training schools, technical colleges, and miscellaneous schools?
Do the results differ for those who took the vocational course in
comprehensive schools rather than in vocational high schools? How
much of the training in the different kinds of institutions is linked
directly to specific occupational qualifications or credentials? How
directly do the programs lead to relevant employment? How satisfied with the training are the graduates and employers? Any significant differences between public and private sectors, and between
rural and urban areas?
Much of the Japanese approach to vocational and technical
education at the secondary school level is different philosophically
and in practice from the American concept and experience. In those
instances where program objectives are similar, it would be interesting to compare student achievement, including level of occupational competence where relevant.

Access to University

How many graduates of the various kinds of upper secondary school vocational programs attempt and how many succeed in gaining admission to universities and at what status levels?

Teachers

How do teachers in vocational programs and schools differ from their colleagues in nonvocational education assignments on the various dimensions (characteristics, education, and so on) set forth earlier in the "Education Profession" section?

National Expenditure

It would be interesting to know the total national expenditure on vocational and technical education within the schools (nonemployer) framework, and the proportion it represents of the total national expenditure for education. While much relevant information is available, apparently the total expenditure has not yet been determined.

Higher Education

The number of aspects worth exploring is virtually unlimited. On various matters much information is available in Japanese and some in English. Several examples of topics that would seem to merit early attention are:

Control

What control does the Ministry of Education have over the various segments of higher education, and how is the control exercised directly and indirectly? How much latitude do postsecondary institutions in the various categories have over their own policies, programs, and growth? How is the budget for national universities developed and allocated among the individual institutions? Within universities, how much autonomy do individual faculties and

departments have? Are there significant differences in internal autonomy between public and private institutions of the same type
and status? What control or influence does the ministry exercise
over the entrance examinations of institutions in the various postsecondary categories?

University Entrance and Flexibility

Dimensions of Examination Issue

Specifically, what and how difficult is the content of the entrance examination? What is the nature and extent of detail in each
subject area? What are representative questions and acceptable answers? What kind and amount of analytical, reasoning, and problem-solving skills and abilities are required in the various subjects?
What proportion of the final score is dependent simply upon re-
call/recognition/memorization?

How many institutions make up the top status category,
how many students compete for how many vacancies in the respective freshman classes, and what is the range of scores and the cutoff point for each of the institutions in the top tier and in the next
few tiers? How many students who fail in their initial effort are
successful on subsequent tries? What proportion of total national
first-year admissions are at stake in the freshman classes of the institutions in the top tier of prestige? How difficult is it to gain entry
to the remaining (majority of) universities? How have the numbers
and patterns changed over the past ten or twenty years? (Much of
the data is available in Japanese.)

Power Structure Views Toward Change

What are the views and sentiments of the Ministry of Education, university faculties, the most prestigious government ministries, and Japan's large companies toward changing the present
university entrance examination system? What modifications appear most likely to be accepted and implemented, and what differences would such changes likely make in precollegiate education?

How will the forthcoming revision of the ministry's
"University Establishment Standards" facilitate or impede change
in university organization, admissions, curriculum, standards,
staffing, and institutional evaluation, and what are the likely

implications for improving the quality of undergraduate education? What is the outlook for increasing flexibility in transfer of credits between departments within faculties, between faculties within institutions, and between institutions, and what arguments are used to defend the rigidity and cost of the status quo?

Applicants Who Just Miss Admissions Cutoff Point

Longitudinal studies are needed of the subsequent life patterns of students who just miss the cutoff point of entrance examinations to the universities in the top few tiers of status and who fail to gain entry on any succeeding attempts. Do they abandon a university education altogether or persist and enter universities at the next lower status level? In either case, how do their subsequent careers compare with their initial competitors who scored just above the cutoff point and gained admittance to the institutions originally preferred? Just how close is the present fit between institutional status and employment status after graduation? How influential is the traditional hierarchical rank of Japanese universities in conferring individual advantage in contemporary Japan--as strong, stronger, or weaker than it was ten, twenty, or forty years ago?

Special Provision for Applicants Who Have Studied Abroad

Several Japanese universities have recently developed a special admissions process for secondary school students who have attended schools abroad for at least two years before applying for entrance to a Japanese university. How widespread is this phenomenon, and what are the institutional variations? How does the special admissions process differ from the regular entrance requirements, and how satisfactory do the universities involved find this new alternative? Do the students admitted fare as well as those selected through the regular process? If so, what are the implications for change in the regular procedures?

Undergraduate Education

Quality

What would careful, systematic study by field and type of institution reveal about the quality of university undergraduate

education in Japan today? For example, what are the specifics of
course and graduation requirements? How much experience do students
have with library and laboratory research and with term paper
writing? How does the grading system work? How do teachers
teach? How would the findings compare with the current quality of
undergraduate education in the United States?

If most of undergraduate higher education is as weak as
generally believed, why do the education authorities, prospective
employers, and the general public expect and accept so little?

Productivity, Prestige, and Wastage

Most of Japanese undergraduate education is believed to
have a low yield in knowledge and skill acquisition. Learning productivity
is believed to be low because of relatively undemanding
performance requirements (to be established--see above). It would
be interesting to try to determine whether productivity varies with
institutional prestige, and if so, how--either directly or, conceivably,
inversely.

It also would be worth trying to pin down just how much of
university undergraduate education in Japan might reasonably be
considered to represent value added beyond the academic achievement
produced in elementary and secondary education. Variations
among fields and faculties would be especially interesting. Have any
universities produced research evidence on the educational outcomes
of their programs? If so, what are the gains in knowledge and skills,
and what changes in student attitudes, objectives, and motivation
are evident?

Further, it would be interesting to explore calculations of the
full cost to the nation of wastage in Japanese undergraduate education
including, among other things, the low yield in knowledge and
skill acquisition (as may be determined above), the cost of *ronin*
(compared with the cost of creating additional places in the universities
so eagerly sought after, or with upgrading the quality of education
in other good institutions in the current second and third tiers
of status), and the "marking time" aspect of much of the rationale
for junior college attendance.

University of the Air

What role does the University of the Air play in postsecondary education: How flexible are the entrance requirements? How up-to-date is the curriculum? How innovative and effective is the instruction? What are the characteristics of the students it attracts, and how do they differ, if they do, from the students at established universities of high ranking? How acceptable does the general public find this alternative form of higher education? What impact is the University of the Air having on conventional higher education in Japan? (At least some of this information is readily available.)

Demographic Change

How is higher education preparing for the substantial decline in the supply of high school graduates that is projected to begin in 1993? What are the prospects for changes in university philosophy and policy regarding serving nontraditional students with conventional programs or new kinds or programs or both?

Research, Development, and Change

Research and Development System

What provisions and capabilities exist for education research and development in Japan at the various levels of government and education, including higher education, and in business and industry? What is the role of the National Institute for Educational Research (NIER) and other education research bodies? How much contact and cross-fertilization in education research are there between the education system and business and industry? How extensive is the Japanese education research community's contact with education research in other countries, particularly the United States? What are Japan's current priorities for education research? What attention is being devoted to such fundamental fields as individual differences, aptitude testing, and diagnosis and treatment of learning disorders? (Some of this information is available.)

How and to what extent does Japanese education provide for field testing of new ideas, methods, and materials? Are certain schools designated for experimentation and demonstration? If so,

how are experiments conducted at the upper secondary level so as
to not compromise student competitiveness on university entrance
examinations? How are new approaches and practices evaluated?
What are the arrangements for systematic dissemination of new
ideas and research results? How do research results get translated
into practice?

Education Change

How mutable is the education system at its present stage?
What is the nature and functioning of the change process? To what
extent is education change in Japan research-based? How does the
change process work with regard to: national and local goals and
policies, requirements, and standard practices; the interaction of national and local authorities; preservice and inservice teacher education; and between and among schools, governance bodies, and
teacher education programs, particularly in modification of certification requirements? How are executive, legislative, and governance
bodies involved at national, prefectural, and municipal levels? What
role is played by individual innovators and local education centers?
How does the Japan Teachers Union fit into the picture? Do *juku*
and *yobiko* contribute anything of significance to experimentation
and innovation in Japanese education?

In addition to directives and guidance from the Ministry of
Education, prefectural, and/or municipal education authorities, are
there other sources and processes through which educators at the
school level and in teacher education learn about new ideas? How
common is it for teachers and teacher educators to follow developments in other countries? What are the principal forces and influences that lead to experimentation and adoption or adaptation of
new ideas, approaches, and techniques? What curriculum changes
are in the offing as a result of the recently completed periodic review by the Ministry of Education's Curriculum Council? What is
the relationship between this council's recommendations and those
of the National Council on Educational Reform?

What aspects of public dissatisfaction with the system do
teachers agree with and would they like to see changed? What aspects do they disagree with and would they resist strongly? What
are the reactions of the Ministry of Education and teachers to the
work of the National Council on Educational Reform?

National Council on Educational Reform

What has resulted thus far from the reports and recommendations of the National Council on Educational Reform? What fundamental change, if any, is being implemented?

Suzuki Method

How is the Suzuki method viewed by mainstream Japanese educators at ministry, prefectural, municipal, school, and postsecondary teacher education program levels? What do they see as its utility and the prospect for incorporating it into the regular school system, particularly during the compulsory education period? To the extent the Suzuki approach is viewed negatively, what is the basis of the objections?

Other

Parent Teacher Association

In addition to its traditional functions as "a forum for the school to explain its policies and expectations to parents and to organize parental assistance for school activities" (Leestma et al. 1987, 32), is the PTA becoming more of an independent force in Japanese education? To what extent is it taking an active leadership role in school reform? To what extent are there differences in the role (whether it be traditional or emerging) of the PTA at the elementary, junior high, and senior high school levels?

Development of Science and Mathematics Education

More needs to be known about the comparative development--respective rise and decline, if you will--of science and mathematics education in Japan and in the United States during the past thirty years. How did elementary and secondary school science and mathematics achieve their current level of excellence in Japanese education? During the same period, how did American science and mathematics education falter or go wrong after the electrifying stimulus of Sputnik and the subsequent major national reform efforts under the auspices of the National Science Foundation and the U.S. Office of Education, among others?

Occupation Legacy

It has been forty-five years since the end of World War II, when Occupation authorities undertook to democratize Japan through major changes in the education system, as well as in other sectors of government and society. It is time for a thoroughgoing, comprehensive analysis of the legacy that remains from the Occupation's various education reform efforts. Wray's study (in press) is likely to help illuminate the subject.

Research Considerations and Approaches

As one reviews the many aspects of the research base that need attention, the importance of certain types of research and design considerations become apparent. To begin with, a more careful determination of representativeness of sample is indicated all along the line. The apparently common assumption that simply picking a school or two at random constitutes a representative national sample needs careful examination. Despite general characteristics of centralization, standardization, and stability, there is reason to believe that contemporary Japanese education probably is more variable and less static than usually represented. Indeed, the nature and extent of variation and the process of change are among the basic aspects of Japanese education that we need to know more about as soon as possible.

More local-level case studies are needed in sufficient depth on a wide variety of issues and aspects. For example, there is no substitute for the kind of basic building blocks of scholarly inquiry represented by the insightful work of culturally sensitive and language proficient researchers like Lewis (1984, 1988), Peak (1987 and this volume), Kotloff (1988), and August (in press and this volume). Such careful studies are needed to produce new knowledge on subjects not previously addressed, to confirm, extend, or modify findings of the small amount of good research previously reported in English, and cumulatively to provide a suitable base for broader generalizations worthy of confidence. Such work also can stimulate cogent ideas for further research (see, for example, suggestions for research on classroom management in Lewis 1988).

An important element in planning and conducting some kinds of classroom research is appropriate involvement of good teachers. Despite the many differences between the United States and Japan, there is no substitute for the insight of experienced teachers in helping understand classroom reality (see, for example, Ohanian 1987) or in explaining to outsiders the philosophy and rationale underlying their own educational practices (see Tobin, Wu, and Davidson 1987).

A more complete understanding of education in Japan will also require larger scale studies of education in action, including ethnographic studies on site. Systematic investigation is needed not just of the realities and dynamics of teaching and learning in different subjects, classrooms, and grade levels in different kinds of schools, but also of individual schools and groups of schools as pedagogical and cultural systems in their own right. We need to know more about student and teacher cultures and those of other education personnel. The school's multifaceted relationships with society must be taken into account. Given the strong influence of culture and tradition, but also the ferment of a society in transition, various studies will require interdisciplinary effort, and sometimes longitudinal dimensions. The cumulative results of both local case studies and larger, more complex investigations will enable foreign researchers to better recognize and understand the difference between *tatemae* and *honne* in Japanese education.

Researchers need to be sensitive to the fact that some issues and problems which normally would be viewed as education matters in the United States are matters of cultural change in Japan. (For example, fundamental change in the university entrance examination system could be considered a serious challenge to some aspects of the society's value system.) Rohlen's *Japan's High Schools* (1983) provides an outstanding example of insightful ethnographic research in broad societal context; it's a landmark contribution by a Western scholar to the fathoming of education in Japan.

A useful approach to the challenge of studying education in societal context is through cooperation between education researchers and specialists in Japanese studies. *Japanese Education Today* provides an example of the potential of such teamwork. The present volume also includes examples of the value of collaboration between U.S. and Japanese scholars on subjects of mutual concern.

Comparative studies that analyze education elements, circumstances, subcultures, and results in equivalent kinds of schools and student populations in Japan and the United States in their local, regional, and national contexts would be very useful for enriching our understanding of fundamental relationships in education and between school and society, how each shapes the other and affects continuity and change in the national character and culture. Indeed, solid comparative data from two such different cultures could contribute to education theory as well as advance the cause of comparative education generally.

Research Opportunities with Special Potential

For such reasons as cost, language, research access, and differences in academic calendar, many American researchers interested in Japanese education are unlikely to have the opportunity to conduct research in Japan. However, there are many possibilities for serious research in the United States, particularly for those able to use Japanese language sources, and thorough preparation in the United States enables one to maximize any time available for fieldwork in Japan. Further, at least some aspects of Japanese schooling can be observed in the United States. There are also potential opportunities not yet widely appreciated for single issue or broader focus research in Japan or for comparative studies of education in both countries.

Japanese Schools in the United States

As of 1987, the Japanese Government recognized and assisted forty-six Japanese schools in the United States: forty-four supplementary (Saturday) schools and two full-time schools (in New York and Chicago) for the compulsory school period, grades one through nine. In the full-time schools, the principals and majority of the teachers are provided by the Japanese Ministry of Education. There is also a private Japanese school in Los Angeles for grades one through nine.

In the supplementary schools, primary emphasis is on the Japanese language along with social studies and mathematics. Most of the enrollment is in the elementary school grades one through six. At the senior high level, only grades ten and eleven are offered,

because almost all twelfth grade students return to Japan to prepare for university entrance examinations. Generally speaking, the
ministry provides the principal of the school if its enrollment is
between 100 and 400.   If the enrollment is over 400, both a
principal and vice-principal are provided. Teachers are secured
locally from the Japanese community.

A recent development of special significance is the emergence of opportunities to secure a Japanese upper secondary (grades
ten through twelve) education in the United States. This was inevitable in light of the rapid growth of Japanese investment in
American business, industry, and finance; the consequent sizable
increase in the number of Japanese executives and their families
residing in the United States; and the great difficulty in entering
Japanese higher education through other than traditional Japanese
preparation for university entrance examinations. During the spring
and summer of 1988 there were announcements of three Japanese
high schools to open in the next few years. All are privately
sponsored.

Meiji Gakuin University, one of Japan's oldest Christian institutions of education, is purchasing the former Tennessee Military
Institute in Sweetwater, Tennessee, and converting the facilities
into a Japanese high school. (Tennessee reportedly has the second
largest number of Japanese companies, after California.) To be
named Tennessee Meiji Gakuin (TMG Academy), the new school
opened in May, 1989.

Musashino Higashi Gakuen Educational Foundation, the
parent body of a private lower secondary school in the Tokyo suburb of Musashino, plans to open an upper secondary school in
Boston in April, 1990.

Keio University, a private university that is one of Japan's
most prestigious postsecondary institutions, has announced plans to
establish a senior high school on the campus of Manhattanville College in New York, to open in the fall of 1990. The school reportedly
will offer a hybrid Japanese and American curriculum drawing on
the best of both and emphasizing preparation for university
entrance.

It also should be noted that some Japanese *juku* already offer programs in the United States.

There is also some early indication of Japanese interest in
purchasing or forming partnerships with small private American
colleges, primarily to increase study opportunities in the United
States for Japanese university students. Some of the early offers

are being made to institutions in Oklahoma, Oregon, Maryland, and West Virginia.

Japan Exchange and Teaching Program

A recent development of impressive size and with diverse research potential both short- and long-term is the Japan Exchange and Teaching Program (JET). Initiated in 1987 by the Japanese government, this far-sighted program is aimed at promoting mutual understanding between Japan and selected other countries, fostering international perspectives among the Japanese generally, and improving foreign language education. The program brings competitively selected college graduates under thirty-five years of age to Japan for a year to "teach English in schools and in local governmental organizations, or to act as international activities coordinators for local Japanese governments" (Embassy of Japan 1988). The participants receive transportation and a salary equivalent to approximately $28,000 (in 1988). The program is conducted in Japan under the cosponsorship of the Ministry of Foreign Affairs, the Ministry of Education, the Ministry of Home Affairs, and the local governments.

The program is off to a promising start. For 1988-89, approximately 1,300 college graduates from six countries (the United States, the United Kingdom, Australia, New Zealand, Canada, and Ireland) were involved, with about 900 of them from the United States. Approximately 1,050 of the 1,300 total were newly selected for the 1988-89 program (620 of them Americans); the remainder were extended a second year from the approximately 400 participants of the preceding year. The program is expected to increase to approximately 3,000 participants annually in 1991.[8]

While JET is not intended as a research program, the participants represent a unique and sizable source of firsthand knowledge about various aspects of Japanese education today and a promising pool from which future research talent might develop. They are also, of course, potential subjects for studies on such topics as attitude formation and change through the experience of living and working in Japan. Depending upon background, interest, skills, and resourcefulness, some of the participants may have engaged in modest research efforts of their own while in service or after completion of their responsibilities in Japan. Then there are obvious possibilities for studies of what effect the influx of foreign teachers will have on internationalizing Japanese education. Other possibilities of research potential in JET may well occur to the reader.

Sister City and State-Prefecture Relationships

As of early 1988, approximately one-fourth of the 800 American cities affiliated with Sister Cities International (SCI) had formal links with approximately 200 Japanese cities, and approximately a dozen American states had formal links with Japanese prefectures.[9] The possibilities for facilitating access to research sites and developing long-term research relationships, particularly for longitudinal and/or comparative studies, are exciting to contemplate, particularly (but certainly not exclusively) for researchers from institutions associated through geographic location or otherwise with the cities and states involved.

To the extent there is sufficient mutual interest among enough of the existing pairings, a unique bilateral data base of considerable size, representativeness, and diversity could be developed that would be useful for various comparative studies over time, including, among other possibilities, research on public and private high schools (see Coleman and Hoffer 1987, as well as Rohlen 1983), and on the development of mutual understanding and the effects of school reform efforts. At an appropriate stage, comprehensive research efforts along such lines as the Eight Year Study (Aikin 1942) and a Study of Schooling (Goodlad 1984), to cite two classic American examples, might be considered, bearing in mind that the two countries do not share all the same objectives in education, nor do their schools (and exams) play the same role in the lives of the students, especially during adolescence. One can conceive of the possibility that selected, long-term comparative studies of unusual potential might benefit from special binational sponsorship. CULCON, for example, was the framework under which the U.S. Study of Education in Japan and the companion Japanese study of selected aspects of American education were conducted (see preface).

It would be interesting to determine the present nature and extent of sister cities' exchange activity in education at the elementary and secondary levels, and to determine what is known about the results to date. What are the institutional partners and participating individuals learning from each other? How are attitudes and perceptions about the other country being affected in school and adult education programs? What difference is the bilateral linkage making in school curriculum development?[10] Other aspects of personal research interest will occur to the reader. (An initial listing of several hundred sister school relationships between Japan and the United States, most of them within the SCI framework, was published in Japanese by the Japan American Cultural Society in 1988. The society plans to produce an English version in 1989 or 1990.)

Regional and Educational Exchanges for Mutual Understanding

Another commendable Japanese initiative involving teachers, Regional and Educational Exchanges for Mutual Understanding (REX), also has interesting research possibilities once the emerging program is established. In brief, beginning in 1990 a small number of carefully selected Japanese teachers of English will spend the first four months of the Japanese school year at Tokyo University of Foreign Studies learning how to teach the Japanese language to native speakers of English. Then they will serve the balance of their special two-year assignment abroad in interested local school districts or state or provincial education departments. They will teach Japanese, primarily at the secondary school level, and serve as resource persons on Japan while at the same time improving their own proficiency in English and learning first-hand about the host country culture.

Costs are shared. The Japanese Ministry of Education funds the special language training program in Japan and the transportation costs, and the Ministry of Home Affairs pays for the substitute teachers who replace the absent REX teachers. The foreign education authorities provide salaries and local accomodation costs for the REX teachers during their period of service in the host country, and the Japanese government covers the remaining expenses of the program.

The program concept includes a few other countries besides the United States (initially Canada, Australia, and New Zealand), and is beginning on a much smaller scale than JET. A total of a dozen or so teachers is planned for the first year and maybe double that number for the second, with approximately half of the total slated for service in the U.S.

The initial linkages will be based on existing relationships such as sister cities or previous exchange programs, but the program concept is flexible. The initiative for developing REX linkages rests with municipal and prefectural education authorities in Japan and their counterparts in the United States and other countries. Further information is available from the Embassy of Japan.

Branch Campuses in Japan of American Universities

There has been a flurry of press coverage about the interest of several Japanese communities and prefectures in helping American universities establish branch campuses in those places. What is the story behind the movement and what is the present situation (by the turn of the decade American branch campuses were being established in Japan at the rate of about one a month)? What is the nature of the institutional partnerships involved? Who do the institutions serve and for what purposes, with what initial and continuing problems and results? A generally helpful initial review of the phenomenon has just become available (Chambers and Cummings 1990). What education research opportunities do these branch campuses offer?

Concluding Thoughts

For all of the reasons given here and in the first volume of the U.S. Study, it is clear that education in Japan is a subject of special interest and value. In research terms, it is far from a mature field, at least so far as work by foreign scholars is concerned. We are much closer to the beginning of an era of serious, systematic, sophisticated work than to any stage resembling completion of the research challenge. Individually and together, there is much yet to be done on a broad and complex front.

Research Cooperation with Japan

Increasing communication and cooperation between foreign scholars and their Japanese research peers merit special emphasis. The value to each side goes well beyond providing or receiving technical assistance or taking out a form of insurance in approaching special challenges of language and culture. Neither Japan, the United States, nor any other nation has a uniformly superior education system for today's world and the foreseeable

future. There are no satisfactory answers yet to some of the
education problems that both nations (and various other countries)
face in common, and neither nation (nor any other) has a monopoly
on good ideas.

Increasing scholarly communication and cooperation is part
of the solution. The potential for learning from each other, in research perspectives and approaches as well as in research results,
is real. More cooperation with Japan--and with other nations--in education research is as important as it is in scientific and industrial
research and in various manufacturing efforts, if not more so over
the longer term. Some of the education answers each nation needs,
for its own purposes as well as for matters of mutual concern, may
be found, or found sooner, through research cooperation. And the
mutual understanding that develops through the process pays continuing dividends for other national interests as well as for future
scholarship.

Consequences of Good Evidence

Obtaining good evidence on the questions raised in this
chapter undoubtedly will lead to revision of some existing views of
Japanese education. For the most part, however, such adjustments
are not likely to entail radical revision of the overall picture summarized in the first volume of the U.S. Study, largely because of the
rigorous effort there to stay within the tenable basic evidence and to
avoid the misconceptions, exaggeration, and hype so often associated with accounts by foreigners of Japanese education. Japanese
education does not need hype, positive or negative. It is genuinely
impressive and fascinating enough to engage and hold attention
without resorting to creative writing or overemphasis on nonrepre-
sentative examples and insignificant aspects.

Additional solid information would help fill some crucial gaps
in our knowledge, add to depth of understanding in diverse areas,
and bring some parts of Japanese education and various relationships into more precise focus. The more good evidence accumulates,
the more accurate a picture can be developed of: the system in the
round, the contributions of the parts to the whole, the dynamics of
the process, the total results, and, of special significance, a more
complete understanding of the full cost--psychological as well as
economic--of the present system. At this juncture, it does not appear
likely that a more thorough cost/benefit analysis would enhance the

luster of the formal school system. In part, this is because much of the available research, at least at elementary and secondary levels, appears to deal more with the strengths of the system than with its weaker and sometimes darker sides.

In the writer's view, Japan's genuine achievements in education will not be diminished by whatever adjustments flow from a more substantial knowledge base and the process of setting the record straight where it may be in error or incomplete. The major successes of Japanese education are real enough, particularly the enormous accomplishment of bringing a larger proportion of the school-age population to a higher level of academic attainment in a shorter period of time than any other nation in history. Among other things, Japanese education in cultural context succeeds in instilling in most children a strong belief that they are capable of learning, a personal sense of responsibility for high level achievement and motivation to do their best; orderliness, diligence, good study habits, and self-discipline; an enduring commitment to a sense of duty, work ethic, and persistence of effort; skill in group cooperation, social harmony, and teamwork; and a personal orientation toward continuing education and lifelong learning. These are formidable achievements by any standard, whatever else may prove to be awry.

Research on the questions raised in this chapter should well contribute to a clearer sense of how much of the net effectiveness of Japanese education can fairly be attributed to the formal school system itself and how much to the combination of:

> the continuing influence of history and tradition;

> the nation's strong consensus on cultural values and education purposes;

> the parental priority given to education and the strong bond between home and school; and

> the continuous reinforcement of the status quo by the prestige of universities and the powerful influence of their entrance examinations; by the interlocking community, occupational, and government contexts in which the school functions; and by the reward structure of society.

A larger body of good evidence, new and old, would enable us to better estimate the answer to the question: What results would such a school system alone likely produce in a different, non-Japanese setting?

Personal Perspectives on Education and Change in Japan

From what is known to date, the probability seems high to this writer that the more we learn about school and society in contemporary Japan, the more important the overall historical and cultural context will prove to be, not just in traditional terms, but also because of complications inevitable in a hierarchical society increasingly caught up in a transition of uncertain proportions. Societal changes include an erosion of some aspects of the national consensus on education and related cultural values, the emergence of a generation gap that continues to widen, and increasing student alienation from formal schooling beyond the elementary level. While of modest proportions in comparison with conditions in various Western countries, such developments are very alarming to the Japanese (Leestma et al. 1987, 66).

Among the factors responsible or otherwise involved are the rising economic affluence; the onset of a consumer culture; the growing appeal for youth of individuality and self-interest, in part because of greater awareness through television and films of the diversity of personal options and more flexible lifestyles of youth in other democracies; declining patience with rigidly prescribed behavior codes and delayed gratification; and increasing disaffection, by parents as well as students, with the exceedingly competitive, high pressure grind for university entrance which dominates the path to economic and social mobility and security.

Yet, as noted earlier, the formal education system has some impressive strengths, including a strong, well-balanced common core of learning during the nine years of compulsory schooling. Much of the most apparent instructional excellence is found at the elementary school level--not unlike the situation in the United States. Indeed, the more closely Japanese education is studied, the more likely it seems that the image of the system beyond the elementary school is likely to suffer (as in the United States). The reasons include increasing recognition of new needs that the present system is not designed to cope with, the growing dissonance in Japanese society, and better understanding of the lack of educational balance at the senior high school level because of the distortions wrought by the university entrance examinations.

It may also be that the special strength of Japanese education does not rest disproportionately with the teachers, competent though they are. While Japanese teachers are often represented as being better qualified than those of other nations, for the most part, the matter of relative capability remains to be determined. The distinctive strength of the teaching force may well lie more in its collective characteristics. Essential elements in effective combination include consistency of approach, conscientiousness in role, peer group teamwork and mutual assistance, continuing professional development through inservice education, and the teaching force being more or less in tune internally and with the rest of a coherent system reinforced from within and without.

The decisive strength of the school system per se appears to lie in an interwoven complex of factors that, in addition to a strong teaching force, includes:

> the widespread societal commitment to high scholastic achievement, in part a manifestation in education of the general Japanese tendency to feel that "competence is a moral duty" (Dore and Sako 1987, 3);

> the general coherence and consistency of the philosophical and pedagogical orientation consisting of psychological concepts, in both cognitive and affective domains; goals and expectations; attention to motivation, effort, and persistence; curriculum content and sequence; instructional patterns; and organizational arrangements;

> the holistic concern, particularly during the compulsory school years, that ties together values, attitudes, feelings, habits, character development, motivation, skills, and achievement within and between the academic and nonacademic aspects of the program;

> the congruence of school efforts with society's general consensus on school purposes and comprehensive reinforcement of school efforts;

> the focusing effect and driving force of university entrance examinations; and, it should be acknowledged,

> the important symbiotic contribution of *juku*, particularly in sup-
plementary and remedial instruction.

However Japanese education may be parsed in efforts to
identify which factors are responsible for what, at this stage of our
knowledge it seems clear enough that in elementary and secondary
education generally, as well as in such components as the teaching
profession, the whole is more than the sum of its parts. It is the
combination and reinforcing interaction of historical and cultural
values; parental involvement; school objectives, education staff, a
standardized curriculum and pedagogical approach; high expectations; out-of-school study; relationship between education credentials
and employment; and total societal surround that account for the
strengths as well as the weaknesses of education in Japan.

Thus, in Japan, more than in most countries, the education
system must be defined more broadly than the school. Indeed, for
practical purposes education and society are generally of a piece,
even as the school system internally is of a piece. So closely are
school and society interwoven that the nature and pace of change in
education appear inextricably dependent upon the nature and pace
of change in society. Yet what once seemed seamless is increasingly
less so. Stress fractures are becoming more apparent at various
points in school and society and the interfaces between them.

Despite growing evidence of change in society and increasing
public disenchantment with the major education system as it
stands, no acceptable education alternatives have yet emerged, because a new consensus has not yet been reached, the system continues to function according to the old one. With the increase in
stress and frustration, it is clear that something has to give, but
what, how, and when remain to be seen. All of this has implications
for education studies in context, as well as for identifying or laying
down valid and reliable base lines soon from which change can be
measured.

With the development of participatory democracy to its present stage, the strong persistence of certain values (including the
importance of education and societal commitment to consensus) and
education concepts, and the lack of a comprehensive superior model
of education elsewhere, the challenge of change in Japanese education today is far more difficult than it was at the time of the Meiji
restoration. It will be interesting to observe the process at work and
see how it all turns out.

Notes

1. Among established American scholars, for example, there are few who rank with Passin (1965) in command of the historical development of Japanese education, with Cummings (1980, 1982) and Rohlen (1980, 1983) in depth of knowledge and insight into contemporary Japanese education in cultural context, with Hess (1981) and Stevenson et al. (1986) in fruitful collaboration with major Japanese scholars on high quality basic research, or with Ranbom (1985) on journalistic inquiry into Japanese education. Few have Duke's personal knowledge and feel for how the Japanese school shapes the "loyal, literate, competent, and diligent worker" (Duke 1986, 24). This line-up should not be construed to mean that the only top flight students of Japanese education are American. Dore (1984, 1987), for example, would make any knowledgeable researcher's short list.

A number of those who have produced some of the best recent research on Japanese education contributed background papers for the first volume of the U.S. Study. As explained in the preface, several of these papers constitute the bulk of this second volume. This book illustrates some good research by individual Japanese and American scholars as well as by collaborative effort between American and Japanese scholars.

2. There is a general worldwide need to improve scholarly access to education research literature produced in languages other than English. While there are some modest international efforts involving a few major languages and some encouraging progress on a highly selective basis in at least three world regions, education lags well behind science and medicine, for example, in having ready access to research literature worldwide. (However, there is now an important breakthrough concerning Japan--see below.)

Research on Japanese education by English speakers, the largest group of foreign scholars pursuing the subject, would benefit greatly from a comprehensive guide in English to sources of reliable information about education in Japan, particularly Japanese language sources and education research literature (see below). Japan's National Institute for Educational Research and Japan's National Institute of Multi Media Education are among the sources that should be more widely known. Sources outside the Ministry of Education are also important for some education sectors. Two examples are the National Institute of Employment and Vocational

Research and the Research and Development Institute of Vocational
Training, both supported by the Ministry of Labor.

It should be emphasized that a wealth of government statistical data and other research information is available on Japanese
education and training, particularly for those willing to dig for it.
However, the data are not all of an equal standard and often need
sophisticated interpretation. One has to know what the numbers
mean as well as what is not there.

Late addition: A few years after the first volume of the U.S.
Study of Education in Japan was published and following completion
of this chapter, including the foregoing portion of this note, a pio-
neering development of special significance for foreign scholars began to emerge from the National Institute for Educational Research
in Tokyo. It merits special mention here because of its potential
value for future research, including introducing Japanese scholarship, researchers, and possible research collaborators to non-
Japanese researchers interested in education in Japan.

In 1988, funded by a grant from the Ministry of Education,
a team of NIER researchers led by Tatsuo Yamada began to develop a computerized database of abstracts in English of research
on education published in Japan during the period 1977-87.
(Virtually all of the research papers included in the database were
written in Japanese.) The purpose was to help respond to the increasing international demand for information about Japanese education by making information about Japanese research on education
more widely known and more easily accessible to education researchers outside Japan. ERIC descriptors were used to the fullest
extent possible to maximize compatibility with the principal international standard.

The field of education was defined broadly for this project.
The 3,500 research papers included in the database were selected
from the research bulletins of thirty-five national colleges and uni-
versities and several major academic societies. The latter are the
Japanese Society for the Study of Education, Japan Comparative
Education Society, Japan Society for Science Education, Japan
Council of Educational Technology Centers, and the Japan Society
for the Study of Adult Education.

The database is located at NIER and is accessible in English
through public telephone lines or via floppy disks. Two of the five
parts of the database have been published in paperback (Yamada
1989 and 1990). Each contains approximately five hundred abstracts. The 1989 volume contains abstracts of papers published by

the national research universities, Kyushu and Hiroshima. The 1990 volume contains abstracts from the research bulletin of the National Center for University Entrance Examination and from the journals of the five associations noted above. The 1990 volume also includes a summary report on the development, characteristics, and methodology of the project itself, from which most of the description in this note is drawn. Publication of the balance of the database is dependent upon availability of funds.

The abstracts in the first two volumes deal with a considerable range of fields and subjects, including a substantial number of entries concerned with aspects of education in other countries and foreign influences on Japanese education. While providing foreign scholars with the most open window yet on educational research in Japan, the material in the first two volumes appears to vary widely in its possible value for foreign researchers--for which the same likely could be said of comparable collections of research on education from any other country with an active research community. It should be noted that the contents of the two published volumes cannot be taken as a representative sample of the entire database or of the full body of educational research in Japan during 1977-87 for reasons explained in the summary report (Yamada 1990, xi-xii).

3. A similar statement could, of course, be made about education research in any country, but the situation in the United States reflects fewer constraints than the situation in Japan. Not only does the United States have many more researchers involved in education and related social science topics and consequently a much larger volume of research activity, but with its diversity of values, more open society, and greater proclivity to challenge old ways and the prevailing order, few, if any, areas of education are off limits to critical investigation.

4. For a comparative analysis of social studies textbooks in Japan and in the United States, see *In Search of Mutual Understanding* (1981), a cooperative effort jointly sponsored by the Japan Textbook Research Center, the International Society for Educational Information in Tokyo, and the National Council for the Social Studies in Washington, D.C., and Becker 1983. In view of textbook developments since this analysis of almost a decade ago, the same sponsors have begun planning to update the project with a review of current texts.

5. Three examples of recent research undertakings on teachers and teacher education:

In the Consortium for Cross-Cultural Research in Education, teams of scholars from seven nations (U.S., England, West Germany, Japan, Singapore, Poland, and Canada) are conducting comparative studies of secondary school teacher satisfaction. The foci include teacher roles and responsibilities, teaching practices, school working conditions, job stress, and satisfaction with teaching as a career. Program coordination is at the University of Michigan School of Education. The consortium is expanding to include universities in China and Israel and possibly in other countries.

A new consortium of ten major American universities and ten major Japanese universities is undertaking cooperative research on teacher education in the two countries. The American universities include Minnesota, Stanford, Vanderbilt, and San Diego State, with the University of Minnesota the lead institution. The Japanese universities include Kyoto, Tokyo, Waseda, and Hyogo University of Education, with Kyoto University the lead institution.

Individual studies by various established scholars continue. For example, Professor Nobuo Shimahara of Rutgers University conducted research on teacher socialization in Japan during a 1988-89 sabbatical year at Tokyo University. The first results were published in Japanese (Shimahara and Sakai 1991).

6. For an effective approach to capturing classroom dynamics at the preschool level through imaginative use of videotapes and subsequent analysis, interpretation, and explanation by the teachers, administrators, students, and parents involved, see Tobin, Wu, and Davidson 1987. The approach included provision not only for eliciting insiders' views of their own schools, but also for gaining the Japanese participants' perspectives on a related videotape of an American preschool in action.

7. An interesting, but not unflawed beginning is reported in a recently published study of the international knowledge and attitudes of a small sample of freshmen and senior education majors in fourteen of Japan's national universities (Cogan, Torney-Purta, and Anderson 1988).

8. In the United States, information on application procedures, selection criteria, and terms and conditions of service are

available from the Embassy of Japan in Washington, D.C., any of the thirteen consulates around the country, or the one in Guam.

9. Further information on the role and programs of Sister Cities International and a directory of current city and state pairings with their counterparts in Japan is available from Sister Cities International, 120 South Payne Street, Alexandria, Virginia, 22314.

10. Still among the more useful resources for teaching about the two countries in schools are the products of the CULCON Education Committee's first major cooperative effort in mutual understanding. The sourcebook produced by the American team for learning about Japan is *Opening Doors: Contemporary Japan* (1979). For a summary of the joint project and the special characteristics of the approach employed, see Bickley, Bullard, and Leestma (1977).

References

Aikin, W. M. 1942. *The Story of the Eight-Year Study*. New York: Harper.

August, R.L. In press. Section on education in R.E. Dolan and R.L. Worden, eds., *Japan: A Country Study*. Washington, DC: U.S. Government Printing Office.

Becker, J.M. 1983. "The Japan-United States Textbook Study Project." *The History Teacher* 16:4, 565-66.

Bickley, V.C., B. Bullard, and R. Leestma. 1977. "Education for International Understanding." *International Educational and Cultural Exchange* 12:4, 10-16.

Chambers, G.S., and W.K. Cummings. 1990. *Profiting from Education: Japan-United States International Educational Ventures in the 1980s*. New York: Institute of International Education.

Cogan, J., J. Torney-Purta, and D. Anderson. 1988. "Knowledge and Attitudes Toward Global Issues: Students in Japan and the United States." *Comparative Education Review* 32, 282-97.

Coleman, J.S., and T. Hoffer. 1987. *Public and Private High Schools: The Impact of Communities*. New York: Basic Books.

Cummings, W. K. 1980. *Education and Equality in Japan*. Princeton: Princeton University Press.

-----. 1982. "The Egalitarian Transformation of Postwar Japanese Education." *Comparative Education Review* 26, 16-35.

Dore, R.P. 1984. *Education in Tokugawa Japan*, 2nd ed. Ann Arbor: Center for Japanese Studies, University of Michigan.

-----, and M. Sako. 1987. *Vocational Education and Training in Japan*. London: Imperial College, Centre for Japanese and Comparative Industrial Research.

Duke, B. 1986. *The Japanese School: Lessons for Industrial America*. New York: Praeger.

Ehara, T. 1989. "The Internationalisation of Japanese Education: Current Situation and Problems." Paper delivered at International Conference on Internationalisation of Japan in Comparative Perspective, University of Sheffield, September 21-23.

Embassy of Japan. 1988. Press release of July 13 on the 1988 Japan Exchange and Teaching Program. Washington, D.C.: Embassy of Japan.

Gallup Organization. 1988. *Survey of Geographic Knowledge*. Washington, DC: National Geographic Society.

Goodlad, J. I. 1984. *A Place Called School*. New York: McGraw-Hill.

Goodman, R. 1990. *Japan's 'International Youth': The Emergence of a New Class of Schoolchildren*. Oxford: Clarendon Press.

Hess, R. D. 1981. In H. Azuma, K. Kashiwagi, and R.D. Hess, *Maternal Attitudes, Behaviors and Children's Cognitive Development: Japan-U.S. Comparative Research*. Tokyo: University of Tokyo Press. (In Japanese).

Holloway, S. D. 1988. "Concepts of Ability and Effort in Japan and the United States." *Review of Educational Research* 58:3, 327-45.

In search of mutual understanding. 1981. Joint report of the Japan/United States Textbook Study Project. Bloomington, IN: Social Studies Development Center, Indiana University.

Kotloff, L.J. 1988. *Dai-Ichi Preschool: Fostering Individuality and Cooperative Group Life in a Progressive Japanese Preschool.* Doctoral dissertation, Cornell University.

Leestma, R. 1979. "Foreword" in L.W. Pike, T.S. Barrows, M.H. Mahoney, and A. Jungleblut, eds., *Other Nations, Other Peoples.* Washington, DC: U.S. Government Printing Office.

-----, R.L. August, B. George, and L. Peak. 1987. *Japanese Education Today.* Washington, DC: U.S. Government Printing Office.

Lewis, C.C. 1984. "Cooperation and Control in Japanese Nursery Schools." *Comparative Education Review* 28, 69-84.

-----. 1988. "Japanese First-Grade Classrooms: Implications for U.S. Theory and Research." *Comparative Education Review* 32, 159-172.

Ohanian, S. 1987. "Notes on Japan from an American Schoolteacher." *Phi Delta Kappan* 68:5, 360-67.

Passin, H. 1965. *Society and Education in Japan.* New York: Teachers College Press, Columbia University.

Peak, L. 1987. *Learning to Go to School in Japan: The Transition from Home to Preschool Life.* Doctoral dissertation, Harvard Graduate School of Education, Cambridge, MA.

-----. In press. *Learning to Go to School in Japan*. Berkeley: University of California Press.

Ranbom, S. 1985. "Schooling in Japan." A special three-part series for *Education Week*, February 20, February 26, March 6.

Ravitch, D., and C.E. Finn, Jr. 1987. *What Do Our 17-Year-Olds Know?* New York: Harper and Row.

Rohlen, T. P. 1980. "The Juku Phenomenon: An Exploratory Essay." *Journal of Japanese Studies* 6, 207-42.

-----. 1983. *Japan's High Schools*. Berkeley: University of California Press.

Shimahara, N., and A. Sakai. 1991. "Nippon ni okeru kyoin kenshu to kyoiku kaikaku" [Japan's teacher internships and educational reform]. *Research Journal of University of Tokyo* 30:1, 83-93.

Stevenson, H., H. Azuma, and K. Hakuta. 1986. *Child Development and Education in Japan*. New York: W. H. Freeman and Company.

Tobin, J.J., D.Y.H. Wu, and D.H. Davidson. 1987. "Class Size and Student/Teacher Ratios in the Japanese Preschool." *Comparative Education Review* 31, 533-49.

U.S.-Japan CULCON Joint Study Team. 1979. *Opening Doors: Contemporary Japan*. New York: The Asia Society.

Wray, H. In press. "Change and Continuity in Modern Japanese Educational History: Allied Occupational Reforms Forty Years Later." *Comparative Education Review*.

Yamada, T. 1989. *English Database on Educational Researches* [sic] *Published in Japan 1977-1987, Vol. 1*. Tokyo: National Institute for Educational Research.

-----. 1990. *Educational Research in Japan 1977-1987*. Tokyo: National Institute for Educational Research.

INDEX

A

Academic pressure. *See*
Examinations, entrance;
Pressure, academic
Academic schools: vs.
comprehensive, 16; vs.
vocational, 16, 27
Academic year, 15
Achievement, relation to
creativity, 227-28
Achievement scores, 2; elementary
schools, 185-88; mathematics,
2, 9, 104-7, 176-80, 181-85,
192, 237; science, 2, 141-55,
166-67, 180-81; science,
opportunity to learn and, 161;
science, variables correlating,
152-55
Activities, special. *See* Special
activities
Admission, university: on
recommendation, 17, 20,
302n.2; *see also* Examinations,
entrance, university
Advanced Mathematics, 116
Advanced Mathematics Concepts,
120
*Algebra and Trigonometry
Structure and Method: Book II*,
120
Algebra Structure and Methods,
119
Amabile, T., 229-35 *passim*
Amae. See Indulgence
Arithmetic, 51, 52; basic number
skills, 39-40, 59, 66; *see also*
Mathematics
Art, 51, 64, 217, 238

Arts, the, 217; creativity in, 255;
traditional Japanese, 54
Assembly, classroom, 84-89
Assignments, summer, 139
Attached schools, 362-63
Attitude, student, 200-1, 252-53,
372-74
Australia, 332, 394, 396
Azuma, Hiroshi, 188-89, 191, 197-
98

B

Ballet lessons. *See* Dance lessons
Basic skills. *See* Number skills,
basic; Reading skills, basic
Battered parent syndrome, 211
Battered teacher syndrome, 211
Behavior, student. *See* Students,
behavior
Biology, 136, 140, 157
Blind. *See* Special education
Boards of education, municipal and
prefectural, 12

C

CAI. *See* Computer Assisted
Instruction
Calculators, 155
Calligraphy lessons, 49, 51, 52, 64
Canada, 332, 394, 396, 406n.5
CEE. *See* College entrance
examination